THE

LORD'S

SERVICE

THE LORD'S SERVICE

The Grace of
Covenant Renewal Worship

Jeffrey J. Meyers

Canon Press ▋ *Moscow*

Jeffrey J. Meyers, *The Lord's Service: The Grace of Covenant Renewal Worship*

© 2003 by Jeffrey J. Meyers
Published by Canon Press, PO Box 8729, Moscow ID 83843
800–488–2034 | www.canonpress.com

07 08 09 10 11 12   9 8 7 6 5 4 3 2

Cover design by Paige Atwood

Printed in the United States of America.

Library of Congress Cataloging-in-Publication Data

Meyers, Jeffrey J.
 The Lord's service : the grace of covenant renewal worship / Jeffrey J. Meyers.
   cm.
Includes bibliographical references and index.
 ISBN-13: 978-1-591280-08-8 (pbk.)
 ISBN-10: 1–59128–008–7 (pbk.)
 1. Worship. I. Title.
 BV10.3 .M49 2003
 264—dc21   2002154033

To my beloved wife Chris,
still a Meyers after 23 years

Table of Contents

Introduction and Acknowledgments

I am amply supplied – Philippians 4:18

When someone called Goethe's attention to the unsettling journalistic practice of undermining the public's confidence in the originality of important men and their works by trotting out all the supposed sources of their inspiration, Goethe responded, "That is very ridiculous. We might as well question a well-fed man about the oxen, sheep, and swine that he has eaten and which have given him strength. We are indeed born with talents, but we owe our developments to a thousand influences of a great world, from which we appropriate to ourselves what we can and what is suitable to us." Goethe's point is twofold. On the one hand, we cannot *reduce* someone's character and work to the sources that have sustained and inspired him. But, secondly, as the Apostle Paul said to the cocky Corinthians: "What do you have that you did not receive? If then you received it, why do you boast as if you did not receive it?" (1 Cor. 4:7).

I confess both truths. I am, of course, responsible for everything in this book, and my own personality, history, education, and idiosyncratic interests are evident throughout. Nevertheless, everything you read in this book I have received from someone else. *Everything.* I have been well fed by a rich feast of liturgies, liturgists, and liturgical theology spread for me by the Church of Jesus Christ. I cannot begin to identify everyone that needs to be thanked; a short list must suffice. First, I want to acknowledge and thank the church and pastors of my youth—the Lutheran Church Missouri Synod. This may seem odd for a Reformed pastor, but I believe it is appropriate and necessary for me to do so. I didn't always appreciate my liturgical heritage.

During my college years I was taught by various campus ministries to despise the formality, predictability, and rigid order in which I was raised. It was all just rote and therefore meaningless repetition, I was told. I was instructed to include in my "testimony" words to this effect: "I never heard the Gospel and didn't get saved until I came to college. No one ever shared the Gospel with me until I met people associated with such-and-such campus ministry." It didn't take long for me to realize that this story was not accurate. Shortly after coming back to the faith of my childhood I would walk into a church service and be able to participate with relative ease. Most churches in the mid-1970's were still liturgically traditional. How did I know how to sing the hymns? Why could I recite the creeds without looking at the words? Why did these prayers sound familiar? What accounts for my being "ready" for the sequence of events in the worship? How did I know these stories that the pastor was reading? It all came back to me. As a child I was trained to worship. It was drilled into me from my infancy. Week after week I participated in the common liturgy of my Lutheran parish.

I may not have appropriated or appreciated the liturgy with maturity until college, but it was there all along. Indeed, in the liturgy of my childhood years, the Gospel was read, preached, sung, and prayed every Lord's Day! I knew it, and I believed it *as a child*. Even today when I occasionally worship with the local LCMS church in our neighborhood (which still uses the older liturgy from *The Lutheran Hymnal* [1941]), I experience freedom that I don't experience in Presbyterian churches that are constantly fiddling with the order and content of their liturgy. I'll say more about *that* later. For now, I simply want to give thanks to God and some long overdue credit to my Lutheran brothers in Christ.

Of course, I am no longer a Lutheran. I am Reformed and Presbyterian, an ordained minister in the Presbyterian Church in America. There are theological and ecclesiastical reasons for my change that cannot be explained here. What I can do is acknowledge the contribution of many former Presbyterian pastors, professors, and friends, especially those men who challenged me to think biblically and theologically about the corporate worship of the local church. After my wife and I joined the First Presbyterian Church of Augusta, Georgia, Pastor John W. Oliver modeled for me the dignified way a minister ought to conduct himself officiating the service of worship. The late Rev. David Winecoff, my pastor and mentor while at Covenant Theological Seminary, spent many precious hours with me and other men personally training us in how to research, construct, and lead worship. I learned from him that the minister's stewardship of the corporate liturgy of the church is equally as important as the preaching ministry. I was also privileged to sit under the teaching of Dr. Robert G. Rayburn at Covenant Seminary before his death. I consider the present work something of an extension of his own *O Come, Let Us Worship: Corporate Worship in the Evangelical Church* (Grand Rapids: Baker Book House, 1980). Dr. Rayburn's solemn warnings about specific liturgical errors commonly made by evangelical ministers in leading the service often echo in my mind when I stand before God's people on the Lord's Day.

In addition, the time I spent at Westminster Presbyterian Church in Tyler, Texas during the mid-1980's was of inestimable value—primarly for the mentoring and later friendship of James B. Jordan, but also for the rich liturgy my family and I entered into every Lord's Day. But Jim Jordan really does need to be singled out. One does not need to read between the lines in this book to see his influence on every page. My book is largely a popularization of his profound biblical, theological, and liturgical insights. So deeply has Jordan's work affected my thought and life that I suspect many parts come perilously close to plagiarism.

The fundamental content of this book began to take shape about a dozen years ago as I wrote a series of essays explaining the meaning of the Lord's Day service. They were first distributed as newsletter articles for Covenant Presbyterian Church, the congregation I served in Houston, Texas. I am grateful to the elders and members of that congregation for the patience they displayed with their young, zealous minister. I revised those articles slightly in the mid-1990's for the congregation of Providence Reformed Presbyterian Church in St. Louis, Missouri where I am presently Senior Pastor. Since that time, my own understanding of the meaning and practice of Christian worship has developed significantly as I have participated in the worship of the Church and continued to study the Bible as well as liturgical history and theology. The elders and members of Providence Reformed Presbyterian church have responded with an enthusiasm and appreciation that often leaves me speechless. No minister could ask for a better session or congregation to lead before the throne of God every Lord's Day.

For many years this book circulated in a spiral-bound edition. Many friends and acquaintances have made numerous suggestions that I have incorporated into this final version. I especially want to thank my associate, Pastor Tommy Lee, for all of his suggestions and corrections. I am grateful the help and encouragement of Brian and Melanie Carter, who read the entire manuscript and found numerous errors. Doug Jones of Canon Press has been extraordinarily kind and supportive throughout the process of publication. I should also mention others who have carefully read earlier editions of this book and provided helpful theological advice: Dr. Peter J. Leithart, Rev. James B. Jordan, Pastor Burke Shade, Pastor Mark Horne, Pastor Jeff Steel, and the many seminary interns at Providence whose tongues have been effectively loosed by the many cigars and beers enjoyed on my back patio over the years. I can't imagine working on such a project without a community of scholars like these men offering encouragement and guidance at every step. A reader familiar with this informal community will see evidence of our "common mind" all through this work.

The original version of this book was written to help explain the Sunday morning service at Providence Reformed Presbyterian Church. At first *The Lord's Service* was a small manual designed to equip the membership of Providence for intelligent participation in worship and also to provide visitors with a biblical and theological rationale for our form of corporate worship. The elders of Providence wanted the inquiring visitor as well as the committed member to know the biblical explanations for our corporate Sunday worship and so be able to worship intelligently with us, experiencing the fullness of reverent worship and praise. We wanted our members and interested visitors to know that we had thought through our worship services, that there were good reasons behind our liturgy. The original, smaller version did not clutter up the text with academic references and extended polemical arguments because it was designed, first of all, as a relatively simple explanation of our service, accessible to any adequately educated member or visitor.

In time the small manual became a much larger work. I developed an expanded edition for the benefit of ministerial students, church officers, and others who needed to dig deeper into the study of worship and liturgy. This larger, beefed-up edition included extensive reference notes as well as additional chapters that dealt with matters important for pastors and seminary students. The book that you now hold in your hands is a revised edition of that expanded version. I have revised it considerably. The book is now divided into three major sections. First, there are eight chapters in which I briefly explain the biblical reasons for the overall order and content of our worship. In Part II we walk through each element of the service step by step as I explain its place and significance in the movement of the liturgy as a whole. Finally, Part III includes an extended bibliographical essay that should be useful to those who are interested in more advanced study, as well as various essays in which I have addressed a few of my concerns about traditional (and untraditional) themes in Presbyterian worship.

Although this book will now reach a much wider audience, I have retained Providence Reformed Presbyterian Church as a model for three reasons. First, it seems appropriate to talk about the worship of the Church from the perspective of one's own liturgical experience. Authors who write on the liturgy or liturgical theology normally do so from within their own tradition. Every pastor must necessarily begin his ministerial service *in medias res* when it comes to the liturgy of the congregation that he serves. Although Providence's worship may not be everything I would want, it is where the Lord has situated me and I am very grateful for it. In my own humble opinion, it doesn't get much better than this in Presbyterian circles. Second, if I were to write about some ideal form of liturgy that has never been learned and lived by any particular church, what good would that do anyone? As it is, I have included enough hints and suggestions here and there in the book to give discerning readers clues about what might be improved. Third, if readers wish to experience what they read, they can visit St. Louis and see and hear how it works. One will discover too, however, that Providence is in many ways an ordinary church with problems similar to those in most ecclesiastical communities.

There are reasons why Reformed congregations ought to behave in certain ways and not others during the Sunday service—sound biblical, theological, and historical reasons. We should not simply follow the dead, musty, liturgical traditions of our fathers. Neither should we clamor to be "trendier than thou," like too many twenty-first-century American evangelical churches seem to be doing these days. I believe the worship I describe in this book is both securely grounded in the Word of God and effectively draws on the wisdom of the historical liturgy, especially the Reformed tradition. I pray that this book will help promote the kind of worship that will please our Lord and effectively expand his kingdom.

Pastor Jeffrey J. Meyers
Trinity Season A.D. 2002

PART I
The Divine Service of
Covenant Renewal:

*The first foundation of righteousness is
undoubtedly the worship of God.*
— John Calvin

The first part of this book (chapters 1–8) deals with biblical and theological fundamentals that are indispensable for addressing questions about the practice of corporate Christian worship. G. K. Chesterton once argued that when things go wrong, we need "unpractical men" who will analyze the problem before rushing in with solutions.

> There has arisen in our time a most singular fancy: the fancy that when things go very wrong we need a practical man. It would be far truer to say, that when things go very wrong we need an unpractical man. Certainly, at least, we need a theorist. A practical man means a man accustomed to merely daily practice, to the way things commonly work. When things will not work, you must have the thinker, the man who has some doctrine about why they work at all. It is wrong to fiddle while Rome is burning; but it is quite right to study the theory of hydraulics while Rome is burning.[†]

---

† G. K. Chesterton, *What's Wrong With the World* (1910), in *The Collected Works of G. K. Chesteron, Volume IV,* (San Fransisco: Ignatius Press, 1987),43.

Too many contemporary pastors rush to solve attendance and interest problems in their churches with "practical" solutions for making worship services more comfortable, relevant, or exciting for modern people. Such ad hoc, often novel, liturgical practices have ignited fiery controversies in Reformed and evangelical circles that some have called "worship wars." Many authors have worked hard to sidestep foundational theological questions so as to suggest without needless delay practical down-to-earth, how-to advice to douse on this blaze. "The church is burning," they cry. "We need water now!" But is all of this practical advice correct? Will all this activity extinguish the fire? It looks like water. It feels wet like water. Nevertheless, it would be a good idea for someone to examine the liquid to determine the validity of these claims. After all, it may be gasoline.

To paraphrase Chesterton, It is wrong to fiddle while a fire rages over worship practices; but it is quite right to study the biblical theology of corporate worship in order to discover the best remedy for quenching the fire. This book's first eight chapters do not contain a great deal of how-to advice. Some would say they are very unpractical. Nevertheless, I am convinced that Christian ministers and people must rediscover the foundational biblical and theological reasons for corporate worship. No pastor should plan or lead a congregation before God's holy presence in worship until he has carefully considered the kind of issues I address in the first part of this book. Ministers who actually compose services, write prayers, choose hymns, and are responsible for ordering the events of a corporate worship service are obligated to make a studied effort to achieve some competency in these matters. Christian men and women who gather together each week for the Divine Service will also find their experience of worship enriched by thinking through these same issues.

1
Why Go to Church on Sunday? Some Popular Answers

When you come together as a church . . .
—1 Corinthians 11:18

Occasionally I walk into a room in my home or even get into my car and suddenly forget why I am there. Why did I come in here? Where am I going? My daughters call this "spacing out." "Dad's spacing out again, Mom." Of course, it normally only takes a few seconds to remember the reason I came into the room or got into my car. I can only imagine what would happen if the reason never came to me. What if I always walked into a particular room of my home without knowing why? Not knowing why one is in a specific place or doing a certain activity is not only embarrassing, but it's also abnormal.

Something like this happens to many Christians when they walk into their church service on Sunday morning. Unfortunately, unlike my temporary amnesia, there is often no recollection of the answer to the question "Why am I here?" because the worshiper never had a clear understanding of the purpose of Sunday morning worship to start with. Some might have a ready answer to the question, but their reason for being in church might be tangential to the purpose of the service as a whole. They come to church because their parents taught them to come to church. They come to church because it is the thing to do on Sunday. Because their children need religious education. Because they meet friends at church. Because they can make productive business contacts. But if asked to explain the purpose of the Sunday service itself, they can do little more than repeat the opaque word "worship."

Many Christians today are confused about the meaning and practice of Christian worship. Before we address all the messy details about what ought and ought not to go on during a worship service, we must answer one foundational question: what is the purpose of a Sunday church service? In other words, *why* does a church come together on Sunday? Why is the congregation gathered together? What are they doing? What is the point? For the next seven chapters we will be exploring answers to these questions.

One way to answer questions about the purpose of Christian worship might be to compose a list of the various activities that we typically engage in during the Sunday meeting. Why are we here? We are here to meditate, sit, kneel, stand, hear, sing, pray, confess, praise, read, think, eat, drink, depart, etc. Of course, with such a list we have not really answered the burning question: *why* do we do those things? To what end? For what purpose? If we say that the purpose of the Sunday service is to gather together and do all these things, the question still lingers: why do we do *these* things? What does all of this hearing, speaking, standing, sitting, singing, praying, eating, and drinking accomplish? Why this particular set of activities and not others? What do we achieve by doing these things? At the end of the service what will have happened? What will have changed, if anything? Are we there for an emotional experience? An educational lesson? To praise God? What is the point of doing all this?

Moreover, if we can ask questions about the grand, overall meaning of the service, we can also ask about the form and content of each specific activity. As we shall see, the two are inexorably related. Why do we do these things and not others? Why do we say these prayers and not others? Why do we sometimes stand, sometimes kneel, and sometimes sit? Why do we say certain words and not others? Why do we sing these hymns and not others? Questions about the sequence of activities must also surface. Why do we do what we do in the *order* that we do them? Why does this come first and that second and this other thing third? Does it matter what order we do things as long as we get everything into the service? Specific questions like these are intimately related to the question of the overall purpose of the whole assembly.

When members of a congregation have answers to these questions they will be able to worship with understanding. Answering these questions, therefore, has great practical value. Every Christian ought to personalize this. Why do *I* come to church on Sunday morning? What am I looking for? What am I hoping will happen? What am I hoping to give? What do I anticipate receiving? What do I expect to be accomplished as a result of my being at church on Sunday morning? Everyone comes for some reason. Do I come for the *right* reasons?

Before we go any farther, then, we must answer this crucial question: What is the *purpose* of our Lord's Day assembly? Why do we come to a church service on Sunday? The answer to this key question will help explain why certain words and actions are included in the church's worship and will also determine the way in which the service is ordered from beginning to end. Unfortunately, there are serious disagreements among modern Christians about the purpose of Sunday worship. There are at least four different popular perspectives on the purpose of the Sunday worship service. In this chapter we will briefly analyze each proposed answer. This brief survey will prepare us for a fifth answer, one that we will begin to unpack in chapter two.

Worship as Evangelism?

First, some Christians and churches believe that the purpose of the Sunday morning service ought to be evangelism. Many "independent" and "community" churches tend to adopt this view, although more and more evangelical Presbyterian and Reformed churches also think that outreach defines the chief purpose of the Sunday service. Such a perspective is not entirely new. Nor is it entirely wrong, as we shall see. But before we can examine the proper place of evangelism in the Sunday service, we have to give some attention to a common distortion. Since the ill-named "Second Great Awakening" in the early nineteenth century, many Protestant churches have embraced evangelistic effectiveness as the foremost criteria for effective worship.[1] The same has been true in some quarters of Presbyterianism since the rise of New School Presbyterians in the early 1800's.[2] Currently, evangelistic effectiveness drives virtually everything in "worship" for many churches that identify with the "church growth movement."[3]

Worship is Not Evangelism. Before moving on to suggest other problems with this perspective we should stop and note briefly the *prima facie* argument against it from Scripture. Evangelism is one thing, worship another. Worship is something you do before God. "Ascribe to Yahweh the glory due his Name; bring an offering and come before him; worship Yahweh in the glory of his holiness" (1 Chr. 16:29). "Worship Yahweh with gladness; come before him

---

[1] Although his work only deals incidentally with worship, Nathan O Hatch's *The Democratization of American Christianity* (New Haven: Yale University Press, 1989) is required reading for pastors and interested laymen who would understand the "mind-set" of modern American evangelical Protestantism toward the role of worship, the Ministry, and the Church.

[2] See Julius Melton, *Presbyterian Worship in America: Changing Patterns Since 1787* (Richmond: John Knox Press, 1967), esp. chapter 3; and Harry S. Stout, *The Divine Dramatist: George Whitefield and the Rise of American Evangelicalism* (Grand Rapids: Eerdmans, 1991). Peter J. Leithart's "Revivalism and American Protestantism," in *The Reconstruction of the Church*, ed. James B. Jordan (Tyler: Geneva Ministries, 1985),46–84, summarizes the deleterious effects of the "revivals" on local parishes in America.

[3] I recommend two insightful critiques of this modern ecclesiastical fad: Douglas D. Webster, *Selling Jesus: What's Wrong With Marketing the Church* (Downers Grove: InterVarsity Press, 1992) and Philip D. Kenneson and James L. Street, *Selling Out the Church: The Dangers of Church Marketing* (Nashville: Abingdon Press, 1997). These do not deal so much with worship per se, but with the foundational philosophical and theological underpinnings of the seeker-church movement. R. Lawrence Moore provides a sociological and cultural analysis in his *Selling God: American Religion and the Marketplace of Culture* (New York: Oxford University Press, 1994).

with joyful songs" (Ps. 100:2). "Worship the Lord your God and serve him alone" (Mt. 4:10). These passages and many more indicate that God is the object of worship. Evangelism, however, has man as the object. The Church evangelizes when she goes *out* from God's presence to proclaim to the world that Jesus is Savior and Lord (Mt. 28:16–20; Acts 1:8).

Furthermore, God's people gather for worship on the Lord's Day in response to His gracious gifts. God summons *His people* to make a command performance before him. Unbelievers do not gather for worship. The Lord's family assembles on the Lord's Day for worship. In Christ the saints have sanctuary access. They are invited into heaven itself. If unbelievers are present, they are nevertheless not the focus of the assembly. They are not "in Christ" and therefore have no heavenly access to the Father. Jesus described the temple as "a house of prayer" (Mk. 11:17). Prayer is offered to God. In Matthew 6:1–13 Jesus warned his disciples about praying "before men." The Pharisees loved to "pray in the synagogues" in order to "shine before men." Jesus, however, commands private prayer. In context that cannot simply mean *individual* private prayer. Jesus did not oppose corporate prayer. But he was concerned that prayer be prayer and not transformed into something else like witnessing and evangelism. "Jesus was not happy with prayer that tried to be a witness. Prayer is not a form of evangelism, addressed to other people. Prayer is addressed to God."[4] Since the whole Christian assembly engages in "common prayer" in Sunday worship, it follows that evangelism per se is ruled out. Even so, as I have hinted in previous paragraphs, there is an important sense in which the Gospel is proclaimed and "evangelism" practiced in the normal Sunday assembly of God's people. The *form* that evangelism takes in a biblically ordered worship service will be noticeably different than what is popular today. But

---

[4] Frederick Dale Bruner, *The Christbook: A Historical/Theological Commentary on Matthew 1–12* (Waco: Word Books, 1987), 233 (cited in James B. Jordan, *Theses on Worship* [Niceville: Transfiguration Press, 1994], 41).

the proper nuancing of this must await further reflection in later chapters.

Worship as Technique. When evangelism becomes the overriding purpose of worship, then what is done in the service easily degenerates into a *technique* for evangelism. Too often, according to this understanding, *results* are what count. Should the effectiveness of a worship service be evaluated based on the number of visiting unchurched people that supposedly get saved or become regular attendees? In many American churches the entire Sunday service has been radically overhauled in order to appeal to the so-called unchurched seekers. "Seeker" appears to function as a pious code word for "religious consumer," a potential client eyeing each particular church to see which one might offer the best product. Unfortunately, many "seeker friendly" churches really do not do much by way of *biblical* evangelism at all. Their services can best be described as pre-evangelistic. If anything like "evangelism" happens within the service, it may come at the end of a chatty, how-to message and take the form of a few sentences about how to believe in Jesus and get saved. Other churches expect that the visitor will feel comfortable enough or even enjoy the service so much that he will return again.[5] Then, at some future date, the unbeliever may be ready to hear and respond to the Gospel.

Fortunately, many churches that have adopted some of the church growth philosophy still retain in their services enough of the elements and order of traditional Christian worship so as not to degenerate into pure neo-pagan, religious consumerism. The conception of the Sunday service as evangelism, however, often

---

[5] James L. Brauer has analyzed the function of music in a contemporary "seeker" service. His conclusions are frightening: "Thus it is clear that music is not seen as a servant of the words (proclamation, prayer, praise), but as a servant of expanding the users of a faith system by getting and keeping the attention of the seeker. Music is there to 'attract' a particular subculture and to 'impress'. . . . As one writer has described the seeker service, 'Essentially it is pre-evangelistic entertainment, a highly entertaining, sixty-minute 'infomercial' for Christianity'" ("The Role of Music in Seeker Services," *Concordia Theological Journal* [Jan. 1998]: 7–20).

continues to stifle any rediscovery of the power of an energetic liturgical service. The kind of liturgical service that I will defend in this book may be much more effective at evangelism than "seeker services." After all, when Paul conjectures about the presence of unbelievers in a Christian service he does not envision them being "comfortable" or "entertained." On the contrary, when the Church behaves properly in worship, the "outsider" who enters "is convicted" and "called to account by all" so that "the secrets of his heart are disclosed, and so, falling on his face, he will worship God and declare that God is really present" in the assembly (1 Cor. 14:24–25).[6] A full-bodied liturgical service in which the people are honestly confessing their sins, carefully listening to large portions of the Bible being read, energetically reciting and singing the Psalms, loudly confessing their faith by reciting the creeds, and so on, ought to have a profound impact on visiting outsiders.

At its worst, however, a church that adopts a consumer-minded posture may end up importing into their Sunday service whatever *techniques* it judges to be most *effective* in attracting local religious consumers. More and more, the rationale for introducing mass-culture into church services is to "break down a person's defenses." Some go so far as to chide traditional (biblical) forms of worship, like the spoken word, as ineffective in twentieth-century culture. "A person's resistance to persuasion is very high when spoken to, but very low when exposed to drama and music," claims Bill Hybels.[7]

Style Matters. Churches that choose evangelistic effectiveness as the criteria by which they evaluate their services tend to look for ways to attract and keep people, and they generally model their services after the broader cultural events (t.v. talk shows, concerts, sitcoms, etc.). Their services are carefully engineered multi-media

---

[6] A common misperception needs to be corrected. 1 Cor. 14:24–25 does not mandate the presence of unbelievers and outsiders in a Christian worship service. It does not even assume that they will be present. In order to expose the chaotic, foolish behavior of the Corinthians during their assemblies, Paul propounds a hypothetical situation.

[7] Quoted in George G. Hunter, *How to Reach Secular People* (Nashville: Abingdon Press, 1992), 153.

events designed to produce the appropriate results. Marketing often plays a key role in determining the shape of the service. The inside of the church may look and feel like a concert hall (with a large band and choir up front), a movie theater (where everything is projected up onto a large screen), or an auditorium (with a "stage" up front). Usually, during the service the people are relatively passive: they function less like a congregation of active worshipers and more like an audience. Generally speaking, what happens in practice in these churches is that most of the traditional forms are jettisoned, and the church unashamedly embraces the dominant and omnipresent entertainment models so prominent in American culture.[8]

These changes are often justified by appealing to the neutrality of different "styles" of worship. I will have more to say about this later, but for now I must detour briefly to insist that these "styles" are not neutral.[9] They embody a distinctly modern American worldview. Evangelism may be the motive for the substitution of pop forms for more biblical and traditional ones in the worship service, but what will the end be? I believe that transforming the worship of the Church using these cultural "styles" and the latest technological innovations in communications and entertainment will affect the mindset and lifestyle of the community that submits to these popular "forms."

The manner in which doctrine is embodied, communicated, lived, and sung is not neutral. Style equals form, and form matters. In other words, the form or manner in which we approach God in worship is not something indifferent (*adiaphora*). The *way* we pray

---

[8] For example, Ed Dobson describes the "seeker church" criteria for music selection: "We wanted a musical style that would elicit a response. Unchurched people come to a service hesitantly. Their mindset is 'you're not going to get me.' Their defenses are up. We felt that a style of music that would get them moving in a physical way (nodding heads and tapping feet) would help break down their defenses. This does not mean that the crowd are on their feet nodding heads and clapping; they seldom clap during a song, but they always applaud at the end" (*Starting a Seeker Sensitive Service: How Traditional Churches Can Reach the Unchurched* [Grand Rapids: Zondervan, 1993],42ff). There you have it: "breaking down their defenses" and the crowds always "applaud at the end."

[9] See Chapter 8 "Corporate Rites and Rituals" for a longer discussion of these issues.

and *how* we worship is inexorably related to who we are, to whom we are praying, and what we believe about the One we engage in prayer and praise. Style (form) and doctrine are mutually conditioning. Or at least they ought to be. What you believe will influence how you pray, worship, and sing. The way in which you worship will impact what you believe. This is just the old principle *lex orandi lex credendi* ("the law of prayer is the law of belief").[10] I maintain that the American church has *not* carefully thought through these issues.

One commonly hears comments like these: "I am not concerned with the style of music, only the doctrine" or "Worship style is just a matter of taste or culture, what is really important is our doctrinal confession" or "As long as you believe correctly it makes no difference what style of worship you choose." I think this is frightening evidence of our sloppy theology of worship and music. What do the forms (styles, etc.) we use uncover and communicate about what we believe? How ought *what* we believe impact upon the forms we use to embody our faith? I cannot advocate strongly enough the need for ministerial students and elders to come to grips with the meaning of American pop culture and technology, especially the subtle danger latent in the Church's capitulation to these supposedly "neutral" forms. [11]

A church that chooses evangelistic effectiveness as the *purpose* of Sunday morning worship may be tempted to judge everything in

---

[10] Chapters 6 and 7 explain this maxim and its application to the Church's liturgy in more detail.

[11] The works of Quentin Schultze deal masterfully with the impact of electronic media on the Church's doctrine and life. I highly recommend his two books. *Televangelism and American Culture: The Business of Popular Religion* (Grand Rapids: Baker Book House, 1991) lays out in horrifying detail the way in which t.v. culture has damaged the life of the Church. *Dancing in the Dark: Youth, Popular Culture, and the Electronic Media* (Grand Rapids: Wm. B. Eerdmans, 1991) explains the effects of the omnipresence of popular "youth" culture on the life of the Church. In addition to these, see Ken A. Myers, *All God's Children and Blue Suede Shoes: Christians and Popular Culture* (Wheaton: Crossway, 1989) and Neil Postman's books: *Technopoly: The Surrender of Culture to Technology* (New York: Knopf, 1992) and *Amusing Ourselves to Death: Public Discourse in the Age of Show Business* (New York: Penguin, 1986).

the light of the results achieved. Furthermore, theological questions about form and order will often give way to utilitarian concerns. Like modern corporations, modern churches feel the need to produce tangible results that can be measured and touted to the present membership. Let the future worry about any possible long-term consequences that might develop because our worship services have been transformed to achieve immediate results.[12] Of course, all of this is baptized with the language of soul winning.

As we shall see shortly, there is a genuine evangelistic dimension to the Lord's Day liturgy. The Gospel is embodied in the liturgy and preached in the sermon. Nevertheless, it is not directed primarily to those outside of the faith, but to the community of believers. If unbelievers visit, they will hear the Gospel, but it will not be on their own terms.

Worship as Education?

Another segment of the Church believes that the Sunday service ought to be for the purpose of communicating truth. Education is the chief end of worship. Churches that have this emphasis tend to degenerate into lecture halls complete with overhead projectors and armies of note-taking members. Even without these educational paraphernalia, however, American conservative churches typically highlight doctrine and teaching in their worship services. The sermon, for example, is elevated all out of proportion as the dominant element of worship. Education becomes the primary goal. Nothing else is of much importance in the service. Most of what comes before the sermon functions as "pre-game ceremonies" for the main event—the sermon. People may like to sing, and singing may make them feel good, but they have not really thought through what purpose, if any, hymns and songs ought to have in the overall structure of the service—besides preparing the congregation emotionally for the sermon.

---

[12] See chapters 6 and 7 for my analysis of the connection between the way we worship and the content of our confession and life.

Once again, however, the Bible appears not to put the emphasis on teaching in worship. "Oh come, let us sing to Yahweh; let us make a joyful noise to the Rock of our salvation! Let us come into his presence with thanksgiving; let us make a joyful noise to him with songs of praise! . . . . Oh come, let us worship and bow down; let us kneel before Yahweh, our Maker!" (Ps. 95:1–2, 6). Not hardening our hearts to the voice of God (Ps. 95:7–8) has a doxological context. Jesus said that the meeting place of his people ought to be a "house of prayer"(Mt. 21:13; Is. 56:7), not a lecture hall. The heavenly hosts are not seated as armies of students armed with note pads and pencils around the throne of the Lamb in Revelation 4 and 5. Rather, we see them "fall down before him who sits on the throne" (Rev. 4:10) and hear them "singing a new song" (Rev. 5:9). If this heavenly scene models for us earthly Christian worship, then the corporate acts of kneeling, antiphonal responses, and singing are fundamental to worship. All of this is not to say that teaching has no place in corporate Christian worship services. We shall see that it does. Nevertheless, it is not the sole or chief reason that Christians should come to church on Sunday.

Worship as Experience?

There are others who emphasize the emotional or inner experience of the congregation in worship. They believe that the Sunday service's function is to produce some kind of beneficial "heart" response in the people. Many church leaders appear to believe precisely this. Religion is reduced to what happens "inside" of us, sometimes even to sentimental and pious feelings. Pastors smile all the time and read poems from the pulpit to help the people feel good about themselves. For those who have embraced this philosophy of worship (a kind of liturgical Pollyanna-ism), the focus of the church is anthropological—that is, on *man*. I recently phoned the office of a church whose biblical orthodoxy is at best questionable and heard the following answering machine message: "Remember God loves you *just the way you are!*" My first thought was that this gets it precisely backwards. In truth, God loves his people in spite of the way they are, because of his Son Jesus Christ. Even so, in all too many Sunday services it appears as if, at all costs, people must leave the service feeling that they are okay and believing that everyone else is too. The Christian faith is reduced to religious sentimentalism. In modern American church services, edification is cut loose from its doctrinal moorings and is blown about by every humanistic, trendy gust of psychological and sociological silliness. It is almost as if the greatest achievement of corporate worship is to engineer within the worshipers some kind of praise-induced emotional or psychological ecstasy.

It would be difficult to prove from Scripture that the principal purpose of the corporate assembly ought to be producing religious and emotional experiences in those who gather. Worshipers gather to perform actions. The biblical language of worship has people *doing things* before God ("offering"[Ps. 4:5]; "prostrating" [Is. 49:7]; "confessing"[Ps. 32:5]; "kneeling"[Ps. 95:6]; "singing"[Ps. 95:1]; bringing "gifts" in their hands [Exod. 34:20]). In addition to this, worship is evaluated not according to the affect it might have on worshipers, but whether it is "acceptable" to God or not (Gen. 4:3–7; Exod. 32; Is. 1; Rom. 12:1–2; 14:17–18; Heb. 12:28–29; 13:16).

Worship as Praise or Exaltation?

We have been considering prominent tendencies in contemporary churches with respect to the purpose of Sunday worship. So far I have identified three possible purposes: evangelism, education, and experience. If one wanted to extend the mnemonic assonance, the word "exaltation" might work. From this perspective the purpose of worship is to gather and give praise to God, to exalt His Name. Churches that emphasize praise as the goal of worship might style their services "celebrations." All of those passages that call believers to "ascribe" or "give to the Lord the glory due to his Name" can be marshaled in support of the truth that the corporate service is a service of praise (Ps. 29:1–2; 96:7–8; 149:1).

This fourth conception of worship is much closer, but still not quite adequate to express the fullness of biblical worship. Certainly there are numerous passages that exhort us to "Praise the Lord" and to "worship" him. I would caution the reader, however, that in many cases the word "worship" has not served us very well. It is not the most faithful translation of the words used to designate "bowing down" or "prostrating oneself" (e.g. Psalm 95:6). For example, when we are called to "prostrate" ourselves before God, this does not exactly correspond with the way we use the word "worship" in modern culture. First, most Protestant Christians in America do not worship God by falling down on their knees or faces. More telling, however, is the fact that falling down before God means allowing oneself to be lifted up by him (Dan. 8:17–18). It is to give one's self over to the Lord's service. In effect, falling down before God puts us in the position to be served by God. Much more, therefore, is often going on in these passages than merely ascribing "worth" or "praise" to God.

Often the giving of praise or glorifying of God is set over against the worshiper's expectation of *receiving* anything from God in church. I will carefully examine the one-sidedness of "worship as praise" in chapter five, but let me say here that not only is the super spiritual sounding assertion that "we just gather together to give praise to God taking no interest in what we might get from Him" unbiblical, it may also easily slip into doxological hubris. Reformed pastors and theologians are particularly vulnerable to this distortion of the purpose of worship. The slogan "we gather for worship to give not to get" has become something of a Reformed shibboleth. We love to beat charismatics and others over the head with it. It makes us feel superior. As if we don't go to church because we *need* anything! We Reformed Christians go to church to *give* God glory and honor, not to *get* something from Him. As I hope to show, this kind of thinking is extremely dangerous.

For us, as creatures of God, there can be no such thing as "disinterested praise." We simply cannot love or praise God for who He is apart from what He has given us or what we continue to receive from Him. We are not His equals. The notion that pure love and worship of God can only be given when it is unmixed with all thoughts of what we receive has no biblical grounding. To be sure, it sounds very spiritual and pious. It even comes across as self-denial. "We just want to praise You for who You are, God. We love You and praise You, O God, not for what we get from You, but just for who You are." In fact, however, there is no such worship in the Bible for the simple fact that we cannot approach God as disinterested, self-sufficient beings. We are created beings. Dependent creatures. Beings who must continually *receive* both our life and redemption from God. Our "worship" of God, for this reason, necessarily involves our passive reception of His gifts as well as our active thanksgiving and petitions. We cannot pretend that we do not depend upon Him. We will always be receivers and petitioners before God. Our receptive posture is as ineradicable as our nature as dependent creatures. We put ourselves in a position to be served by Him. Recognizing this is true spirituality. Opening one's self up to the need for God's service is the first movement in our "worship," indeed, the presupposition of all corporate worship. It is faith's posture before our all-sufficient, beneficent Lord. Praise follows *after this* and alone can never be the exclusive purpose for our gathering together on the Lord's Day.

Conclusion

Obviously, there is some truth in each of these four perspectives. A Christian service that does not proclaim the Gospel, engage the emotions of the congregation, teach God's word, and ascribe to God praise and honor will likely be a distorted, dangerously truncated service. All four of these options, however, err to the extent that they *reduce* the purpose of the Sunday service to one or another dimension. Additionally, those who embrace only one of the first four purposes often tend to see the Sunday service as primarily a *technique* for producing a particular effect on the members of the congregation, either on their will, mind, or emotions. All four of these dimensions—evangelism, preaching, edification, and praise—are in and of themselves essential. They each have their proper place in the worship service. But the overall purpose of a biblical worship service should not be *reduced* to any one of them. Moreover, the purpose (and practice) of our Lord's Day worship service must never degenerate into an attempt to engineer or manipulate some desired effect in the congregation. Worship must not be understood as a technique. William Willimon says it well:

> The Protestant cleric who used to look down on the manipulation and forced emotionalism of the old-time tent revivalist does not shrink from using modern liturgical gimmickry such as balloons, dance, clowns, drama, and contrived gestures of intimacy to induce various emotional states in his own congregation. "Anything to shake them up a bit" was the justification given by a pastor recently after subjecting his congregation to a forty-minute barrage of taped screams, slides of malnourished children, and his own "prophetic" sermonic scoldings. The use of worship for managerial ends and cheap emotional highs is not new in Protestantism. Utilitarian, pragmatic, motivational manipulation of people during Sunday morning worship is as old as Charles Finney's "New Measures" in revivals for prodding people down to the altar. As C. S. Lewis said, "The charge is feed my sheep not run experiments on my rats." When worship is reduced to a pep rally for the pastor's latest crusade or to a series of acts that contain the minister's own hidden agenda, our concern for worship is called into question.[13]

Every conception and form of liturgy that focuses on man will eventually degenerate into intellectual or psychological manipulation. As we will discover, only when we pattern our worship according to the structure of God's covenantal relations as revealed in Scripture will we experience the fullness of God's gracious work for us in corporate worship.

---

[13] William H. Willimon, *Worship as Pastoral Care* (Nashville: Abingdon Press, 1979), 17.

2
Covenant and Worship

*The counsel of Yahweh is for those who fear
Him, for He makes known to them His covenant.*
—Psalm 25:14

Why then are we called together as a church on the Lord's Day?
What is the purpose of our Sunday assembly? What happens at
church? I have already suggested that the word "worship" cannot adequately express what happens during the Lord's Day assembly. Indeed, we do worship and praise God, but that is not
the whole story. In the previous chapter I also argued that the
point of the Sunday service should not be reduced to evangelism,
education, or experience. How can we avoid a similar reduction-
ism in defining the purpose of our Sunday assembly? Only by
identifying a biblical purpose that includes everything we experience and do in Christian corporate worship. God's covenant
provides the key. Simply stated, the purpose of the Sunday service is covenant renewal. During corporate "worship" the Lord
renews His covenant with His people when He gathers them together and serves them. But what exactly is a covenant and how
does covenant renewal take place? We must take some time to
examine what the Bible means by "covenant" before we
dive into a discussion of covenantal corporate worship. The

distinctive manner of God's covenantal relations with His people will provide us with the basic order and structure of the corporate worship service.

Here at the outset I should emphasize that the end or goal of God's covenant is always a feast. God invites us to a meal. We come to church on Sunday to eat with Jesus and one another, to feast in His presence. I wonder how many American Protestant Christians come to church in order to feast with God and his people at a common Table. Who would deny that this is the eschatological goal of all of God's covenantal works—the marriage supper of the Lamb (Rev. 19:6–10)? Even so, when God renews His covenant with His people in history it always climaxes with a common meal. But I am jumping too quickly to the conclusion. Before we get there we have to discuss covenant making and renewal in the Scriptures.

No Simple Definition

I would solicit the reader's patience at this early place in the book. There is no one biblical passage I can point to that will lay out a definition of the covenant. There is no proof text that says, "Worship is covenant renewal." The components of a covenant and the contours of covenant renewal events will have to be carefully built up from an analysis of a variety of covenants, covenantal documents, and covenant rituals and rites described in the Scriptures. In the next few chapters I will demonstrate that the covenantal documents as well as the sequence of events by which God covenants and renews covenants all follow a similar pattern. God's covenantal initiatives normally take the same form, following a similar sequence of related actions. After I have discussed the covenant, the covenantal sacrifices, and the Trinitarian shape of the Christian worship service, the reader should experience the cumulative effect of this body of evidence and come to some cognitive rest on the content and sequence of covenant renewal worship.

The Bible uses the word "covenant" over three hundred times in the Old and New Testaments to describe the way in which God relates to his people. God enters into, remembers, and renews His covenant with His people (Gen. 6:18; Deut. 5:3; Ezek. 16:60; Lk.1:72; 22:20; Heb. 8:10). The people for their part must not break, but remember and renew their covenant with God (1 Chr. 16:15; Ps.103:18; Hos. 6:7). There are covenant making rituals (Gen. 15:1-21; 21:27; Exod. 24:7–8; 34:27; Jer. 34:18), covenant documents (Exod. 34:27–28; the Decalogue, Deut. 31:9, 26; the entire book of Deuteronomy; Heb. 9:4), covenantal laws (Exod. 21–23; Ezra 10:3), covenant signs (Gen. 9:12; 17:9–14), covenant meals (Lk. 22:20; 1 Cor. 11:25), covenant mediators (Heb. 12:24); covenant sacrifices (Exod. 24:8; Heb. 9:18–20; 10:29), covenant memorials (Gen. 9:15–16; Exod. 20:24; Josh. 4:7; 1 Cor. 11:25), covenant promises (Ps. 105:9–11; Heb. 8:6), covenant curses (Deut. 29:21; 30:1; Josh. 8:34), covenant witnesses (Deut. 31:26; Mal. 2:14), and more. Nevertheless, a good many Christians, even life-long Presbyterians, are often mystified by the concept of the covenant. We denominate our churches and schools with this word "covenant," but when asked to define it for outsiders words fail us. In days past, in early American social life, one could not live too many days without hearing the word "covenant" uttered by all sorts of people applying it to many different kinds of situations. Some legal documents could be described as covenants. A civil magistrate covenanted with God and the people to serve them as ruler. Covenants were written up and signed by nations outlining international agreements. Employers entered into covenants with their employees. And men and women would stand before pastors and judges on their wedding day and repeat these words:

> I, Jeffrey, take you, Christine; To be my wedded wife; And I do promise and covenant; Before God and these witnesses; To be your loving and faithful husband; In plenty and in want; In joy and in sorrow; In sickness and in health; As long as we both shall live.

Unfortunately, except in certain legal contexts where "covenant" and "covenanting" is still used as "legalese" we do not live in a culture that speaks this way anymore. The word covenant has even disappeared from our marriage ceremonies.

One reason why so many are mystified by the word covenant and the concept of covenanting is that it is almost impossible to *reduce* it to a slogan or nice neat definition. The word describes a multidimensional reality that cannot be captured by a simplistic description. There is no straightforward definition of a covenant in the Bible. Think about this. Perhaps God didn't provide us with a succinct definition of a covenant so that we would be driven to examine the multifaceted details of his covenantal relations with us. In other words, by not giving us a cute little ten-word definition, God forces us to come to grips with the astonishing richness of his covenants with mankind.

Furthermore, there is no replacement word that can easily stand in for the word "covenant." One cannot simply substitute the word "contract" or "agreement" or even "promise" for "covenant," even though some have tried to do so. We might illustrate this with the marriage covenant (Prov. 2:10–17; Ezek. 16:6–14; Mal. 2:13–16). Unless I am mistaken, Christians do not normally talk about the marriage contract or the marriage agreement or the marriage compromise because we know that marriage is so much more than these. Like the marriage covenant God's covenant with us cannot be reduced to an agreement or a contract. The covenant is certainly not a deal or an agreement. It is not solely about law and legal status. It is not simply a promise. And it is much more than friendship. These words may express *something* of the meaning of a covenant but they fail to embrace its fullness. There is no simple definition of a covenant.

The Language of Personal Relationship

Although God's covenants with us are "personal" and rightly describe "relationships" between God and us, nevertheless, biblical covenants are not adequately described or defined as simply "personal relationships." Regrettably, many in the Church have chosen to ape popular American culture and describe our relations with God using the language of "personal relationship." This phrase has become a popular substitute for the word covenant. The first problem with this kind of language is that it is much too ambiguous. These days a "personal relationship" can be used to describe almost anything. People experience personal relationships with their spouses, workmates, friends, casual sex partners, pets, and even their cars. All one needs to have a personal relationship is at least one person. Furthermore, the precise nature of the "relationship" is left amorphous. So what does it mean when Christians talk about their "personal relationship" with God? It is often hard to know. This kind of trendy lingo is too fluid and for that reason can be quite misleading. To describe the worship of the Church as a time when people engage in or enrich their "personal relationships" with God can mean almost anything.

What is worse, I fear, is that Christians sometimes unwittingly give people the wrong impression when they use wooly terminology like "personal relationship" to talk about their closeness to God. Consider the word "relationship." It is much too thin and flimsy to support the weighty character of biblical covenants. In our culture the word "relationship" likely conjures up images of television sitcoms such as *Friends* and *Seinfeld*. In modern parlance a "relationship" is an informal, non-binding association or friendship. A relationship might last for a while, but maybe not. People enter into a variety of relationships for personal fulfillment and happiness, just as they leave them when these conditions are not being met. These kinds of relationships can be on one day and off the next. They involve no formal or binding responsibilities. They bend, sway, and stretch according to the desires of the individuals involved in these "relationships." They have no objective shape or form. This is not the case with covenantal relationships in the Bible.

For example, there is a television commercial for the book *Power For Living* in which a famous football player talks about how difficult life is and how hard it is to be alone in the world. The solution offered is that you can have a "personal relationship with God." Accept Jesus and you can experience a wonderful and exciting personal relationship with Him. Great. But what exactly does that mean? I wonder what non-Christians who hear that kind of language think they will get or experience if they accept Jesus. The implication is that you will be able to experience companionship with God just like you experience "personal relationships" with family and friends. Are these associations accurate and helpful? Even though there are similarities, there are also huge differences.

Having a personal relationship with God is not the same as having a personal relationship with another human person. Consider the fact that God does not talk to us face-to-face. We do not *immediately* experience his presence like we do when we relate to other people in the flesh. No one has face-to-face relations with Jesus anymore—no one on earth, at any rate. He is *absent* in a very real and significant sense. A large part of the purpose of Jesus' "upper room discourse" (Jn. 14-17) has to do with preparing his disciples for his *departure*. Since his ascension, we cannot touch, see, or hear Jesus speak apart from the mediation of other people. A Christian's relationship with Jesus, therefore, is not immediate, but mediate. No doubt the "real absence of Jesus" ought to be explained in more detail, but my point is pretty simple: the language of "personal relationship" does not best describe the precise way in which the Lord and His people relate to one another. I'm not denying that God's interaction with us is a "relationship" or that it is "personal," but when you combine those two words the resulting phrase has connotations that do not really help us understand how God and man relate to one another.

The biblical word "covenant" is much better. When we hear it we are reminded that God's relations with us have a particular *form*. Indeed, a covenant is a *formal* personal relationship, if you will. That is not an adequate definition, of course, but it reminds us that covenants possess definitive content and structure. The covenant is the *form* or *shape* of God's personal relations with us.

The Order and Structure of God's Covenant

God has not given us a simple sentence definition of a covenant; rather, He has told the story of how He has entered into covenant with man so that we can appreciate the richness of His covenantal relations with us. He has also left us with covenantal documents that exhibit the form of His covenant (the book of Deuteronomy being one of the most helpful). Without a simple definition we are driven to contemplate the multi-dimensional form or structure of His covenantal initiatives, acts, and speech as revealed in the Bible. These concrete, historical events and literary documents therefore become the paradigms (or models) of what the covenant is and ought to be. I should hasten to add that God Himself, especially as He exists eternally as three Persons in relation, is the ultimate archetype of the covenant. The origin and ground of the covenantal form we see displayed in the biblical events and documents we are about to investigate can be traced back to the formal, personal bond that exists between the Persons of the Father, the Son, and the Holy Spirit. This is precisely why it is so difficult for us to define the covenant with simple formulas. The covenant partakes of the richness of God's eternal Trinitarian life.[1]

Thankfully, the structure of God's covenant has been a major research project in biblical studies for about a century. Great strides have been made in our understanding of the covenant with the introduction of the discipline of "biblical theology" in the twentieth century. Much scholarly attention has been given to the way that God inaugurates, sustains, and perpetuates His covenantal relations

---

[1] See Ralph A. Smith, *The Eternal Covenant* (Moscow: Canon Press, 2003).

with his people. My brief discussion here presupposes these recent advances in biblical theology.[2]

In order to understand covenant renewal worship we have to examine the order and structure of God's covenant with man. We should begin with the very first covenant, the covenant of creation, especially God's covenantal relation with Adam in Genesis 2:4b–17. God's relations with Adam are covenantal from the start. Here in Genesis 2 we discover the basic form of God's covenant with man. For pedagogical purposes I will analyze God's covenant under five headings: 1) God takes hold, 2) God separates and makes something new, 3) God speaks, 4) God grants ritual signs and seals, and 5) God arranges for the future.

First, in initiating the covenant, Yahweh (note the personal, covenantal name of God) takes hold of the ground (Gen. 2:4b). He is Lord over His creation. In the beginning He created all things and so had sovereign control over that initial formless, empty, and dark matter (Gen. 1:1–3). He took hold of it and began to form his creation (Gen. 1:4ff). So now also God takes hold of the dust in order to form it into something new.

Second, Yahweh separates out of the dust material to form a new being. There is a separation. This is extremely significant. Every covenant in the Bible after this will involve a separation of some portion of the old "material" so that it can be formed into something new. Here in Genesis 2, after taking hold of the dust of the ground,

---

[2] Helpful introductory works on the covenant include Cornelis van der Waal, *The Covenantal Gospel* (Neerlandia: Inheritance Publications, 1990); James B. Jordan, *Covenant Sequence in Leviticus and Deuteronomy* (Tyler: Institute for Christian Economics, 1989); *The Law of the Covenant: An Exposition of Exodus 21–23* (Tyler: Institute for Biblical Economics, 1984); *Through New Eyes: Developing a Biblical View of the World* (Brentwood: Wolgemuth & Hyatt, 1988); Norman Shepherd, *The Call of Grace: How the Covenant Illumines Salvation and Evangelism* (Phillipsburg: Presbyterian & Reformed, 2000); W. J. Dumbrell, *Covenant & Creation: A Theology of the Old Testament Covenants* (Grand Rapids: Baker Book House, 1984); O. Palmer Robertson, *The Christ of the Covenants* (Grand Rapids: Baker, 1980), Meredith Kline, *The Structure of Biblical Authority*, revised edition (Grand Rapids: Eerdmans, 1972), John Murray, *The Covenant of Grace* (London: Tyndale Press, 1954); and John Calvin, *The Covenant Enforced: Sermons on Deuteronomy 27 and 28*, ed. James B. Jordan (Tyler: Institute for Christian Economics, 1990).

God makes a new being—the breath of life is united with the dust of the ground. God separates and then He unites. A separation and a union produce something new. What was once merely dust is now transfigured into a new creation—Adam. Every covenant involves some kind of separation and a union resulting in a new creation. God Himself, the covenant Lord, Yahweh, takes the initiative and graciously inaugurates this process. He takes hold and transfigures the old into something new. This is how every covenant is made and renewed: God graciously inaugurates the process.

Appropriately, this new creation is then given a new name. God gives the man his name "Adam." According to Genesis 2:7, "Yahweh God formed *Adam* from the dust of the ground." Adam is, however, also named and defined as "a living being" in the same passage (literally, a "living soul"; Heb: *nephesh hayim*). God names and therefore defines his new creation. Implicit in this covenantal arrangement thus far is a proper hierarchy: Yahweh is God and Lord, man is a dependent creature under Yahweh and answerable to Him. Yahweh is the one who took hold of the dust, united it with the breath of life, brought about this new being, and gave it a new name. He is the covenant Lord, Yahweh. And Adam is now therefore in a living covenanal relationship with Yahweh, his Creator and covenant Lord. Covenants always involve new names and new lines of authority fitting for the new covenantal arrangement.

Thirdly, God *speaks* to Adam. Words are essential for personal, covenantal relations. God's speech to Adam informs him of God's gracious arrangement with him. God's word to Adam also constitutes their personal relations. All personal relations are constituted and maintained by verbal communication. Yahweh talks to him about what he is to do ("serve and guard the Garden"). Furthermore, Adam is told that he is free to eat of any tree in the Garden (which must include, by the way, the Tree of Life, v. 9). Words inaugurate and sustain all covenantal relations. For his part, Adam is to hear and heed the instructions of his covenant Lord.

Fourth, covenantal arrangements involve tangible signs and seals (often accompanied by public oaths of loyalty) with promises of blessing for faithfulness and threatened curses for disobedience. More importantly, however, it is about *food*. Here in Genesis 2:16 Yahweh commands Adam not to eat from the Tree of the Knowledge of Good and Evil. Two trees are singled out from the rest to serve as "sacramental" signs and seals of the covenant. This should not surprise us since food and meals function this way in virtually every covenant in the Bible. But the important point here is that essential to every biblical covenant are these public, very physical memorials of the covenant. There is a sign of the covenant, something physical and tangible to remind God and Adam of the covenant: the two trees in the Garden. Faithfully maintaining the covenant demands that Adam and Eve maintain a faithful relation to these two trees. Faithfulness to God means being faithful in relating to these two trees. This same pattern is found throughout the Bible: keeping God's covenant means faithfully performing the covenantal rituals established by God.

The fifth and final aspect of the covenant of creation is God's arrangement for its succession. In other words, God arranges for the perpetuation of the covenantal relation. It will not end with Adam. Here in Genesis 2 this aspect of the Adamic covenant is shown by God's surprising gift of a woman to help Adam and ensure the continuation of the human race through childbearing. So Genesis 2:18–24 embodies this fifth element of God's covenantal arrangement. Arrangements for the continuation and expansion of the covenant are normally the final moment in covenant making and renewal rituals and documents.

Voila! We have a covenant: God's first covenant with man. What was once plain old dust is graciously taken hold of by Yahweh, separated from the ground, brought into a new state of existence, and given a new name. There is a new order and a fitting line of authority—Creator over creature. God inaugurates and maintains this new covenant with Adam by speaking to him, and Adam is encouraged to find blessing and life in obedience to his gracious covenant Lord by thankfully eating from the Tree of Life, confessing his dependence on God's grace, but dutifully avoiding the Tree of the Knowledge of Good and Evil for a time.[3] Finally, God graciously provides for the succession of the covenant by making a wife for Adam. God and Adam are in covenant with one another. We call this "the creation covenant" or "the covenant of life."[4]

Now, let us review what we have discovered in our analysis of the first creation covenant. Yahweh's covenant with Adam contains in seed form everything that will go into the other covenants in the Scriptures. There will be some important changes, of course, after the fall of man, but the post-fall covenants are not ad hoc, novel arrangements, but renewals of the creation covenant. Our outline of the form of God's covenant includes five dimensions:

1. As covenant Lord, Yahweh takes hold of His creation in order to do something new with it.

2. The Lord effects a separation. What God grasps is then transformed from one state to another, from the old to the new: a new creation. This new union (dirt and life-giving breath of Yahweh) receives from God a corresponding new name, which implies a new hierarchical relationship. There is a covenant head (Yahweh) and there are those who are dependant on that covenant head (human creatures).

3. A new verbal communication of stipulations is expressed by the covenant Lord, a way of life fit for the new covenantal situation, a gracious enumeration of how to live fully and joyfully in this new covenant.

---

[3] See James B. Jordan, *Primeval Saints: Studies in the Patriarchs of Genesis* (Moscow: Canon Press, 2001), "Rebellion, Tyranny, and Dominion in the Book of Genesis," in *Christianity & Civilization* No. 3, ed. Gary North (Tyler: Geneva Divinity School Press, 1983), 38–80, and *Through New Eyes*, 133–163.

[4] It is also sometimes called the "covenant of works," but this can be misleading if one thinks that Adam's fundamental relationship with God was not founded on God's gracious gift of life but rather on his "meriting" God's favor. Adam is not required to work for God's love and favor, but to continue in the life he has been given by faithfully and joyfully doing his duty as God's servant, a "light" yoke that he tragically throws off (Gen. 3:1ff).

4. The Lord offers His covenant partners a fellowship meal. He gives the gift of signs and seals of the covenant (two trees) together with a setting forth of blessings for grateful faithfulness and curses for ungrateful disobedience.

5. The Lord arranges for the future succession of the covenant, which in this covenant involves marriage and children.[5]

A Five-Fold Sequence and Structure

It is appropriate now to examine in summary form the other biblical covenants and see how they also fit this basic pattern.[6] We will see that these same dimensions (and, of course, more) are present in every covenantal initiative that God makes with his people—from Noah to Christ. I will not examine these covenants in great detail, but will attempt to establish the presence of this basic pattern. My goal is to show in the end how the covenant renewal service on the Lord's Day embodies this carefully ordered pattern and sequence.

[5] Stated more abstractly, these five steps have been conveniently described in terms of the acrostic THEOS: Transcendence (God the great and sovereign king mercifully takes hold of His subjects), Hierarchy (God breaks down the old [and sinful] and restructures it into something new), Ethics (God graciously informs us how we are to live our new life), Oath (God confirms His promises and warns against curses by oaths, memorials, and other signs), and Succession (God commissions His people and insures their future protection). See Ralph A. Smith, *The Covenantal Structure of the Bible*, available from <http://www.berith.org/essays/bib/> (Sept. 29, 2002).

[6] I need to make a few qualifying comments here. I do not mean to suggest that this five-fold way of enumerating the dimensions of covenantal arrangements is the only way to slice the pie of this rich relationship that the Bible calls a covenant. There have been other Reformed theologians who have analyzed this covenantal sequence using a three-fold, a four-fold, a six-fold, a seven-fold, even an eight-fold model (for an overview and references see James B. Jordan, *Covenant Sequence in Leviticus and Deuteronomy* (Tyler: Institute for Christian Economics, 1989). Models like these are helpful in that they quantify for us something of the amazing richness of God's covenantal dealings with man. They also, like maps, help us navigate the complex covenantal landscape by giving us some identifiable features from which to orient ourselves. Although different Reformed authors slice the pie of the covenant differently, they are agreed that "covenant" characterizes God's relation with us and that the form or structure of the covenant consists at least in God's sovereign, gracious initiation of the covenant, His establishment of the terms or stipulations, His promise of blessing and threat against breaking the covenant, and His arrangement for the covenant's future continuance and expansion.

Consider the first marriage covenant that God arranges between Adam and his bride, Eve. The original ordeal of Genesis 2:21–24 clearly manifests a covenantal form and order.

1. Yahweh God causes Adam to fall into a deep sleep and takes hold of him in order to make something new.

2. Adam falls into a deep sleep and "dies" to his old existence, his aloneness. While he is sleeping Yahweh separates out part of Adam's side (his flesh and bones). Thus there is a *separation*, a movement from the old to the new. Then, that which has been separated is built up, transfigured into something new and glorious, and brought to Adam by Yahweh to be united with him. Adam then *speaks* to his new bride. He gives her a new name (woman; Heb. *'ishah*). In fact, he himself now becomes something of a new man in some profound sense because of this new relationship with her. They are "one flesh." There is a new authority structure. The man has the role of being the "head" or "leader" of the new family.

3. God then tells us (Gen. 2:24) what all this means. There is a new mandate, a new *torah* (way of life) established by God. Men will leave their old life and be united to form a new family unit. They will cleave to a wife and become one flesh with her. Here we have the ethical requirements of marriage in a nutshell.

4. The "sacrament," if you will, or physical memorial of this marriage covenant is the sexual union between a man and his wife ("they were both naked and not ashamed," v. 25). This becomes the physical sign and seal of the marital covenant.

5. Finally, God has made provision for the perpetuation of the covenant. This is implicit in the narrator's comments in verse 24. There will be other men and women who will come together in marriage. Where will they come from? Genesis 1:26–28 tells us. The man and the woman will have children. In this way the covenant of marriage perpetuates not only the marital covenant but also the covenant between God and mankind, ensuring that other humans will also come into existence and experience Yahweh's covenantal grace.

After the fall of man every covenant God makes with man is a gracious covenant in a heightened sense. Even more so than the first creation covenant. This is so because every covenant God establishes after the fall involves God's merciful intervention in spite of man's deserving condemnation and rejection. Second, this means that the initial establishment of the covenant, God's sovereign separation of the new from the old will always involve a death and resurrection. The separations are now very traumatic. Sin must be dealt with, which means that someone must die to suffer the judicial punishment for man's sin.[7] Each time God separates out for Himself a people He must both *atone* for their sin, which is why every post-fall covenant is founded upon vicarious sacrifice, and He must tear them from their old life and renew them. I cannot call attention to this in each and every covenant, but the reader should not fail to notice these new aspects of every post-fall covenant. This will be crucial to our understanding of covenant renewal worship in that all biblical covenantal renewals are sacrificial in nature.

Consider the Noahic covenant in Genesis chapters 6–9:

1. God graciously takes hold of Noah. He finds "favor in the eyes of Yahweh." (Gen. 6:8)

2. After singling out Noah, God takes hold of him and his family and separates them out from the old, dead world that is under judgment. This separation is a death and resurrection. The old world dies under the

---

[7] I believe that the meaning of sacrificial death goes beyond punishment for sin. Just as I am not convinced that the form of death imposed by God upon Adam as punishment for his transgression exhausts the meaning of death. There is a kind of "dying to self" that God Himself models in His divine communal life as Father, Son, and Holy Spirit. Was there sacrifice before the fall? I believe there was. I will have a bit more to say about this later when I discuss the Lord's Supper. Suffice it to say for now that God created man in order that mankind would mature into the kind of life and community that God the Father, Son, and Holy Spirit are. The Triune life was the eschatological goal of Adam and his posterity. This would mean that he had to learn the kind of self-giving service, obedience, and "death to self" that characterized the divine community. In other words, the Persons of the Godhead live sacrificially, and it was God's intention that mankind mature into this kind of life as well. When Adam tossed off this plan at the Tree of the Knowledge of Good and Evil, God forcefully imposed it on him. If you won't patiently learn sacrifice through loving service to me and to your wife, then I will judicially impose it on you. You will die, whether you like it or not. And you will give of yourself both to the ground and to one another in order to live and grow. The challenge for us is to relate the two "kinds" of "death"—the "normal" inter-Trinitarian "death" whereby each Person of the Godhead "dies" to self and lives for the other(s) and the curse of death imposed on Adam because of his rebellion. I believe it is appropriate to suggest that because Adam failed to willingly "die" to self and serve his wife God therefore imposed death on him as punishment/training. "If you won't chose to die, I will train you to

judgment of God while Noah and his family pass through the waters and enter a new creation. Noah then emerges as a new Adam, with a slightly different hierarchical arrangement in this new society than before. All commentators will note the emphasis now on human government in dealing with mankind's proclivity for murderous violence. Noah has matured and God has therefore given him more authority.

3. God speaks to Noah and gives him a new word fit for his new situation. Under the Noahic covenant, there is a slightly altered, new way of life.

4. There are new signs and seals of this new covenant: first, a sacrificial system that involves the use of every clean animal (Gen. 8:20); and second, a rainbow to remind God of his covenant. (Gen. 9:8–17)

5. God sets up an arrangement for the succession of this covenant when he makes a promise that he will never again flood the earth (Gen. 8:21–22) and establishes a priestly nation (the Shemites) to minister to the seventy nations of the world. (Gen. 10)

Next, we have the Abrahamic covenant (Gen. 12, 15, 17, 22).

1. Abram is taken hold of by Yahweh in order to do something new with him. (Gen. 12:1)

2. The Lord graciously separates Abram and his family from their old country and their old family (Gen. 12). There is a death to the old world and a "new creation."[8] He is united with a new land (Canaan) and given a new name (Abraham). The people of God are now called "Hebrews" (from Abraham's ancestor Eber, Gen. 11:16). God reveals Himself by a new name: El Shaddai or "God Almighty." As a result there are new lines of authority (revealed when Abraham must conquer the existing "lords" of the land in Gen. 14).

---

do it my way." But even if post-lapsarian man's death was a curse, it was still the way of maturity and eschatological fullness of life. And, of course, God the Son came not only to take upon himself the curse of death, but to do so as God, embodying the divine way of dying to self and living for the other.

[8] Throughout this book I will sometimes use the phrases "old world," "old order," and "old creation" to designate the time from Adam to Christ. The Bible describes Jesus' work as ushering in a new world order, even a new creation (Mt. 19:28; Gal. 6:5; Eph. 1:10). The animal sacrificial system and the central sanctuary, for example, are replaced with decentralized, human communities gathered in the Spirit around the Word and the Lord's Table for covenant renewal, sacrificial worship. For more on the recreation of the world in Christ, see Peter J. Leithart, *The Kingdom and the Power: Rediscovering the Centrality of the Church* (Phillipsburg: Presbyterian & Reformed Publishing Co., 1993), especially chapters 1–6.

3. God speaks to Abraham, granting him new, more detailed promises (a seed that will bless all the nations and the possession of the land, for example). One of the most important new ways in which Abraham is to be faithful has to do with his waiting patiently for God's promise of a child.

4. There is a new sign and seal of the covenant: circumcision (Gen. 17). Blessings and curses are associated with this covenantal sacrament.

5. And, of course, God's promise of an heir for Abraham will ensure the perpetuation of the covenant. To this end God has chosen Abraham, "so that he will direct his children and his household after him to keep the way of Yahweh by doing what is right and just so that Yahweh will bring about for Abraham what he has promised." (Gen. 18:19)

After the Abrahamic covenant comes the Mosaic covenant (Exod.).

1. The people of God are graciously regarded by Yahweh, who takes hold of them and their situation in order to do something new. (according to his covenant promises made to Abraham, Gen. 15:12–21)

2. The people of God are torn from Egypt, separated from the death of slavery to Pharaoh, and cross the Red Sea as a new creation. They are bound together into a new entity—a nation with a new name: Israelites. God reveals himself with a new name: Yahweh (Exod. 3:14–15). There is now a new authority structure for the new nation: Moses, Aaron, priests, Levites, and elders are newly installed as rulers.

3. God speaks to the people, graciously providing them a new word from Him fit for their new estate—the Ten Commandments and what is called "the law of the covenant" (Exod. 20–23). The people then hear and respond with oaths of loyalty.

4. Not only does God utter the Ten Words from Mt. Sinai, but He also provides them with new signs and seals of His covenant: the tabernacle, the priesthood, and the sacrificial system. Not surprisingly, associated with these sacramental tokens of His presence are all sorts of blessings promised to those who faithfully perform them and curses for those who faithlessly violate the covenant rituals.

5. Finally, the entire book of Deuteronomy renews the covenant with the second generation of Israelites in the wilderness just before they cross the Jordan into the Promised Land. The whole book is concerned with the maintenance of the Mosaic covenant under the leadership of Joshua. (see especially Deut. 32-34)

[handwritten margin note: Oaths of Loyalty to the Law of the Covenant]

I could make similar observations about the form of the Davidic Covenant as well as what has been called the Restoration Covenant (after the return of the Jews from exile in Babylon) but I will resist the temptation. I think the reader can see the pattern. Finally, we move to the New Testament and consider the final "new covenant" in Christ.

1. God takes hold of his creation to do something new. Jesus takes on our flesh in order to faithfully execute the covenant promises.

2. In Christ we have the fulfillment of all the typological death and resurrection events in the Old Testament. Jesus and His people united to Him die to the old Adamic world and rise again as a new creation. God's people are mercifully separated out from the old world in union with Christ. This is also a marriage: the Husband leaves his family to secure for himself a bride, and the Church is separated out from the old world to be united to her new covenant Lord. The people of God, therefore, are now united to Christ and become a new creation in Him. We become the Church, the body of Christ, a new reality. Furthermore, we are baptized into the newly revealed name of God: the name of the Father, Son, and Holy Spirit. The people of God now are given new names: Christians. All of this means that there is a new hierarchy, new lines of authority: Jesus is Lord and as Head over His Church has instituted a government which represents Him on earth: pastors, elders, and deacons. (Eph. 4)

3. God speaks anew to His people, now through His Son (Heb. 1:1ff). There's a "new" way of life for those in covenant with God through Christ—the way of love and sacrificial living. This is all laid out for us in the new covenantal documents that we call the "New Testament [Covenant]."

4. The public face of the covenant has changed too. Gone are circumcision and the animal sacrifices. New, non-bloody signs and seals of the covenant are instituted—the Lord's Supper and Baptism. These are now the memorials of God's new covenant.

5. Finally, provision is made for the succession of the covenant with the ordination of ministers, elders, and deacons, and Christ's charge to them to make disciples by baptizing and teaching the nations.

The ritual of the Lord's Supper is explicitly identified by Jesus as a covenant renewal rite: "This cup that is poured out for you is the new covenant in My blood" (Lk. 22:10). That means we should find the same covenantal order and shape here as well. The Lord's Supper is a covenant memorial meal. Every week at this meal the covenant is renewed when the Lord takes us through the order of covenant renewal:

1. Jesus took hold of the bread and gave thanks. He did the same with the cup.

2. He broke the bread and poured out the wine giving them new names ("my body" and "my blood"), and as Lord and Master distributed them to His followers.

3. He taught them while they ate and spoke of the new covenant that would result from His death and resurrection. (Jn. 14–17)

4. He told them to "do" what He did and so memorialize His life, death, and resurrection to the Father in this ritual meal.

5. After they ate and enjoyed the bread and wine, the disciples were strengthened for the mission to which they were being called. They sang a psalm and departed.

The covenant is formally inaugurated with disciples at Baptism. An analysis of the rite of Baptism shows that this same covenantal order is present:

1. The child (or adult) is called by God.

2. He is then separated from his old way of life (natural parents). God takes hold of the person being baptized, tearing him from his old world and bringing him into a new life in the Church. United to Christ and his Body, the Church, the child is given a new name (disciple/Christian) and placed under the authority of the pastors and elders of the church.

3. As a disciple the person now learns to listen to and heed God's Word.

4. He is admitted to the covenant memorial meal where he must learn to live faithfully and experience the blessings of the covenant.

5. Finally, he grows to learn the importance of perpetuating the covenant by means of evangelism, marriage, and the faithful nurture of covenant children.

Conclusion

Now we have a basic outline of God's way of covenanting with His people. Of course, there is a great deal that I have not covered about God's covenants. One thing that comes to mind is how each covenant develops and transforms previous covenants. God takes His people from glory to glory, the New Covenant being the most glorious of all. Another dimension of biblical covenants that will become clearer as we move forward in this book is their *social* character. Covenants are never merely formalized individual relationships; rather, they always involve families and communities of people. Covenant renewal worship happens when God takes hold of us as a community, a church, and not simply as a gaggle of isolated individuals that happen to be in the same room on Sunday.

Much more could be said about the character and structure of God's covenantal relations with us. But enough has been said so far to suggest that when God calls His people together to enter into covenant or to renew His covenant with them this event has a basic order or shape. If the corporate worship of the Christian Church is such a covenant renewal event, then we should expect it to have a similar shape. This is precisely what we find in traditional Christian liturgies.

1. Call to worship: God comes near and calls His people out of the world to gather in His presence. He graciously takes hold of us and brings us near to Himself.

2. Confession and Forgiveness: God reminds us what He has done for us in Christ and declares His interest in restoring us again to his favor in Christ. We confess our sins and God absolves us of guilt. God graciously reminds us that we bear the name Christian and are members of His family in Christ. He tears us from our old sinful ways and renews His love for us in Christ.

3. Scripture Readings and Sermon: God speaks to us through his Word. His people respond by giving themselves and their gifts as a fitting offering.

4. The Lord's Supper: God invites us to commune with Him at his covenant meal, and we respond by memorializing His covenant and enjoying His faithful provisions at the family feast.

5. The Benediction and Commissioning: God blesses us and charges us to extend His kingdom into the future and into the world, making disciples of all nations. We are dismissed from God's special presence, renewed and equipped for this task.

We should also be careful to note that the fourth slot in this covenant renewal sequence occupies the climactic position in this process. As I mentioned at the beginning of this chapter, God invites people to church on Sunday for a meal. Eating and drinking together with the Lord caps off the service. It is the *goal* of the Lord's Service. The Lord's Supper should never be something occasionally tacked on to the end of a Christian worship service. One of the chief reasons why so many distorted answers are given to the question "why do I come to church on Sunday" is that the Communion meal has not figured prominently into much of American evangelical worship. In many churches the Lord's Table may never even be set for Sunday morning worship. It gets pushed off to a weeknight or Sunday evening celebration for select Christians who decide they might have some pious use for the ritual. We come together as the Church for the Lord's Supper. If we are not coming together to eat with Jesus at this common Table, then we deserve the rebuke of the Apostle Paul (1 Cor. 11:20).

It is more than coincidence that this traditional order of Christian worship tracks with the order of God's covenantal relations in Scripture. Traditional liturgies have not typically been labeled "covenant renewal services" largely because the covenant has not been adequately appreciated or understood until recently. How then did the Church "know" to order her services in this way? There are a number of possible answers. First, whether one explicitly identifies these patterns and sequences that we have been examining as "covenantal," the fact remains that they are deeply embedded throughout the Scriptures. One can recognize from Scripture the manner and order in which God draws us near to Himself and seek to follow it in corporate worship without necessarily calling it "covenantal." Whether the word "covenant" is used or understood, these covenantal patterns have profoundly influenced the historic liturgies of the Church. Moreover, I believe that an explicit link can be found in the sacrifices. The Spirit has led the Christian Church throughout her long history to explain and pattern her worship using *sacrificial* categories. As we shall see in the next chapter, covenant and sacrifice are inexorably connected. What is sacrificial is covenantal, and visa versa.

3

Covenant Renewal: Worship as Sacrifice

For the word of God is living and active, sharper than
any two-edged sword, piercing to the division of soul
and of spirit, of joints and of marrow, and discerning
the thoughts and intentions of the heart.
—Hebrews 4:12

God's personal relations with us take the form of a covenant. In other words, the covenant structures God's personal relations with us. I argued in the last chapter that we do not merely have a personal relationship with God or with Jesus. That might mean almost anything. To some it simply means that Jesus is going to take them to heaven when they die because they prayed a prayer or walked down an aisle in church. To others it might mean more, so that they talk to Him when they are in trouble or come to church to think about Him occasionally. A covenantal relationship, however, is a *formal* relationship between God and us. Like marriage (which is a human covenant modeled after the God's covenant with his church, Eph. 5:22–33), God's covenant with us has a definitive form and content. Furthermore, there is a distinctive way of renewing covenantal relations in the Bible, and that is by way of sacrifice (Gen. 8:20–9:17; Gen. 15:8–18a; Exod. 24:4–11; 34:15; Lev. 2:13; 24:1–8; Num. 18:19; 1 Kgs. 3:15; Ps. 50:5; Lk. 22:20; Heb. 9:15, 18; 9:20; 12:24; 13:20).

According to the Scriptures, in corporate Christian worship the people of God are engaged by the Spirit and drawn into the Father's presence as living sacrifices in Christ (Eph. 2:18). This is how God renews His covenant with His people. He draws near to draw us near. And in drawing us near to Him we are renewed through sacrifice. Christian worship is sacrificial; when we say Christian worship is covenant renewal worship we mean that it takes the form of sacrifice and offering. Although we will develop this in more detail throughout the next chapter, the same five-fold covenantal pattern can be discerned in the way the details of the sacrificial ritual unfold. The first offering of Leviticus 1:1–9 illustrates this:

1. Call to Worship: God calls the worshiper to draw near. In response to God's call the worshiper comes with the appropriate animal. (Lev. 1:1–2)

2. Confession and Absolution: God requires that the worshiper die in the representative animal. The worshiper leans on the animal and identifies with it. After which it is slaughtered, the blood separated out and splashed on the altar as a public presentation to God that the worshiper/animal has been slain. (Lev. 1:3–5)

3. Consecration: God moves the priests to cut up the animal, making it fit to ascend the altar into God's fiery presence. The worshiper/animal must not only die, but it is necessary that he be properly prepared for God's holy presence. (Lev. 1:6–7)

4. Communion: The worshiper as represented now by the animal ascends into God's glory-presence (the fire on the altar) and becomes food for God. In effect, the animal has been turned into smoke and incorporated into God's glory cloud presence symbolized by the fire and cloud at the top of the altar. This is a communion meal.

5. Commissioning: Once the sacrifice is over, Yahweh sends the worshiper out renewed and empowered for service in the kingdom. (Num. 6:22–27)

The Lords serves us when He draws us near to Himself through "knife and fire" (Gen. 3:24), that is, by making us living sacrifices. This means that our reasonable liturgy, as the apostle Paul says in Romans 12:1–2, is to offer ourselves as "living sacrifices," to submit to the Lord's transforming knife and His fire. The assertions made in these introductory paragraphs will take many pages to explain and prove from the Scriptures, but we dare not move too quickly.

Abrogated or Fulfilled? Synagogue or Temple?

Before we move on to analyze the details of the sacrificial rituals and their application to the question of the form of Christian worship, I must stop and dispel a widespread misunderstanding in Reformed and Evangelical circles. In the remainder of this chapter I will present arguments for the continued relevance of the Old Testament's sacrificial rituals. The way of sacrifice has not been abrogated; *animal* sacrifices have. Discussion of the revocation of the sacrificial system has not always been carefully nuanced. The meaning and application of the Old Testament animal sacrificial system cannot be exhausted by referring it all to the historical work of Christ on the cross. This is a real weakness in post-Reformation Protestant theology (see the Westminster Confession of Faith 6:5, 8:5–6, and 29:1–2 for examples of this one-sided emphasis on the abrogation of sacrifice). In the New Testament sacrificial language is *not* confined to the historical work of Christ on the cross (Eph. 5:2; Heb. 9:26; 10:12). The author of Hebrews, for example, tells us that the entire Old Covenant sacrificial system "was symbolic for the present time" (Heb. 9:9–10).

As I shall illustrate shortly, much of the language used to describe the Church and the Christian life in the New Testament is derived from the tabernacle, temple, and sacrificial system. Contrary to some authors, the topic of the synagogue and its worship barely arise. This means that the reality of *life* in the new age was pre-figured in the sacrificial rituals of the old age. The life and worship of the Church of Jesus Christ do not so much derive from the synagogue (which was largely a peripheral institution in the old world),[1] but rather from the tabernacle/temple symbolism and rituals, as they are understood to be fulfilled by and in Christ.

---

[1] Donald D. Binder, *Into the Temple Courts: The Place of the Synagogue in the Second Temple Period* (SBL Dissertation Series 169; Atlanta: Society of Biblical Literature, 1997).

Jerusalem was not the only place God commanded worship. According to Yahweh's explicit directions, every Sabbath day was to be a "holy convocation," one of the "feasts," according to Leviticus 23:1–3. Such a mandate demands local, weekly worship, and not in Jerusalem, but decentralized in the towns. This is surely the origin of what would later be styled "synagogues." The Sabbath services in the local gatherings were not explicitly regulated. In other words, God doesn't lay out a how-to list for synagogue worship like he does for sacrificial worship in the book of Leviticus. The absence of detailed regulations, however, did not mean freedom to do anything. Wise Levitical pastors and elders in the local towns would have understood that the regulations of the Temple and sacrificial system applied *mutatis mutandis* to the local services.[2] We know for a fact that synagogue practice was modeled on the temple, and by the time of Philo and Josephus synagogue worship was explicitly described in templar terms (e.g., prayers were described as "sacrifices," as in the New Testament, and the synagogue itself was considered holy space).[3]

Nevertheless, no first-century Jew would have failed to note a dramatic change in synagogue worship. Even though the pre-Christian synagogue services were modeled on the temple liturgy, the one thing they could never do during their weekly services was partake of the sacrificial meals. One memorialized Yahweh and experienced covenant renewal at the great feasting hall of the temple. In the new world, however, after the death and resurrection of Christ, the Church is the New Temple. She feasts with the King of Kings every week when she gathers. The fact that the covenant renewal meal is an integral part of weekly Christian worship was a dramatic experience for the first-century Jews. They understood the

---

[2] See Peter J. Leithart, "Synagogue or Temple? Models for Christian Worship," *Westminster Theological Journal* (forthcoming), and *From Silence to Song: The Davidic Liturgical Revolution* (Moscow: Canon Press, 2003), especially chapter 6.

[3] Ismar Elbogen, *Jewish Liturgy: A Comprehensive History* (Raymond Scheindlin, trans.; Philadelphia: Jewish Publication Society, 1993).

change: the Church was the New Temple (1 Cor. 3:16–17; 2 Cor. 6:16; Eph. 2:18–22; Heb. 8:1–2; 1 Pet. 2:5; Rev. 21:3).[4] When the early Christians met they ate (Acts 2:42, 46; 20:7, 11; 1 Cor. 5:8; 10:16–17; 11: 17–34; Rev. 3:20). If the synagogue in the old world derived much of its liturgical structure from applying the details of the animal sacrifices to the gathered communities' ritual worship, the post-Pentecost Church now understood herself to be the fulfillment of both temple and synagogue. In her worship all the sacrificial types of the old world were fulfilled.

Accordingly, Hebrews 10:1 identifies the ritual/sacrificial system as the "shadow of the good things to come." The model for the Church was the sacrificial order prescribed in the Scriptures of the Old Testament, not the first-century practice of the Jews. [5] Jesus' sacrifice not only did away with the old animal offerings, it also illumined for the Church the true meaning of the sacrificial rituals for life and liturgy. Jesus was not only our substitute, but also the forerunner (Heb. 6:20). In union with Him we are drawn into God's presence as living sacrifices. In Him the Church is holy space, the environment in which living sacrifices are offered. Geoffrey Wainwright explains:

> A final point must be made in connection with the "novelty" of Christianity and the way in which it may nevertheless be said to "fulfill" the Old Testament and, *mutatis mutandis*, the other religions. The Jesus of St. Matthew claimed to have come not to abolish the Law but to fulfill it (Mt. 5:17). Jesus fulfilled the profound intentions of the Law in a way which Jewish practice had been powerless to achieve: this is the view which may underlie the apparent *double entendre* of St. Paul in Romans 10:4, where he says that "Christ is the end, *telos,* of the Law;" such a view seems in any case necessary in order to reconcile St. Paul's positive appreciation of the Law

---

[4] See Roderick Campbell, *Israel and the New Covenant* (Philadelphia: Presbyterian and Reformed Publishing Co., 1954), especially chapter 17, "The New Temple."

[5] Paul F. Bradshaw explains that ". . . although the sacrificial imagery of the Temple certainly did continue to figure in early Christian thought, and more strongly from the fourth century onwards in actual liturgical practice, the source for this was the literary description of the Temple liturgy in the Hebrew Scriptures rather than the first-century institution itself" (*The Search for the Origins of Christian Worship: Sources and Methods for the Study of Early Liturgy* [New York: Oxford University Press, 1992],15.)

(e.g. Rom. 7:12; 13:8-10) and his more familiar recognition of its bankruptcy as an instrument whereby to achieve salvation. The German word *Aufhebung* would allow us to make the point that there may be an "abolition" which is also an "assumption;" the deep values of the Law are taken up into a new and efficacious reality by which their forms are transfigured. According to Hebrews, the animal sacrifices of the Old Covenant—divinely appointed, but "shadows," and of limited effectiveness, 7:18ff; 8:5f; 9:1–10:4—are fulfilled and transcended by the self-offering of Christ, "who through the eternal Spirit offered himself without blemish to God" (9:14; cf. 10:5–10) and inaugurated a new and everlasting Covenant (7:22; 8:6–13; 9:15; 12:24). Believers now enter into the movement of their Forerunner and High Priest (6:20) and are summoned "continually to offer up through him a sacrifice of praise to God" (13:15a). The Christian Eucharist is traditionally called *sacrificiam laudis*. It focuses "the tribute of lips"— and of lives (9:14; 10:24; 13:1–6; 13:16)—"that acknowledge God's name" (13:15b).[6]

I believe that incipient Marcionite presuppositions plague much of modern Christian scholarship so that a deep-seated aversion to the ordering and ritual of the Old Testament surfaces in a great deal of "New Testament" scholarship.[7] Not surprisingly, too many Christian leaders look exclusively in the New Testament for directions for worship. How often have we heard that the Old Testament may have been liturgical and structured, but the New Testament church is unstructured and free? After all, "there are no liturgies in the New Testament." One would think that the Old Testament order anachronistically embodied a Roman Catholic formalism from which Jesus heroically freed us. Rob Rayburn offers this telling criticism of such sloppy thinking:

---

[6] Geoffrey Wainwright, *Doxology: The Praise and Worship of God in Worship, Doctrine, and Life* (New York: Oxford University Press, 1980), 174–175.

[7] See Henning Graf Reventlow's *The Authority of the Bible and the Rise of the Modern World* (Philadelphia: Fortress Press, 1985) for an account of this Marcionite propensity in post-Reformation England; and Peter J. Leithart, "Marcionism, Postliberalism, and Social Christianity," *Pro Ecclesia* 8 (Winter, 1999): 85–96, for a discussion of how Marcionism infects modern theological investigation.

Part of the reason why so many Christian worship services have no logic, no order, no movement, is because those who superintend those services of worship have not paid attention to the Bible's main instruction in the formation of a worship service *because that instruction is found in the Old Testament*. . . . It is this disregard for the importance of what is done in the worship of God and the order or logic with which it is done that has lead to the common pejorative use of the words "liturgy" and "liturgical" in many evangelical and even Reformed circles. This is a mistake in more ways than one. Every church service is a liturgy, if it has various elements in some arrangement. That is what liturgy is. Liturgical churches are churches that have *thought* about those elements and their proper order. Nonliturgical churches are those that have not. It is no compliment to say that a church is a nonliturgical church. It is the same thing as saying it is a church that gives little thought to how it worships God.[8]

In his analysis of the liturgy in the book of Revelation, Philip Carrington registers his surprise that so many Christian scholars have failed to see the connection between the sacrificial system and life in the New Covenant:

I am astonished to find so few discussions on the temple ritual, not only in connection with the Revelation, but also in connection with the Palestinian background of the New Testament generally. The recent advance in this study has concerned itself with the eschatological literature, and the oral teaching of the Rabbis; it has neglected the temple, its priesthood, and worship. But in the New Testament period the temple system was central; after its destruction the Rabbis organized a new Judaism on enlightened Pharisee lines. But it was a new religion, not the old. The old religion died in the year A.D. 70, and gave birth to two children; the elder was modern Judaism without temple or priest or sacrifice; the younger was Christianity, which was proud possessor of all three. What links Hebrews with Revelation is its insistence on this fact. Christianity is the true heir of the old faith. To it have been transferred the priesthood and her sacrifice.[9]

---

[8] Robert S. Rayburn, "Worship From the Whole Bible," in *The Second Annual Conference on Worship: The Theology and Music of Reformed Worship, February 23–25, 1996* (Nashville: Covenant Presbyterian Church, 1996),22–23.

[9] "The Levitical System in Revelation," in Philip Carrington, *The Meaning of Revelation* (London: SPCK, 1931).

Living Stones & Sacrifices

Consider the birth of the New Covenant church on the day of Pentecost in Acts chapter two. In the old world, when the glory cloud descended upon the tabernacle and temple, the fire of God ignited the wood on top of the altar for the purpose of sacrifice. At the inauguration of the new creation in Christ, the glory cloud descends upon the new temple of God in Acts 2 and the fire of God is ignited over the heads of the Apostles, the new *human* temple of God, enabling them to offer their lives as living sacrifices (Eph. 2:21; 1 Pet. 2:5). The animals in the Old Covenant symbolized human beings. Once Jesus offers Himself as the human sacrifice that fulfills every animal offering in the old order, the typological animal rituals fall away. Since Christ's death and ascension, what is left is the reality that sacrificial animals always symbolically represented— human beings offering themselves to God. The Church of Jesus Christ is the New Temple and as such the worship and ministry of the Church is in some profound sense "temple service."[10]

What, after all, was the point of all of the animals and furniture and lamps and rocks and poles and curtains and tables and altars in the Old Covenant? God was not really concerned about holy animals and objects, was He? Was it the fat of oxen and lambs burned on the altar that *really* pleased Him? Absolutely not! All these things were ultimately about people. God's real temple is made up of human beings (Jn. 2:19; 1 Cor. 3:16; 2 Cor. 6:19; Rev. 3:12). *Things* do not draw near to God, *people* do. Isn't this exactly the point of the prophetic criticism of the Israelites in the days of faithlessness and apostasy? The people of Israel failed to apply the deeper meaning of the animal sacrificial rituals in their own community (Ps. 40:6; 51:16; 54:6; 66:15; Is. 1:11; Jer. 6:20; Hos. 3:4; 4:13; 6:6; 8:13; 12:11; 13:2; Amos 4:5; 5:22).

---

[10] See Roderick Campbell, *Israel and the New Covenant* (Philadelphia: Presbyterian & Reformed Publishing Co., 1954), especially chapter 17, "The New Temple," 150–156.

What happens to the sacrificial animal symbolizes what happens "spiritually" to the worshiper himself as God draws him near. Only this connection makes sense of Yahweh's own polemic through His prophets against *mere* animal sacrifice. The people of Israel were not making the connection. They were to offer themselves as living sacrifices through the offering of the covenant memorial animal sacrifices. Quoting Psalm 40:6, the author of Hebrews writes, "Therefore, when he [Jesus] came into the world, he said: 'Sacrifice and offering you did not desire, but a body you have prepared for me'"(10:5). Jesus embodied God's requirements as outlined in the sacrificial system. He was the true and faithful Israelite who offered Himself as was required. His acts of obedience, prayer, and self-denial fulfilled the true intention of animal sacrifice.

But even before Jesus, there were those like David who glimpsed the true meaning of sacrifice when he himself approached God according to the sacrificial way symbolized in the sacrifices: "For you do not desire sacrifice, or else I would give it; you do not delight in burnt offering. The sacrifices of God are a broken spirit, a broken and a contrite heart—these, O God, You will not despise" (Ps. 51:16–17). There is plenty of evidence in the Old Testament itself that sacrificial language was applied to liturgical acts other than animal sacrifice.[11] The symbolic connection between the sacrificial animal and the human worshiper ought to have been well-known to the Israelite (e.g., the ram substituted and represented Isaac on the altar, Gen. 22:13). All animal sacrifice symbolized human sacrifice. The prophet Micah, for instance, encourages the kind of devotional conclusions that every Israelite ought to have discerned from the symbolism of the liturgy of animal sacrifice:

> With what shall I come before Yahweh, and bow myself before the High God? Shall I come before him with burnt offerings, with calves a year old? Will Yahweh be pleased with thousands of rams, ten thousand rivers of oil?

---

[11] See Peter J. Leithart, *From Silence to Song: The Davidic Liturgical Revolution* (Moscow: Canon Press, 2003), especially his discussion of "regulation by analogy."

Shall I give my firstborn for my transgression, the fruit of my body for the
sin of my soul? He has shown you, O man, what is good; and what does
the LORD require of you but to do justly, to love mercy, and to walk humbly with your God? (Mic. 6:6–8)

God did not *ultimately* take pleasure in animals slaughtered,
chopped up, and turned into smoke on the altar, did He? No! God
really delights in the sacrifice of his people. This is why we say that
the foundational sacrifice of Christ has not simply put an end to all
sacrifice and offering, but instead has manifested its true meaning.
Jesus shows us the way of sacrifice, true human sacrifice, in His life
and self-giving death on the cross.

The sacrifice of Christ has indeed put an end to the entire system
of animal sacrifice, but not to sacrifice per se. United to the sacrifice of Christ we are enabled to be living sacrifices, a notion that was
symbolized in the Old Covenant fleshy rituals. Brian Gerrish's insightful summary of Calvin's comments on Numbers 19 shows us
how Calvin was able to understand the place of "sacrifice" in the
New Covenant:

In his commentary on a passage in the Book of Numbers (Num. 19:1–10),
Calvin too speaks of "offering Christ," and he means by the expression much
the same as Luther. He is trying to uncover the obscure spiritual meaning
of the Lord's commandment to slay a red heifer, which was then to be
burned outside the camp together with its skin and dung. Calvin dismisses
the fantasies of those who speculate on the details ("I would rather be ig-
norant than assert anything doubtful"), but he does not doubt that the
ritual was a figure whose truth was fulfilled in Christ. What catches his attention in particular is that the whole people were instructed to bring the
heifer for sacrifice. And this suggests to him the fact that each of us should
offer Christ to the Father (*necesse est ut Christum quisque Patri offerat*). "For
although he alone offered himself, and indeed once for all, nevertheless a
daily offering, effected by faith and prayers, is commanded of us." Calvin
hastens to add that this is not the kind of offering that the papists have invented, who turn the Supper into a sacrifice, imagining that Christ must
be daily slain if his death is to profit us. Rather, by the offering of faith and
prayer we apply to ourselves the virtue and fruit of Christ's death. According to Calvin, there is, in fact, a clear distinction between two offerings in

this passage. Though they bring it, the people are not permitted to slay the heifer; that is the peculiar office of the priest. The people made their offering indirectly (mediate), by the hand of the priest. And that is how it is today: "To propitiate God, we set Christ before his face. But it is necessary for Christ himself to come between and to discharge the office of a priest."[12]

If these assertions were true, we would expect to see the ritual language and symbolism of the sacrificial rites applied to the people of God in the New Covenant. The positive sense of offering and sacrifice should arrive at the fullness of its meaning in the New Testament. In other words, not only does the death of Jesus fulfill the meaning of the sacrificial ritual in that He suffers the wrath of God for our sin, but that same death, combined with His resurrection, ascension, and on-going life also has sacrificial significance that goes beyond penal satisfaction. In His death Jesus shows us the way to live in imitation of His self-denial and self-giving love for others. "If anyone would come after me, let him deny himself and take up his cross daily and follow Me" (Lk. 9:23). In union with Christ His people also share in this sacrificial way of living. This is exactly what we find when we look carefully at the language of the New Testament.

A Survey of the Language of Sacrifice in the New Testament

The popular opinion that the Old Testament temple and sacrificial system have nothing to do with life and worship in the New Testament can find no justification in the New Testament itself, except perhaps from a very superficial reading of the book of Hebrews. A brief tour through the New Testament Scriptures ought to establish the fact that the way of sacrifice has not been abrogated, but fulfilled—not only by the work of Christ *for us*, but also through the work of Christ *in us*.

Sacrifice describes the essence of the Church's mission in the world: "You also, as living stones, are being built up a spiritual

[12] B. A. Gerrish, *Grace & Gratitude: The Eucharistic Theology of John Calvin* (Minneapolis: Fortress Press, 1993),153–154.

house, a holy priesthood, *to offer up Spiritual sacrifices acceptable to God through Jesus Christ.*" (1 Pet. 2:5). Notice how similar this is to Paul's description of the activity and life of the church in Philippi. He calls their work "the sacrifice and priestly service that arises from your faith" (Phil. 2:17). The language of sacrifice is used as a description of the Christian life (Rom. 12:1). The fact that Paul speaks of "living sacrifices" should alert us to the fact that there is a *positive* dimension to the sacrificial ritual in addition to the idea of penal, substitutionary execution. The self-denying, generous lives of Christians are sacrifices. The author of Hebrews admonishes the church, "But do not forget to do good and to share, for with such sacrifices God is well pleased" (Heb. 13:16). This life of love is a sacrificial life that we live in union with Christ's sacrificial offering, according to Ephesians 5:2: "And walk in love, as Christ also has loved us and given Himself for us, an offering and a sacrifice to God for a sweet-smelling aroma." Augustine's way of linking Christ's actions and ours is to remind us that the *totus Christus* (the "total" or "whole Christ") includes Head and Body or Husband and Bride, if you will (Rom. 12:5; 1 Cor. 12:12, 27: Eph. 5:23).[13] We can therefore say that both Christ and those united to Him as His Body offer sacrifice. We are priests "in Christ" (Rev. 1:6; 5:10; 20:6). We sacrifice "in Christ" (Rom. 12:1; Heb. 13:5).

Furthermore, as living sacrifices we give off a smell. According to 2 Corinthians 2:15–16, "We are to God the fragrance of Christ among those who are being saved and among those who are perishing. To the one we are the aroma of death leading to death, and to the other the aroma of life leading to life. And who is sufficient for these things?" First, like the typological Old Testament animal sacrifices offered by faith, Christians that live sacrificial faithful lives of love and good works "smell good" to God the Father (Gen. 8:21; Exod. 29:18; Lev. 1:9, 13). "We are *to God* the fragrance of Christ," Paul says. Second, we smell good to each other and to those God

---

[13] See Augustine, *City of God*, X. 5–8 (trans. by Henry Bettenson [Middlesex: Penguin Books, 1984], 377–380).

is drawing near to Himself; but we will not smell like barbecue beef or lamb to everyone. We smell like burning flesh to some, the aroma of death unto death. This hearkens back to the two smells that filled the air in the environs of the tabernacle and temple—the gut-wrenching smell of death and blood, as well as the pleasing aroma of the flesh of these animals being cooked as food on the altar.

Sacrificial language is also used to describe the sanctifying work of the Word of God in our lives. "For the Word of God is living and powerful, and sharper than any two-edged sword, piercing even to the division of soul and spirit, and of joints and marrow, and is a discerner of the thoughts and intents of the heart" (Heb. 4:12). This is a reference to the priestly knife that chopped up the animal sacrifice after its death, preparing it for its ascent into God's presence as smoke. When we hear the Word of God read and preached we come under the knife, as it were, and are made living sacrifices by the Spirit's work (Eph. 6:17; Rev. 1:16; 2:12).

The exemplary, self-giving service of apostles and pastors is described as a priestly service (Rom. 15:16), using sacrificial language (Phil. 2:17; Col. 1:24–25). Paul describes the lives of believing Gentiles as offerings to God. He strives to "be a minister of Jesus Christ to the Gentiles, ministering the gospel of God, that the offering of the Gentiles might be acceptable, sanctified by the Holy Spirit" (Rom. 15:16).

The monetary gifts of Christians are said to be offerings well pleasing to God, according to Philippians 4:18: "Indeed I have all and abound. I am full, having received from Epaphroditus the things sent from you, a sweet-smelling aroma, an acceptable sacrifice, well pleasing to God."

Finally, the worship of the people of God is explicitly described as sacrificial (Ps. 50:8, 14, 23), and the language of sacrifice is used to describe the liturgical service of Christians: "Therefore by Him let us continually offer the sacrifice of praise to God, that is, the fruit of our lips, giving thanks to His name" (Heb. 13:15). The corporate prayers of God's people are described using the sacrificial

imagery of smoke ascending (Rev. 8:1–5). Even the Lord's Supper
is a memorial offering. Paul describes the communion meal as a fulfillment of the Passover sacrifice when he says, "Let us keep the feast"
(1 Cor. 5:8). The imagery and language of the Supper is the language of the peace (or fellowship) offering ("Do this as my memorial," Lk. 22:19; 1 Cor. 11:24–25). We should note also that the
bread (body) and wine (blood) are *separated* in the rite of Communion just as they are in the sacrificial animal rites of the Old Testament. The body and blood appear on the Lord's Table already
divided. The death of Christ has already taken place in the past.
What remains is for us to partake of the benefits of his sacrifice and
to be transformed ourselves into living sacrifices in union with his
body and blood. I will have much more to say about the meaning
of "covenant memorials" later in my analysis of the Lord's Supper.
My point here is that sacrificial categories and terminology are freely
used to describe the practice and meaning of the New Covenant
communion meal.

We could continue with sacrificial references in the New Testament. I have only listed some of the more obvious ways in which
the New Testament speaks of the sacrificial rituals being fulfilled by
the people of God. There are also more subtle ways in which the
Spirit has incorporated the ritual symbolism of sacrifice throughout the entire New Testament corpus. My point is that in both Old
and New Covenants the details of the sacrificial ritual always had
reference ultimately to Christ *and* His people. Calvin argues in the
Institutes that there are two dimensions to the offerings in the Old
Covenant rituals:

> We know that, according to the consistent usage of Scripture, what the
> Greeks sometimes call *thusia,* sometimes *prosphopa*, sometimes *telete*, is called
> "sacrifice." Generally understood, this includes every sort of thing offered
> to God. We must therefore make a distinction, yet in such a way that this
> distinction may bear an anagogical interpretation, from the sacrifices of the
> Mosaic law, under the shadows of which the Lord willed to represent to his
> people the universal truth of sacrifices. But although these were of various

forms, still they can all be referred to two classes. For either an offering was made for sin by some kind of satisfaction, by which guilt was redeemed before God; or it was a symbol of divine worship and an attestation of religion—sometimes, in the mode of supplication, to ask God's favor; sometimes, of thanksgiving, to testify gratefulness of heart for benefits received; sometimes, of the exercise of simple piety, to renew the confirmation of the covenant. To this latter sort belonged burnt offerings, libations, oblations, first fruits, and peace offerings.[14]

Conclusion: The Trinitarian Origin of Sacrificial Relations

Sacrifice and offering, therefore, constitute major metaphors for Christian worship and living in the Bible. I use this word metaphor, not precisely, but loosely to mean something like a comprehensive symbol, a global outlook that shapes and explains the whole of the Christian life. According to Gordan Wenham, "The pattern of OT sacrifices may thus provide a pattern of truly Christian worship. Worship should begin with confession of sins, a claiming of Christ's forgiveness, and a total rededication to God's service, before going on to praise and petition."[15]

Contrary to popular Christian opinion, the New Testament does not abrogate sacrifice, but rather, Jesus Christ fulfills and establishes the genuine meaning and practice of sacrifice and offering. Sacrificial images and rites are part of the *central core* of the biblical revelation of the personal relations between God and man (from Gen. 3:21 through Rev. 21:22–27), possibly even constitutive of the personal relations within the Godhead.

In the unity of the Godhead, the Persons of the Trinity are united in this sacrificial dynamic of mutual giving and receiving. For the Son to "sacrifice" Himself to the Father for us, therefore, was not

---

[14] *Institutes of the Christian Religion* (1559 edition), ed. John T. McNeil, trans. Ford Lewis Battles, vols. 20–21 of *Library of Christian Classics* (Philadelphia: Westminster Press, 1960), 4.18.13. Even though Calvin rightly distinguishes these two dimensions of sacrifice (satisfaction and eucharist), his explanation fails to note that every individual sacrifice also embodies both dimensions.

[15] Gordan Wenham, *The Book of Leviticus*, The New International Commentary on the Old Testament (Grand Rapids: Zondervan, 1979), 66.

a foreign or merely human act, but instead His self-giving death manifests something about the very way in which the divine Persons are constituted in unity with one another. Sacrifice is a divine act, an inter-Trinitarian way of life.[16] The personal relations within the Godhead are relations of reciprocal giving and receiving. Geoffrey Wainwright, writing on the paradigmatic nature of Christ's sacrifice for the liturgy of the Church, makes this theological observation:

> In Christian eyes, this sacrifice stands at the heart of the communion between humanity and God; it may even correspond, within the sphere of time, to that eternal perichoresis by which, according to highly developed Trinitarian theology, the divine Persons empty themselves into each other and receive each other's fullness. At any rate, the classical movement of Christian worship has always meant a participatory entrance into Christ's self-offering to the Father and correlatively being filled with the divine life.[17]

The way of sacrifice, therefore, transcends the Mosaic institution of animal sacrifice. Better yet, the sacrificial rituals of the Old Testament are not merely ad hoc arrangements, but rather are grounded in the rich relational life of Father, Son, and Holy Spirit. Sacrifice reveals something of the nature of what it means for God to be personal (Father, Son, and Holy Spirit relate to one another self-sacrificially) and, therefore, also of the way in which personal relations are constituted between God and man, as well as between man and man in human communities.

This explains my assertion that sacrificial language and imagery are not merely fulfilled in the work of Jesus Christ, but also serve

---

[16] For more on Jesus' death as an instance and revelation of the divine way of dying, see Jeffrey J. Meyers, "Does God Suffer? Are We Theopascites?" (lecture delivered at the annual Biblical Horizons Bible Conference, July 2000), P.O. Box 1096, Niceville, FL 32588.

[17] *Doxology*,23. See also Colin Gunton, "The Sacrifice and the Sacrifices: From Metaphor to Transcendental?" in *Trinity, Incarnation and Atonement: Philosophical and Theological Essays*, eds. Ronald J. Feenstra and Cornelius Plantinga, Jr. (Notre Dame: University of Notre Dame Press, 1990),210–229; and Anne Hunt, *The Trinity and the Paschal Mystery* (Collegeville: The Liturgical Press, 1997).

to define and shape the life of the believer in Christ. In the pre-cross world both the work of the Messiah *and* the work of those who trust in the coming Messiah are couched in the symbolic structures of animal sacrificial rites and all the accompanying things—altars, bowls, knives and other assorted hardware. In the New Testament the old animal sacrificial typology is fulfilled *by* Christ and *in* the believer who is united to Christ by faith. In union with Christ—who offered Himself as *the* Sacrifice—we not only have the penalty for sin removed, but we are also being made into acceptable sacrifices by faith. The promise is that if we by faith offer ourselves to the Father through Christ in the Spirit we will become what God has destined us for—men and women remade in the image of God.

4

The Sacrificial Liturgy of Covenant Renewal

Gather to me my faithful ones,
who cut a covenant with me by sacrifice.
—Psalm 50:5

We have identified the purpose of the Lord's Day corporate assembly as covenant renewal.[1] But as we have explained, and are about to explore in much more detail, God accomplishes covenant renewal through sacrifice. Therefore, we might also say that Christian worship is sacrificial. The way in which God renews His covenant with us is the way of sacrifice. Our reasonable *liturgy*, the apostle Paul says, is to "offer ourselves as living sacrifices" (Rom. 12:1–2). On the Lord's Day God Himself draws near to draw His people near. The flaying knife of God's Word and the transforming fire of his presence reconstitute and restore the

---

[1] Christian worship may be profitably understood from a number of theological and practical perspectives. I have chosen to analyze the Sunday service from the perspective of covenant renewal sacrifice because the preponderance of biblical evidence supports this frame of reference, but one might also consider the whole service as prayer, performance, family time, praise, drama, play, death and resurrection, dialogue, sermon, etc. Michael Scott Horton, for example, in his new book *A Better Way: Rediscovering the Drama of*

congregation, making them fit for life in His presence and work in His kingdom.[2] In response to God's covenantal initiative—His drawing near to us—we submit to His sacrificial work; that is, we confess, thank, praise, and pray as we are renewed through the Spirit and enabled to give unto our Covenant Lord the glory due His Name. And it all culminates with a meal. The Lord serves us bread and wine at the Table, where we experience as a community His *shalom*. This is the progression we must carefully examine in this chapter. Exactly how does this happen? The details, particularly the order of the sacrificial rituals so carefully described in the Old Testament, contain the divine pattern or liturgy for the people of God assembled for worship.

Learning to Like Liturgy

Before we begin to examine the covenantal, sacrificial order of Christian worship a defense of the word "liturgy" may be in order. The word "liturgy" is a Bible word and ought not to scare us, if we properly understand and qualify its meaning. In Romans 12:1, for example, we are urged, in response to God's mercy, to offer our bodies as living sacrifices. Such a course, we are told, is holy and pleasing to God; it is our "reasonable service." The word translated "service" (or "worship" in some translations) is the Greek word *latreia*, which refers to the sacrificial "service" or "liturgy" by which

---

God-Centered Worship (Grand Rapids: Baker Books, 2002) chooses to organize his discussion under the overarching theme of "drama," and in so doing is able to incorporate satisfactorily these other perspectives (including covenant renewal). To my mind, however, covenant renewal sacrifice faithfully incorporates all of these other aspects and offers a better overall orientation to the movement of the liturgy as a whole. For more on the various aspects of worship see James B. Jordan, *Theses on Worship: Notes Toward the Reformation of Worship* (Niceville: Transfiguration Press, 1994).

[2] Note that what we customarily call the "Lord's Day" might also be identified as "the Day of the Lord," which is its grammatical equivalent. Once we see this, we can read the Old Testament prophetic descriptions of the Day of the Lord and learn about what happens on Sunday. Every Sunday is a prototypical Day of the Lord. The Lord draws near to deliver His people and judge His enemies. The Last Day will be a cosmic, super Sunday.

the worshiper presents himself to God (Phil. 3:3; Heb. 9:9; 10:2; 12:28).

In Acts 13:2 the Antioch church's worship on the Lord's Day is described as follows: "On one occasion, while they were engaged in the liturgy of the Lord and were fasting, the Holy Spirit spoke to them" (my translation). Many newer translations speak of the church "ministering" to the Lord. The word "ministering" means "serving," and the Greek word used here is *leitourgeo*, which refers to public, congregational service—whether God's service to the people or the people's before God is hard to know. The language of Acts 13:2 ("the Lord's liturgy" or "service") is ambiguous, maybe purposefully so. It might refer to the service rendered *to* the Lord by the people or the service performed by the Lord *for* His people. Whether it is one or the other, or possibly both, one thing is sure: the assembled congregation at Antioch was engaged in what we would today call a "worship service." Like the Antiochene Christians we gather on the Lord's Day as the church, not to serve ourselves, but to be served by and to serve God. This is the "liturgy of the Lord."

In Hebrews 9:6 the word "liturgy" (*latreia*) refers to the ceremonies or rites of the priests in the old creation tabernacle and temple. In the new age God's people as a whole are priests. United to Jesus our high priest, the entire congregation has sanctuary access as "saints." A "saint" is a "holy one," a term that has special connotations. In the old order one who was holy could cross boundaries and enter into the tabernacle or temple without fear of punishment. Regular priests were invited into the Holy Place (Exod. 28:9) and High Priests into the Most Holy Place (Lev. 16:3; Heb. 9:25). After the ascension of Jesus into the heavenly tabernacle everyone united to Him has full sanctuary access as holy ones ("saints"). Therefore, as New Covenant priests the people of God perform priestly service (*latreia*) inside (not outside) God's house. This mode of "sacrificial living" *coram deo* ought to characterize our daily lives, to be sure, but on the Lord's Day there is a special sense in which we are gathered together by God as the body of Christ in order to be drawn into God's holy presence as "living sacrifices."

The meaning of "liturgy," therefore, is intimately connected with the biblical practice of "offering" and "sacrifice" at the holy tabernacle and temple. More important than finding the word "liturgy" in the Bible is the recognition that God has established a carefully delineated way of approaching Him. God's way of graciously drawing us into his presence is not arbitrary, but follows a predictable sequence that is controlled by His holy and merciful character as the Triune God. According to the New Testament, the way or order in which God drew the sacrificial animals into His presence in the Old Testament symbolizes God's appointed way of drawing sinful human beings into His holy, but life-giving presence in His Son. By means of the sacrifice of "a son of the herd" (Lev. 1:5; literal translation) with the priest's help, Yahweh drew faithful worshipers near. Now in the new creation faithful worshipers are brought near in the Son with the help of the Spirit. This is the way of sacrifice. Sacrifice answers the question: "How are we drawn into God's presence?" The sacrifices are *qorban*, "that which is brought near" (Lev. 1:2; 2:1; 3:1–2; 4:23; 5:11; 7:38). Furthermore, the Hebrew verb "to sacrifice" or "offer" (*qrb*) is related and means, "to cause to draw near." The worshiper who offers a sacrificial animal draws near to God. Biblical sacrifice is not a technique invented by man in order to secure something from God or to draw down his favor. Rather, God has graciously provided man with a way of entering into His presence in His Son by His Spirit, and that way is the way of sacrifice.[3]

---

[3] "For Israel, the sacrifice is based on the gracious will of God by which He has entered into a covenant relationship with his people, and the Lord therefore says concerning the blood of the offering in Leviticus 17:11: 'I have given it to you . . . on the altar.' In contrast to the position taken by Köhler, the sacrifice here then cannot be seen as a result of a human attempt to ascend to the 'unknown God,' for in it God rather descends to humankind in order to lead it back to himself. At the same time, it is made clear that this reestablishment of life in communion with God can proceed only by way of death. The sacrifice is thus given by the grace of God as a means of atonement . . ." A. Noordtzij, *Leviticus*, translated by Raymond Togtman (Grand Rapids: Zondervan, 1982), 20–21.

The way of sacrifice, therefore, is God's appointed way of mercifully bringing the worshiper near to Himself by means of the
substitute/representative animal. Ultimately, this is the way of Jesus
Christ's life, death, resurrection, and the resulting incorporation of
His (and our) humanity into the Trinitarian family life of the
Godhead. Jesus Christ offered Himself by the Spirit to the Father
once for us all, and we, too, united to Christ, follow this pathway.
By the Spirit we are drawn into God the Father's presence united
to Jesus Christ.[4] This is what happens every Lord's Day in the worship service. This is the way of sacrificial worship—united to Christ
we are not only brought together by the Spirit, but by the same
Spirit we are drawn into the Father's presence in His Son by cleansing, consecration, and communion.

The Sacrificial Pathway

The primary focus of this chapter is on issues surrounding the
order of the service. I am referring to how the service progresses—
what comes first, second, third, etc., and why *this* ought to follow
that, and *that* follow *this.* Even though this temporal dimension
of biblical worship has been largely neglected in our own tradition
(the emphasis instead being on the "elements" of worship), I believe
that explaining the biblical order or sequence of man's approach to
God in the service may be the key to resurrecting a hearty Bible-
based liturgy in our churches.

I am sorry to say that you will find very little help from our own
tradition in this area. We talk a lot about "elements" and what is permitted or forbidden in worship, but questions about proper *order*
or *sequence* remain for the most part unaddressed in our circles.
Many Reformed theologians and pastors, of course, do have a

---

[4] "There is a movement of grace (creation, revelation, salvation) from God toward the
world—from the Father through the Son and in/by the Spirit; and there is a movement of
grace (faith, love, obedience) from the world to God—to the Father through the Son and in/
by the Holy Spirit" (Peter Toon, *Our Triune God* [Wheaton: Victor Books, 1996], 37).

general sense of how a worship service should be ordered, but they usually have not thought through *why* this order is appropriate.[5] I believe that the traditional Christian liturgical order arose in the early Church from a gut-level familiarity with the biblical way of approaching God, even if Church theologians have not always explicitly identified the biblical source of their intuitions. After all, the Church's roots are Jewish. If Gentiles joined the people of God they were grafted into an olive tree that had been growing for many generations (Rom. 11:17, 24). The Apostles went "to the Jew first" (Rom. 1:16) so that the community that developed was thoroughly familiar with the temple meal rituals and would have naturally applied these to the new covenant meal. How else would they have done it? What I offer here is a reasonable biblical explanation of how the traditional order of Christian worship developed as the corporate, sacrificial, covenant renewal service of God.

Without going into too much detail up front, an outline of the temporal progression of sacrificial/covenantal worship ought to be established before we proceed to explain the service in detail. One might think of the three major "sections" or "movements" within the service as three "steps." The movement of the liturgy is an *ascent* into God's presence along the pathway He has established. Just as every sacrificial animal passed through three "zones" and underwent three major "operations" on its way up the altar and into the presence of God, so also the human worshiper travels the same sacrificial pathway up the "holy mountain" into God's presence. By faith we understand our progress during the Lord's Day service to be God's graciously drawing us into His presence, making us fit in

[5] D. G. Hart and John R. Muether, for example, devote a little more than two pages (out of 190) to questions of order and sequence in worship. The sequence they commend is quite traditional, but their rationale for such an order is rather flimsy. They repeat the old saw that "Scripture does not provide a fixed order of worship" (*With Reverence and Awe: Returning to the Basics of Reformed Worship* [Phillipsburg: Presbyterian and Reformed, 2002], 97) and go on to suggest that the service ought to be ordered according to a "gospel logic." I have no problem with this as long as we remember that the gospel is grounded in the covenantal patterns and sacrificial system graciously given by God to His people in the Bible. If that fact were granted, then we could begin to think through the liturgical implications of the sequence of events performed in the sacrifices.

Christ for fellowship with Him. In drawing us near God performs three big sacrificial "operations" on us.

The three operations or steps can be conveniently identified as *Cleansing, Consecration, and Communion.* These are just handy labels that we attach to the three major operations performed on the sacrificial animals as the Lord drew them (and the worshipers represented by them) into His presence. As it ascends into the Lord's presence each sacrificial animal is always :

> 1. slaughtered and its blood splashed on the altar (cleansing and forgiveness), then
> 2. skinned, cut up, washed, and arranged in proper order on the altar grill (consecration), and finally
> 3. transformed into smoke and incorporated into God's presence as food (communion).

This is the sacrificial pathway that every animal/worshiper experienced as God elevated him to Himself. The animal/worshiper is cleansed of the guilt of sin through the death of a substitute, consecrated and made ready for God's presence, and finally incorporated into God's glory cloud theophany that symbolically occupied the center and top of the altar. Remember, the bronze altar was a miniature "Holy Mountain," a portable Mt. Sinai, if you will.[6] The three main zones where the three operations are performed on the animal (in front of the altar, the walls or sides, and the fiery center and top) correspond to the three zones on Mt. Sinai (Exod. 19:12–25; 24:1–18) and to the three rooms in the tabernacle (Courtyard, Holy Place, and Most Holy Place). The animal's entrance into the fire and its transformation into smoke represents the worshiper's entrance into the Holy of Holies and his incorporation into the glory cloud of God's presence, the eschatological goal of redeemed

---

[6] Exodus 20:18–26 makes the symbolic link explicit. The smoky, fiery top of Mt. Sinai corresponds to the center and top of the altar.

humanity.[7] In other words, the animal/worshiper moves symbolically from outside to inside, from below to above. He is taken up
and into the life and fellowship of God.

Interestingly enough, in addition to the three "steps" taken by (or
"operations" performed on) each sacrificial animal, there were also
three main types of sacrifices that were part of the normal taber-
nacle/temple liturgy of Old Testament worship: a Purification
Offering, an Ascension Offering (sometimes mistakenly called a
"whole burnt offering"), and a Fellowship (or Peace) Offering.[8]
Each specific type of sacrifice highlights one of the three major
operations:

> 1. *The Purification Offering* highlights and expands on the cleansing or
> purification dimension of sacrificial offerings. That is why it is called a pu-
> rification offering. The offering accents the animal's slaughter and the
> display of the blood on the altar. For example, Leviticus 17 (the day of
> atonement) is an elaborate Purification Offering where the act of confes-
> sion and forgiveness is highlighted. The other two aspects are present, but
> downplayed.

---

[7] Jacob Milgrom explains: "The equivalence of the Tabernacle to Sinai is an essential,
indeed indispensable, axiom . . . . The Tabernacle, in effect, becomes a portable Mt. Sinai,
an assurance of the permanent presence of the deity in Israel's midst" (*Leviticus 1–16*, vol. 3
in *The Anchor Bible* [New York: Doubleday, 1991],574; see also 134ff). See also James B.
Jordan, "The Whole Burnt Sacrifice: Its Liturgy and Meaning," *Biblical Horizons Occasional
Paper* No. 11 (March 1991), and Mary Douglas, "The Eucharist: Its Continuity with the
Bread Sacrifice of Leviticus," *Modern Theology* 15 (April 1999):220–1. See chapter 20, "The
Ascension Offering Examined," in Part III for a thorough discussion of the steps involved
in the animal's ascent.

[8] Actually, there are five basic types of animal sacrifice in the Old Testament, but one of
them—the Trespass Offering—was an "occasional" offering and not part of the normal cycle
of offerings. Trespass Offerings were offered as the reparation for unlawful encroachment or
assaults against God and His holiness. There, of course, is much more to the Trespass
Offering than this. See James B. Jordan, "The Death Penalty in the Mosaic Law," Biblical
Horizons Occasional Paper No. 3 [Niceville: Biblical Horizons, 1988]). The Tribute and
Drink Offerings were always offered *with* other sacrifices and never alone. The regular, daily
offerings at the tabernacle are called "Ascension Offerings" in Numbers 28:3. This seems to
be the most basic, the "mother" of all other sacrifices. The Tribute Offering (*mincah*) was
always "attached" to the Ascension Offering.

2. *The Ascension Offering* expands on the element of consecration and the ascension of the animal/worshiper into God's presence. That's why it is named *'olah* (Hebrew for "ascension"). The entire sacrifice is made fit to ascend. The Ascension Offering highlights the acts of skinning, cutting up, washing, and then the transforming of the entire representative animal by fire and its incorporation into the cloud of God's special presence at the tabernacle.

3. *The Communion or Peace Offering* expands on the element of union and communion with God. Once again, fellowship with God is a crucial dimension of all sacrifices, but it is highlighted in this offering. The Hebrew word *shalom* connotes communion, peace, and fellowship. *Shalom* is experienced in the meal. In this offering the food aspect of the sacrifice is emphasized. The sacrifice is the "bread of God" (Lev. 21:6). In the Peace Offering, communion and peace with God are not merely symbolized by the sacrifice being turned into smoke and assimilated into the glory-cloud presence of Yahweh. In this sacrifice fellowship with God is communicated by means of a common meal. There is cleansing and consecration, but the focus in this offering is on the common meal that the worshiper enjoys with Yahweh, the priests, and his family by means of the sacrifice.

Furthermore, these three types of sacrifices are always offered in the same order: Purification Offering (cleansing), Ascension Offering (consecration), and Peace Offering (communion meal). Worshipers are purified, ascend into God's presence, whereupon they eat and drink with the Lord. The inauguration of the priesthood of Aaron in Leviticus 9 shows us the order in which each of these three sacrifices were offered in the tabernacle liturgy.[9] Thus, we have clearly revealed an order or liturgy of approach to God not only in each individual sacrifice, but the same pathway is manifest in the liturgical order by which the three ordinary sacrifices were regularly offered.

[9] For more on the importance of the ritual order in which these sacrifices were offered, see my "Excursus on the Significance of the Ritual Order of the Sacrifices" at the end of this chapter.

The Three fold Gift of God

Another biblical way to think about these three steps in the service is to consider them as God's three ways of serving us or God's three gifts given to us on the Lord's Day. These are His gifts of glory, wisdom, and life. They correspond to the three hidden gifts locked away in the tabernacle's Most Holy Place (Num. 17:10; Heb. 9:4): Aaron's rod with almond blossoms (transformed person), a copy of the Torah (wisdom), and a pot of manna (life). What was hidden in the Old Testament is now revealed in Christ (Exod. 16:31–34; Eph. 3:9; Col. 1:26; 2:3; Heb. 9:3–4; Rev. 2:17). He is the final and faithful high priest (the greater Aaron). He is the Word of God incarnate (the true wisdom of God). And Jesus is the heavenly manna, the bread of life come down from heaven to give life to the world. These three gifts correspond with the three ways in which God services us as He draws us along the sacrificial pathway into His presence.

Glory

| Aaron's Rod Blossomed | Sin Offering | Confession and Restoration |

Wisdom

| Decalogue Tablets | Ascension Offering | Consecration by the Word |

Life

| The Pot of Manna | Peace Offering | Communion Meal |

During the first stage of the service God reconstitutes us in our personal, covenantal relationship with Him. We are granted the gift of the forgiveness of sins and the clothing of the righteousness of Christ. We receive from God a renewal of our standing in His holy presence. We are fully restored as kings and priests in Christ who have the authority to come boldly into the Father's presence by the Spirit. This corresponds to the first operation performed on the sacrificial animal—he is executed and his blood must soak the altar from top to bottom, thus opening the door in heaven from God to man. It also correlates with the "sin (or purification) offering," which is the *first* sacrifice when all three of the normal sacrifices are offered. Blood must be shed. The animal (worshiper) must die. The blood must then be applied, splashed on the sides of the altar (the way of ascent into God's presence) from top to bottom.[10] The presence of the blood opens up a pathway into God's holy presence. No one dare come into God's presence without confessing sin and reappropriating the efficacy of the shed blood of Christ. There is no sanctuary access without confession and forgiveness.[11]

Second, God speaks to us from His Word as the pastor reads, then explains and applies the Bible to the listening congregation. Hearing the Word of God, we hear the Spirit's guidance for our lives. The double-edged sword of the Word chops us up and rearranges us as living sacrifices (Lev. 1:6). The sword of the priest, which earlier had slaughtered the animal, now serves to prepare him for his transformation into smoke by the fire on the altar. The sword and the fire on the altar do not destroy, but transform. This is a crucial point. The penalty of death has been rendered by the knife when the animal was slaughtered. The fact that *more* happens to the animal than merely his death tells us that from that point on the animal is being made fit for God's presence. The animal, which represents the worshiper, is now being prepared for his transformation into smoke on top of the altar when he is incorporated into God's

[10] The evidence of the death is the blood. Without the public presentation of the blood, there is no access to God (Exod. 12:21–23; Lev. 17:11; Heb. 9:22). The presentation of the blood is the evidence that the sentence of death has been carried out (Gen. 37:31–34; Exod. 22:13). For that reason blood cleanses (Lev. 16:19; Deut. 21:1–9).

[11] Commenting on Exodus 29:38–46 and the prophetic meaning of the animal sacrifices, Calvin notes: "We may not, therefore, doubt but that He has been altogether propitiated to us by the sacrifices of His only-begotten Son, and has remitted our sins. But although Christ was once offered, that by that one offering He might consecrate us for ever to God, yet by this daily sacrifice under the Law, we learn that by the benefit of His death pardon is always ready for us, as Paul says (2 Cor. 6:2) that *God continually reconciles Himself to the church* when He sets before it the sacrifice of Christ in the Gospel" (John Calvin, *Commentaries on the Four Last Books of Moses*, trans. by Charles William Bingham, volume 2 [Grand Rapids: Wm. B. Eerdmans, 1950],297, emphasis mine).

glory-cloud presence. The New Testament makes clear that the transforming sword of God is the Word, the instrument used by the Spirit to transfigure Christ's people (Heb. 4:12). The reading and preaching of the Word, therefore, are the major operations in this second step of sacrificial worship. We should note that the Tribute Offering (sometimes called the "Grain" or "Meal Offering"), which symbolizes the offering of the worshiper's work, is placed on top of the animal sacrifice just as it is being turned into smoke. This corresponds to the collection of tithes and offerings from the people after the reading and preaching of the Word and before the communion meal.

The third and climactic step in the sacrificial/covenantal renewal liturgy is the Lord's Supper. In the Old Covenant this was symbolized when the animal was turned into smoke, ascended, and was assimilated into God's glory cloud, which corresponds to the worshiper's being drawn into the nearest possible relation to God. This union with God may also be seen in the third and last sacrifice offered in the liturgical sacrificial sequence—the Fellowship or Peace Offering. There is no more intimate symbol of the close fellowship between God and man than the covenant meal. From Genesis to Revelation the meal remains the preeminent symbol of God's intimate love and presence with mankind in Christ. God and man are at one (at-one-ment) and at peace around the table. Ultimately, this is the reason we have been invited into God's presence—to enjoy a fellowship meal with Him. The common meal not only occupies the climactic slot in the covenant renewal sequence on the Lord's Day, a communal feast will cap off all of history as the redeemed Bride of Christ participates in the festive marriage supper of the Lamb (Rev. 19:9, 17).

In our order of worship once the congregation has received the forgiveness of sins and experienced the transforming ministry of the Word of God, then the Lord provides them with his assurance of peace—a covenantal memorial meal. Sacrifices are "food" (lit. "bread" in Hebrew) for God (Lev. 3:11, 16; 21:6;

Num. 28:2; and in Lev. 6:10 the fire is said to "eat" the sacrifice) and "food offerings"[12] (over 25 times in Leviticus alone). God does not *need* food (Ps. 50:7–15), but He takes pleasure in "tasting" His people. Being eaten is symbolic for being incorporated into fellowship with God. The Lord delights in those whom He draws near.

This sacrificial, covenantal order or sequence of approach to God appears throughout the Bible. We might have established essentially the same order from the various examples of what happened when men and women were drawn into God's special presence in the Bible (Gen. 15:1–21; Exod. 3:4ff; 19:1ff; 24:1ff; Ezek. 1:1–3:15; Is. 6:1ff; Rev. 1:9–20) or from an examination of the form and structure of the covenant itself or even from reflection upon the logic inherent in the Gospel as it is expounded by Paul in epistles like Romans and Ephesians.[13]

The oft-repeated slogan "The Bible does not give us an order of worship" is therefore dangerously misleading. Obviously, God has not provided us with a sample bulletin or a laundry list of the elements of worship and their proper order. And yet, how much clearer does it need to be? The force of these biblical commands, principles, and examples firmly establish the prescribed way of approaching God in worship. Some have argued that texts like those we have been examining were never intended by God to provide a required order of worship for the New Testament church. But this raises the question about just what God *did* intend by them. If the covenantal structure, the sacrificial system, and the personal examples of men and women drawn into the Lord's presence do not instruct the Church in the proper way, the proper order in which to approach God, then what are they there for? If these passages don't count as liturgical instruction for the Church, what would?

---

[12] On the meaning of *'ishsheh* as "food offering" see G. J. Wenham, *The Book of Leviticus* (Grand Rapids: Wm. B. Eerdmans, 1979),56.

[13] Terry Johnson, *Leading In Worship* (Oak Ridge: The Covenant Foundation, 1996),15-18.

Conclusion

Based on this analysis, we can now offer a synopsis of the service as a whole. The congregation is served by God as they move from prostration (confessional obeisance in response to being called into God's presence) to standing (praise for God's renewed forgiveness) to sitting (in order to hear and learn from the Word) and then, finally, to reclining at the Table (to enjoy table fellowship with God). The basic threefold pattern of God's service to us may be outlined as follows:

> God cleanses and restores us through confession and absolution
> (Purification Offering).
> God consecrates us by the Word (Ascension Offering).
> God communes with us at the Table (Fellowship Offering).

Our response to God's work (our service to Him) corresponds to His service to us and gives us this threefold sequence:

> We confess our sins, receive absolution, and respond with praise.
> We hear the Word of God and offer our works and lives to Him.
> We eat and drink at peace with God at His Table.

If we put this all together and include the call to worship at the beginning and the blessing or commissioning of God at the end, then we have the following fivefold order of sacrificial or covenant renewal worship:

> God Calls Us—We Gather Together and Praise Him
> God Cleanses Us—We Confess Our Sins and are Forgiven in Christ
> God Consecrates Us—We Respond in Prayer and Offering
> God Communes with Us—We Eat God's Food at His Table
> God Commissions (Blesses) Us—We March out to Serve God

We might also designate the major moments in the language of the three biblical sacrifices we have examined in this chapter:

The Entrance
The Purification Offering
The Ascension Offering
The Fellowship Offering
The Benediction and Exit

The liturgy moves from tension to rest, from death to life, from mourning to joy.[14] God calls us together, cleans us up, tells us how to live, fuels us for service in His kingdom, and sends us forth to do His work. We strip off our soiled garments, are washed clean by the blood of Christ, are given white robes of holiness which serve as wedding garments of glory for the meal, and finally, as a result of our worship, we are outfitted with armor to carry out our mission in the world.

We have now come full circle and can link this sacrificial order with the fivefold order of covenant renewal as we outlined in chapter two. This expanded fivefold order corresponds to one of the primary ways that covenant making, covenant renewal, and covenant documents are often structured in the Bible. The covenant renewal sequence can be seen, for example, in Deuteronomy where God

1. initiates the covenant renewal process through Moses His representative, 1:1–5;
2. rehearses Israel's rebellion and need for renewal, 1:6–4:43;
3. instructs the Israelites in their covenantal obligations, 4:44–26:19;
4. promises blessing and threatens curse, 27–30; and
5. commissions Joshua to lead them into the promised land, 31–34.[15]

---

[14]The sequence of covenant inauguration and covenant renewal through sacrifice also corresponds to the temporal patterns of the course of human history and the biographies of individuals. James B. Jordan has sought to uncover these deep connections in his provocative series of essays *From Bread to Wine: Toward a More Biblical Liturgical Theology*, draft edition 1.1 (Niceville: Biblical Horizons, 2001).

[15] See James B. Jordan, *Covenant Sequence in Leviticus & Deuteronomy* (Tyler: Institute for Christian Economics, 1989).

This fivefold covenant model moves like this: God graciously takes hold of (calls) His people, forgives their sins, instructs them in the way of righteousness, assures them of His blessing (by oaths and signs), and finally commissions them and secures their future success as the covenant renewal rite is concluded. This is what happens to us in sacrificial, covenant renewal worship. More precisely, this is how God *serves us* in covenant renewal worship.

****

Excursus on the Significance of the Ritual Order of the Sacrifices

To some readers it might seem odd or perhaps novel that I would draw liturgical lessons for the Christian church from the order of the sacrificial rituals of Israel. Even so, discovering in the ritual order of the animal sacrifice a liturgical order for Christian worship is not new with me. Many Reformed and Evangelical commentators have made similar connections. For those who may need collaboration for this procedure, I offer the following samples from an assortment of Bible scholars and commentators. A. F. Rainey notes:

> The formal inauguration of the whole Israelite cultus is portrayed in a *narrative description* (Lev. 9); it was obviously intended to serve as a precedent just as was the preceding chapter concerning the priests . . . . That the liturgy of Leviticus 9 was grounded in actual temple procedure is demonstrated by the account of Hezekiah's great cleansing and restoration of the temple (2 Chr. 29:20–36). An extensive sin offering was made first (vv. 20–24); next there followed the burnt offering, the ritual of which was accompanied by elaborate acts of worship in music and song (vv. 25–30). At this stage the king announced that the people had "committed themselves to [a state of holiness vis à vis] the Lord" (v. 31). They were therefore in a state of purity that qualified them to engage in further sacrifices (vv. 31–35) of devotion (more burnt offerings) and thanksgiving (peace offering).[16]

[16] A.F. Rainey, "The Order of Sacrifices in the Old Testament Ritual Texts," *Biblica* 51 (1970): 497.

Rainey goes on to argue that this liturgical order:

> Is the key to understanding the religious significance of the sacrificial system. First of all, sin had to be dealt with; the appropriate offering (sin and/or guilt) had to be made. This was closely linked with a burnt offering that followed it immediately (with its accompanying cereal and drink offerings as stated in many instances) and thus completed the self-committal required for full atonement. Afterwards the supplicant(s) was qualified ritually for the last stage of the liturgy. This crowning phase was the presentation of burnt and peace offerings (with their cereal and drink offerings, of course). The former include both the voluntary gifts of individuals and the calendral offerings (symbolizing the constant devotion of the people as a whole). The peace offerings represented the communal experience in which the Lord, the priest and the worshiper (along with his family and the indigent in his community, Deut. 12:17–19) all had a share. The ritual approach was therefore: expiation, consecration, fellowship.[17]

Gordan Wenham maintains, "The pattern of OT sacrifices may thus provide a pattern of truly Christian worship. Worship should begin with confession of sins, a claiming of Christ's forgiveness, and a total rededication to God's service, before going on to praise and petition."[18] R. K. Harrison agrees:

> The order of sacrifices described in the ritual prescriptions constitutes an important guide for Christians with regard to the principles of spirituality underlying divine worship. Of the three concepts enunciated, the one that had priority concerned cleansing from sin, denoted by the sin offering. When proper atonement had been made the worshiper was to surrender his life and labor to God, as indicated by the burnt and cereal offerings. Finally, he was to enjoy fellowship with God within the context of a communion meal, which the peace offering furnished . . . . Some early Gentile Christians at Corinth, who were unfamiliar with the spiritual conditions governing Jewish worship, did not observe this order and so were not able to discern the Lord's body. (1 Cor. 11:20–21, 29)[19]

[17] Ibid., 498.
[18] Gordan Wenham, *The Book of Leviticus* in *The New International Commentary on the Old Testament* (Grand Rapids: Zondervan, 1979), 66.
[19] *Leviticus: An Introduction and Commentary*, (Downers Grove: InterVarsity Press, 1980),106–7.

In addition to these modern evangelicals—Wenham and Harrison—one will have to consult older commentators, since they often seem less afraid to confess the essential unity of the Old and New Testaments. A few examples will suffice. The German commentator C. F. Keil explains the meaning of the order of sacrifices this way:

> The sacrificial law, therefore, with the five species of sacrifices which it enjoins, embraces every aspect in which Israel was to manifest its true relation to the Lord its God. Whilst the sanctification of the whole man in self-surrender to the Lord was shadowed forth in the burnt offerings, the fruits of this sanctification in the meat offering, and the blessedness of the possession and enjoyment of saving grace in the peace offerings, the expiatory sacrifices furnished the means of removing the barrier which sins and trespasses had set up between the sinner and the holy God, and procured the forgiveness of sin and guilt, so that the sinner could attain once more to the unrestricted enjoyment of covenant grace.[20]

Commenting on Leviticus 9:8–21 and the ritual order of the sacrifices, Keil and Delitzsch note:

> The sin-offering always went first, because it served to remove the estrangement of man from the holy God arising from sin, by means of the expiation of the sinner, and to clear away the hindrances to his approach to God. Then followed the burnt-offering, as an expression of the complete surrender of the person expiated to the Lord; and lastly the peace-offering, on the one hand as the utterance of thanksgiving for mercy received, and prayer for its further continuance, and on the other hand, as a seal of covenant fellowship with the Lord in the sacrificial meal.[21]

---

[20] Cited in James G. Murphy, *A Critical and Exegetical Commentary on the Book of Leviticus* (Andover: Warren F. Draper, Publisher, 1872),20–21.

[21] C. F. Keil and F. Delitzsch, *Commentary on the Old Testament*, 10 vols. trans. by James Martin (Grand Rapids: Wm. B. Eerdmans, 1973), 1:345–346.

Two quotations from Samuel H. Kellog make the same point: [22]

The significance of this order will readily appear if we consider the distinctive meaning of each of these offerings. The sin offering had for its central thought, expiation of sin by the shedding of blood; the burnt offering, the full surrender of the person symbolized by the victim, to God; the meal offering, in like manner, the consecration of the fruit of his labors; the peace offering, sustenance of life from God's table, and fellowship in peace and joy with God and with one another. And the great lesson for us now from this model tabernacle service is this: that this order is determined by a law of the spiritual life.

Let us then, on no account, miss this lesson from the order of this ritual; before the peace offering, the burnt offering; before the burnt offering, the sin-offering. Or, translating the symbolism, perfect fellowship with God in peace and joy and life, only after consecration; and consecration only possible in fullness and only accepted of God, in any case, when the great Sin offering has been first believingly appropriated, according to God's ordination, as the propitiation for our sins, for the canceling of guilt. [22]

W. Robertson Nicholl concurs:

The significance of this order will readily appear if we consider the distinctive meaning of each of these offerings. The sin offering had for its central thought, expiation of sin by the shedding of blood; the burnt offering, the full surrender of the person symbolized by the victim to God; the meal offering, in like manner, the consecration of the fruit of his labors; the peace offering, sustenance and life from God's table and fellowship in peace and joy with God and with one another. [23]

[22] Samuel H. Kellog, *The Book of Leviticus* (London: A. C. Armstrong and Son, 1899), 222, 228.

[23] W. Robertson Nicholl, *The Expositor's Bible*, vol. 1 (Grand Rapids: Eerdmans, 1943), 1:293. See Nicholl's extended discussion of the importance and meaning of the ritual order of the sacrifices (293–295).

Peter Lange comes to the same conclusion:

In the order of the offerings of Aaron both for himself and the people is clearly expressed the order of the steps of approach to God; first, the forgiveness of sin, then the consecration completely to God, and after this communion with Him, and blessing from Him.[24]

Finally, even the *NIV Study Bible* gets this just right:

When more than one kind of offering was presented (as in Num. 6:16–17), the procedure was usually as follows: (1) sin offering or guilt offering, (2) burnt offering, (3) fellowship offering and grain offering (along with a drink offering). This sequence furnishes part of the spiritual significance of the sacrificial system. First, sin had to be dealt with (sin offering or guilt offering). Second, the worshiper committed himself completely to God (burnt offering and grain offering). Third, fellowship or communion between the Lord, the priest and the worshiper (fellowship offering) was established. To state it another way, there were sacrifices of expiation (sin offerings and guilt offerings), consecration (burnt offerings and grain offerings) and communion (fellowship offerings— these included vow offerings, thank offerings and freewill offerings).[25]

[24] Johann Peter Lange, ed., *Leviticus* in *Commentary on the Holy Scriptures*, trans. by Philip Schaff (Grand Rapids: Eerdmans, n.d. [reprint, 1876]), 80.

[25] From the chart "Old Testament Sacrifices," in *The NIV Study Bible* (Grand Rapids: Zondervan, 1985), 150.

5

The Lord's Service and Ours

What do you have that you did not receive?
—1 Corinthians 4:7b

In view of the one-sided emphasis in some Evangelical and Presbyterian circles that the congregation gathers to *give* praise to God and not to *get* anything, I must insist on the lopsided, impoverished nature of this posture. We have been told by well-meaning teachers, even otherwise orthodox Reformed theologians, that it is downright wrong to come to church in order to get something. A popular shibboleth has it that Reformed or Presbyterian worship stands apart from other theologies of worship in that we do not come to church to *get* anything but to *give* praise and honor and glory to God. Regrettably, many modern Reformed works on worship take this position. The first sentence in John Frame's popular book on worship is: "Worship is *the work of acknowledging the greatness of our covenant Lord.*"[1] He assumes this definition throughout the book. I could

---

[1] John Frame, *Worship in Spirit and Truth* (Phillipsburg: Presbyterian & Reformed, 1996), 1 (his emphasis).

quote other recent Reformed authors to the same effect. Most of them define worship as what the people of God do, the work they perform on the Lord's Day, specifically the adoration, praise, and honor that they ascribe to God. This notion must not be permitted to go unchallenged. It is only half of the truth, and the *second* half at that.

First, and above all, we are called together in order to get, to receive. This is crucial. The Lord gives; we receive. Since faith is receptive and passive in nature, "faith-full" worship must be about receiving from God. He gives and by faith we receive. The Lutheran scholar Vajta is surely correct:

> Faith will never reach that degree of maturity where it could live without receiving. A grateful reception of God's gracious gifts will always remain the task of Christian worship, for it is impossible to evolve a church service out of the spiritual assets of the believers.[2]

By faith Christians are given and receive God's forgiveness, Word, nourishment, and benediction in worship. We come as those who receive *first* and then, second, only in reciprocal exchange do we give back what is appropriate as grateful praise and adoration. More and more I am discovering, especially in our modern context, how crucial such a conception of worship is. Too often in conservative churches, worship or liturgy is described first of all as the "work of the people." While I do not deny that we "work" during worship, I do regard this definition as dangerously one-sided. Whatever we "do" in worship must always be a faithful *response* to God's gifts of forgiveness, life, knowledge, and glory—gifts we receive in the service. Without this perspective, the purpose of the Lord's Day assembly degenerates into an opportunity for Christian people to gather together and offer human devotion to God.

---

[2] Vilmos Vajta, *Luther on Worship* (Philadelphia: Muhlenberg Press, 1958), 129.

Slouching Towards Pelagiansim

Stating it this way calls attention to two more related problems with this conception of worship. First, it is dangerously Pelagian. As Calvinists we should be able to see the Pelagian danger lurking in such a one-sided conception. Sadly, too often Calvinistic churches have embraced Calvin's *soteriological* reformation without also adopting or even understanding his correlative *liturgical* reformation. Hughes Oliphant Old explains, "What Calvin has in mind is that God is active in our worship. When we worship God according to his Word, he is at work in the worship of the church. For Calvin the worship of the church is a matter of divine activity rather than human creativity."[3]

And since Pelagianism goes hand in hand with a Unitarian understanding of God, it is no surprise that worship framed in these terms tends to ignore the Trinity. In the traditional liturgy the service of God on our behalf has a very definite Trinitarian shape to it. I will explore this in more detail in the next chapter, but for now it is enough to call attention to the fact that God *serves us* when He graciously draws us into the presence of the Father in spiritual union with His Son. This Trinitarian content and shape safeguards against Pelagian conceptions of the liturgy. When the liturgy embodies the service of the Triune God—not simply service to the Triune God, but Father, Son, and Holy Spirit's service for and in us—we are not likely to slouch towards Pelagianism. During the Divine Service the congregation is taken up into the giving and receiving that characterizes the inter-trininitarian relations between the Persons in the Godhead. God's eternal tri-personal life of loving give and take is the origin and ground of all such human activity in the liturgy.

Interestingly enough, not even God gives without the expectation of receiving something in return. First of all, within the

---

[3] Hughes Oliphant Old, "John Calvin and the Prophetic Criticism of Worship," in *John Calvin & the Church: A Prism of Reform*, ed. by Timothy George (Louisville: Westminster/John Knox Press, 1990), 234.

society of the Trinity, the Father gives to the Son with the expectation that the Son will "give back" love and submission. The same
thing can be said of each of the inter-personal relations within the
Godhead. Secondly, God gives to his creatures with the expectation
of receiving back from them love, fellowship, and submission. The
Father gives the Son to us, and the Son, united as He is to humanity, is Himself humanity's reciprocal gift. The offering [back] of humanity to God the Father is accomplished by the Spirit in the
humanity of Jesus. We participate not only in receiving the gift of
the Son but also in the Son's mediation of humanity's response to
God. So then, giving in the hope of receiving does not imply a con-
tractual understanding of personal relationships, either within the
social life of the Trinity, or between God and man, or man and man.
The word to describe the "rules" or "form" of this reciprocal giving
and receiving is the word "covenant".[4]

Much of what goes by the name "contemporary" worship has
evacuated the Sunday service of God's service to man as well as the
proper Trinitarian context of our response. It is all about what *we*
do. The reduction of Christian worship to "praise" and "giving
worth to God" by well-intentioned conservative pastors desirous of
purging the Church of superficial worship forms will only continue
to feed the very thing that they oppose.

The Pastor as Jesus' Representative

For example, to name one side effect of this kind of thinking, the
disappearance of the minister as the Lord's representative and

---

[4] Some very interesting philosophical and theological work has been done here by John
Milbank. See his "Can a Gift be Given? Prolegomena to a Future Trinitarian Metaphysic,"
Modern Theology 11:1 (Jan. 1995):119–161 and "The Ethics of Self-Sacrifice," *First Things*
90 (March 99): 33–38. Milbank's articles, however, will be very difficult reading for almost
anyone. Milbank aims at bringing radical Trinitarian orthodoxy to bear upon the current
philosophical and societal question of what constitutes genuine personhood. As William T.
Cavanaugh explains, "Milbank provides a corrective [to the notion of 'pure' gift] . . . in point-
ing out that a certain kind of exchange does take place in the divine gift. Although it is true
that we can never make a return to God, 'since there is nothing extra to God that could return to him,' in the economy of the divine gift we participate in the divine life, such that the

spokesman, the ordained man through whom the Lord gives His gifts, is linked to this error. Many pastors no longer lead the worship service. This departure of the leadership of the pastor in contemporary worship follows from the kind of one-sided conception of the Lord's Day service that I have been critiquing. If what the people are doing in worship is merely getting together to praise and pray and offer God all kinds of human devotion, then we can all just do it together and anyone can lead us. If, however, the Lord himself is meeting us and giving us His gifts, then the ordained minister will be prominent so that the people can be left in no doubt that it is the Lord Himself who is speaking, forgiving, baptizing, offering us food and drink, and finally blessing us and sending us out into the world to further His kingdom. In traditional Christian theology and worship the minister is ordained to represent Christ to His Bride. The pastor's actions, therefore, in the Divine Service mediate to the congregation the acts and words of Christ.

This is why the pastor who leads worship must be an ordained *man*. By virtue of his office, he must represent the Husband to the Bride. A woman cannot do so. It would upset the entire fabric of God-ordained role relationships within the church and home for a woman to speak and act for Jesus in corporate worship. The symbolism of male headship must be maintained in the corporate liturgy of the Church. The Church submits to her Lord as she receives

---

poles of giver and recipient are enfolded into God . . . . The gift is not alienated from the giver, but the giver is the gift, goes with the gift. For this reason . . . a return is expected, but this is never a mere contract, since the return is not pre-established, but comes in an unpredictable form at an unpredictable time, bearing the character of a counter-giver. In the divine economy, this type of giving is perfected as the dualism of giver and recipient are collapsed; Christ is the perfect return of God to God . . . . We receive the gift of Christ not as merely passive recipients, but by being incorporated into the gift itself, the body of Christ. As members of the Body, we then become nourishment for others—including those not part of the Body—in the unending Trinitarian economy of gratuitous giving and joyful reception" ("Beyond Secular Parodies," *Radical Orthodoxy*, eds. John Milbank, Catherine Pickstock, and Graham Ward [London: Routledge, 1999], 109).

from him the Word and Sacraments by the mouth and hands of her ordained pastors. The pattern of male headship is rooted deeply in the created order (Gen. 2:15–24; 3:15–19; 1 Tim. 2:11–15; 1 Pet. 3:1–7) as well as in the re-created order of the Church (1 Cor. 11:3–16; 14:33–35; Eph. 5:22–33). These role relationships are nonnegotiable.[5] C. S. Lewis makes this telling observation:

> I am crushingly aware how inadequate most of us are, in our actual and historical individualities, to fill the place prepared for us. But it is an old saying in the army that you salute the uniform not the wearer. Only one wearing the masculine uniform can (provisionally, and till the *Parousia*) represent the Lord to the Church: for we are all, corporately and individually, feminine to Him. We men make very bad priests. This is because we are insufficiently masculine. It is no cure to call in those who are not masculine at all. A given man may make a very bad husband; you cannot mend matters by trying to reverse the rolls. He may make a bad male partner in a dance. The cure for that is that men should more diligently attend dancing classes; not that the ballroom should henceforth ignore distinctions of sex and treat all dancers as neuter.[6]

All of this is not to say that the Lord serves us in worship *exclusively* through the pastor, since the Lord is at work even in the corporate praying, reciting, and singing of the congregation. How many times have we been truly served by God as we listened to and joined in with the united voice of the church in prayer and praise? The Lord, then, serves us on the Lord's Day as His Spirit speaks through *both* the voice of the minister *and* the voices of His people. We should never lose sight of the primacy of the Lord's service to us when we gather to Him on the Lord's Day.

---

[5] See George W. Knight, *The Role Relationships of Men and Women* (Chicago: Moody Press, 1985); John Piper and Wayne Grudem, eds., *Recovering Biblical Manhood and Womanhood: A Response to Evangelical Feminism* (Wheaton: Crossway Books, 1991); Eric L. Johnson, "Playing Games and Living Metaphors: The Incarnation and the End of Gender," *Journal of the Evangelical Theological Society* 40 (June 1997): 271–285; and Vern Sheridan Poythress, "Gender in Bible Translation: Exploring a Connection with Male Representatives," *Westminster Theological Journal* 60 (Fall 1998): 225–53.

[6] Cited in *Credenda Agenda* 11/2 [1999]: 3.

Christian worship provides the occasion for God's service to the Church; that is, in the liturgy *God serves us* by granting us the gifts of the kingdom, which includes, but is not limited to knowledge. We gather to receive. The Lord gives. I have argued that the diminishing place of the pastor in the Sunday service corresponds to the deformation of the service from what God does for us to what we do before God. When the robed pastor is prominent, the people are left in no doubt that God is speaking and acting through the instrumentality of the office of the Ministry to deliver His gifts to the congregation. [7]

Terminological Turmoil: Worship or Service

Moreover, the terminology we use to describe what happens on the Lord's Day can be confusing. We have inherited the designation "worship service," which, to my mind, tends to introduce confusion. "Service" comes from the Latin *servitium*, as in *servitium Dei* ("the service of God" or "God's service"). This older way of designating the Christian liturgy is delightfully ambiguous. In the "Divine Service" or "the service of God" who is serving whom? Is God serving us? Or are we serving God? Or is it both? Classically, the "Divine Service" was thought to include both God's service to us and our service to God. Even so, our fathers in the faith considered God's service to us (the forgiveness of sins, the ministry [service] of the Word, the Sacraments, etc.) as primary and our service to Him as secondary response. But this emphasis is exactly what is lost when we call our corporate, Sunday assembly "worship." This term comes to us by way of the Anglo-Saxon word "worth-ship," which simply meant to accord someone his proper worth. What we appear to be emphasizing with this term is not God's gifts and ministry to us through His Word and Sacraments, but our ascribing "worth" to Him. Some Reformed writers have a tendency to miss this. We are too ready to accept the misleading definition of liturgy as "the work

---

[7] For more on this see chapter 14 in Part III entitled "The Place of the Minister in the Lord's Service."

of the people," which, as we have seen, is a severely truncated view of what happens in the Divine Service.[8] What happens on Sunday is the continuation of the service of the ascended Lord Jesus for His people. "For who is greater: the one at the table or the one who serves? The one at the table, surely. Yet here am I among you as the one who serves." (Lk. 22:27; see also Mt. 20:28; Jn. 13:5–16; Phil. 2:7–8).

If our service is primarily *for* God, then our worship inevitably degenerates into Pelagianism with a thin Calvinistic veneer. To combat this problem we must understand the proper *order* of things. First, we receive *from* God. Then, *secondly*, we give back *to* Him with gratitude precisely that which He graciously continues to give us. Everything we are and have we received from Him (1 Cor. 4:7). He stands in no need of our service or praise. He has not created us primarily to get glory for Himself, but to distribute and share the fullness of His glory with His creatures. He is not like the pagan gods who need to suck up as much glory and praise as they can. With the true God the determination of the amount of glory possessed by Him and us is not a "zero sum game." If He has all glory, this does not imply that we have none. If we possess glory, it does not come at the expense of His glory. Only when we refuse to acknowledge the source of our glory and assert our own over against His do we then fall under the condemnation of the prophets. Thomas Howard rightly challenges this distortion:

> If God alone is all-glorious, then no one else is glorious at all. No exaltation may be admitted for any other creature, since this would endanger the exclusive prerogative of God. But this is to imagine a paltry court. What king surrounds himself with warped, dwarfish, worthless creatures? The more

---

[8] Even a good work like Robert G. Rayburn's *O Come, Let us Worship* (Grand Rapids: Baker Book House, 1980) misses this important distinction. Reformed ministers would do well to study carefully what the Lutherans have said about God's service to His people on the Lord's Day. See Peter Brunner, *Worship in the Name of Jesus* (St. Louis: Concordia Publishing House, 1968), especially chapters 6–8; and Norman Nagel, "Whose Liturgy Is It?" *Logia* 2/2 (April 1993): 4–8. Other Lutheran authors also make this important point (see the Lutheran works cited in my bibliographic essay).

glorious the king, the more glorious are the titles and honors he bestows. The plumes, cockades, coronets, diadems, mantles, and rosettes that deck his retinue testify to one thing alone, his own majesty and munificence. He is a very great king to have figures of such immense dignity in his train, or even better, to have raised them to such dignity. These great lords and ladies, mantled and crowned with the highest possible honor and rank are, precisely, his vassals. This glittering array is his court! All glory to him, and in him, glory and honor to these others.[9]

In contrast to this, it is the other cruder form of the "all glory be to God" doctrine that is too often the popular view. Even worse, this zero-sum glory game is regularly taught as the distinctive Reformed theological perspective on worship. If anyone has an ounce of glory, then God must confiscate it. Far from being truly Reformed, such a perspective is implicitly pagan. As Christians we must say that if anyone has an ounce or two pounds of glory, it has been *bestowed* by God from the plentitude of His own glory and so all glory in the world must ultimately redound to Him. "For of Him and through Him and to Him are all things, to whom be glory forever. Amen" (Rom. 11:36).

If the Church's worship is the place where God glorifies his saints by distributing his life-giving Word and Sacraments, if it is the occasion for God to *serve* the congregation, then with this understanding we can, to some degree, transcend the rigid dichotomy regarding the purpose of the Sunday service—is it for evangelism or worship? Why do we have to choose between one or the other? Is worship for the people of God or unbelievers? Well, primarily for the people of God, but if unbelievers are present they may be served as well. If through the liturgy God graciously delivers gifts of forgiveness, life, and salvation, then He offers them to everyone present, the people of God as well as those who are not yet part of His people. Inasmuch as the Lord's Day service is the place and time where God comes through His Word and Sacrament to serve

---

[9] Thomas Howard, *Evangelical Is Not Enough* (Nashville: Thomas Nelson, 1984), 87.

people, it is obviously beneficial to both. The Spirit can enliven any unbeliever present and use His Word as it is read, prayed, sung, and preached to bring them new life. What else is this but evangelism?

Conclusion

I do not mean to suggest that our response is not also included in God's gracious provision in Christ. It is. It is not as if God works but then stops just where our human response begins, which is to say that the gift-response dynamic is not a zero-sum game either. Rather, God's grace includes our human response to the extent that our human response takes place "in Christ." God is at work in us even when we are at work praising Him. We "work" at thanking and praising Him because He is at work in us (1 Cor. 12:3; Rom. 8:26; Phil. 2:13). The entire process of covenant renewal or sacrificial worship can only be performed as we are graciously given to participate in the kingly and priestly work of Jesus Christ. Our offering of ourselves as Christians will always be a participation in Jesus' own offering of his humanity to the Father in the Spirit.[10] John Calvin understood that this give-and-receive dynamic comes to a climax at the Lord's Table:

> Calvin's own perception of the Sacrament [is] in fact the occasion for two acts of self-giving: Christ's giving of himself to the church and the church's giving of itself to God. It is this double self-giving that makes the Supper

---

[10] For a helpful exposition of this notion of doxological participation, see Alan J. Torrance, *Persons in Communion: An Essay on Trinitarian Description and Human Participation* (Edinburgh: T & T Clark, 1996), especially his conclusion (chapter 5), 307ff. The first two-thirds of this book may be tough work for those who have little familiarity with (or interest in) Karl Barth and modern Trinitarian theological issues. The introduction and conclusion, however, can be profitably mined by any ministerial student for provocative theological insights bearing upon liturgical theology. James B. Torrance's *Worship, Community & The Triune God of Grace* (Downers Grove: InterVarsity Press, 1996) outlines a similar emphasis for a more popular audience. He sums it up like this, "There is always a double movement in worship—a God-humanward movement and a human-Godward movement—and both must be understood in terms of the gift of grace, the gift of the God of grace who provides for us a way of loving communion" (60).

both embody and represent the perpetual exchange of grace and gratitude that shapes Calvin's entire theology. The sacred banquet prepared by the Father's goodness is the actual giving, not merely the remembering, of a gift of grace, and precisely as such it demands and evokes the answering gratitude of God's children.[11]

The issues discussed in this chapter lead me to believe that describing the Lord's Day service as "covenant renewal" and "sacrificial" improves upon the language of "dialogue" that was in use for a while in the last few decades of the twentieth century. On the one hand, the word "dialogue" has the advantage of calling attention to the *verbal* interchange between God and man. In worship God's speaks and we respond with our own voices. Both God's service to us and our service to God takes the form of words received and given back. The problem, however, is that "dialogue," as it is used today, often connotes conversation between equals, and it is usually used to describe "an exchange of different ideas." James A. DeJong makes this point:

> . . . the idea of dialogue has certain deficiencies. Dialogue is usually between equals. In worship God convenes the meeting and remains in charge through his appointed delegates. Like invited dinner guests, God's people attend worship by divine initiation. Dialogue may ramble. Worship does not; its exchanges are prescribed.[12]

On the Lord's Day God graciously operates on us first and our actions are in grateful response to God's activity. Indeed, our words and actions are energized by His Spirit's ongoing operations throughout the service. The fundamental purpose of the corporate Sunday service, therefore, is to *receive* by faith God's gracious service in Christ and then to respond with thanksgiving in union with Christ *praising* the Living God. This is what we call "covenant renewal worship."

---

[11] B. A. Gerrish, *Grace and Gratitude: The Eucharistic Theology of John Calvin* (Minneapolis: Fortress Press, 1993), 156.

[12] James A. DeJong, *Into His Presence* (Grand Rapids, Board of Publications of the Christian Reformed Church, 1985), 14-15.

6
The Trinity and Covenant Renewal Worship

Part 1 – The Nexus Between Worship and Confession

In vain do they worship me, teaching as
doctrines the commandments of men.
—Isaiah 29:13 & Mark 7:7

At numerous pivotal places in the first five chapters I have alluded to the fact that covenant and sacrifice are ultimately grounded in God's eternal tri-personal communal life as Father, Son, and Holy Spirit. The eternal personal relations between Father, Son, and Holy Spirit are covenantal. The mutual love, obedience, and self-sacrificial giving and receiving that characterizes the relations of Father, Son, and Holy Spirit in eternity is the origin and ground of God's covenant with us and our covenantal relations with one another. The bond of love between the Persons of the Trinity has been graciously extended to embrace human creatures.

We must give careful attention to the fundamentally Trinitarian character of genuine Christian covenantal worship. It is made explicit in Ephesians 2:18, "Through Christ we . . . have access in one Spirit to the Father," but it is embedded in the entire record of Scripture. I will maintain throughout this book that it is precisely this Trinitarian dynamic that is jeopardized in so much of what passes for Christian worship in modern churches. In the next two chapters I will argue that our liturgy must exhibit an explicitly Trinitarian content and shape if it is to be genuinely and recognizably *Christian* worship.[1] First, I will make a case for a deep, inexorable connection between the *form* of worship and our doctrinal confession. In the following chapter I will unpack the significance of this nexus for the order and substance of our worship.

If worship is reduced to evangelism, education, experience, or even praise, the Persons of Father, Son, and Holy Spirit need not play a vital role except possibly as objects of worship. In contrast, covenant renewal worship has the Father effectually calling His people into His presence by the Spirit and then renewing His Church in Jesus Christ His Son. The gathered Church, as it receives this service from the Triune God, then responds by the enabling power of the Spirit with thanksgiving and praise in Christ directed to their heavenly Father. The Spirit has been sent by the Father to bring us to the Son, and with the Son to Himself. A liturgy that embodies this reality will be ineradicably Trinitarian in "both directions"—as God serves us and as we serve God.

Lex Orandi, Lex Credendi

In Jaroslav Pelikan's delightful dictionary, *The Melody of Theology*, he cites this "shocking" passage from an appendix to Adolf von Harnack's *History of Dogma*: "The history of dogma in the first three centuries is not mirrored in the liturgy, as far as we know it, nor is the liturgy a clearly emerging basis of the dogmatics." Harnack

---

[1] The substance of these two chapters was originally presented at the Connecticut Valley Conference on Reformed Theology on March 15, 1997, and subsequently published as one essay in *Christendom Essays*, ed. James B. Jordan (Niceville: Transfiguration Press, 1997), 11–28.

misses something essential here, according to Pelikan. Harnack's bold assertion, Pelikan insists, "needs to be offset by a far greater recognition of the role that liturgy and the *lex orandi* of Christian worship have played in the development of doctrine as the *lex credendi*"[2]

Harnack's one-sidedness is quite typical of a kind of modern theological intellectualism that fails to see the complex nexus between the *life* of the Church and the *confession* of the Church, between liturgy and dogma, worship and doctrine. Not just any old connection, but a particular kind of connection. Pelikan refers to the common Latin theological tag *lex orandi, lex credendi. Lex* means law or rule. *Orandi* is prayer.[3] Here the *lex orandi*, the rule of prayer, refers to the corporate, liturgical prayer of the Church in worship. *Lex credendi* means "rule of belief" or "confession." One can hear the word *credo* ("I believe") in this Latin word *credendi*. In its most general sense, then, *lex orandi, lex credendi* means "the rule of prayer influences the rule of belief" (*lex orandi, lex credendi*).

Confession Regulates Worship

Reformed Presbyterians may not be familiar with how this slogan is used in liturgical theology. We typically reverse the common order to *lex credendi, lex orandi*. If Reformed Protestants accept the slogan at all, then this is the way we usually interpret it. With this interpretation, doctrine is normative for worship in that what the Church believes *ought* to determine the content and practice of worship. In other words, biblical and systematic theologians ought to be self-consciously engaged in determining the doctrinally correct form and content of worship. The *lex credendi* of the Church must be used to establish the *lex orandi* of its worship. Any liturgical practice or prayer that violates biblically-derived doctrines or established creeds may not be allowed. This much at least is sloganized in the famous "regulative principle" of Reformed

---

[2] Jaroslav Pelikan, *Melody of Theology* (Cambridge: Harvard University Press, 1988), 113.
[3] Compare: *Ora et labora* ("pray and work"); *ora pro nobis* ("pray for us").

worship.[4] Doctrine ought not to be derived from liturgy; rather, liturgy must be built upon sound doctrine. Calvin articulates this particular link between doctrine and worship in his *On the Necessity of Reforming the Church*:

> There is nothing to which all men should pay more attention, nothing in which God wishes us to exhibit a more intense eagerness than in endeavoring that the glory of his Name may remain undiminished, his kingdom be advanced, and the pure doctrine, which alone can guide us to true worship, flourish in full strength.[5]

Luther expresses something like this in his admonition to the clergy of Lubeck in 1530: "Do not begin with innovations in rites . . . . Put first and foremost what is fundamental in our teaching . . . . Reform of impious rites will come of itself when what is fundamental in our doctrine has been effectively presented and has taken root in our pious hearts."[6] Luther's formulation, however, hints at a more subtle sense in which the *lex credendi* influences the *lex orandi* of worship. Here we might speak of the inevitable influence that the doctrinal presuppositions of any given Christian community will exercise upon their practice of worship. Such theological convictions may not even be self-consciously or actively applied to liturgical matters by theologians and pastors, but they will inescapably "influence" the form and content of a particular community's *lex orandi*. There are, no doubt, aspects of the *lex orandi* which worshipers, pastors, and even theologians might not notice as members of a certain worshipping community, but which later generations will pick out as originating in some deep-seated, not

---

[4] What is commonly called the "regulative principle of worship" is summarized in the Westminster Confession of Faith, chapter 21, articles 1–3, and the Westminster Larger Catechism, Questions 108 and 109. See my discussion in chapter 16 on "The Regulative Principle of Worship" in Part III.

[5] Quoted in Carlos M. N. Eire, *War Against the Idols: The Reformation of Worship from Erasmus to Calvin* (Cambridge: Cambridge University Press, 1986),199.

[6] *D. Martin Luther's Werke: Briefwechsel* (Weimar, 1930–1970), vol. 5, 220–21.

always verbalized, doctrinal presuppositions shared by the entire community. We are often blind to our own presuppositions, as the saying goes.

An historical example would be the way baptismal liturgies and prayers were gradually transformed under the influence of the new Reformation doctrinal commitments.[7] The rite of the Lord's supper developed similarly, according to the various doctrinal commitments in each Reformation community. Thus, there would appear to be a behind-the-scenes "influence" that the *lex credendi* of any particular community has upon its worship, and this often without the community itself even recognizing such an operation at work. Why, for example, does the modern Evangelical Church refuse to practice the Lord's Supper weekly? If this intimate nexus between doctrine and liturgy exists, then the question is: what doctrinal presuppositions fuel such a departure from the historic practice? In other words, what do we believe about the Lord's Supper that has caused us to marginalize its practice in the life of the worshipping Church? A church will inevitably embody in its corporate worship, in its manner of prayer, what it believes, teaches, and confesses. *Lex credendi* influences *lex orandi*. I believe that this constitutes a fruitful area for theological research, but it is not exactly the question that I want to pursue here.

Worship Regulates Confession

That is the way Protestants typically understand the relationship between worship and prayer, liturgy and doctrine. Doctrine must and does influence liturgy. But this is not the precise relationship between doctrine and worship that the phrase was originally intended to describe. Protestants have transposed the direction of influence. Historically the slogan has been understood to mean that the rule of prayer is an appropriate norm for or inevitable source of

---

[7] See Hughes Oliphant Old, *The Shaping of the Reformed Baptismal Rite in the Sixteenth Century* (Grand Rapids: Eerdmans, 1992).

the Church's doctrinal confession. From *lex orandi* to *lex credendi*. Liturgy functions as a norm or source in the development of Christian dogma. For Roman Catholics the slogan functions as a kind of "liturgical regulative principle" for dogmatic development—the principle of *lex orandi, lex credendi* enables them to appeal to past liturgical practice to justify a particular doctrinal development. For example, both the Roman dogmas of the immaculate conception (promulgated by Pius X in 1854) and the assumption of Mary (1950), although formulated and defined as Church dogma late in Christian history, are said to have been present in seed form in the early liturgical practice and prayers of the Church in accordance with the rule "law of prayer is the law of belief." The *lex orandi, lex credendi* principle, therefore, authorizes the magisterium of the Roman church to formulate dogma based on the liturgical tradition of the Church. This is how the formula has been used by the Roman Catholic church—in this *procedural* way, justifying the derivation of doctrine from the liturgical life of the Church.

Of course, Reformation Christians have trouble with this understanding. We deny that the *lex orandi* of the Christian community ought to be used as an authoritative source for the *lex credendi* of the Church, that the liturgy ought to function as a normative fountainhead for doctrinal formulations. On this understanding, liturgical tradition operates as an authority, occupying a special, if not equivalent position alongside the Bible as a source for doctrinal definitions. Reformation Christians, however, confess the absolute authority of the Bible over all other sources, including tradition, and therefore cannot accept the Roman understanding of the use of this maxim.

Worship Influences Confession

Once again, however, there is a more subtle sense in which *lex orandi, lex credendi* might be affirmed by Reformation Christians. Unfortunately, the overreaction of many Protestants to the Roman Catholic understanding often clouds some very fruitful investigations into the influence of liturgy upon theology. We at least ought to recognize that the *lex orandi* will inevitably influence the development of the Church's *lex credendi*. We might call this the hidden or secret influence interpretation. Here is how it works. The way a community of faith worships will inexorably, though not always obviously and almost never immediately, affect the content of the worshipping community's confession of faith. What I mean by "hidden" is that the lines of influence may not always be clear enough for a contemporary member of the community to say, "Ah, yes, one day we will believe such-and-such because we are in the habit of praying or worshipping in such-and-such a manner." The lines of influence remain "hidden" until the doctrinal implications make their appearance in the form of public teaching and confession.

Furthermore, it may be easier for us to do a historical study of the influence of the *lex orandi* on the developing *lex credendi* of the Church than for us to understand how contemporary changes in a Church's liturgy will effect the emerging *lex credendi* of the future. The reason I put "hidden" in quotation marks is that what is hidden from one generation is often only too clear to the next which has to live with the doctrinal effects of the worship of their forefathers, whether advantageous or deleterious. So Prosper of Auquitatine, in the early fifth century, defended the Augustinian doctrine of sin and grace against the Pelagians by appealing to the *lex orandi* of the undivided Church. Augustine and his disciple Prosper both appeal to the form and content of the traditional baptismal liturgies to bolster the Scriptural argument against the Pelagian contention that children are born into the world without original sin. Look, Augustine says in effect, the way we have always baptized babies proves that the universal Church has consistently confessed in her liturgy that infants stand in need of the forgiveness of sins.[8] Prosper could not appeal to any ecumenical conciliar or creedal formulations since

---

[8] Augustine, "On the Merits and Forgiveness of Sins, and on the Baptism of Infants," in Philip Schaff, ed., *Saint Augustine: Anti-Pelagian Writings*, trans. Peter Holmes and Robert

the councils of Nicea, Constantinople, or Ephesus never dealt directly with these questions. Prosper appealed to the existing liturgical customs and practices, particularly the prayers, to prove the antiquity of Augustine's views. This is how the Church has always prayed (*lex orandi*), Prosper argued, therefore, the doctrinal formulations (*lex credendi*) of Augustine should not surprise anyone as novel. Augustine's doctrine is just the creedal, confessional flowering of our Church's traditional way of prayer and worship. Prosper's comment, *legem credendi lex statuat supplicandi* ("let the law of prayer establish the law of belief") is the source of the formula that we have been discussing.[9]

We might say the same thing about the Trinitarian creedal formulations of Athanasius, the Cappadocians, the Nicene-Constantinopolitan Creed, and Apostles' Creed. These doctrinal formulations developed in the context and with the full support of the Church's worship. The doctrine of the Trinity was *first* a way of worshipping and praying to the true God in Christ by the Spirit. The passages in the New Testament that distinguish most clearly between the Father, the Son, and the Holy Spirit are those that deal with the worship of the Church, prayer, the Lord's Supper, and Baptism. When Paul writes about prayer, he reflects upon the manner in which Christ and the Holy Spirit enable us to approach the Father. It is through Christ that we have access by one Spirit to the Father (Eph. 2:18). "And because you are sons, God has sent forth

---

Ernest Wallis, vol 5 of *A Select Library of Nicene and Post-Nicene Fathers of the Christian Church* (1887; Grand Rapids: Eerdmans, 1971). Of course, what Augustine is doing here is *interpreting* the ancient *lex orandi* of the Church. To Augustine, the *lex credendi* implied in the *lex orandi* seems transparent enough. The fact that the sacrament of remission of sins has been applied to infants necessarily implies that they have something to be forgiven; and since they have committed no personal sin, it must be for the guilt of original sin that they are washed in the laver of regeneration. Augustine argues that Pelagius knows full well that his position is a *novelty* asserted against "the ancient ingrafted opinion of the church."

[9] See Prosper's "Official Pronouncements of the Apostolic See on Divine Grace and Free Will," in *Prosper of Auquitaine: Defense of St. Augustine*, trans. De Letter, vol. 32 of the *Ancient Christian Writers* (New York: Newman Press, 1963), 183, 234.

the Spirit of His Son into your hearts, crying out, "Abba, Father!" (Gal. 4:6). Only by the Holy Spirit are we given access through the Son to the Father's presence. These passages describe our doxological approach to God in prayer (*lex orandi*). Out of this dynamic Trinitarian language of worship and prayer, the dogmatic confession of the doctrine of the Trinity eventually emerged.

One can see, therefore, that causal connections may be hidden to a contemporary observer, but the fact that liturgy influences belief is true, regardless of whether one can ascertain the precise way in which the process proceeds. Here we would insist with Pelikan, contra Harnack, that the liturgy often is an emerging basis for Church dogma, a powerful force in the life of the Church's dogmatic development, and one that must be carefully considered.

Jesus Exposes the Nexus

A question might arise at this point: Does the Bible support this particular understanding of the relationship between worship and doctrine? Rather than cite a list of proof texts that might support this dynamic connection, we shall examine one passage in the Gospel of Mark that makes it clear just how potent ritual can be in doctrinal development, for better or worse. In Mark 7:5, the Pharisees and Scribes of the law interrogate Jesus: "Why do Your disciples not walk according to the tradition of the elders, but eat bread with unwashed hands?" They were right to confront Jesus since He was their leader. The disciples were doing what Jesus had taught them. Not only did Jesus Himself ignore many of the religious practices of the Pharisees and Scribes, He often displayed outright contempt for the whole structure of their oral tradition. Public contempt. Open defiance. Jesus and His disciples publicly flouted the rituals and ceremonies that they considered so essential. Why? What could it hurt to follow these traditional washing rituals that had developed over the years? Jesus answers the Pharisees and Scribes' question with what is in effect a two-part answer. First, citing Isaiah 29:13 He argues that they have elevated their own traditions to the level of the commandments of God. By elevating these extra-biblical rituals, they have managed to excuse themselves and others from the genuine requirements of the law of God (Mk. 7:6–13).

The second part of Jesus' answer is extremely relevant to our current investigation. It's not merely that people are led to despise and break the commandments of God. That certainly is bad enough. There is more! Jesus calls the multitude together and announces to them: "Hear Me, everyone, and understand: There is nothing that enters a man from outside which can defile him; but the things which come out of him, those are the things that defile a man'" (Mk. 7:14–15). Why does Jesus now begin to talk about what "goes into" a man? Remember the whole episode began as a controversy over how to eat bread, not over the laws of clean and unclean meats (Lev. 11).[10] Where would anyone get the idea that what "goes into a man" makes him unclean? The answer is: these Pharisaical rituals led people to believe that man's problem is what comes from outside of him into him. Jesus explains how the oppressive oral law rituals requiring scrupulous and continuous washing before eating had a very dangerous effect on the way people thought about man and sin and ultimately salvation. Rituals eventually influence what one believes. Over time *how* one worships, the ceremonies one performs, will determine *what* one believes. This is the principle *lex orandi, lex credendi*.

For Better or Worse

Now this principle can work for good or it can work for evil. When one worships according to God's prescription, then God's rituals will cultivate a true understanding of the relationship between God and man. If one carefully followed the Old Testament laws of ritual cleanness and meditated on them day and night, one would never arrive at an environmental understanding of man's

---

[10] For a discussion of how the laws concerning the eating of unclean meats relates to this passage, see James B. Jordan, "The Mosaic Dietary Laws and the New Covenant" Studies in Food & Faith, No. 11 (Niceville: Biblical Horizons, 1990).

predicament. When Jesus proclaimed, "What comes out of a man, that defiles a man. For from within, out of the heart of men, proceed evil thoughts, adulteries, fornications, murders" (Mk. 7:20–21), He was not promulgating some new doctrine. Rather, He was only unpacking the doctrinal significance of the divinely prescribed rituals of Leviticus, which dealt with uncleanness arising from all sorts of skin eruptions and emissions.

But now what happens when the rituals that God has established are replaced with man-made rituals? What effect will they have on what the worshiper believes and confesses? Well, that is always hard to say beforehand. Introducing new rituals into the worshipping community is always a dangerous gamble. One cannot know what the effect might be on the confession of the people in the future. But we can look back and learn our lesson: the laws that were spun out of the brains of the religious leaders of Israel, that had no grounding in the law of God, led to dangerous doctrinal misunderstandings—misconceptions that touched on the conception of man's fundamental problem before God. Jesus here is trying to expose doctrinal error that has infected the Jewish church *because of* the introduction of these oral law rituals about washing and cleansing.

Conclusion: A Reformed Distinctive?

There is, therefore, a much more profound interplay between worship and doctrine than most Reformed Protestants are ready to admit. Neither is the interplay as one-sided as most Reformed scholars would have us believe. Without denying for one moment the importance of the normative influence of doctrine upon worship, it must be insisted that the relationship is more like a two-way street, the movement from the current *lex orandi* of the worshipping community to the future *lex credendi* of the believing community may not be as visible and quantifiable as the opposite movement, but we ignore it at our own peril.

Carlos M. N. Eire argues that it is part of the genius of Reformed theology to affirm what Harnack denied—precisely the profound, complex connection between worship and doctrine that we have been discussing. "Religion is not merely a set of doctrines, but rather a way of worshipping, and a way of living. 'True piety begets true confession.' This is enormously significant. One may even argue that it becomes the fundamental defining characteristic of Calvinism."[11] *True piety begets true confession.* Eire is quoting Calvin![12] Concerning disputes about the form and content of the liturgy, Calvin astonishes us with an affirmation of the vital, intimate connection between the Church's worship and confession: "For it is not true that we dispute about a worthless shadow. The whole substance of the Christian religion is brought into question."[13]

What is this but *lex orandi* begets *lex credendi*? And Eire says that this becomes a "defining characteristic of Calvinism." If this is part of the genius of Reformed theology, a "fundamental defining characteristic" of Calvinism, I think someone ought to tell contemporary American Reformed and Presbyterian churches and especially the seminaries. Why then do our Reformed seminaries ignore *liturgical* theology? Liturgical forms are considered *adiaphora* ("something indifferent") by many Reformed institutions that train ministers. While Reformed seminarians are busying their brains with Hodge and Berkhof, are the seeds of the destruction of our distinctive doctrinal commitments being sown in our churches every Sunday as our people are blown to and fro by every wind of liturgical fad? What they *do* in church every Sunday may actually undermine what they confess in their confessional standards and learn in the classroom.

[11] Eire, *War,* 232–33.
[12] *De fugiendis, Corpus Reformatorum* 5:244.
[13] *On the Necessity of Reforming the Church,* cited in Eire, *War,* 232.

7

The Trinity and Covenant Renewal Worship

Part 2 – The Trinitarian Shape of Christian Liturgy

Through Christ we . . . have access
by one Spirit to the Father.
—Ephesians 2:18

More than thirty years ago Karl Rahner noted that it was an undeniable fact that many churches "notwithstanding their exact profession of the Trinity, are almost alone as 'monotheists' in the practice of their religious life. One can even risk claiming that if the Trinity should have been suppressed as false doctrine, a great part of the religious literature could still remain unchanged after this occurrence."[1] Robert W. Jenson warns that we are on the verge of losing our identify as the church: "a religious fellowship in which the differentiating relations between Father, Son, and Spirit had ceased to shape ritual and theology would no longer

---

[1] Karl Rahner, *The Trinity*, trans. by Joseph Donceel (New York: Crossroad Publishing Company, 1997 [1967]),11.

be the church, no matter how otherwise dedicated it was to one or another Christian value or slogan."[2]

Tragically, these astonishing charges appear to be accurate. The reality of God as Trinity often has little influence on the shape and content of much modern Evangelical and Reformed worship. Now that we have discussed the nexus between worship and confession, it is time to make some specific applications about the way we worship as Christians.

How We "Teach" the Trinity

A parishioner once approached me inquiring about the Trinity. One of his workmates was a member of a nominally Christian sect that denied the dogma of the Trinity. This member was genuinely surprised that his friend was so adamantly anti-Trinitarian in his opinions. Now you have to understand something about my parishioner. He had been a member of our church for less than a year. Before joining with us he was a member of a typical, American independent church for over fifteen years. He and his wife came to me after they were married looking for the proverbial middle road between Catholicism and Independency. They were both professing believers. She had become a believer in his old church, but she could not stomach the "free church" worship on Sundays. That is the background.

As I said, this man came to me one day asking about the Trinity. He said, "You know, Pastor, I've noticed since I've been here how much this church emphasizes the Trinity. Why is that?"

---

[2] Robert W. Jensen, *Systematic Theology: Volume I, The Triune God* (New York: Oxford University Press, 1997),113–4. The following works make significant contributions to the study of the relationship between the Trinity and the worship of the Church: James B. Torrance, *Worship, Community & the Triune God of Grace* (Downers Grove: InterVarsity Press, 1996); Alan J. Torrance, *Persons in Communion: An Essay on Trinitarian Description and Human Participation* (Edinburgh: T & T Clark, 1996),307–371; *The Forgotten Trinity: The Report of the B.C.C. Study Commission on Trinitarian Doctrine Today* (London: British Council of Churches, 1989); Thomas F. Torrance, "The Mind of Christ in Worship: The Problem of Apollinarianism in the Liturgy," in *Theology in Reconciliation* (London: Geoffrey Chapman,

Now I know what some readers may be thinking: here is a pastor that is a graduate student in systematic theology looking forward to a dissertation on the Trinity; he is probably always preaching and teaching on the Trinity. But I'm not, I assure you. At the time of this member's question I had preached only occasionally on the Trinity, mostly when the Church year sets aside Trinity Sunday to address this issue. So when this man said to me, "Why does this church emphasize the Trinity so much," I was a little surprised.

"What do you mean?" I asked. "We don't use the word "Trinity" all that much do we?"

He said, "No, no, that's not it. It seems like the Father, Son, and Holy Spirit always show up in our prayers, creeds, and hymns. I'm not used to that. I don't really understand it. Why is that so important? In my old church we never recited the Apostles' Creed or the Nicene Creed. I had never even heard of these creeds until I began to worship here. We never sang the hymns that you sing here either. So many of them have the Trinity in them. We never sang the Doxology or the *Gloria Patri* or the *Te Deum*. We never prayed in unison using printed prayers. Those who were so moved offered up most of our prayers informally. They were not carefully composed. We prayed in Jesus name, but, to my knowledge, no one ever ended a prayer with . . . what is it?"

I said, "You mean praying to the Father 'through Jesus Christ who lives and reigns with You and the Holy Spirit, one God, world without end. Amen'?"

"Yeah, that's it!"

1975); George S. Bebis, "Worship in the Orthodox Church," *Greek Orthodox Theological Review* 22 (1977):429–443; John Thompson, *Modern Trinitarian Perspectives* (New York: Oxford University Press, 1994), esp. chapter 5, "The Trinity and Worship,"94–105; James M. Houston, "Spirituality and the Doctrine of the Trinity," in *Christ in Our Place: The Humanity of God in Christ for the Reconciliation of the World* (Exeter: Paternoster Press, 1990); and Geoffrey Wainwright, *Worship with One Accord: Where Liturgy and Ecumenism Embrace* (New York: Oxford University Press, 1997), chapter 14, "Trinitarian Worship,"237–250.

The upshot of all of this is that this man had always thought the Trinity was a *doctrine* that served primarily to mark the line that divides Christianity and the cults, but he never quite understood the significance of the doctrine beyond that for his life and worship. Unfortunately, I think this is how the doctrine of the Trinity functions too often at the popular level—it is little more than a boundary marker against error and heresy. If that! Dorothy Sayers suggests that the average churchgoer's conception of the doctrine of the Trinity is more like a parody of the Athanasian Creed: "The Father incomprehensible, the Son incomprehensible, and the whole thing incomprehensible. Something put in by theologians to make it more difficult—nothing to do with daily life or ethics."[3] Timothy Lull wondered if the Trinity should be subtitled "the guilt producing doctrine" because we cannot quite muster the theological enthusiasm of the ancient Athanasian Creed.[4] Modern Christians feel guilty confessing the Athanasian anathema ("if anyone does not believe it faithfully and firmly, he cannot be saved") because we really don't know what difference the doctrine makes. Our confession of the Trinity appears to float out at a safe distance from our normal lives. The way we worship, the way we pray, the order and content of our liturgy, indeed, the way we live—these are not adequately shaped by our Trinitarian convictions. Our *lex orandi* does not sufficiently reflect our *lex credendi*.

Like so many American Evangelicals, this man had no appreciation for the doctrine of the Trinity because he was not accustomed to worshipping the Father through the Son in the Spirit—at least not explicitly and formally. His *lex credendi* was deficient because his *lex orandi* was deficient; the rule of prayer influenced his habits of mind. I'm not suggesting that he did not in fact worship the Father, Son, and Holy Spirit in his free church tradition. Rather, I am

---

[3] Dorothy Sayers, "The Dogma is the Drama," in *The Whimsical Christian: 18 Essays by Dorothy L. Sayers* (New York: Collier Books, 1987),25.

[4] Timothy F. Lull, "The Trinity in Recent Literature," *Word and World* 2.1 (Winter 1982): 61.

proposing that he was not used to worshipping the Triune God explicitly and liturgically. The corporate worship of his old church did not structure his mind and heart so as to understand what he was doing on the Lord's Day. Consequently, his *confession* of God was inadequate and dangerously skewed, leaning towards Unitarianism.

How Should We Then Worship

Reformed pastors and scholars must begin to study the enormously significant connection between confession and liturgy. We could then also begin to follow the example of Augustine's liturgical program in Hippo, which Peter Brown summarizes as, "removing habits that give rise to false opinions."[5] Surely it is reasonable to assume that the routines of life and liturgy will naturally affect the routines of the mind, as we have seen demonstrated in the preceding chapter. The way we now worship, the way we pray, the way we approach God in corporate worship in our churches will determine what our spiritual grandchildren one day will believe, teach, and confess. Shouldn't the way we worship and pray as a corporate body be inculcating habits that give rise to orthodox convictions? Shouldn't the *lex orandi* of the Church be more thoroughly Trinitarian in its content and shape?

That is my burden in this chapter. I am deeply concerned that contemporary Evangelical and Reformed churches are in danger of losing the rich Trinitarian life and structure of the Church in corporate worship. I fear that the Trinity is being marginalized in the corporate, Lord's Day worship of our churches. Remember Karl Rahner's observation. What difference would it make in your church if the doctrine, the confession of the Trinity were to disappear? Would anybody even notice that it happened? What difference, if any, would the loss of the doctrine of the Trinity make in the liturgy, the content and manner by which the assembled church approaches God?

---

[5] Peter Brown, *Augustine of Hippo* (Berkeley: University of California Press, 1967), 345.

What we do on the Lord's Day in God's presence defines who we are. We are most authentically the Church when we gather around the Word, the Table, and the ordained minister on the Lord's Day in corporate worship. St. Paul makes a telling remark when he rebukes the Corinthian church. He says, "In the following directives I have no praise for you, since *you come together* not for the better, but for the worse. In the first place, I hear that when *you come together as the church*, there are divisions among you . . . . *When you come together*, it is not the Lord's Supper you eat" (1 Cor. 11:17–21, emphasis mine). Paul is concerned that their "coming together as the church" manifests what they truly are and believe. The church gathered for worship will reveal in her words and actions what she really is and believes. Philip Butin reminds us that this was Calvin's understanding: "The Worship of the visible Church, theologically speaking, is pivotal in the divine-human relationship for Calvin. This is because it is the event in which the visible community of believers . . . is most authentically the church."[6] In 1989, the British Council of Church's published the results of a study commission on the Trinity, called *The Forgotten Trinity*. The work begins with the corporate worship of the Church. "It is in our worship that most of us become aware of the doctrine of the Trinity."[7]

The Trinity, then, is not primarily a doctrine about which we think, reflect, dispute, and write scholarly monographs. All of these activities are important and have their place. They are all ways in which faith seeks understanding, according Anselm's to memorable tag: *fides quaerens intellectum*. Nevertheless, foundational to all of our second-level discourse *about* the doctrine of the Trinity is our faith, our trust (our *credo*) *in* the Triune God, our praising His name, and our speech to Him. True Christian worship can only be offered to God the Father, Son, and Holy Spirit. More specifically,

---

[6] Philip Butin, *Revelation, Redemption, and Response: Calvin's Trinitarian Understanding of the Divine-human Relationship* (New York: Oxford University Press, 1995), 101.

[7] *The Forgotten Trinity: The Report of the B.C.C. Study Commission on Trinitarian Doctrine Today* (London: British Council of Churches, Inter-Church House, 1989), vol. 1.

true worship is offered to the Father through the Son in or by the Holy Spirit. Anything else is sub-Christian at best. First we hear the Triune God talking to us and so we learn to talk *to* the Father, Son, and Holy Spirit, only then do we begin to learn to talk *about* them.

Think about how we begin our Christian life among the assembled people of God—when we are named and claimed by the Triune God at the baptismal font. The Father adopts us in His one and only Son by means of the washing of regeneration, giving us a new life in His redeemed family. We then gather together weekly as the Spirit-anointed royal priests and are enabled to boldly approach the Father through the Son and experience the closest possible communion with the Triune God. The Spirit of God makes the reading and preaching of the Word of God an effectual means of leading the people through the Son to the Father. The Father then invites His children to partake of the richness of His grace at the Table, where, first, we give thanks to the Father in the Spirit for the gift of His Son, and then through the miraculous work of the Holy Spirit we are made partakers of the life-giving flesh and blood of His Son. And this is just a rudimentary outline of the rich Trinitarian experience of the Church in worship. Everything the Church experiences in corporate worship has a Trinitarian shape and content.

Worship Coram Deo *and in* Trinitate

Moreover, the Church's worship is not merely a performance *coram deo* ("in the presence of" or "before the face of God"). We do not simply assemble *coram Trinitate* ("in the presence of the Trinity") on Sunday. Corporate worship is even richer than we suppose and our marginalization of the Trinity's significance for worship has greatly impoverished our conception of the work (liturgy) of worship. Worship is not merely something we do for God or to God or in God's presence. Worship is something God does for us in the person of Christ through the power of the Spirit. Worship is not primarily our act, but foundationally the gift of God. As we noted in chapter five, our English word "worship" does not include this idea like the Lain *servitium Dei* or the German *Gottesdienst* ("the service of God" or "God's service" or "the Divine Service"). These phrases are gloriously ambiguous. Is the "service of God" the service of man to God or the service of God to man? Is it an objective or subjective genitive? Yes. First, God serves us in worship. God gathers us together and ministers to us, drawing us into His life of love and fellowship. In this way, secondly, we serve Him.

Furthermore, this service of God in our behalf has a very definite Trinitarian shape to it. God's service to us is to graciously draw us into the presence of the Father in Spiritual union with the God-man Jesus Christ. The man Jesus Christ is the only mediator between God and man. He is *the* King and Priest. He offers Himself as man before the Father and He does so as the Representative Man, the High Priest of redeemed humanity. John Thompson says it well: "Jesus Christ is thus the one true worshiper....By the Holy Spirit we are drawn into the worship and response Christ offers to the Father. Ours is a response to a response. The Spirit enables this and so gives what He demands, the worship of our hearts and lives."[8] Another perspective on this complex Trinitarian reality is that the Spirit unites the Bride to the Son, who then brings us to the Father. Here the Spirit functions as the Priest, and the Son as the King.[9] In either case, these Trinitarian considerations insure that worship or *Gottesdienst* is not foundationally what we do; rather, it is what we are graciously given to do in Christ. Worship is the service of the Triune God to the congregation.

Worship is principally *God's Service*, not our service to God. It is what we are graciously *given* as well as what we are *given to do* in Christ. Worship is the service of the Triune God to the congregation. James B. Torrance is right I believe when he says that there is something grotesquely Unitarian, even Pelagian, about the

---

[8] John Thompson, *Modern Trinitarian Perspectives* (New York: Oxford University Press, 1994),100.

[9] See James B. Jordan, "What is the Covenant?" *Biblical Theology Basics*, nos. 1–2 (Jan. & Feb. 2002).

popular view of worship in Evangelicalism. There are two views of worship:

> ... a unitarian view that worship is what we, religious people, do to try to please God, and a Trinitarian one, where worship is the gift of grace to participate through the Spirit in the incarnate Son's communion with the Father—the way of joy and peace and confidence. The church which takes her eyes off Jesus Christ, the only mediator in worship, is on the road to becoming apostate. There is no more urgent need in our churches today than to recover the Trinitarian nature of grace—that it is by grace alone, through the gift of Jesus Christ in the Spirit that we can enter into and live a life of communion with God our Father.[10]

Sadly, this "unitarian" way of worshipping seems to be prevalent in Reformed churches as well. God is at a distance and we come and do all kinds of things before Him to please Him. As I warned in an earlier chapter, this is dangerously close to being pagan. There is a real sense in which genuine Christian worship can never simply be *coram Deo* or *Coram Trinitate* or even *ad Deum* or *ad Trinitatem*, but *in Trinitate*. (The Latin preposition "in" here should be understood in the richest possible sense to include both the instrumental ["by means of"] as well as the spatial sense of "in").

Worship and the End of Creation

A Trinitarian conception of worship, therefore, recognizes the two movements of God: 1) God to humanity—from the Father through the Son by the Spirit to redeem man; and 2) humanity to God—in reverse direction—by the Spirit through the Son to the Father.

The Trinitarian shape of Christian liturgical worship partially embodies and always looks forward to the eschatological wedding feast of the Lamb. Our worship is a foretaste of glorious things to come. Consider Jonathan Edwards's profound explanation for creation:

[10] Torrance, *Worship,* 59.

> The end, the ultimate end of the creation of God was to provide a spouse for His Son, Jesus Christ, that might enjoy Him, and on whom He might pour forth His love.
>
> Heaven and earth were created in order that the Son of God might communicate His love to His spouse and bring that bride into the very family life of the Trinity.
>
> There was, as it were, an eternal society or family in the Godhead, in the Trinity of persons. It seems to be God's design to admit the church into the divine family as his Son's wife.[11]

These are marvelous statements. In Christ humanity has been drawn up into the very life of the Triune God. By faith we are there now (Col. 3:1–3), all the while longing for the day when faith becomes sight and experience (Col. 3:4). By the Spirit we are graciously granted communion with the Son who presents us to the Father. The doctrine of the Trinity arose not only from the Scripture's objective witness to the truth, but it also arose from the church's participation in the life of God, a participation granted by the Spirit through the Son. By grace we become members of the Triune family. This participation ought to be experienced, albeit only partially, every Sunday by Christians participating in the corporate liturgy of the Church.

Where are these Trinitarian realities embodied in the worship, the *lex orandi* of our Churches? Where is the evidence in our churches of the reality that every Lord's Day the congregation is being led by the Spirit to the Son and into the Father's presence? Is anybody even aware that it is happening? Are our prayers consistent with this reality, both in form and content? Do we pray to the Father through the Son in the Spirit? Do we make this explicit and routine so that the congregation can be trained in orthodox habits of prayer that

---

[11] *Miscellanies*, 710, 103, and 741. See Amy Plantinga Pauw, *The Supreme Harmony of All: The Trinitarian Theology of Jonathan Edwards* (Grand Rapids: Wm. B. Eerdmans Publishing, 2002).

will endure? Is the order of our approach to God (the sequential order in our liturgy) consistent with the Triune God's service to us? What about the hymns and songs we sing? Are they explicitly Trinitarian as corporate sung prayers of petition and praise? The Reformers, especially Luther, were sensitive to this. Originally for children, Luther's hymn "Lord, Keep us steadfast in thy Word," is a particularly good Trinitarian prayer:

> 1. Lord, keep us steadfast in thy Word
>   And curb the Turks' and papists' sword
>   Who Jesus Christ thine only Son
>   Fain would tumble from off thy throne.

> 2. Proof of thy might, Lord Christ, afford,
>   For thou of all the lords art Lord;
>   thine own poor Christendom defend
>   That it may praise thee without end.

> 3. God Holy Ghost, who comfort art,
>   Give to thy folk on earth one heart;
>   Stand by us breathing our last breath,
>   Lead us to life straight out of death.[12]

Understanding the Creeds

What about the ecumenical creeds? What has happened to them? Do we recite these creeds in corporate worship? Some Reformed theologians have criticized the Nicene and Apostles' Creeds. The most notable and referenced critic of the Apostles' Creed in our circles is the Scottish Presbyterian theologian William Cunningham. After a string of criticisms, his conclusion is that "the Apostles' Creed, as it is called, is not entitled to much respect, and is not fitted to be of much use, as a summary of the leading doctrines of Christianity."[13] His fundamental objection to this

---

[12] Jaroslav Pelikan and Helmut T. Lehmann, eds., *Luther's Works,* American Edition (St. Louis: Concordia Publishing House; Philadelphia: Fortress Press, 1955–86), vol. 53, 305.

[13] William Cunningham, *Historical Theology* (Edinburgh: The Banner of Truth Trust, 1960 [1862]),90.

creed is that it says nothing about "justification by faith." This is a very weighty objection, but it arises from a fundamental misunderstanding of the language and purpose of these creeds. These creeds are not designed primarily to be a list of doctrines to which Christians give their assent. Neither the Nicene nor the Apostles' Creed may be characterized as a list of propositions to which we subscribe. On the contrary, they are public, personal confessions of trust in God the Father, Son, and Holy Spirit, acknowledging God's work of creation, redemption, and sanctification for us. They contain doctrinal propositions, of course. And we assent to the truth of these statements. Nevertheless, when the congregation recites these creeds they are *not* saying something like, "We hold this opinion on this subject," or "We think that these ideas and concepts are true." Not exactly. Other ecclesiastical documents fulfill this purpose. We have confessions and catechisms that function this way. The Westminster Shorter Catechism is filled with abstract definitions of doctrinal terms (Q. What is justification? A. Justification is . . .). There is nothing inherently wrong with this, but it is not how the Nicene and Apostles' Creeds have been written.

The first two words of these creeds are often dangerously misunderstood. These creeds begin with the words "I believe." Unfortunately, in the minds of many Christians this assertion is basically equivalent to "I think" or "I am of the opinion." The word "creed," however, comes from the Latin verb *credo*—the first word in the Latin creeds. The Greek translation of the creeds uses the word *pisteuo*, which is precisely the word that is used for "faith" in the New Testament (Jn. 3:16, 36; Rom. 10:10). When you say, "I believe [*credo, pisteuo*] in God the Father Almighty," you are not stating an opinion or even assenting to a doctrine; rather, you are confessing your personal trust, your faith in the Father Almighty. "I believe [*credo, pisteuo*]" is exactly equivalent to the language of personal trust used in the New Testament: "I believe in" or "I place my faith in" or "I trust in" ("Believe [*pisteuo*] on the Lord Jesus Christ, and you will be saved, you and your household," Acts 16:31).

No one is justified merely because he assents to the Reformation doctrine of justification. Unfortunately, many people even in our own churches are convinced that they are justified merely because they believe the *doctrine* of salvation by grace alone. This is a common, but deadly mistake. Only those who place their faith and trust in God the Father, Son, and Holy Spirit are justified. Believing the doctrine of justification by faith will save no one. The creeds provide opportunities to verbalize one's faith and trust in the God who justifies us in Christ Jesus through the work of the Holy Spirit. There is no doctrine of justification by faith articulated in the creeds because the creeds express the faith of justified sinners. *Credere in Deum* or better *Credere in Trinitatem* constitutes the very life of the Church *coram deo* or *coram Trinitate*. In response to the Father's beneficent creating, the Son's incarnation, and the Holy Spirit's work of sanctification, the Church speaks: *Credo*. I believe. I place my faith in. I *trust* in Father, Son, and Holy Spirit.

Confessing the Apostles' or Nicene Creed during the Divine Service reminds us that we are gathered together, in opposition to the world, as those who trust in the one true God as Father, Son, and Holy Spirit. If these creeds really are personal confessions of faith and trust, if they really do embody the core biblical teachings about God and His work, then you and I ought to recite these creeds wholeheartedly and energetically. When the pastor calls to the congregation, "Christians, what do you believe?" or better "Christians, in whom do you trust?" the people should respond with a vigorous, loud recitation of the creed. Faithfulness to the true and living God is a life-long calling. The challenge of remaining loyal to God the Father, Son, and Holy Spirit engages the Church as her most arduous and adventurous task. Reciting the creeds during the service effectively reminds us of this every week.

Conclusion

We could—indeed, we should—go through the entire *lex orandi* of the contemporary Reformed church and in the light of the doctrine of the Trinity think through our liturgical practice at every level. This needs to be done. The rite of Baptism, the celebration of the Lord's Supper, the Trinitarian form of order and authority—all of these and more ought to be subjected to a thorough-going Trinitarian critique by Reformed liturgists. By now I hope the point is sufficiently clear. We began by noting the apparent lack of concern for the Trinity in contemporary American Evangelical Christianity. What is the solution to this problem? How do we rejuvenate the Trinitarian *lex credendi* of the church? Write more books and articles? Deliver more lectures and write more scholarly monographs? Or form a committee to study the matter? What good would that do? The only lasting solution lies in restoring the Trinitarian *lex orandi* of the worshipping Church.

In his work on the Trinity, *The God of Jesus Christ*, Walter Kasper says, "The only answer to the modern God-question and to the situation of modern atheism is the God of Jesus Christ and the Trinitarian confession, which must be brought out of its present *existential* obscurity and turned into a grammar for theology as a whole." [14] Permit me to tweak this quotation just a little and unpack that adjective "existential": The only answer to the modern God-question and to the situation of modern atheism is the God of Jesus Christ and the Trinitarian confession, which must be brought out of its present liturgical and creedal obscurity in American Evangelicalism and turned into a grammar for worship and church life as a whole.

---

[14] Walter Kasper, *The God of Jesus Christ*, trans. by Matthew J. O'Connell (New York: Crossroad, 1996), ix (emphasis mine).

8

Corporate Rites and Rituals

I will show you a more excellent way.
—1 Corinthians 12:31b

Before I begin to analyze and explain the liturgy in detail, I must pause to explain and defend the *corporate* nature of the liturgy, specifically the use of coordinated, congregational prayer and praise in covenant renewal worship. I am referring to the responses and prayers the people recite or sing together. If we want our worship to be corporate (from the Latin *corpus*, "body"), then it must involve the entire local body of Christ. We must say and do things *together*. My goal in this chapter is to discuss and defend the use of set or fixed congregational prayer and praise—that is, prayer and praise voiced in unison by the congregation. Should we use precomposed prayers and responses in our worship? What is the origin of the traditional practice of reciting prayers and responses in unison during the service? Why do we stand and sit together? Why bother with all these external, physical postures? Are these practices distinctively Roman Catholic? Are we violating the Reformation principle of "the priesthood of all believers" when we worship like this? Wouldn't it be safer to avoid these external rituals altogether? Isn't it obvious that spontaneous, free prayer and praise is more genuine and spiritual? Since corporate prayers and ritual actions structure the entire covenant renewal service, it will be advantageous to answer these objections and questions before we go any further.

Patterns From Above

Jesus taught us to pray "Thy will be done on earth as it is in heaven" (Mt. 6:10). He thereby, over against the man-made, oral law tradition of the Pharisees and Sadducees, reestablished heaven as the pattern for what is done on earth. This pattern is symbolized in many places in the Old Testament, beginning in Genesis 1:1–2. But this priority is consistently present: the heavenly pattern must be followed on earth.[1] This is especially true for the worship of the people of God. Moses is warned by Yahweh to model the worship of the tabernacle exactly "according to the pattern" shown him on Mount Sinai (Exod. 25:9, 40; Heb. 8:5). Similarly, in the new age, since Christ's death, resurrection, and ascension, heaven and earth are united when the Lord gathers his Church to worship on Sunday. There is a real sense in which the assembled Church worships in heaven (Heb. 12:22). The Lord's Day is an eschatological foretaste of heavenly existence. The book of Revelation, for example, narrates the link between what happens in heaven and the Church's worship on earth. Geoffrey Wainwright and Ethelbert Stauffer orient us to the significance of the book of Revelation for Christian liturgy:

> At the beginning of the book of Revelation, St. John tells us that he "was in the Spirit on the Lord's Day" (1:10). Exegetes commonly hold that the visionary's ensuing accounts of life and events in the heavenly Jerusalem reflect in some ways the worship practices in the churches of his time, either in the regular Sunday gathering or at Easter (depending on the sense of "Lord's Day"). By divine inspiration St. John's experience of contemporary Christian liturgy was "heightened" into the vision of worship in the city

---

[1] James B. Jordan expounds this biblical theme with brilliant systematic consistency in his *Through New Eyes: Developing a Biblical View of the World* (Brentwood: Wolgemuth & Hyatt, 1988).

of God. In turn, the inspired writer's heavenly vision has helped to shape the understanding and performance of worship in the earthly church down through the centuries.[2]

The historical function of the early Church finds its fulfillment in worship. (But the significance of her worship finds its mature expression in the Apocalypse.) John, the liturgiologist among the apostles indicates the place that the worship of the Church has in universal history. The Church on the mainland of Asia assembles for worship on the Lord's Day, while John is . . . on the island of Patmos. But then all earthly limitations are removed and the heavenly temple itself is opened to the inward eye, as once it was opened to Isaiah. John saw the "tent of witness," the "ark of the covenant," the "altar," the "seven lamps," the "censer of sacrifice," whose smoke filled the whole temple. Men and beasts alike prostrate themselves before God and the Lamb and adore. Angels and martyrs play on their eternal harps. The lonely figure on Patmos is both witness of and sharer in the worship of heaven itself. The heavenly trumpets sound. The *Trisagion* is sung. The praises sung by the creatures, the stars and the worlds surge around the Creator like some fugue of Bach's that knows no end. The heavenly choir sings the *Agnus Dei*. The drama of salvation rolls onward like Palestrina's Marcellus Mass. The 144,000 voices sing a new song in words no human ear can learn. The angel proclaims an eternal gospel in unearthly glory like the final chorus of Handel's Messiah. The final Church comes together for the "great Eucharist," a Church of priests who are to serve God throughout eternity. That is the liturgy of universal history that the seer of Patmos knew and shared in. But the brotherhood is also gathered round Him, invisible, here and now a Church of priests. It receives the heavenly epistle and shares in the heavenly worship with its solemn "yea" and "amen" and "maranatha," "even so, come quickly Lord Jesus." So the apocalyptic liturgist understands the doxology of the persecuted Church in the framework of a liturgy that embraces all worlds and times.[3]

---

[2] Geoffrey Wainwright, "The Church as a Worshipping Community," *Pro Ecclesia* (1994):57.

[3] Ethelbert Stauffer, *New Testament Theology* (London: SCM Press, 1963),202; cited in Eugene H. Peterson, *Reversed Thunder: The Revelation of John & The Praying Imagination* (New York: HarperCollins, 1988),198. Chapter 5, "The Last Word on Worship" in Peterson's *Reversed Thunder* is also well worth consulting.

Surely these scholars are correct: the manner in which worship
is conducted in heaven functions as a model for the Church on
earth. When the Apostle John was privileged to observe heavenly
worship, as he records for us in the Revelation, he saw an orderly,
formal service performed by angels, living beings, and the twenty-
four elders. They repeated various rituals and ritual responses
(Rev. 4:9–11). They alternated responses antiphonally (Rev. 5:11–14).
They sang hymns in unison (Rev. 5:9). They fell down together (a
prearranged liturgical action), and they jointly recited prayers of
praise and thanksgiving that must have been precomposed and
memorized. How else would they have all prayed and sung simul-
taneously? Here, then, we have a biblical model for corporate Lord's
Day prayer and praise in our worship services. G. K. Beale makes
this point in his recent commentary on the Revelation. He argues
that too many modern commentators miss the point of Revelation
4–5 when they try to identify sources for the various elements in
John's vision from within the worship of the first-century synagogue
and/or Church. "John intended the readers to see what is told of in
the vision [Rev. 4–5] as a heavenly pattern that the Church is to reflect in its worship rather than the other way around (just as the
heavenly pattern of the tabernacle shown to Moses on the mountain was to be copied by Israel in the construction of their own
tabernacle)."[4]

An Unwarranted Assumption

Consider the manner in which the question about precomposed,
memorized prayers is often asked. Even though the question is often put in terms like this: Why does the congregation read these
prayers? I must counter with a fact: the congregation does not merely
read these prayers, they pray them. Moreover, since these prayers are
part of the ordinary liturgy of the congregation, they don't have to

---

[4] G.K. Beale, *The Book of Revelation: A Commentary on the Greek Text* (Grand Rapids /
Cambridge: Eerdmans/Paternoster Press, 1999), 312.

read them because they have memorized them. One could just as well question the manner of praying in some churches where the pastor does all the praying from the pulpit: Why does that congregation merely listen to the pastor pray throughout the service? That would not be fair. The very way in which the question is put prejudices the case from the outset. Presumably, a congregation is able to pray *with* the pastor while he prays. The same ought to be true when the congregation *recites* prayers. Surely the congregation is able to do more than merely recite these prayers. They can make the corporate prayer their own. They can pray sincerely. In fact, I believe, practically speaking, that it is easier to pray sincerely when one actually takes up a prayer on one's own lips, than when one merely listens to another person pray. Many have found it easier to daydream when one is listening—eyes closed—to another pray than when one's attention is focused on voicing a prayer oneself.

The Road to Rome or Canterbury?

Isn't this the kind of thing Roman Catholics do? There is a tendency in our circles to jump to conclusions about whether a liturgical practice is Romanism or Episcopalian. Let me give you an example of how quick we are to jump to the wrong conclusions. I was approached once after a service by a worshiper who was sure that we had lapsed into Catholicism because we had prayed for the dead in our service. Actually, the prayer did not explicitly mention "the dead" nor offer petitions for them; rather, it was a prayer of thanksgiving in remembrance of those who have died. The exact wording of the petition is as follows:

Minister: We remember with thanksgiving those who have loved and served You in Your Church on earth, who now rest from their labors (especially those most dear to us, whom we name in our hearts before You). Keep us in fellowship with all Your saints, and bring us at length to the joy of Your heavenly kingdom;

People: **We ask you to hear us, good Lord.**

Read the petition carefully. Notice that this prayer is not a prayer *for* the dead. We are not asking God to do something for the dead. We are not praying for their release from purgatory or for a second chance. In this petition we are giving thanks for the faithful Christians whom we have known and from whom we have learned so much. We are thanking God for their love and faithfulness. We are thanking God for godly parents and relatives, who have meant so much to us, who have now gone to be with Christ. We are thanking God for departed teachers, elders, and pastors who have been a positive example to us of the Christian life. We are giving thanks to God for the exemplary lives of the great pastors, teachers, and missionaries of the past. And finally, we are petitioning God to give us the grace to follow their example of faith and perseverance. We pray the same thing when we sing the fourth stanza of Reginald Heber's "The Son of God goes forth to war." The last petition is "O God to us may grace be given to follow in their train." [5] When properly understood, then, this is a very appropriate and powerful prayer. Unfortunately, this may not be the kind of petition that we might spontaneously offer. Thus, it serves as an excellent example of the principle I have explained above. We must be trained to pray like this.

There are many ways to express this petition that we might be conformed to the faithful saints of former days. Here is another example from the older Presbyterian *Book of Common Worship* (1946):

> O Lord God, the Light of the faithful, the Strength of those who labor, and the Repose of the blessed dead: We give Thee thanks for all Thy saints who have witnessed in their lives a good confession, for all the faithful departed, and for those dear to our hearts who have entered into rest . . . . Grant us grace so as to follow their good example, that we may be one with them in spirit, and, at last, together with them, be made partakers of Thine eternal kingdom; Through Jesus Christ our Lord . . . .

[5] Hymn #489 in the *Trinity Hymnal* (Philadelphia: The Committee on Christian Education, Inc., The Orthodox Presbyterian Church, 1961).

Back to the objection: but all of this talk about responses and printed prayers seems more Episcopal, Lutheran, and Catholic than Presbyterian. Yes, Catholics, Lutherans, and Episcopals practice similar forms in their worship services. So what? Does that make it wrong? Roman Catholics and Episcopals kneel for prayer; does that make kneeling dangerous or wrong? I always chuckle a little inside whenever I call the congregation to worship on Sunday morning using Psalm 95: 6, "Oh, come let us worship and bow down; let us kneel before the Lord our Maker." And then, what do we do *after* I read these words? We stand up! Why don't we kneel in worship like the Bible directs? I suspect that one of the reasons is that we are afraid we might look like Roman Catholics or Episcopalians. As far as I'm concerned, that is a pitiful reason for not obeying the Bible.

Biblical Bodily Postures

Of course, we would need kneelers in our pews to kneel for prayer. During the confession of sin the congregation ought to be on their knees, but, alas, our tradition has largely ignored the need for kneelers because it has failed to guard and pass on the traditional Christian teaching and practice regarding the importance of bodily posture throughout the entire worship service. I have heard people say that God is not interested in the posture of our bodies, but only the attitude of our hearts. Well, that's not exactly what the Bible says. There are too many references in the Bible to outward bodily postures in worship to dismiss kneeling as mere formalism. Even the Hebrew and Greek words that we translate as "worship" (*shacha, proskuneo*) mean "to bow down" or "to prostrate oneself" before another (Gen. 22:5; Exod. 32:10; Ps. 22:27, 29; Mt. 2:2; 4:9; Jn. 4:20–24; Heb. 11:21; Rev. 4:10).

What many people fail to recognize is that one's bodily posture will both express, as well as help establish, the posture of one's heart. When we are humbled, we hang our heads. When we are joyful, our arms and head fly up and we begin to move. More often than not, the reason most American Protestants don't kneel in worship is not because they are too humble, but too proud. It is all too convenient for us to keep to ourselves and not reveal our true selves in such bodily postures. This is pride. After citing numerous biblical references, Robert S. Rayburn notes,

> The position of the body is itself an act of worship. When you kneel or stand because you are in the presence of the Almighty and are to speak to him, you are honoring him with your entire self, with your soul and body together expressing reverence. In Holy Scripture, whenever men or women came face to face with God, they always immediately and instinctively assumed postures which were appropriate for a creature and a sinner before the living God . . . If we are really worshipping God as his children, then we are to worship him not with half ourselves but with our whole selves and our bodies ought to be as involved as our souls . . . . This was the feeling of the church in the days of the Reformation. A failure to take proper positions of body in the church was regarded as an act of irreverence.[6]

Rayburn then quotes from a sixteenth-century Reformed manual of worship and order, the *Book of Discipline of the French Reformed Church* (1559):

> That great irreverence which is found in divers persons, who at public and private prayers do neither uncover their heads nor bow their knees shall be reformed; which is a matter repugnant unto piety, and giveth suspicion of pride, and scandalizes them that fear God. Wherefore all pastors shall be advised, as also elders and heads of families, carefully to oversee, that in time of prayer all persons, without exception do evidence by these exterior signs the inward humility of their hearts and homage which they yield to God; unless anyone be hindered from doing so by sickness or otherwise. (Chapter 10, Art. 1)

---

[6] Robert S. Rayburn, "Worship and the Whole Man," *The Second Annual Conference on Worship: The Theology and Music of Reformed Worship, February 23–25, 1996* (Nashville: Covenant Presbyterian Church, 1996), 42–43.

Reformation churches knelt for prayer. Reformed pastors and theologians rebuked people that refused to do so. It would have been hard for them to conceive of any other posture for prayer (besides standing, of course). Nobody sat for prayer. Calvin and Luther would have been baffled at our arrogant refusal to practice what the Bible instructs merely to avoid being identified with another branch of the Church, however wrong that church may be about other doctrinal matters. Many mistakenly think that avoiding rituals like kneeling is evidence of simple faith and humility. C. S. Lewis, however, analyzes this assertion: "The modern habit of doing ceremonial things unceremoniously is no proof of humility; rather it proves the worshiper's inability to forget himself in the rite, and his readiness to spoil for everyone else the proper place of ritual."

The fact that Catholics and Episcopals practice congregational and responsive praying and kneeling might make such practices suspicious in our eyes, but we must be careful not to define how we ought to worship primarily in reaction to what Rome or Canterbury does. We might very well end up throwing out the baby with the bath water, which has been done all too often in the history of Protestant worship. It may be helpful to review briefly the liturgical renewal of the sixteenth-century Reformation and the rationale behind it.

The Reformation and the Priesthood of All Believers

One of the central intentions of the sixteenth-century Reformers remains virtually unknown in many of our churches today. The Reformers to a man, especially Luther and Calvin, sought to correct the late medieval distortions of worship by restoring congregational participation. The late medieval mass was hardly a congregational worship service at all. The service was said in Latin, which very few laymen understood. There was virtually no congregational participation in the service beyond watching the visual "performance" by the priest at the altar. The bread, (supposedly) transformed into Christ's real body and held up for the people to adore, was the climax of the mass. The people almost never partook of the Communion elements; only the priest ate and drank. There was no congregational praying, singing, or reciting of the creeds. The congregation merely watched and listened. They were largely passive. As individuals they may have performed private devotions completely independent of what the priest was doing up front, but as a community they did not participate in the liturgy.

To the Reformers this was a gross distortion of biblical and early Church (second and third century) worship practices. One of their greatest achievements was to restore intelligent, unified participation by the body of Christ in worship. They transformed the people from uncomprehending observers of the worship of the sacrificing priests into an active royal priesthood. Calvin, echoing the early Church fathers, insisted that "each Christian bears the exalted title of sacrificer," and therefore has a rightful place in the offering of praise and prayer in the liturgy. It is not the priest alone who has access into the heavenly sanctuary, but rather every member of the body of Christ has heavenly access into God's throne room on the Lord's Day. In the New Covenant there are no degrees of nearness (as there were in the Old Covenant), but every worshiper is a "saint," that is, one who has sanctuary access.

This, of course, is the great Reformation principle of the priesthood of all believers. The principle manifestation and evidence of the reality of this fundamental truth takes place during corporate worship as the whole congregation *participates* in offering to God prayer and praise. The congregation prays, praises, and communes with God. The pastor does not worship *for* them as a proxy; the people worship as the pastor *leads* them. What this means is that the priesthood of all believers demands a corporate liturgy.

> One value of a thoughtfully considered liturgy is that it enforces the idea that we are worshipping as the church, not as individuals or home groups. We are the Ship of Orthodoxy, not three-hundred fifty separate rafts in a lagoon. In many evangelical circles this is a great temptation. An individual may soar into the heavenlies and, oblivious to everything and everyone

around him, dance and shout to his heart's content. However, when we gather as the church, we can never be oblivious to those around us (1 Cor. 14). A home group may sing, testify, confess, sing some more, laugh, break for coffee, and come back together for teaching; but when we gather as the church, we must remember we are in God's Throne Room, not our living room. This is not coffee with our buddies but a royal audience with the King of the universe. This is of particular relevance because so many Christians today approach church worship as an extension of their prayer closets.[7]

Thus, the Reformers restored many of the pre-medieval practices of the post-apostolic church. They intentionally sought to recover what has been called "Old Catholic" forms of worship while bypassing the distortions of medieval *Roman* Catholic liturgical rites. The Reformers restored frequent Communion. They all sought to re-introduce weekly Communion at every Lord's Day worship service. They all effectively revived preaching and teaching so that the people could be instructed by God's Word every week. They all brought the recitation of the creeds by the congregation back into the worship service. They all rediscovered the inspired Psalms as the prayer book and hymnbook of the Church.

Moreover, congregational singing was resurrected and became one of the hallmarks of Reformation worship. Calvin discusses music and singing under the heading of prayer. The people were taught to sing the Psalms in corporate worship, since the Psalter is the inspired prayer book of the Bible. All the Reformers wrote model liturgies and prayers for use in the churches. This revival of congregational prayer was based squarely on the priesthood of all believers, which demanded that the people participate in the prayers and not just listen to them. In fact, the liturgies of the Reformers, Calvin included, were much more fixed than we modern Americans would feel comfortable with. The point I am trying to make

---

[7] Monte E. Wilson, "Church-O-Rama or Corporate Worship," in *The Compromised Church: The Present Evangelical Crisis*, ed. by John H. Armstrong (Wheaton: Crossway Books, 1998),76.

here, though, is that congregational praying of precomposed prayers, either spoken or sung, has a long and venerable history in Reformation churches and ought not to be jettisoned merely because they are not familiar forms to twenty-first century American Evangelical Protestants.

Exposing an Absurd Objection

Why, then, do so many American Christian people object to precomposed prayers recited by the congregation? I often hear a complaint that runs like this: "How can I pray what someone else wrote? These words are being forced on me. They are not coming from my heart and so I should not be made to pray them. I am against all forms of liturgies that are imposed on the congregation. They put the Spirit in a straight jacket." This kind of objection is often sincere and well meaning, but (to be frank) it is easily reduced to absurdity. It is an attack on the inspired Psalter, which has been given to the people of God as a corporate prayer book. Even worse, it is an attack on the use of the Lord's Prayer.

If the only prayer that a participant in the congregation can pray during a worship service is one that comes spontaneously from the individual worshiper's heart, then, first of all, congregational worship as such is ruled out. People must do things together in congregational worship. The people of God gather together as a community, to offer unified prayer and praise to the Father through the Son in the power of the Holy Spirit. If all prearranged liturgies and prayers per se are impositions on the individual worshiper's freedom, then the only thing left is for everyone to gather and worship the Lord spontaneously as individuals. But even then you run into trouble. If worship must be free in the sense that no external forms are allowed whatsoever, then no one, not the pastor nor anyone in the congregation could ever be allowed to impose any form on anyone in the congregation, except possibly if a unanimous vote was taken each time a suggestion was made. To press a little more, someone would have to determine the time to begin the service and this would be an artificially imposed regulation that would shackle the Spirit's freedom. After all, some people many not be ready to worship at 9:00 A.M. Why restrict their freedom in the Spirit?

We must be clear on this point. If one objects to precomposed prayers because one believes they unnecessarily bind the conscience of the believer to a particular form, then logically one must also reject all hymns, all prayers spoken by the pastor, and, indeed, any order of service whatsoever. If precomposed spoken prayers are a hindrance to the spontaneity of the Spirit, then so are precomposed sung prayers—hymns. After all, hymns are prayers—precomposed prayers. Singing is just a heightened form of speech—glorified and beautified speech. Not many people ever really think clearly about this. There is essentially no fundamental difference between a congregational prayer recited in unison by the people and one that is sung in unison by the people. Make no mistake about it, hymns are precomposed prayers of praise or petition written (usually) by someone outside of the congregation and "imposed" on the people by whoever prepares the bulletin. These hymns (to continue our *reductio ad absurdum* argument) then become an imposed, alien form which stifles the freedom of the Spirit and hinders all heartfelt spontaneity. Logically, as I indicated above, one would also be forced to reject all prayers by the pastor as well, since the pastor's prayers are nothing but an external form of prayer imposed on the congregation. I think you get the point now. Formal prayer is not necessarily the same as formal*ism*.

Corporate Prayer in the Bible

Precomposed prayers are biblical. This practice is not merely some leftover from Roman Catholicism. Our use of set prayers is very self-conscious. The historical Church got the idea from the Bible, particularly the Psalms and the book of Revelation, but not exclusively so. The Old Testament is filled with examples of how the saints used set forms of prayer to confess and praise God (Deut. 26; Ezra 3:10; Neh. 12:24; Ps. 136). David appointed Levites to compose prayers and songs to be used in the corporate worship of Israel (I Chr. 6:31–48; 15:16–24; 16:4–6; 25:1–5). These prayers and songs were then preserved for corporate use by the Israelites during their weekly and annual worship services (Lev. 23). Moved by the Holy Spirit, David himself composed prayers for corporate and individual use (I Chr. 16:7). Do not miss my point. The Holy Spirit moved David to compose and preserve for posterity a corporate prayer book for the saints. David in his Spirit-guided wisdom appointed Spirit-filled men to compose a song book/prayer book for the people to aid them in their public as well as private worship.

The Psalm titles, contents, and structure all witness to the fact that they were given by the Spirit to the covenant community to use in corporate worship. Just scanning through the Psalms one finds that many of them begin with words like "A Psalm for the Sabbath Day" (Ps. 92) or "To the Chief Musician: A Psalm of the sons of Korah" (Ps. 47). The *content* of many of the Psalms also witnesses to their intended use in public worship: hymns of praise (Ps. 95, 145–150), community confessions (Ps. 78, 105, 106, 135), and Psalms to be sung as the people ascend to Jerusalem for worship (Ps. 120–134).

Notice the many references to *specific postures* of worship within the Psalms (Ps. 5:7, Ps. 63:2–3, Ps. 95: 6, "O come let us worship and bow down, let us kneel before the Lord our Maker"). Even the very structure of the poetry supports its appropriateness for responsive and antiphonal recitation and singing in worship. They were written for congregational recitation and singing. Their structure testifies to the fact that the Spirit composed them to be recited and sung responsively or antiphonally in congregational worship (Neh. 12:24). Psalm 136 is an obvious example, cast as it is in the form of a litany.

So, when we use the Psalms in worship, whether we are reciting them in unison, reciting them antiphonally or responsively, or whether we are praying them by singing them, we are following

God's appointed forms of worship. Furthermore, when we include in the service Psalm-like prayers to be said by the congregation in unison, we are seeking to follow biblical guidelines that enable the congregation to participate together as a community in the activity of worshipping the Lord.

These kinds of prayers also help to guide and train the congregation in the art of biblical praying. We do not "naturally" know how to pray. The fact that one is a Christian does not guarantee that he will know how to pray. There is a silly myth that goes pretty much unchallenged in American Evangelicalism—worship comes "naturally." As someone has nicely put it: "Christians have to be taught everything from how to study the Bible to how to love their wives, husbands, and children. But when it comes to worship, evangelicals are nervous about someone teaching them prayers, chants, and even a set form of worship. Worship is supposedly the one thing that every living, breathing Christian automatically does the right way." This is a myth, a dangerous myth. When I look at the Bible I see all kinds of instruction and forms given to help us learn how to approach the King of kings properly. Coming into God's presence is different from anything else we do, and, furthermore, it is one of the most difficult activities we do.

The other problem with not having set and regular prayers is that it has the effect of excluding children, the mentally handicapped, and senile older adults. What is most prominent and sometimes over exaggerated in our circles—the sermon—is largely inaccessible to small children and others who may not have the intellectual capacity for messages dominated by discursive reasoning. Sadly, Reformed churches often pitch their services to the highly educated and thereby exclude all others. One has to be able to "read" to participate. One has to be able to "think logically" to understand sermons and articulate the finer points of sacramental theology, to sit at the Lord's Table.[8] In other words, the worship service is not

---

[8] All baptized Christians, young and old, articulate and inarticulate ought to be at the Lord's Table. See chapter 21, "We All Partake of One Loaf" in Part III.

accessible to the whole body of Christ, but only to a certain caliber of people—the young, intellectual, and literate portion of God's people. If, however, we would use set prayers and forms of worship every Sunday, children would learn to pray these prayers. And when members of the congregation begin to lose their mental capacities as they get older, they would still be able to participate in the service because these prayers, responses, and creeds would have been burned into their souls through constant use every Lord's Day.[9]

Consider again what we discover when we look into *heaven* and see how worship is conducted there. Lo and behold, we hear prayers spoken or sung *in unison* by great throngs of people and angels (Rev. 4-5). Notice that heavenly worship is conducted with set prayers and responses. How else would they all know what to say and when to say it? In heaven the saints triumphant pray responsively and antiphonally in concert with the angels. Remember that Jesus taught us to pray "Thy will be done on earth as it is in heaven." Earthly congregational praying ought to be modeled on heavenly congregational praying.

Conclusion: The Usefulness of Congregational Prayers

Finally, summing up our argument so far, precomposed, congregational prayers are a very valuable aid to worship. How so? First, we don't know how to pray, and precomposed prayers can help train our minds to pray biblically. Good prayers guide us and assist us in composing our own prayers, both with respect to content and structure. Almost all the phrases from all the prayers that we use in our worship come right out of the Bible. Thus, ultimately, we are praying God's Word. There *are* biblical ways to pray, and these precomposed prayers, used consistently, will help you *learn* how to pray. Surely this is the reason why so many prayers are recorded for us in the Bible. The traditional prayers of the Church offer the

---

[9] Leonard Payton argues this masterfully in his lecture "Liturgical Piety: Enduring to the End" given at the First Annual Pre-General Assembly (PCA) Conference on Reformed Liturgy (available from Biblical Horizons, P.O. Box 1096, Niceville, FL 32588).

worshiper guidance and direction, oftentimes by utilizing the language and structure (order of prayer) lifted right from the Bible itself.

Second, prayers sung or said in unison manifest the unity of the Church in prayer. We all pray together as the corporate body of Christ, not just as a bunch of individuals. Corporate worship is not designed merely as an aid to each individual's devotions. We don't come into church to worship merely as individuals with our own private tubes to God. We come together as the body of Christ, and as the body of Christ we confess our sins, pray, and praise God together. The Spirit recreates us into a community.

Third, printed prayers ensure congregational participation in the prayers. Remember worship ought not to be something you come to watch or hear, rather you come to perform worship yourself. Think about this: it is very difficult to get distracted when you are saying a prayer out loud. It is hard to do anything else but pray the prayer. A set prayer insures your participation and guards against your mind wandering.

Now, of course, someone could merely read the prayer. It is possible that a recited prayer could become rote (that is, a reading mechanically recited from memory without understanding). Nevertheless, when everything is said and done, I submit to you that it is much more difficult for your mind to wander when your attention is focused on reading and saying a prayer that you are familiar with than it is when you have your eyes closed and are merely listening to the pastor pray. Let's face it—most people find it very difficult to concentrate on praying when someone else is saying a long prayer. If you aren't familiar with the prayer that you are reading or hearing, then you will have to evaluate it as you are praying. And how much more effective would it be to recite prayers that you trust and know by heart? I will have a bit more to say about this in the introduction to Part II, but for now I would suggest that there is a freedom that comes from a set liturgy, a freedom to let go and participate without having to evaluate every word that you hear and say. Learning the liturgy is like learning the steps to a dance. Once one learns the ritual, one can participate with freedom and joy.

Fourth, no church can avoid prayer rituals altogether. You either have *good* prayer rituals or you have *bad* ones, helpful or dangerous ones, but it is impossible to be free from all forms in a church's corporate prayer life. Congregations that never use prayer books or set prayers, nevertheless, do develop, sometimes unknowingly (which is unfortunate), certain habits with respect to praying. You know very well what happens when there is no guidance or direction to the prayers. Prayers become tedious: "I *just* want to thank you, Lord . . . and I *just* want to ask . . . and I *just* want . . ." Or they become trivial and down right silly: "O Lord, help us to *be all that we can be*" (the Army Prayer) or "Lord, help us to *reach out and touch somebody* this week" (the AT&T prayer).

Obviously, we are not obliged to use all kinds of pretentious words and grandiose phrases in order for our prayers to be acceptable to God. I'm not trying to put down anyone's prayer merely because it is not as well structured and manicured as someone else's. God is pleased with the meager and unsophisticated prayers of His people, just as He is pleased with a young child's. But—and here's the important point—if the child never grows up and learns how to pray biblically, if the content of his prayers remains the same, then it is not so cute anymore. God may be pleased with a childlike prayer, but He is not satisfied with it. He expects us to grow up and learn how to pray like adults, to conform our prayers more and more to the models He has given us in the Scriptures.

Some churches never get beyond praying for sick people and saying grace at the table. That's fine as far as it goes, but have you ever noticed that the Bible does not contain a whole lot of prayers for sick people and pretty much assumes that we know how to give thanks for our food? Again, I'm not talking here about a fancy, flowing style. My concern centers on the *content* of the prayers: confession of sin; thanking God for creation and providence; thanking God for the person and work of Christ; praying for strength in the midst of temptation; praying that His kingdom would be protected from all its enemies and extended throughout the world. These are petitions that do not come "naturally" to us. We need to be trained. Printed, set prayers help to discipline and educate us. They help us to grow up and pray as mature Christians.

PART II
The Lord's Service Explained

*God never frustrated his worshipers, but ever received
them graciously, provided they came to him in sincerity.*
— John Calvin

Chesterton's witty observation usually holds: "As is common in
most modern discussions the unmentionable thing is the pivot
of the whole discussion."[1] The unmentionable thing in discussions of worship in many Protestant circles is "liturgy." I have
broken the verbal taboo numerous times already in this book.
One of my seminary professors, the late Dr. Robert G. Rayburn,
never tired of reminding us that *every* church has a liturgy. Not
every church uses the word liturgy, but every church orders its
worship service according to some rationale. It is impossible not
to have an order of service. Even if the order is not well thought
out or is insufficiently prepared beforehand by the pastor, some
order of worship will prevail during the Sunday morning worship hour.

Unfortunately, many American Protestant churches, in their
zeal to abandon anything that smacks of Roman Catholicism
with its formalism and fixed liturgies, end up with a haphazardly

---

[1] G. K. Chesterton, "What's Wrong With the World," in *The Collected Works of G.
K. Chesterton*, vol. 4 (San Francisco: Ignatius Press, 1988),215–16.

thrown together worship service that consists of various elements dropped into the program here and there without any biblical rationale.[2] Sometimes practical reasons are given for such a random "order." A hymn follows a prayer because the congregation needs to stand up and stretch after sitting for a while. A solo follows a Scripture reading just to add some variety to the service. Ordinarily spontaneity is elevated as more "spiritual" than preplanned arrangements. Whatever the case may be, the one thing that is normally missing is any biblical/theological reflection on how the church ought to approach the living God.

"There are good reasons for having an established liturgy and these reasons have often been recounted," according to Hughes Oliphant Old.

> In the first place liturgical forms are a good means of teaching the essentials of the Christian faith. When familiar liturgical forms and texts are used again and again, it gives us the opportunity to meditate on them and to penetrate their meaning more deeply. When there are well established procedures with which everyone is familiar, it makes it easier to concentrate on content rather than on outward form. Any athlete understands the importance of mastering form. Such simple things as breathing must be done correctly, but this is essential so that eventually they can be done spontaneously, without effort, without thinking about them. The concentration must be on other things. Forms are a means to an end, and if they are constantly changing they obscure the end rather than lead to it.[3]

---

[2] Liturgical worship and theology have fared much better in what we would consider largely liberal or neo-orthodox Presbyterian churches (like the PCUSA or even the Church of Scotland), a fact that may even contribute to confessional Presbyterians' suspicion of all things liturgical. If these churches like liturgy, then it must be bad. See the Presbyterian Church (USA) *Book of Common Worship* (1993) and the recent essays on it in Bryan D. Spinks and Iain R. Torrance, eds., *To Glorify God: Essays on Modern Reformed Liturgy* (Grand Rapids: Eerdmans, 1999).

[3] Hughes Oliphant Old, *Worship That Is Reformed According to Scripture*, Guides to the Reformed Tradition (Atlanta: John Knox Press, 1984),162.

I have heard liturgical worship contemptuously described as "worship by recipe," a reference to our practice of following a basic order and our repeated, but not slavish, use of various printed prayers, confessions, and other congregational recitations within the service. My response is: what is wrong with recipes? A recipe is "a set of directions with a list of ingredients for making or preparing something" or "a formula for or means to a desired end." Is having a "recipe" for worship something bad? I doubt that anyone prefers to eat dinners that are not made according to a recipe? No doubt some of our favorite dishes are very thoughtfully prepared and carefully cooked according to detailed recipes. Does anyone really want their chef (or wife or husband) to spontaneously prepare and cook their meal? The only way this would work is if the cook had, through extensive experience, internalized the "rules" for cooking. Every meal is the product of some recipe just as every worship service will inevitably follow some order or liturgy.[4]

I question the wisdom of not having consistently recurring patterns in our Sunday morning service. C. S. Lewis called the constant itch for novelty in worship the "liturgical fidget." Repeatedly changing the form and content of each Sunday service is actually an obstacle to worship. Lewis points out that a worship service "is a structure of acts and words through which we receive a sacrament, or repent, or supplicate, or adore." He uses ballroom dancing to illustrate his point. Just as one must "know" the steps in order to dance, so also one needs to be thoroughly at home with the liturgical form in order to perform the action that the form is meant to enable. "As long as you notice, and have to count the steps, you are not dancing, but only learning to dance." In the same way, if the worshiper is confronted with novelties in the service, he will be distracted from the very point of the service. The best liturgy "would be one we were almost unaware of; our attention would have been on God. But every novelty prevents this. It fixes our attention on

[4] See D. G. Hart, "Why Evangelicals Think They HATE Liturgy," *Modern Reformation* 5 (Jan/Feb 1996): 17–20.

the service itself; and thinking about worship is a different thing from worshipping." Lewis concludes with a call for "permanence and uniformity" in the Sunday service, explaining that he could "make do with almost any kind of service whatever if only it would stay put. But if each form is snatched away just when I am beginning to feel at home in it, then I can never make any progress in the art of worship. You give me no chance to acquire the trained habit."[5]

The real question is not whether but what kind of established liturgy (or recipe, if you prefer) does the congregation follow. Is it a good liturgy? Which is to say, is the liturgy self-consciously biblical in form and content? Since, as we have seen, the liturgy is chiefly God's service to us, we must first inquire of any "liturgy": Does this liturgical order and content embody God's service to His assembled Church? Is this the biblical way in which God draws His people close to Himself by way of sacrifice, weekly renewing His covenantal love for them? And because worship also consists in the congregation's active praise before God, the second question we ask is: Does this order and content of worship enable the congregation to respond appropriately to God's gracious service, gratefully giving back to God worship and praise that is pleasing to Him?

Here, then, is a good rough-and-ready definition of liturgy: *the orderly, biblical way in which the congregation is drawn into God's majestic, life-giving presence.* As we have seen, the biblical way is the way of sacrifice and the purpose is covenant renewal. God has informed us in Scripture concerning the manner in which He serves His people and His people serve Him on the Lord's Day, and we must be very careful to follow His guidance. The movement of the worship service corresponds to our movement into God's presence, or better, the order corresponds to *the way in which God draws us into his presence.* The Bible reveals how God graciously draws men and women into His loving fellowship and this sacrificial "order"

[5] C. S. Lewis, *Letters to Malcom: Chiefly on Prayer* (New York: Harcourt, Brace, and World, 1964), 4–5.

or "way" by which God brings us near and renews His covenant informs the order of our corporate service on the Lord's Day. This order of approach, this movement into God's presence is what we call the "liturgy" or the "Divine Service" or, in our case, the "Lord's Service."

A Morning Service from Providence Reformed Presbyterian Church

The Sunday morning covenant renewal service follows a similar order and pattern each week. Each element of the service is briefly explained in the next four chapters, with special attention given to its place in the overall order of worship.[6] The titles given to the various movements (Ascension Offering, etc.) in the sample order given below are not always exactly the way they appear in the Sunday bulletin, but the substance of each of the elements and their relative order remain regularly constant, with a few noted exceptions.[7] A **bold** style signals congregational responses and prayers. The cross (†) indicates when the people stand.

---

[6] I will resist the temptation to make too many suggestions for improving our current liturgy. Every pastor must necessarily begin his ministerial service *in medias res* when it comes to the liturgy of the congregation that he serves. Significant liturgical changes can only be made when he has gained the trust of his elders and people. A little liturgical humility ought to be exercised as well since most pastors have not received adequate training in Reformed liturgical theology in seminary. That means, of course, that some portion of the first ten years of the young pastor's ministry must be devoted to filling out his knowledge of biblical and historical liturgical theology. Even when the pastor comes to firm, informed liturgical convictions, he must know that the process of reforming a congregation's liturgy takes much longer than he is likely to expect, almost surely *generations*. We pastors often learn this the hard way.

[7] More examples of our Morning Service as the order appears in our bulletins can be found at Providence Reformed Presbyterian Church's website (http://www.prpc-stl.org).

Covenant Renewal Worship
The Morning Service - August 4, 2002
Pentecost Season

Preparation For Worship: *Psalm 90 & 100*
*Organ – Mr. Bill Hoover
Welcome & Announcements – Pastor Jeffrey J. Meyers

The Entrance

Call to Worship: *Psalm 100:4–5*   Pastor Jeffrey J. Meyers
†Hymn #304 "Open now thy gates of beauty"   *Trinity Hymnal*
†Salutation & Responsive Scriptures

†Pastor: In the Name of the Father, and the Son, and the Holy Spirit!
     Congregation: **Amen!**   *Matthew 28:19*

  The Lord be with you!
     And also with you!   *Ruth 2:4*

  Our help is in the Name of the Lord
     Who made heaven and earth!   *Psalm 124:8*

  The eyes of all look to you,
     And you give them their food in due season.

  You open your hand;
     You satisfy the desire of every living thing!   *Psalm 145:15–16*

†Pastor: Let us pray:

  **Almighty God, unto whom all hearts are open, all desires known, and from
  whom no secrets are hid, cleanse the thoughts of our hearts by the inspiration of your Holy Spirit, that we may perfectly love you, and worthily
  magnify your glorious Name, through Jesus Christ our Lord. Amen.**

The Sin Offering

†Call to Confession

  Beloved in the Lord! Let us draw near with a humble heart and confess our
  sins to God, our Father, imploring him in the name of our Lord Jesus Christ
  to grant us forgiveness:

  Blessed is the man against whom the Lord counts no iniquity!
     And in whose spirit there is no deceit.   *Psalm 32:2*

  I said, I will confess my transgressions to the Lord,
     And you forgave the guilt of my sin.   *Psalm 32:5*

Almighty God, who art rich in mercy to all those who call upon you; hear me as I come to you humbly confessing my sins, and imploring your mercy and forgiveness. I have broken your holy laws by my deeds and by my words, and by the sinful affections of my heart. I confess before you my disobedience and ingratitude, my pride and willfulness, and all my failures and shortcomings toward you and toward my family and friends. Have mercy upon me, most merciful Father; and of your great goodness grant that I may hereafter serve and please you in newness of life; grant me this, I pray, through the mediation of Jesus Christ my Savior and Lord. *Silent Prayer.* **Amen.**

†Pastor: Now lift up your heads and hear the good news! God, our heavenly Father, has had mercy on us. He has given his only Son to die for you, and for his sake forgives you all your sins. Therefore, as Christ's minister and by his authority, I declare to you the entire forgiveness of all your sins; in the Name of the Father, and of the Son, and of the Holy Spirit.

Congregation: **Amen!**

The Ascension Offering

†Pastor: Lift up your hearts.
We lift them up to the Lord.

†Let us give thanks to the Lord our God.
It is proper and right to do so.

†Truly it is proper, right, and salutary, that we should at all times, and in all places, give praise to you O Lord, holy Father, almighty and everlasting King. Therefore, with angels and archangels and all the company of heaven, and with the church on earth, we praise and magnify your glorious Name, evermore praising you and singing:

†Hymn #219 "Blessing and honor and glory and power" *Trinity Hymnal*

The Old Testament Reading: *1 Kings 19:1–20* Pastor Tommy Lee

This is the Word of the Lord.
Thanks be to God.

The Epistle Reading: *Galatians 2:11–21*

This is the Word of the Lord.
Thanks be to God.

†The Psalm: *Psalm 90* (recited responsively)

Yahweh, You have been our dwelling place
In all generations.

Before the mountains were brought forth, or ever you had formed the earth and the world,
Even from everlasting to everlasting, you are God.

You turn man to destruction,
And say, "Return, O children of men."

For a thousand years in your sight
Are like yesterday when it is past, and like a watch in the night.

You carry them away like a flood; they are like a sleep.
In the morning they are like grass which grows up:

In the morning it flourishes and grows up;
In the evening it is cut down and withers.

For we have been consumed by your anger,
And by Your wrath we are terrified.

You have set our iniquities before you,
Our secret sins in the light of your countenance.

For all our days have passed away in your wrath;
We finish our years like a sigh.

The days of our lives are seventy years;
And if by reason of strength they are eighty years,

Yet their boast is only labor and sorrow;
For it is soon cut off, and we fly away.

Who knows the power of your anger?
For as the fear of you, so is Your wrath.

So teach us to number our days,
That we may gain a heart of wisdom.

Return, O Yahweh! How long?
And have compassion on your servants.

Oh, satisfy us early with your mercy,
That we may rejoice and be glad all our days!

Make us glad according to the days in which you have afflicted us,
The years in which we have seen evil.

Let your work appear to your servants,
And your glory to their children.

And let the beauty of Yahweh our God be upon us,

And establish the work of our hands for us; yes, establish the work of our hands.

†The Gospel Reading: *Luke 6:17–26*

This is the Gospel of our Lord Jesus.
Praise be to you, O Christ.

†The Nicene Creed

I believe in one God, the Father Almighty, Maker of heaven and earth, and of all things visible and invisible. And in one Lord Jesus Christ, the only-begotten Son of God, begotten of his Father before all worlds: God of God, Light of Light, very God of very God, begotten, not made; being of one substance with the Father, by whom all things were made: Who for us men and for our salvation came down from heaven, and was incarnate by the Holy Spirit of the virgin Mary, and was made man; and was crucified also for us under Pontius Pilate. He suffered and was buried; and the third day he rose again according to the Scriptures, and ascended into heaven, and sits on the right hand of the Father. And he shall come again with glory to judge both the living and the dead, whose kingdom shall have no end. And I believe in the Holy Spirit, the Lord, and Giver of Life, who proceeds from the Father and the Son, who with the Father and the Son together is worshipped and glorified; who spoke by the prophets. And I believe in one holy catholic and apostolic Church. I acknowledge one baptism for the forgiveness of sins. And I look for the resurrection of the dead and the life of the world to come. Amen.

Sermon: THE FAITHFULNESS OF JESUS THE MESSIAH   Pastor Jeffrey J. Meyers
   VIII. EXPOSITION OF PAUL'S LETTER TO THE GALATIANS

The Tribute Offering

†Hymn #83   "We praise thee, O God"   *Trinity Hymnal*
We Offer Ourselves Through Tithes and Offerings
†Prayer of Dedication and Bidding Prayer for the Church

Pastor: Let us pray for the whole Church, that our Lord God would defend her against all the assaults and temptations of the adversary and keep her perpetually on the true foundation, Jesus Christ:

Congregation: Save and defend your Church universal, purchased with the precious Blood of Christ. Give it pastors and ministers according to your Spirit, and strengthen it through the Word and the sacraments. Make it perfect in love and in good works, and establish it in the faith once delivered to the saints. Sanctify and unite your people in all the world, that one holy Church may bear witness to you, the God and Father of all. Amen.

Pastor: Let us pray for our missionaries:

Send forth your light and your truth into all the earth, O Lord. Raise up, we pray, faithful servants of Christ to labor in the Gospel at home and in distant lands. Grant strength and perseverance to all of our missionaries. Grant that they may rejoice in a rich harvest of souls for your kingdom. Support them in times of trial and weakness, and make them steadfast, abounding in the work of the Lord. Bring the nations into your fold, pour out your Spirit on all flesh, and hasten the coming of the fullness of the kingdom of your Son Jesus Christ our Lord. Amen.

Pastor: Let us pray for all those in authority that we may live quiet and peaceable lives in all godliness and honesty:

O merciful Father in heaven, because you hold in your hand all the might of man and because you have ordained, for the punishment of evildoers and for the praise of those who do well, all the powers that exist in all the nations of the world, we humbly pray you graciously to regard your servants, especially the President and the Congress of the United States, the Governor of Missouri, and all those who make, administer, and judge our laws, that all who receive the sword as your ministers may bear it according to your Word; through Jesus Christ, our Lord. Amen.

Pastor: Let us pray for those who are in any way afflicted, oppressed, or troubled in body or soul:

God of mercies, we pray that you would comfort with the grace of your Holy Spirit all who are in sorrow or need, sickness or adversity. Remember those who suffer persecution for the faith, especially those whom we name in our hearts before you . . . . Have mercy upon those to whom death draws near. Bring consolation to those in sorrow or mourning. And to all your people grant a message of your love, taking them into your tender care. Amen.

Pastor: Finally, let us offer the prayer that our Lord has taught us:

Our Father, who art in heaven, hallowed be thy Name, thy kingdom come, thy will be done, on earth as it is in heaven. Give us this day our daily bread. And forgive us our debts as we forgive our debtors. And lead us not into temptation, but deliver us from evil. For thine is the kingdom, and the power, and the glory, forever and ever. Amen.

†The *Gloria Patri*

The Peace Offering

†Prayer of Thanksgiving for the Bread
The Words of Institution for the Bread
The Distribution of and Communion in the Body of Christ
The Communion Hymn#310 (*Psalm 53*) "Hallelujah"   *Trinity Hymnal*
The Words of Institution and Prayer for the Cup
The Distribution of and Communion in the Blood of Christ
Pastoral Benediction

The body and blood of our Lord strengthen and preserve you steadfast in the true faith to life everlasting. In the Name of the Father, and the Son, and the Holy Spirit.
Congregation: **Amen.**

†The Song of Simeon (*Nunc Dimittis*): *Luke 2:30–32*

Lord, now lettest thou thy servant depart in peace, according to thy word; for mine eyes have seen thy salvation, which thou has prepared before the face of all people; A light to lighten the Gentiles, and the glory of the people of Israel. Glory be to the Father, and to the Son, and to the Holy Ghost, as it was in the beginning, is now, and ever shall be, world without end. Amen.

Pastor: Give thanks to the Lord, for he is good.
Congregation: **And his mercy endures forever!**   *Psalm 136:1*

Pastor: O God our Father, Fount and Source of all goodness, who in loving-kindness did send your one and only Son to take on our flesh, we thank you that for his sake you have given us the assurance of pardon and peace in this service; and we ask you not to forsake your children, but evermore to rule our hearts and minds by your Holy Spirit, that we may be enabled constantly to serve you; through Jesus Christ, our Lord, who lives and reigns with you and the Holy Spirit, ever one God, age after age.

Congregation: **Amen.**

The Benediction and Exit

†Hymn #124   "At the Name of Jesus every knee shall bow"   *Trinity Hymnal*
(Ralph Vaughan Williams tune)

†Benediction: *Numbers 6:24–26*
        Congregation: **Amen.**

†We Bless the Lord: Hymn #7 (*Psalm 72:18–19*)

> **Now blessed be the Lord our God, the God of Israel,**
> **For he alone doth wondrous works in glory that excel.**
>
> **And blessed be his glorious Name to all eternity:**
> **The whole earth let his glory fill. Amen, so let it be.**

†Postlude
†Greet One Another.

9
Entrance and Call to Worship

I have calmed and quieted my soul,
like a weaned child with its mother.
—Psalm 131:2a

We move now to explaining the service one line at a time, from entrance to departure. These chapters are written both for ministers and the worshipping congregation. I will, therefore, sometimes address pastors regarding their duties, at other times I will admonish worshipers directly in the second person ("you") in order to explain how the congregation ought to think and act during each of the movements in the covenant renewal liturgy.

We often identify the first step in God's service to us as the Call to Worship. Although this name keeps up the alliteration of "C's" (call, confession, consecration, communion, and commission), what we label each movement in the service is not as important as what actually happens as God renews His covenant with His people in these five divine actions. One should not forget that our worship always begins with and presupposes *God's* service to us. In the first movement of God's five-fold covenantal action, He graciously takes hold of us, effectually calls us together before Him, and thereby distinguishes us from the world as His own peculiar people. Before He can begin His sacrificial work, we must appear at the threshold in response to His summons. We process through His gates and into His courts with praise. But even our initial prayers and hymns of praise can only be a response elicited from us by the Lord's gracious invitation and enabling presence.

Preparation and Entrance

Every effort should be made to prepare oneself and, if applicable, one's family for the worship service. Many people act as if it is sufficient to strut into God's presence with an attitude like this: "Hey, God! How's it going? Here's a song or two and a few bucks. Have a nice day!" Such an attitude often permeates modern laid-back, trendy worship services. No preparation is required, so none is made. No preparation is necessary because the worshiper often doesn't really do much of anything. He is a spectator, a part of an audience. With our understanding of worship, however, preparation is necessary. What we experience as a congregation on the Lord's Day should not be confused with our other, normal activities. This is the special time that the Lord has set aside to meet with His people. We ought to follow the example of Mary and not of her harried sister Martha. Jesus commends Mary when she ceases from her normal work and prepares herself by sitting at Jesus' feet in order to attentively listen to Him: "Mary has chosen what is needful, and it will not be taken away from her" (Lk. 10:42).

In this section I am encouraging the congregation to prepare, but the minister who officiates must also make appropriate preparations for leading the service. These should begin hours before the Call to Worship and include a thorough reading of the service as a whole, especially the extended Scripture readings that will be used, prayer for himself and the congregation, and his arrival at the sanctuary with enough lead time to set up and prepare himself for the beginning of worship without being rushed. The prayers that the minister will offer during the service ought to be carefully considered, if not written out in advance.

Prayer of Preparation

To steel yourself against the wicked disposition illustrated earlier, stop a moment and pray on Saturday night that God would put you in the proper frame of mind in the morning to worship Him. Go to bed early enough to provide a good night's rest. Give yourself enough time in the morning so you do not have to rush out the door. You might even make the atmosphere different on Sunday morning for the family by playing some appropriate music on the stereo as your family dresses and gets ready for church. Sit down for a few minutes (no need to overdo it, just a *few* minutes) open your Bible, read through a Psalm, and say a brief prayer out loud—something like this: "O Lord, enable me this morning to worship You sincerely and in truth. Help me, Father, to receive again Your gracious service to me in the Word and Sacraments. Assist me also so that I can give to You the kind of praise and adoration appropriate to the One who loves me, sent His Son to die for me, and continues to provide all things for me. Amen." You may do this alone or with your family.

Be on time. Now, of course, there will be Sundays when something goes wrong at home and we are providentially hindered from arriving on time. The Lord knows and understands when things happen that are out of our control. But the Lord is not amused when, for no good reason, you stroll into His Majestic Presence after everyone else has properly approached Him in prayer and confession. Dare anyone saunter into the worship service after the confession of sin? Is it not pure presumption to imagine that God will be pleased with this kind of carelessness? If any important human official were to invite you to a special meeting, surely you would try your best to be on time. You wouldn't presume to walk in late to a meeting with the President or the Mayor, would you? Why, then, when the King of the universe summons you into His presence, do you treat it so casually? Do you *really* think that God is meeting with you on Sunday morning? If you do, then you will heed His summons from heaven and make a command performance at the time He specifies.

The Prelude

When the piano or organ starts to play, this is the signal that you should take your seat, quiet your children, stop all conversations, and engage in silent prayer and/or meditation. An appropriate Scripture meditation may be provided at the top of each morning service in the bulletin (see our model service). Take advantage of these guides for preparation. Normally the Scripture meditation is connected with the Call to Worship so that you can again remember and reflect upon your momentary entrance into heaven itself, into the very presence of the Lord of the universe.

Ministers must be careful to oversee the prelude music, both the kind of music selected and how it is played. Music sets and alters moods. The wrong kind of prelude music can jeopardize whatever care God's people have made in preparation for the beginning of the service. Some types of music, for example, have associations that clash with worship. I will leave this admonition vague and not try to give a list of musical styles that might be counter-productive. Likewise, the way the prelude is played may also endanger the opening of the service. This is not the time for flamboyant, concert-like performances. The organist or pianist must not call attention to him or herself. Ministers are charged with oversight over the whole liturgy, including the prelude. They should not leave the music entirely to others who may not have the requisite liturgical knowledge and sensitivity.[1]

Announcements

Announcements come before the beginning of the worship service because they are not directly related to public worship. Everything done after the Call to Worship is done for a reason and

---

[1] The minister, however, should welcome the opportunity to work with the music staff in order to help them gain the requisite liturgical knowledge and sensitivity. Because skilled, well-educated musicians may feel themselves to be more qualified than the minister in matters of music, they may be reticent to accept the minister's oversight in this area. It may require tact on the part of the minister to help church musicians realize that musical service in the church requires liturgical training and oversight as well as musical excellence.

in its proper place. We should not simply stick things here and there in the service merely to get them done. The announcements are important, but they have no proper place in the biblical order of worship. I find mid-worship announcements such as committee reports, financial updates, and other sorts of ecclesiastical "news" items offensive and annoying since they have no legitimate function in the order of covenant renewal. More often than not, they function like commercial or advertisement breaks intruding into the flow of congregational worship (assuming that there is such a flow in the service). When placed before the official beginning of the service, however, as a part of the preparation for worship, announcements may serve to remind us that we are being called into God's presence as a body, not just as individuals. To hear about what is going on in the community of God's people, to make eye-to-eye contact with others in the congregation, might, if received with the right frame of mind, prepare us for the commencement of our corporate liturgy.

The Call to Worship

God Himself calls us to worship. He summons us from heaven to assemble. We do not decide to gather together and then ask God to be present. There is no "invocation" at the beginning of the service. To "invoke" God's presence may be suitable before a football game or a session of Congress, but it makes no sense at the start of a Sunday service. This is the *Lord's* Day. We don't gather together and ask Him to be with us. He commands us from heaven to enter into His presence, and we respond in obedience as the Spirit effectually enables us.

That we do in truth enter into God's special presence in the midst of his gathered congregation must never be slighted or forgotten. The reality of God's special presence with his people on the Lord's Day has come under considerable attack in recent years. All of life is worship, we are told. God is present everywhere all through the week; therefore, what we do on Sunday is not really different than what we do on other days. God cannot be more present on one day or in one place over against another. What are we to think about this kind of reasoning? True, God is present everywhere. But His omnipresence is not what I am referring to here. God has promised to be present with his people in a special manner when they gather on Sunday. The one who skips church for the golf course or shopping mall or state park may not argue from God's omnipresence to justify his not being in church. Sure, God is present on the golf course, just as He is present in hell. But this general presence of God doesn't do the people in hell much good. God is present in heaven and hell, but He is not present in the same way in each of these locations. There is a huge difference.

Even if we cannot define it precisely, God is nonetheless present in a heightened special sense when His people gather as the Church on the Lord's Day. For one thing, He is present there *pro nobis* ("for us"). This is the place and time where He gathers His people around the Word and Sacraments. He has promised to be there *for us* when His people gather. It is not so much that God was not present in, say, China, when the pillar and fire led the people of Israel out of Egypt or when His presence filled the tabernacle upon its completion; rather, the Lord was at these appointed places in a special, life-giving way. The people of Israel were given singular signs of God's special presence as they gathered around Mt. Sinai and the tabernacle. Similarly, it is not that God is absent from the food court in the mall on Sunday; rather, He has promised to be present in a special way, the way of salvation and blessing, at the Communion Table in church. The bread and wine are singular signs designed to assure us of His special, gracious presence with us. He has not promised to be in the mall on Sunday *for you*. Actually, if you refuse to heed the Lord's summons to gather with His Church, He may be present there *against you* so that you could very well experience His judgment and curse, rather than His promise of blessing, life, and salvation.

Moreover, when we are in God's special presence every week, receiving from Him His promise through His Word and Sacrament, we can go forth out of church into the world with the full assurance that God will be with us and for us wherever we may be during the week. Without being in the Lord's special presence we have no assurance of His omnipresent help in every situation and location (see Gen. 3:8; 4:16; Exod. 33:14–15; Deut. 4:37; Deut. 12:7, 18; 14:23, 26; 15:20; Judg. 18:6; 2 Kgs. 13:23; 17:18–23; Mt. 18:20; 1 Cor. 5:4; 11:18ff).

Normally, the minister voices God's call. Seeing and hearing God's ordained spokesman, the congregation should know by faith that God Himself calls them. Nevertheless, even if we use one of the Psalms where the worshipers call each other into God's presence, the presupposition is that God is summoning us through the voice of another. That external voice will normally be that of the pastor (or an officiating elder or intern), but it also may come from the congregation itself. In either case, we respond to the call that comes from outside of us as the very voice of God.[2]

Typically the pastor utilizes some portion of God's Word (maybe a passage from the Psalms) that contains a clear Call to Worship, authoritatively summoning the congregation into God's presence. Psalm 135:1–3 is a good example of a passage that may be used as a Call to Worship:

> Praise Yahweh! Praise the name of Yahweh;
> Praise him, O you servants of Yahweh!
> You who stand in the house of Yahweh,
> In the courts of the house of our God.
> Praise Yahweh, for Yahweh is good;
> Sing praises to His name, for it is pleasant.

In our sample service we have used Psalm 100:4–5:

> Enter His gates with thanksgiving,
> And His courts with praise!
> Give thanks to Him; bless His name!

---

[2] See chapter 15, "On Hearing God's Voice *Extra Nos* " in Part III.

For Yahweh is good;
His steadfast love endures forever,
And His faithfulness to all generations! [3]

Our Response to God's Call

The Lord has now called us into His special presence. He has taken hold of us by His Word and separated us out from the world as His people. This is the first step in the order of covenant renewal worship. The congregation now stands before Him poised to respond to His call and receive His gracious gifts. The sacrifice begins.

The Opening Hymn of Praise. Singing is our first response to God's words and actions in the worship service. Remember, the entire service moves forward as God speaks and the congregation responds. It is something of a conversation between God and His Church. God calls and we respond. God speaks and we listen. God gives and we receive. God acts and we thank Him. We say "amen" each time the Lord speaks to us or acts for us. The dialogical pattern is found throughout the Bible when men find themselves in God's presence (Is. 6:1–12; Jer. 1:4–8; Rev. 4–5, 19:5–10). It is the biblical way to approach God in worship. So, here, at the beginning of the service, the Lord calls us and we gather to praise Him.

Normally, then, we enter into God's presence singing. The opening hymn is almost always a Psalm of praise or a hymn of adoration. This song is addressed to God, which means it is a prayer. This first hymn will usually highlight some aspect of the character and/or work of God thereby giving concrete form to the congregation's adoration and praise. It is appropriate that we should "enter His gates with thanksgiving and His courts with praise" (Ps. 100:5). The gathered congregation is herself now the house or temple of the

---

[3] For more examples of appropriate Scripture passages to use as a Call to Worship, see Robert G. Rayburn, *O Come, Let us Worship* (Grand Rapids: Baker Book House, 1980), Terry Johnson, *Leading in Worship: A Sourcebook for Presbyterian Students and Ministers Drawing Upon the Biblical and Historic Forms of the Reformed Tradition* (Oak Ridge: The Covenant Foundation, 1996), and Hughes Oliphant Old, *Leading in Prayer: A Workbook for Worship* (Grand Rapids: Eerdmans, 1995).

Lord (1 Cor. 3:17; Eph. 2:21; 1 Pet. 2:5), indeed, the "city of God" (Heb. 12:22). Just as the Israelites passed through the gates of Zion singing, we too enter that which these types symbolized with songs of praise.[4]

Our Initial Trinitarian Confession. The minister proclaims: "In the Name of the Father, and of the Son, and of the Holy Spirit." The people then respond with a hearty, "Amen!" Here we are carefully identifying ourselves and our worship as Christian. As baptized believers we bear the Name of Father, Son, and Holy Spirit. This is the God we worship. This is the God under whose authority and in whose presence we live and die. This is our Lord who serves us in worship. By faith we will be receptive to this God throughout the entire morning service. The Bible clearly admonishes the faithful: "Whatever you do in word or deed, do all in the Name of the Lord Jesus, giving thanks to God the Father through Him. (Col. 3:17; also Eph. 2:18; 1 Cor. 12:3). The liturgy includes this right up front so as to ensure that we remember and publicly proclaim that everything that happens in the Divine Service occurs under the sign of our gracious three-personed God. We solemnly and publicly call God and the world to witness that we are "gathered together" in His Name (Mt. 18:20), and in that Name alone we offer our prayers, praise, and thanksgiving (Jn. 16:23).

The Name of God—Father, Son, and Holy Spirit—is liturgically non-negotiable. Not only does God's Trinitarian life structure our service throughout, as we have seen in previous chapters, but the very Name of the Trinity must never be compromised. Even as I write these words the Methodist Church in England has broken with centuries of Christian tradition, not to mention biblical fidelity, and included a prayer to "God the Mother" in its worship book for the new millennium. This new prayer appears in

---

[4] One possible variation on the order I have presented here would be opening the service with a processional hymn of praise. The congregation would sing as the minister(s) processed into the sanctuary to gather in the presence of God. The congregation herself might even process behind her minister into the place of worship, if space and architecture allowed.

one of the Communion services: "God our Father and Mother, we give you thanks and praise for all that you have made . . ." This prayer is idolatrous. God's Name is not Mother.

The proper Name of God is Father, Son, and Holy Spirit. The Trinitarian Name is the fulfillment and eschatological expansion of the Lord's personal proper name in the Old Covenant—Yahweh. Designating our God as "Father" and "Son" is not the result of our comparison between earthly fathers and sons and the deity. These are not anthropomorphic metaphors that we have projected onto an unnamed deity. God is first and foremost a Father *not* in relationship with His creatures, but in relationship with His Son. And God the Son is Son not by virtue of His likeness to created sonship, but because of His eternal relations with God the Father. This is what the Apostles' and Nicene Creeds make clear: "I believe in God the Father . . . and in his Son, Jesus Christ our Lord."

The language of Father and Son has its origin in eternal inter-Trinitarian relationships. These divine Names describe relations that exist within the Trinity quite apart from any consideration of the world of human familial structures. According to Ephesians 3:15, the Father of our Lord Jesus Christ is the Father "from whom every fatherhood [*pasa patria*] in heaven and on earth is named." It is not merely that God has revealed himself as *a* father, or *like* a father. More than this, he is *the* Father. He is the first, eternal, and original Father. God is the original Father; all other human "fatherhoods" are created images of His Fatherhood. Otherwise stated, "Father" is not anthropomorphic language—language drawn from the world and forms (*morphe*) of man (*anthropos*) and then applied to God. Rather, what we have in the word "Father" is *theomorphic* language. The reason we have fathers on earth is because they share some characteristics of the first and original Father. So the designation "Father" is not really a metaphor at all. Moreover, "Father" is not merely an attribute of God; it is His *Name*, a proper name. The same is true for the Son and the Holy Spirit. These are the names to which God responds. They are the familiar terms of address that He has given His family to use when we speak to Him.

God likes His Name. This is the Name into which every Christian is baptized, the Name that they dare not bear in vain. [5] God responds to His Name, but not to other names. His personality and honor are associated with this Name.

All of this means that you may call upon "Sophia" with all your might or you may pray to the "Heavenly Mother" every day or raise your hands toward heaven and say, "Hear me "Goddess/Mother," but if you pray like this, you should know that you are not talking to the God and Father of our Lord Jesus Christ. He doesn't respond to these prayers. Nobody is listening (except perhaps a demon or two who may decide to take a special interest in you). If, however, we address the Father through the Son in the Spirit, then we are addressing the Christian God in the way in which He has revealed Himself. We can know to whom we are talking. And we can be confident that we have the attention of the Father of our Lord Jesus Christ who dwells in us by His Spirit.

The Salutation. The salutation is a greeting, a salute. The pastor hails the congregation, "The Lord be with you." and the people respond, "And also with you." This Hebrew form of greeting and response arises out of the covenantal promise of Emmanuel, "God with us." We see it in the book of Ruth. When Boaz arrives at work he greets his harvesters with "The LORD be with you," and they respond, "The LORD bless you!" (Ruth 2:4). This was a common greeting exchanged between people in Israel. Even the Lord and His angels greet people in this way (Judg. 6:12; Lk. 1:28). In the New Testament it becomes common among Christians as well (Jn. 20:19; cf. 2 Thes. 3:16; 2 Tim. 4:22). By the end of the third

---

[5] It also follows that people who have been immersed or sprinkled with water in the name of some other god (i.e.,Creator, Redeemer, and Comforter) have not undergone Christian Baptism and must therefore be brought to the font and baptized in the Name of the true God. For more on the non-negotiable character of the Name of God, see Alvin F. Kimel, Jr., ed., *Speaking the Christian God: The Holy Trinity and the Challenge of Feminism* (Grand Rapids: Wm. B. Eerdmans, 1992) and Geoffrey Wainwright, "Trinitarian Worship," in *Worship With One Accord: Where Liturgy & Ecumenism Embrace* (New York: Oxford University Press, 1997),237–250.

century it had become an almost universal practice in the liturgies of the churches. It was the greeting that signaled the beginning of the worship service.

Aside from the obvious fact that it is more dignified and reverent than "Hello" or "Good morning," this salutation has a meaningful function in the inauguration of the Divine Service. When the minister says, "The Lord be with you," he declares his intention to lead the people in worship: he desires and prays that the Lord would bless the congregation as they worship under his leadership. The minister acknowledges that he will be the instrument by which the Lord is present with and serves His people during the service. When the people respond, "And also with you," they verbally affirm their pastor's leadership as well as their desire to see him blessed as he performs his pastoral office. The bond of trust and love between the pastor and the congregation having been renewed, the people are now ready to receive the Lord's service and gifts as they are delivered to them through the instrumentality of their pastor. In addition to the receptivity of the congregation, the pastor himself should now be ready to become transparent as a vehicle of the Lord's voice to His people.

Votum and Responsive Scriptures. The salutation is normally followed by the *votum. Votum* means "prayer" or "petition" in Latin. The *votum* is a short initial prayer expressing our need for the Lord's help in order to worship Him properly. The minister says, "Our help is in the name of the Lord," and the people call back, "Who made heaven and earth." These are the words of Psalm 124:8. By reciting this Scripture at the beginning of the worship service we confess that without the Lord's assistance we dare not enter His presence. We cannot genuinely worship God "in the flesh," for without His enabling power all our worship is worthless (Jn. 6:63; 15:5; Phil. 2:12–13; 4:13). He Himself is the One who "helps" us enter His presence.

Other appropriate Scriptures are often added to the salutation and *votum*. In our model service two verses from Psalm 145 are included. During special seasons of the Church year, Scriptures that highlight the events being memorialized should be used. For example, during Advent, passages that speak of the coming King should be recited.[6]

Opening Prayer. The pastor now leads the congregation in a short prayer of adoration and petition that extols the Lord's greatness and requests His continuing service and presence throughout the service. Traditionally, this prayer is a *collect*. In our model liturgy we have chosen the well-known and well-loved prayer for purity from the Anglican service of Holy Communion.[7] Such a prayer "collects up" (Latin: *collecta*) the petitions of the congregation into one common prayer.[8]

This form of prayer, unique to the liturgies of the Western churches, has a peculiar literary form that usually includes five parts:

1) an address to God ("Almighty God");
2) an acknowledgment of some aspect of God's nature or character ("unto whom all hearts are open, all desires known, and from whom no secrets are hid");
3) the petition itself ("cleanse the thoughts of our hearts by the inspiration of Your Holy Spirit");
4) the aspiration ("that we may perfectly love You, and worthily magnify Your holy Name"); and finally,
5) the memorial pleading ("through Jesus Christ our Lord, Amen.").[9]

---

[6] For examples of seasonal scriptural recitations, see the *Book of Common Worship* (Louisville: Westminster/John Knox Press, 1993), 165–400.

[7] From Thomas Cranmer's first *Book of Common Prayer* (1549) in *The First and Second Prayer Books of Edward VI* (London: Dent, 1910), 212.

[8] For more on collects see L. E. H. Stephens-Hodge, *The Collects* (London: Hodder and Stoughton, 1961) and the wonderful collection of Cranmer's collects in, C. Frederick Barbee and Paul F. M. Zahl, *The Collects of Thomas Cranmer,* (Grand Rapids: Wm. B. Eerdmans, 1999).

[9] The minister who chooses the prayers ought to have adequate liturgical resources close at hand to help him select or compose appropriate prayers for the service. See my bibliographical essay for publication information. I would suggest at least the following resources: the old (1946) and the new (1993) *Presbyterian Book of Common Worship* , the various older

Further Observations and Options

Much of the initial response to God's call remains the same from service to service. That which remains constant is called the *ordinary* in liturgical theology. We designate that which might change from week to week the *propers*. Even though we change the opening hymn every week, and periodically use different responsive Scriptures and collects, the bulk of the opening liturgy remains the same every Lord's Day. Some may object to the regularity of this weekly ritual. Saying the same thing over and over again may become rote and meaningless, we are often warned. Well, it may, but it does not have to. We have not thought very carefully about the place of repetitive rituals in our lives or in our worship. Our tradition makes us suspicious of certain kinds of repetitious rituals. Some things strike us as too Catholic or Episcopal. All the while, without much serious reflection, we develop rituals of our own—rituals that remain unexamined theologically and biblically.

Once again, it might be helpful to note that repetition is not inherently bad. I say, "I love you" to my wife over and over again without much variation. I kiss her every day and usually the same way. Our family sits down to eat, going through the same rituals every night. I introduce myself and extend my hand for a handshake the same way as everyone else. These activities are not meaningless simply because they are repeated without much variation. Just the opposite. The uniformity and continuity of these repeated rituals provide stability, security, and structure to our lives. This is what living is all about. We inevitably dispose our lives ritually. Ritual repetition is evidence of life! Chesterton makes just this point quite well:

---

and newer editions of the *Episcopal Book of Common Prayer*, the *Lutheran Service Book and Hymnal* (ALC, 1958), the *Lutheran Hymnal* (1941), *Lutheran Worship* (LCMS, 1982), and *The Lutheran Book of Worship* (LCA, 1978). All of these contain liturgies and prayers that Reformed pastors may freely ransack for ideas. You may, for example, want to use a prayer of confession just as it is from one of the Lutheran services, or you may want to slightly alter the content of any of the prayers to make it fit with whatever Scripture reading you may be using. There is something to be said for the Reformed way of liturgical freedom: it gives us

The sun rises every morning. I do not rise every morning; but the variation is due not to my activity, but to my inaction. Now, to put the matter in a popular phrase, it might be true that the sun rises regularly because he never gets tired of rising. His routine might be due, not to a lifelessness, but to a rush of life. The thing I mean can be seen, for instance, in children, when they find some game or joke that they specially enjoy. A child kicks his legs rhythmically through excess, not absence, of life. Because children have abounding vitality, because they are in spirit fierce and free, therefore they want things repeated and unchanged. They always say, "Do it again"; and the grown-up person does it again until he is nearly dead. For grown-up people are not strong enough to exult in monotony. But perhaps God is strong enough to exult in monotony. It is possible that God says every morning, "Do it again" to the sun; and every evening, "Do it again" to the moon. It may not be automatic necessity that makes all daisies alike; it may be that God makes every daisy separately, but has never got tired of making them. It may be that He has the eternal appetite of infancy; for we have sinned and grown old, and our Father is younger than we. The repetition in nature may not be a mere recurrence; it may be a theatrical encore. Heaven may encore the bird who laid an egg.[10]

We inexorably move through life ceremonially. It is reoccurrence and repetition that make life worth living. If rituals like the salutation, *votum*, or even the Lord's Supper become for us meaningless and boring, it is not the fault of ritual per se but of the one doing the ritual.[11]

Only the Lover Sings

Ideally we should sing these responses—everything from the *votum* to the creeds has traditionally been sung by the people.

---

free access to all of the best of every Christian liturgical tradition. We are free to use, not to lose the rich liturgical tradition handed down to us. In addition to these service books, you will find some prayers and Scripture readings in Robert G. Rayburn's older work, *O Come, Let us Worship* (1980), Terry Johnson's *Leading in Worship: A Sourcebook for Presbyterian Students and Ministers Drawing Upon the Biblical and Historic Forms of the Reformed Tradition* (1996), and *The Collects of Thomas Cranmer* (1999).

[10] G. K. Chesterton, *Orthodoxy* (New York: Image Books, 1959), 60–61.

[11] I highly recommend reading Thomas Howard's refreshing treatment of ritual in *Chance or Dance? A Critique of Modern Secularism* (Wheaton: Harold Shaw Publishers, 1969).

After all, why *say* it when you can *sing* it? James Hastings Nichols describes the typical Reformation service in the sixteenth century: "In classical Reformed worship the 'liturgy' in the strict sense, the people's part, was all sung. It is not the spoken prayers, taken by the minister, but the sung liturgy of the people which must be studied in the first instance to comprehend the meaning of early Reformed worship."[12] That may come as a surprise to modern Reformed folks. We typically *say* everything but the hymns. Colossians 3:16, however, commends us to let the word of Christ dwell in us "richly" by singing "psalms, hymns, and Spiritual songs." The Word dwells in our midst richly or gloriously when it is sung. Singing glorifies and beautifies speech. When you love someone you use heightened, glorified poetic speech and you sing those words to your lover. Somewhere Augustine sloganizes this fact: *Cantare amantis est* ("only the lover sings"). Lovers don't merely talk, they *sing*. Love beautifies. We sing to those we love. We sing about that which we love. Just as poetry is glorified written communication, singing is appropriate whenever plain talk is not enough.

The Lord's Day service is the context where we express our gratitude and love for God. Here we are called to glorify God with our speech. Adoration is a state of the soul that only singing can appropriately express. Follow the progression. Poetry is glorified words. Glorified words are glorified still more when they are sung. The union of many voices makes singing even more glorious. Still again, complex harmonies glorify congregational singing. Finally, the sung word is made yet more glorious when accompanied by instrumental music.

Such a rich conception of congregational participation is true to the best in Reformation theology and practice. For example, a steady stream of men were trained in Calvin's Geneva and sent out as

---

[12] *Corporate Worship in the Reformed Tradition* (Philadelphia: Westminster Press, 1968), 35.

missionaries into all of Europe to establish the Gospel. The Reformation was not simply an intellectual, doctrinal movement—a mere attempt to propagate ideas or doctrines. The Reformation, whether led by Luther or Calvin, was a full-fledged *liturgical* reformation. You didn't just come to Geneva in the 1500's to learn doctrine; you came to learn how to worship God. You came to be formed into a worshipping community. You were trained to sing. To sing your faith. To sing the Apostles' and Nicene Creeds. To sing the *Te Deum*. To sing your prayers. To sing the Lord's Prayer. Especially, to sing the inspired hymnbook of the Church, the Psalter. You were trained in a new manner of living fitting for the Gospel. You were trained to be incorporated into a Christian army of Psalm-singing worshipers. You came to Geneva or Wittenberg or Strasburg in the mid-sixteenth century and you experienced what Paul meant in Colossians 3:16, "Let the word of Christ richly dwell among you, with all wisdom teaching and admonishing one another with psalms and hymns and spiritual songs, singing with thankfulness in your hearts to God." *This* is what it means to be a Reformation Christian. You are a singing Christian, a participant in a congregation of singing, justified believers. The bottom line is that we should learn to sing more of the Divine Service.

10
Confession and Absolution

The blood of Jesus Christ His Son cleanses us from all sin.
—1 John 1:7

The next step in covenant renewal worship is one that many con-temporary Christian churches have dropped altogether.[1] All sorts of reasons might be advanced for why this is so. Our concern, however, will be to explain the crucial place that confession and absolution have in every self-consciously and consistently Christian worship service. To seek an entrance with God Almighty without humbly confessing sin and faithfully receiving His for-giveness in Christ is sub-Christian at best. "If I regard iniquity in my heart, the Lord will not hear me" (Ps. 66:18). The Psalmist's instincts have been formed by generations of sacrifices in the tab-ernacle and temple. There is a way to approach the Holy God of Israel, and the first step is purification from sin. This is the first gift of God, the first service God renders to His people when they are gathered before Him. God's initial service to us consists

---

[1] See for example R. Kent Hughes, "Free Church Worship: The Challenge of Free-dom," in *Worship by the Book*, ed. D. A. Carson (Grand Rapids: Zondervan, 2002), 177–188. Hughes provides three examples of "Morning Corporate Worship Services" from College Church in Wheaton, Illinois. Not one of them contains a corporate confession of sin.

in cleansing us from the guilt of our sin. Confession and absolution correspond to and fulfill the Purification Offering in the old world of animal sacrifices. This critical stage in our ascent into God's presence will bring us near to God and properly situate us in heaven so that we can praise Him with the heavenly company of angelical beings and departed saints.

The Purification Offering

According to the Bible, when men are ushered into the presence of Almighty God, they are made painfully aware of their own sinfulness and guilt. Consider Isaiah's experience. His translation into heaven and his vision of God's majestic holiness had an immediate effect: Isaiah cries out, "Woe is me, for I am undone! Because I am a man of unclean lips, and I dwell in the midst of a people of unclean lips; for my eyes have seen the King, the Lord of hosts" (Is. 6:5). Essentially the same thing happened to Ezekiel when he had a vision of the glory of God by the river Chebar. "When I saw it," Ezekiel explains, "I fell on my face" (Ezek. 1:28). The beloved Apostle John, the disciple who was so "close" to Jesus during his earthly ministry, when confronted with the glorified Lord Jesus Christ, "fell at his feet as dead" (Rev. 1:17).

These examples are given so that we might learn the proper way to approach God's majesty. In each case (and we could cite many more) those that are "undone" in the presence of God are not unbelievers or even particularly heinous sinners who might have reason to fear God's wrath. Rather, they are those who are in covenant with God, but nevertheless experience the holiness of God upon approaching Him. They have not apostatized or fallen out of covenant with God and therefore do not need to be brought back in. God's covenantal grace provides for the ongoing forgiveness of sins for His people.

The Israelite people, for example, after having been delivered from Egypt and graciously brought to Mt. Sinai (Exod. 20:1), nevertheless experience the presence of Yahweh on Mt. Sinai with much fear (Exod. 20:18–21). The Lord's response is to give them a way of access at the altar through sacrifices of Ascension and Shalom offerings (Exod. 20:22–26). The process by which God enters into (or renews the Abrahamic) covenant with the delivered people of Israel follows the overall pattern of covenant renewal worship:

1. Yahweh calls them to Mt. Sinai and declares His intentions. (Exod. 19–20:17)
2. Yahweh graciously provides them an altar (slaughter-site) in order to memorialize His Name. (Exod. 20:18–26)
3. Yahweh preaches the application of the law. (Exod. 21–23)
4. The covenant is ratified with a meal. (Exod. 24)

In the Divine Service, therefore, after we are brought face-to-face with the Lord of Glory at the beginning of the service and are made conscious of our own unworthiness and are sensitive to the guilt and pollution that adheres to us because of our sin, it follows that *the first and most appropriate act* for us as God's covenant people is to confess our sins. Remember, every animal (symbolizing the worshiper) that makes the ascent to God in the sacrificial ritual must first be slaughtered at the threshold and his blood be splashed on the altar as a public, visible sign that God's judicial punishment for sin has been satisfied. Only after this does God begin to draw the animal near and prepare him for his ascent into God's glorious presence in the cloud at the top of the altar. In the same way, every Christian worshiper, at the beginning of the service, must beseech God the Father for the forgiveness of sins on the basis of the death of His Son, the Lamb of God who takes away the sins of the world.

Drawing Near With A Humble Heart

I have learned from experience that modern people often grumble at the thought of being reminded of their sins up front in the worship service. They bristle when reminded of them anywhere in the worship service. This is too heavy for them. Too negative! Modern pagan Americans are not comfortable with being reminded of their guilt when they appear in God's presence. For this reason, many contemporary church services simply omit confession and absolution. Just because the "unchurched" feel uncomfortable with confessions of sin, should we drop them from the order of worship? Who said that unbelievers ought to feel comfortable and at ease in a Christian worship service? If they are not brought face-to-face with their sins, how can they be brought to the place where they "fall on their faces and say, 'God is really among you!'" (1 Cor. 14:24–25).

1 Corinthians 14:24–25 is *the* proof text used by "seeker service" advocates who want to adapt the worship service to make it more acceptable to unchurched people. I have heard this argument used over and over again: "Look, we see in 1 Corinthians 14 that Paul expected unbelievers to be present in the worship of the early Church. Therefore, we should be careful that what we do in worship does not offend or upset them. In fact, we should find out what kind of church service the unchurched people in our area want and then change our service to make it more appealing." One Presbyterian pastor I know took a survey around the neighborhood and asked a sampling of "unchurched" people what they would like to see in a Sunday service. What should we do to make it interesting enough to get you to visit our church? He took the results of the survey and built up a Sunday service specifically designed to attract these unbelievers to church. I saw the service. It was designed to make the visitor want to come back and therefore full of all kinds of interesting and entertaining activities, but it would never have led to the effect that Paul envisions in 1 Corinthians 14:24–25: "But if an unbeliever or an uninformed person comes in, he is convinced by all, he is judged by all; and thus the secrets of his heart are revealed; and so, falling down on his face, he will worship God and testify that God is truly among you."

When it comes to the liturgy the principle question for us must never be, "Will it make our church user unfriendly for the unchurched," but rather, "Is it biblical to confess one's sin when entering into God's holy presence?" Does anyone in the Bible stroll into God's presence singing, "I've got joy, joy, joy, joy down in my heart"? They may eventually express their joy, but their *first* response is always confession of sin. Are contemporary worship services really training people how to worship, how to pray, how to enter into God's presence if they omit corporate confessions of sin? Robert G. Rayburn's comments about this are timely:

> One of the serious weaknesses of our modern worship lies in the fact that we have failed to make clear the inflexible holiness of our God. It is true that he is the God of all grace, that he is infinite in his kindness and mercy toward us, but he is also a God of manifest righteousness who cannot look upon sin. Entirely too many ministers give the impression that all we must do is rest in the lovingkindness of God, knowing that he will always supply all the healing and strength that are needed. The Christian life is not as simple as that. The believer must honestly and reverently deal with sin in his life continually day by day. Before we presume to worship God, we must remember the clear teaching of the Word of God, "If I regard iniquity in my heart, the Lord will not hear me" (Ps. 66:18). Until we have truly and sincerely confessed our sin before the Lord, our worship will not be acceptable in his sight.[2]

A Corporate Confession

Furthermore, the confession of sin is a *corporate* prayer. It is the prayer of the whole local church, and therefore the best forms for this prayer are those that emphasize the corporate nature of the prayer. Prayers prayed in unison by the whole congregation, responsive prayers (called "litanies"), responsive praying of penitential Psalms (32, 51, 130, etc.), and hymns of confession are all well suited for use as prayers of repentance at this point in the service.

Like every other element of worship, the congregational confession of sin comes as a response to God's call. The Lord has called us into His glorious presence and in so doing graciously grants us the opportunity to confess our sins and receive forgiveness once

---

[2] Robert G. Rayburn, *O Come, Let Us Worship: Corporate Worship in the Evangelical Church* (Grand Rapids: Baker Book House, 1980), 187.

again. Generally speaking, the very layout of the service in the bulletin helps to remind you of the dialogical nature of all of worship. God speaks through His ordained servant and then the people respond in obedience to that call. Consider an example of a portion of a typical Sunday morning bulletin:

†God Calls us to Confession: *1 John 1:8–9*
    We Confess Our Sins (*in unison*)
    Almighty and most merciful Father, I have erred, and strayed from your ways like a lost sheep. I have followed too much the devices and desires of my own heart. I have offended against your holy laws. I have left undone those things which I ought to have done; and I have done those things which I ought not to have done; and there is no health in me. Have mercy upon me a poor miserable sinner, O Lord. Spare me, O Lord, as I confess my faults. Restore me for I repent of my sins. Renew me according to your promises declared unto mankind in Christ Jesus my Lord. And grant, O most merciful Father, for Christ's dear sake, that I may hereafter live a godly, righteous, and sober life; to the glory of your holy Name. *Silent Prayer.* Amen.

In this example, which is slightly different than the model service we have been referring to, God calls us to confession when the minister reads 1 John 1:8–9, and we obediently respond with a prayer of repentance. Even the layout helps reinforce the order— the response of God's people is indented to visually remind you that you are responding to God's Word. The confession of sin in this case is a precomposed prayer of repentance prayed in unison by the congregation.

Our model service uses another form. It begins with a general summons from the pastor to the congregation and then engages the congregation to recite a portion of Psalm 32:

†Call to Confession
    Beloved in the Lord! Let us draw near with a humble heart and confess our sins to God, our Father, imploring Him in the name of our Lord Jesus Christ to grant us forgiveness:

Blessed is the man against whom the Lord counts no iniquity.
And in whose spirit there is no deceit. *Psalm 32:2*

I said, I will confess my transgressions to the Lord,
And You forgave the guilt of my sin. *Psalm 32:5*

Almighty God, who art rich in mercy to all those who call upon you; hear me as I come to you humbly confessing my sins, and imploring your mercy and forgiveness. I have broken your holy laws by my deeds and by my words, and by the sinful affections of my heart. I confess before you my disobedience and ingratitude, my pride and willfulness, and all my failures and shortcomings toward you and toward my family and friends. Have mercy upon me, most merciful Father; and of your great goodness grant that I may hereafter serve and please you in newness of life; grant me this, I pray, through the mediation of Jesus Christ my Savior and Lord. *Silent Prayer.* **Amen.**

Ideally, when possible, the congregation should be bowing down on their knees making their confession.[3] If they are not on their knees, then they should continue to stand after the Entrance.

The congregation should be instructed that the public confession of sin is not designed to be an exercise in breast-beating. An intensely personal expression of your abhorrence of yourself and your sinful tendencies is, of course, appropriate for private or silent worship. The confession of sin, however, in a public, corporate worship service is more like the confession of faith, like reciting the Apostles' or Nicene Creeds. As someone has aptly put it, the corporate confession of sin "is a statement in which we confess that we are sinners, whether we feel particularly rotten at the moment or not."

After the corporate, formal prayer offered by the congregation, there is usually a time of silence to provide each member of the congregation an opportunity to confess his or her sins individually and privately. Each worshiper should use this time of silence to repent of particular sins. The confession of sin ought to be a very important part of your weekly routine. It offers a recurring opportunity for Christians to "come clean" before our Heavenly Father.

[3] See the discussion of kneeling and bodily posture in chapter 8, "Rites & Rituals".

God Forgives Our Sins

After the confession of sin we hear the pastor proclaim the Lord's forgiveness to all who have publicly confessed their sin and trusted in Jesus Christ alone. This gracious declaration of God is proclaimed by the minister, using a traditional formula of absolution or a portion of God's Word that announces God's love and favor toward those who humbly admit their need of Christ. This is God's word of assurance to us, and we need it every week.

This element of worship (in conjunction with the confession of sin) has largely vanished from contemporary evangelical worship. Typically, no public confession of sin ever finds its way into a modern evangelical worship service (after all, it wouldn't sit right with the visiting "religious consumers" who do not believe they are sinners), and so, consequently, no declaration of God's forgiveness of the past week's sins ever shows up either. Thus, God's people often miss out on one of the central blessings of the Lord's Day: the opportunity for weekly cleansing and covenant renewal—the *assurance* of God's grace authoritatively proclaimed by the minister to believers who repent of their sins.

There are a variety of ways to communicate the assurance of pardon. The pastor may use a Scripture passage that announces God's grace, but he may also add to it a brief explanation and application of the passage. Some Presbyterian liturgies contain a brief declaration that can be used at this point in the service. Here is an example from the older Presbyterian *Book of Common Worship*:

> †Pastor: Almighty God, who does freely pardon all who repent and turn to Him, now fulfill in every contrite heart the promise of redeeming grace; remitting all our sins, and cleansing us from an evil conscience; through the perfect sacrifice of Christ Jesus our Lord.

Our model worship service uses a slightly different form that begins with a call to "rise up" (from kneeling) or at least to "lift up your heads and hear the good news." The congregation then responds with a hearty "Amen" to God's declaration. They thereby confess that they believe what the minister has declared is the very verdict of God.

> †Pastor: Now lift up your heads and hear the good news. God, our heavenly Father, has had mercy on us. He has given His only Son to die for you, and for His sake forgives you all your sins. Therefore, as Christ's minister and by His authority, I declare to you the entire forgiveness of all your sins; in the Name of the Father, and of the Son, and of the Holy Spirit.
>
> Congregation: **Amen.**

I have called this an "absolution." Is that terminology proper? Well, that depends upon what one means by absolution. It may not be an absolution in the Roman Catholic sense. The pastor does not have any special power to remit sins (as some mistakenly believe), but he does have the office entitling him to proclaim authoritatively God's forgiveness of sins to all who truly repent. There is a difference. Protestant, especially traditional Lutheran and Reformed churches, have understood the Scriptures to teach that the pastor has been ordained by God to represent Christ to the people during the worship service. He thus has the authority to proclaim God's forgiveness, but he does not have the power personally to pardon anyone (Mt. 16:17–20; 18:18; Jn. 20:21–23; and the *Westminster Confession of Faith*, chapter 30).

When Calvin explains the significance of Jesus' commissioning of the apostles as "ordinary ministers of the Gospel" in John 20:19–23 he makes the following observations:

> We now see the reason why Christ employs such magnificent terms, to commend and adorn that ministry which he bestows and enjoins on the Apostles. It is, that believers may be fully convinced, that what they hear concerning the forgiveness of sins is ratified, and may not less highly value the reconciliation which is offered by the voice of men, than if God himself stretched out his hand from heaven. And the church daily receives the most abundant benefit from this doctrine, when it perceives that her pastors are divinely ordained to be sureties for eternal salvation, and that it must

not go to a distance to seek the forgiveness of sins, which is committed to their trust."[4]

Ministers have been given to the people of God so that they need not "go to a distance to seek the forgiveness of sins" but can hear the word of forgiveness from their pastors and know that these men have been "ordained as a surety for eternal salvation." This means that the pastor can (indeed *must*) make a powerful and authoritative declaration of God's redeeming love in Christ to the congregation. Tender consciences often need such a weighty pronouncement. Just as the Apostle John can write to assure the saints, so the pastor may also proclaim the forgiveness of sins in Christ to his people (1 Jn. 2:12).[5]

I once challenged a regular visitor to our church about her sporadic attendance on the Lord's Day. "Why is this?" I asked. She said something like this: "I just don't feel worthy. When I come into church and see all those godly men and women and families, I don't feel like I should be there. I know myself, Pastor. I am no saint. I cannot seem to prepare myself, get myself adequately cleansed and ready to come to church and worship. I know I'm guilty. I *feel* guilty even coming to church!" I said to her, "Jill, think about this. You don't come to church because you are guiltless. Rather, you come to church guilty because you need forgiveness. You come to the service to hear Jesus Christ say to you, 'Your sins are forgiven!' So does everyone else." I reminded her that our liturgy always included a confession of sin up front, followed by the declaration of forgiveness by the minister. "What do you think that's all about?" I asked her. She said that she had not thought very much about it. She thought that she was the only one who needed the assurance of God's love and forgiveness in Christ every week.

---

[4] John Calvin, *Commentary on the Gospel According to John*, volume 2, trans. by William Pringle (Grand Rapids: Baker Book House, 1981 [1848]), 272.

[5] For more on this see chapter 14, "The Place of the Ministry in the Lord's Service" and also chapter 15, "On Hearing God's Voice *Extra Nos*" in Part III.

The Grace of Weekly Forgiveness

I have heard prominent men in Presbyterian circles deny the need for a confession of sin during the Sunday service. The argument runs something like this: If our sins are already forgiven in Christ, why is it necessary to ask forgiveness each week? If we have been justified "once and for all" the moment we believed, then why do we need to seek forgiveness on a weekly (daily) basis? John Frame makes this argument in his book *Worship in Spirit and Truth*.[6] First, he skews the case against a covenantal order of worship using the unfortunate, prejudicial term "reenactment liturgy" to describe it. Next, he argues: "An important theological point is obscured by the reenactment liturgy. That is that redemption is in the past, accomplished once and for all." He also cites the post-Resurrection situation to make his case. He argues that we don't need to confess our sins every Sunday because Jesus has died and been resurrected and our sins are forgiven.

Stop for a minute to think about this. What difference does the post-Resurrection situation make when it comes to confession of sin? This is incredible. Our sins are already forgiven, so we don't have to confess them when we appear in God's presence? After all, 1 John 1:9 ("If we confess our sins, he is faithful and just to forgive us our sins and cleanse us from all unrighteousness") is a *post*-Resurrection proclamation made to Christians! Calvin argues that a continual reception of justification is necessary, that God must "repeatedly" acquit us if we are to be saved in the end:

> Therefore God does not, as many stupidly believe, once for all reckon to us as righteousness that forgiveness of sins concerning which we have spoken in order that, having obtained pardon for our past life, we may afterward seek righteousness in the law; this would be only to lead us into false hope, to laugh at us, and mock us. For since no perfection can come to us so long as we are clothed in this flesh, and the law moreover announces death and judgment to all who do not maintain perfect righteousness in works,

---

[6] John Frame, *Worship in Spirit and Truth*,(Phillipsburg: Presbyterian and Reformed, 1996), 68–70.

it will always have grounds for accusing and condemning us unless, on the contrary, God's mercy counters it, *and by continual forgiveness of sins repeatedly acquits us.* (*Institutes*, 3.14.10; emphasis mine)

In addition to his post-Resurrection argument, Frame also argues about the "emphasis" of the service. In answer to the question, "Why don't you have corporate confessions of sins and assurances of pardon?" Frame responds, "Because our main emphasis is joy in achieved forgiveness." So what? How does that answer the question? I would hope that the joy of forgiveness is also our emphasis in worship. But a worshiper will not experience the joy of forgiveness if he or she does not confess sin.

It seems to me that if you confess your sins each week early on in the worship service and then hear the proclamation of forgiveness in Christ from the Word of God announced by the minister, this would, in fact, set the stage for a joyous worship service. But we don't want to emphasize "mourning for forgiveness," Frame says. And we don't want this kind of thing to "dominate our worship service." Fine. Who said it has to dominate the service? In my experience, these acts of worship typically take about five minutes! How is this a "main emphasis" or something that "dominates" the worship service? Who said a corporate confession of sin up front in each service is the same as emphasizing excessive "mourning for forgiveness?"

The corporate confession is simply an honest and thoughtful recitation before God of one's sins; the sole purpose of which is to allow us to receive forgiveness and enable us to enter fully into the joy of His presence. And why do these elements (confession and forgiveness) have to work "to the exclusion of other biblical emphases" as Frame argues? Again, they are just two elements of the liturgy. How can confession and forgiveness be at odds with other biblical emphases? Unless, of course, they filled the whole service! But we have already said that it need not take more than five minutes.

The *real* problem here is that modern people don't like to be reminded of their sins up front in the worship service. This is too heavy for them. It turns people away. It even offends self-righteous Christian people. Some writers have also claimed that confession and absolution is "unintelligible" to modern people. I doubt if these rituals are unintelligible. Rather, modern pagan Americans don't like to be reminded of their sins when they appear in God's presence. They don't appreciate all this "fuss" about sin. Again my response is so what if they do not feel comfortable in a service that includes a corporate confession of sin. The covenant renewal service is for the people of God, not unbelievers. If unbelievers are present, let them observe humble Christians confessing their faults and receiving forgiveness from God their Father. How much more "evangelistic" can you get? Are contemporary worship services really training people how to worship, how to pray, how to enter into God's presence if the congregation does not confess their sins up front? Are they really modeling the Gospel before the world if they drop confession and absolution?

11
Consecration and Ascent

The Word of God is sharper than any two-edged sword.
—Hebrew 4:12

Having confessed sin and been cleansed by the blood of Jesus, the congregation is now prepared to begin the second major moment in the covenant renewal rite. Just as the priestly sword was at this point trained on the sacrificial animal to prepare him for his ascent into the Lord's presence, and the fire on the altar was stoked up to purify and transform him for fellowship with a holy God, so also now the fiery Spirit will use the Word of God during this part of our service to "chop" us up, wash us, and transform us into holy people prepared to meet our holy Lord (Heb. 4:12; 12:14; Ps. 24:4; Eph. 5:26–27). During this stage of the liturgy the Lord serves us through His Word and we respond by obediently hearing and submitting to the priestly sword of the Spirit: "For the word of God is living and powerful, and sharper than any two-edged sword, piercing even to the division of soul and spirit, and of joints and marrow, and is a discerner of the thoughts and intents of the heart" (Heb. 4:12).

The Sursum Corda

After the absolution, God's purified people are invited to come nearer. Just as the sacrificial animal is brought near the altar in preparation for his being drawn into the fire as food for God and, likewise, just as the Ascension Offering follows the Purification offering, so now the Christian worshiper ascends into heaven to praise Father, Son, and Holy Spirit, and to hear the Lord's verbal instruction in preparation for his fellowship meal with God. Appropriately, therefore, the *sursum corda* (Latin: "lift up your hearts") comes at this point in the service.

> †Pastor: Lift up your hearts!
> **We lift them up to the Lord!**
>
> †Let us give thanks to the Lord our God!
> **It is proper and right to do so!**
>
> †Truly it is proper, right, and salutary, that we should at all times, and in all places, give praise to you O Lord, holy Father, almighty and everlasting King. Therefore, with angels and archangels and all the company of heaven, and with the Church on earth, we praise and magnify Your glorious Name, evermore praising You and singing:
>
> †Hymn #219   "Blessing and honor"   *Trinity Hymnal*

The "heart" here stands for the center of the whole man. The purpose of the *sursum corda*, therefore, is not to elicit an "emotional" response. We are not being summoned to work up "feelings" about the Lord. We may experience certain emotions at this point in the service or not. But how we feel must be transcended by what we know by faith is happening in the liturgy. In the *sursum corda* the congregation is being summoned to accept by faith our heavenly positioning in Christ. The Lord has forgiven us and now invites us "in close" to praise Him and hear His life-giving Word. This is objectively true whether we feel like it or not. Although everything may still "look" the same, by faith we understand that the roof of the Church has been rolled back not only to expose the heavenly service in progress but also to incorporate us into it. Cherubim and seraphim, angels and archangels, together with the church triumphant are now "visible" to the eye of faith. Heaven and earth are now joined and we have been ushered into the festal assembly gathered around the throne of the Lamb (Heb. 12:22–24; Rev. 4–5). We lift up our hearts to the Lord.[1]

Following the *sursum corda*, the people give thanks to God the Father for His glorious grace. This prayer, led by the pastor, reminds them that they are now joining in the chorus of praise before the throne of God. When one makes the ascent into God's presence one starts singing. Singing is a means of ascent.[2] This is when the the music and singing began in the temple liturgy—when the Ascension Offering begins.

> Then Hezekiah commanded that the Ascension Offering be offered on the altar. And when the Ascension Offering began, the song to Yahweh began also, and the trumpets accompanied by the instruments of David king of Israel. The whole assemble worshipped, and the singers sang and the trumpeters sounded. All this continued until the Ascension Offering was finished. (2 Chr. 29:27–28)

Now is when we sing the *Sanctus* ("Holy, Holy, Holy") or another hymn that provides the congregation with the opportunity to participate in the praise offered around the throne of God and the Lamb in heaven. Hymns of praise based on the Revelation 4:8

---

[1] In traditional Reformed liturgies, beginning with Calvin, the *sursum corda* is often placed immediately before the Lord's Supper. But this has the effect of dividing the service in two, as if something different is happening when we come to the Communion Table. In fact, the covenant renewal service is a seamless whole with three movements (Confession, Consecration, and Communion), not two. See James B. Jordan, *Theses on Worship: Notes Toward the Reformation of Worship* (Niceville: Transfiguration Press, 1994), especially Thesis 22: "Eliminate the Divided Service," 109–112.

[2] See Peter J. Leithart, *From Silence to Song: The Davidic Liturgical Revolution* (Moscow: Canon Press, 2003), chapter 4.

("Holy, Holy, Holy, is the Lord God Almighty"), Revelation 4:11 ("Worthy are you, our Lord and God"), or Revelation 5:9 ("Worthy is the Lamb who was slain") are particularly appropriate. Chanting these Scriptures would be even better.[3] The hymn selected in our model service ("Blessing and honor and glory and power") is Horatius Bonar's paraphrase of Revelation 5:9–14. We might also sing Reginald Heber's "Holy, Holy, Holy" or the *Te Deum* here.

The *Te Deum*'s title comes from the first two words of this ancient Latin hymn: *Te Deum laudamus, te Dominum confitemur* ("We praise thee, O God; we acknowledge thee to be the Lord"). In this hymn we join with the angels, apostles, martyrs, departed saints, and the whole universal Church to confess and praise Father, Son, and Holy Spirit. Shamefully, this great hymn has largely disappeared from modern worship. It ought to be sung energetically with full conviction of faith![4]

Singing the *Te Deum* also reminds us of the rich heritage that has been entrusted to us. As we worship the Lord, we are united not only with each other in our particular local church, not only with all the orthodox Christians alive on earth at the moment, but we also have union with all the departed Old and New Testament saints in heaven, who worship God *with* us on the Lord's Day.

---

[3] On the value of chanting see James B. Jordan, "How to Chant the Psalms," *Rite Reasons* 61 (January 2000): 1–4, and "Four Liturgical Concerns," lecture given at the Second Annual Pre-General Assembly (PCA) Conference on Reformed Liturgy, June 19, 2001 (Biblical Horizons, P.O. Box 1096, Niceville, FL 32588).

[4] The best way to sing the *Te Deum* is to chant it. The best chant is found (of all places!) in the older Presbyterian hymnal *The Hymnbook* (Philadelphia: 1965), 460–461 (transpose the key from C major to A major). But you have to have a music leader, accompanist, and congregation that are ready and willing to learn this chant. The next best musical setting is Hymn #2 in the *Anglo-Genevan Psalter* (Winnipeg: Premier Printing, 1984), 318. This Genevan Psalm tune played at an appropriately lively tempo provides a surprising vehicle for bright, energetic confession and praise. The old and new *Trinity Hymnal* contain versions of the *Te Deum* set to the well-known Scottish Psalter tune DUNDEE, but this music is not as bright and vigorous as the others.

Hearing the Word of God

The Lord has now prepared his people to hear His Word as it is read aloud by the pastor. We pause in silence to prepare to listen while God speaks. The pastor announces, "This is the Word of God. Pay careful attention." The call to hear God's Word can take several forms, but it always includes the solemn reminder that what the congregation now hears is the very voice of God speaking to them. Nothing we say or do during the service can compare in importance with our thoughtful, open-hearted reception of God's spoken Word. This is why at the close of each reading the congregation should respond loudly with "Thanks be to God." when the pastor announces the end of the reading with "This is the Word of the Lord."

The modern church has failed to appreciate the centrality of the public reading and hearing of the Word of God. One might sit through an entire "worship" service (even in "Bible-believing" churches) and only hear a verse or two of the Bible read before the sermon. This is inexcusable. Among other things, it will ensure that the next generation will be biblically illiterate. Most of the Bible was written to be read aloud in the congregation. Private Bible reading and study must certainly be encouraged, but such an individualistic appropriation of the Word is not the Spirit's primary way of illuminating and sanctifying the minds of Christians. The Spirit uses the oral reading and preaching combined with the congregation's hearing of the Word in church to bring life to His people.[5] The biblical command is "hear the Word of God" (Amos 4:1; Lk. 11:28).

"Hearing" the Word of God creates an orderly community of love and mutual submission. The Bible comes to us audibly as we

[5] The question of which texts to read each week may be left to the minister and the elders. I consider the debate about the use of the Church year to be primarily a pragmatic question about how best to order the Sunday morning Scripture readings and prayers. Since no new "ceremonies" need to be added for a moderate use of the ecclesiastical calendar, there is no violation of the regulative principle of worship involved. See my parabolic analysis of this issue in Chapter 18, "Is the Church Year Biblical: A Parking Lot Parable" in Part III.

are gathered in community, most notably when read by the pastor in the corporate worship service. We don't choose what part of the Bible comes to us. We are commanded to "hear." The whole Word of God is brought to bear upon us, and we are called to submit ourselves by faith to the authority of the Word of God. God speaks; we listen. Speaking and hearing God's Word is the most fundamental ritual activity in the Church. When the pastor reads the lessons everyone should hold their head up and listen intently to the reading.

The Recitation of God's Law

It is also proper at this juncture for the congregation to recite the law of God or a Psalm, either in unison, responsively (with the pastor), or antiphonally (divided into two). Our model service has the congregation reciting Psalm 90 responsively, but a recitation of the Decalogue or some other summary of God's standards may also be performed here. After receiving forgiveness and restoration in Christ, it is appropriate to rise and recite the covenant law of God. We might recite the Decalogue, a Psalm, or even a portion of the New Testament that describes our duty to God as redeemed men and women. Why should we recite the law at this point in the worship service? Does it make any difference where the recitation of the law is placed?

According to the Bible, the law has at least three foundational purposes: first, widespread public knowledge of the law functions to restrain sin. This is sometimes called the law's *political* use because the knowledge of the law and its penalties will help restrain the wickedness of fallen men in society, even if they are not believers (Deut. 13:11; 17:13; 19:20; 1 Tim. 1:3–10). Certainly the recitation of the law of God in a public worship service can have this effect on those who may not truly be members of the Church of Jesus Christ, but this is not the chief reason for putting the law of God in our worship service, neither does it explain its place in the order of worship.

The second purpose of the law is sometimes called its *pedagogical* use. The commandments teach us to look to Christ for justification since "through the law comes the knowledge of sin," and without the knowledge of sin no one will flee to Christ for forgiveness and grace (Rom. 3:19–20; Gal. 3:24). The law, then, teaches believer and unbeliever alike that no one makes himself righteous in God's eyes by means of the works of the law. "For whosoever shall keep the whole law, and yet offend in one point, he is guilty of all" (Jas. 2:10). Consequently, it is not inappropriate for us to use the law *before* the confession of sin in the order of worship. Nevertheless, this is not the best place for it in the liturgy, because the pedagogical purpose of the law is not the law's chief function.

The so-called third use of the law reveals its most basic purpose. The law serves to teach us what God expects from us, to inform us of God's holy standards. This third function of the law is usually called its *didactic* use. The commandments originally given to Adam and Eve—till the ground, guard the garden, be fruitful and multiply, cleave to your wife, do not eat from the tree of the knowledge of good and evil, etc.—were all given in the context of God's loving instruction. After the fall, the law took on added significance, but the didactic function takes priority. Instruction (Hebrew, *torah*) is the first and most basic function of the law of God (Ps. 1:2; 19:7; 119:1).

Furthermore, if we look carefully at the Old and New Testaments, we discover that the law of God is always given in the context of grace. Take the Ten Commandments, for example. Are they given to teach people how to earn God's favor? No. Are they a republication of the "covenant of works"? Hardly. How do they begin? "And God spoke all these words: 'I am Yahweh your God, who brought you out of Egypt, out of the land of slavery.'" (Exod. 20:1–2). We begin with grace. *After* this announcement of His redeeming grace to Israel, God summarizes their duty as redeemed saints.

This grace-then-law pattern appears throughout the Bible: God redeems, then gives His redeemed people the law. God saves His people in order that they might obey Him (Eph. 2:8–10). This is the most fundamental structure or order of God's covenant. Even the New Testament epistles are structured this way. They are covenantal documents. Romans is not best divided into doctrinal (1–11) and practical (12–16) chapters, as if Paul was working with a Greek conceptual distinction between theory and practice. This ignores the Old Testament covenantal precedents. Rather, Paul's letters are ordered with a covenantal logic. Romans is a covenantally structured document where grace and redemption in Christ (chapters 1–11) provide the context for laying out the duties of those privileged with such a deliverance (chapters 12–16). The same is true with Ephesians: redemption in Christ (chapters 1–3) is followed by what God requires of us (law) in view of His mercy (chapters 4–6). Incidentally, our Westminster Larger and Shorter Catechisms have also been arranged the same way.

We are now in a position to answer the question: why do we recite the law at this point in the liturgy? According to the configuration of the covenant, law follows grace. So, as we make our way through the covenant renewal liturgy, after the Lord has graciously forgiven and restored us, we are ready to listen to His righteous requirements. Ready to hear and obey. Ready to respond in thanksgiving to God's forgiveness in Christ. God's law is a delight and a blessing to the believer saved by grace. He is to meditate on it and find happiness in the knowledge of it, as both Old and New Testament believers testify (Ps. 112:1; Rom. 7:22, "I delight in the law according to the inner man"; and 1 Jn. 5:3, "His commandments are not burdensome"). The law is a gracious gift of God, and the worshiper gratefully acknowledges it to be so. I have a book in my library with a title that gets it just right: *The Grace of Law*.[6] Its three

---

[6] Earnest F. Kevan, *The Grace of Law: A Study in Puritan Theology* (Grand Rapids: Baker Book House, 1976). This is a point that most confessional Lutherans can't seem to grasp. See David S. Yeago's penetrating critique of the classical Lutheran antithetical construal of Law/Gospel in "Gnosticism, Antinomianism, and Reformation Theology: Reflections on the Costs of a Construal," *Pro Ecclesia* 2 (1993): 37–49. See also Andrew Sandlin's timely warning "Lutheranized Calvinism: Gospel or Law, or Gospel and Law," *Reformation and Revival Journal* 11 (Spring 2002): 123–135.

hundred pages are devoted to a historical study which details the Reformation and Puritan insistence that the law of God was a gracious gift to man. The grace of God leads us to embrace the commandments of God. "Oh, how I love your law, it is my meditation all the day" (Ps. 119:97).

The Creed

It is also fitting to confess our faith at this point in the service, thereby reciting aloud God's great covenantal acts in history, especially the incarnation, death, and resurrection of the Lord Jesus Christ. Reciting a creed at this point in the service is a response to the reading of God's Word and a proclamation that publicly identifies us as a church of Jesus Christ. The word "god" means all kinds of things to all kinds of people these days. Without an identifying creed, the world may be left wondering which god we worship and serve. The Apostles' and Nicene Creeds publicly proclaim that *this* is the God we worship—Father, Son, and Holy Spirit. We will tolerate no other gods before Him. We serve Him alone. We will not waffle in our public confession. We will be clear, courageous, and precise in our confession of faith. The first commandment demands as much.

Moreover, the congregation should recite these creeds vigorously as confessions of *faith*. The first two words of these creeds are often dangerously misunderstood. These creeds begin with the words "I believe." As I have argued in chapter 7, in the minds of many Christians this assertion is basically equivalent to "I think" or "I am of the opinion." The word "creed," however, comes from the Latin verb *credo*—the first word in the Latin creeds. The Greek translation of the creeds uses the word *pisteuo*, which is precisely the word that is used for "faith" in the New Testament (Jn. 3:16, 36; Rom. 10:10).

Therefore, when the worshiper says, "I believe [*credo, pisteuo*] in God the Father Almighty," he is not stating an opinion or even assenting to a doctrine; rather, he is confessing his personal trust, his faith in the Father Almighty. "I believe [*credo, pisteuo*]" is exactly equivalent to the language of personal trust used in the New Testament: "I believe in" or "I place my faith in" or "I trust in" ("Believe [*pistueo*] on the Lord Jesus Christ, and you will be saved, you and your household," Acts 16:31). Both the Apostles' and Nicene Creeds provide us with an opportunity to recite our trust in the persons of the Trinity and their work on our behalf. We should enthusiastically and energetically proclaim our God's gracious saving work for us in Christ.[7]

The Sermon

Too many American Christians think that everything that comes before the sermon is little more than "pre-game" ceremonies. Unfortunately, in many contemporary services this is exactly how the pre-sermon activities are viewed, even by the pastor or worship leader. Churches treat the "liturgy" as a collective term for everything that is not important in the service. For Reformed pastors it is all the fluff that comes before the sermon.

Liturgy means the fillers to round things out, the icing on the cake, or, even more bluntly, the window-dressing for the proper stage-managing of sermons and collections. And so we have "opening" and "closing" liturgies, but the meat of the sandwich is somewhere else. If liturgy is simply decorative, it is of course basically trivial. Since in this view it has no theological substance of its own, it naturally becomes the plaything of psychology, sociology, "cultural" this and that, and of course "the arts."[8]

The sermon becomes the big event. All kinds of stuff is placed before the sermon (announcements, solos, hymns, testimonies, dramas, etc.) with little or no thought to the question "why?" The order in which these events occur is meaningless; they simply fill up

---

[7] For more on the use of these creeds in worship see chapter 13, "Whom Do You Trust: The Use of the Apostles' and Nicene Creeds in Worship" in Part III.

[8] Kurt Marquart, "Liturgy and Evangelism," in *Lutheran Worship: History and Practice* (St. Louis: Concordia Publishing House, 1993),58–9.

the time so that everybody has a chance to get settled in by the time the sermon begins. It doesn't matter if we come in a little late, as long as we hear the sermon. Everything else is superfluous. It is not uncommon to sit through the first half hour of an evangelical service without ever hearing the Word of God read until immediately before the sermon. In a biblical, covenant renewal worship service, however, the entire worship service is saturated in the Word of God. We read, sing, pray, and recite the Word of God from the opening of the service. Therefore, the entire service is in some sense sermonic. If our worship is sacrificial, God has been wielding the sword of the Spirit, His Word, throughout the liturgy, and we have been responding to His voice from the moment we heard Him call us into His presence.

Of course, I am not suggesting that the sermon is unimportant. It has crucial significance, but it has taken on an importance out of proportion to the rest of the Lord's Day service in too many churches. This is because it has not been properly situated in the overall context of sacrificial, covenant renewal worship. It has become a big rhetorical event—an opportunity for the pastor to make a big impression. I think that James B. Jordan makes a telling point:

> Since all that is left [in contemporary evangelical worship] is preaching, the act of preaching takes on dimensions foreign to the Bible. Preaching has become a great rhetorical event. Sermons ought to open with a stunning introduction, proceed through three alliterating points, and conclude with a gripping application. People should be stirred, moved, etc. The full-orbed worship of Scripture, with congregational prayer, singing, and the Supper has been lost, and this leaves the people psychologically starved, so the preaching must make up for it. The history of the church becomes the history of preachers. People leave one church and seek another on the basis of who is preaching. If one is in a church with bad preaching, there is nothing else to look forward to in going to church: no worship, no real singing the Word, no Sacrament. Everything hangs on a man, and that man is not the Lord Jesus Christ.[9]

[9] James B. Jordan, *The Sociology of the Church* (Tyler: Geneva Divinity School, 1986), 225–6.

The sermon ought to be the time when Christ personally speaks to His Bride through the ordained pastor (Eph. 4:11–13). We sit down and listen to our Husband speak to us through His appointed representative (Eph. 5:26). The pastor has studied and prepared his sermon so as to instruct God's people (2 Tim. 2:15). This means that the purpose of the sermon is not primarily evangelistic, at least not in the narrow sense. Of course, the good news of forgiveness and grace should always be prominent in the sermon, but I am not convinced that the sermon in the midst of covenant renewal worship ought to be directed to unbelievers. On the Lord's Day *believers* "come together as the church" (1 Cor. 11:18). We need the Gospel applied to our lives.

If unbelievers are present when the Church gathers together, that is fine (1 Cor. 14:23), but they are not the reason why the Church congregates. The Church congregates as the temple of the living God, an assembly of priests offering the sacrifice of praise to their Savior (1 Pet. 2:5, 9). Visiting unbelievers will hear the Word of God expounded and applied. They will hear of Jesus Christ, His grace and His law. But they need to realize that apart from faith in Christ they are not members of the priestly assembly. I am especially opposed to dumbing down the sermon (and the liturgy, for that matter) so that "seekers" will feel comfortable. When unbelievers are present in the worship service, the apostle Paul does not expect them to feel at home, but precisely the opposite. If the service is a genuine *worship* service, then an unbeliever will be "convicted" and "judged," with the result that "he will fall down and worship God, exclaiming, 'God is really among you.'" (1 Cor. 14:24–25).

That is all well and good, but the primary audience addressed on the Lord's Day is the people of God who have just now been reconstituted as God's covenant community. On this particular day at this special time God's people are in the process of being offered as "living sacrifices" (Rom. 12:1). One of the essential means of sacrificial consecration is the "renewing of the mind" so that it will not be "conformed to the pattern of this world" (Rom. 12:2). The Word of God is the priestly knife that chops us up and prepares us as sacrificial "food for God" (Heb. 4:12). Therefore, after we have praised God, confessed our sins, accepted Christ's forgiveness, thanked God for His love in Christ, recited His law, and entered His presence boldly to pray—*after* we have done all of this—then we are ready to listen to the pointed and sharp voice of God from the Scriptures. This powerful Word of God is able to "pierce even to dividing soul and spirit, joints and marrow, judging the thoughts and attitudes of the heart" (Heb. 4:12).

The sermon is the time when the pastor ought to explain the Word of God and bring it to bear upon the life of the congregation. His job is to keep the congregation's nose in the Book. The Word of God is more important than the pastor's stories, illustrations, mannerisms, or rhetorical skills. As a pastor, I want my people to learn the Bible. This has been a central aspect of the Reformed tradition. This is why we preach through books of the Bible. We believe that the congregation needs to know "every Scripture" in order to be "complete, thoroughly equipped for every good work" (2 Tim. 3:17). Hopefully, when I concluded my sermon series on the book of Haggai, for example, the members learned something about the prophecy of Haggai. When I finished the book of Ruth, they should have been able to read Ruth with fresh insights and convictions.

I know that sounds rather simplistic, but in the past I have sat through numerous sermon series and at the conclusion wondered whether I really learned anything about the book the pastor supposedly expounded. Did the pastor explain the book of the Bible? Or did he merely use the book to serve his own purposes? This is a real danger in evangelical circles. I know the temptation. My calling is to "preach the Word" (2 Tim. 4:2), not my own clever ideas. My job as the called Teaching Elder of this congregation is to teach the Bible and to exhort from it. That's what the sermon is for. When the pastor announces, "This is the Word of our God," then stir yourself up to listen intently. You ought to be poised to hear the marching orders of the King of kings. If you are a genuine member of Christ's flock, you should be anxious to hear God's Word preached. "My sheep listen to my voice; I know them, and they follow Me" (Jn. 10:27).

The Tribute Offering

This is the final element in our consecration to God (the second "step" in our three-step sacrificial entrance into God's presence). The presentation of our tithes and offerings to God marks the completion of God's corporate sanctifying work. The Word has done its proper work in our lives, if by the Spirit and from the heart we offer ourselves and our works to God. This is the meaning of the tribute (meal/grain) offering that was placed on top of the Ascension Offering in the order of Old Testament sacrificial worship (Lev. 2:1–3; Num. 15:8–10). The offering is an act of corporate worship. As a sign of her thankful dedication to the Lord, the Church offers to the Father a tenth of the profit with which the Lord has gifted her (Gen. 14:20; Lev. 27:30–32; 2 Chr. 31:5–6; Neh. 10:37–38; 13:12; Mal. 3:10; Mt. 23:23) and any freewill offerings that are over and above the tenth required by God (Lev. 22:29; 2 Cor. 8:2–4).[10]

Bringing the World into The Church

Occasionally one hears that the Christian should leave behind the "world" as he or she comes into the Sunday morning service. Is this correct? Surely we should purify our minds and hearts from the fallen values and concerns of our culture as far as we are able before we come into the service on Sunday (Rom. 12:2; Col. 3:1–2; 1 Jn. 2:15; Jas. 4:8). Indeed, this ethical/moral understanding is often the meaning of the "world" in the New Testament (Jn. 15:19; 1 Jn. 4:5; Eph. 2:2; Jas. 4:4). Apparently, however, this is not

---

[10] For a thorough examination of the place and significance of the Tribute Offering in Scripture, see James B. Jordan's lectures on this subject in *The Twelfth Annual Biblical Horizons Bible Conference: The Inspection of Jealousy, June 22–26, 2002* (P. O. Box 1096, Niceville, FL 32588).

exactly what "leaving the world behind" usually means. It is as if Sunday worship means escaping from the worldly occupations, physical possessions, and other so-called material concerns that dominate our weekly routines.

This kind of dualism between spiritual and physical, religion and everyday life must not be allowed to stand. We are drawn into God's presence to present our "bodies" as living sacrifices, which means that by the Spirit we present our entire being in Christ to the Father, including the work that we have accomplished at home and in the marketplace during the week. God accepts our work offered to Him by faith. We are not merely giving money during the offering, we are gratefully giving ourselves, the token of which is our tithes and offerings that we freely give (2 Cor. 8:1–5).

The offering ought to be part of the corporate service. It is not merely an opportunity for individual Christians to give their tithes and offerings, but also a corporate act of the body of Christ. As the body of Christ we present ourselves for service in God's kingdom. If every person individually dropped a check in a bucket in the foyer of the church, the act would not rise to the level of corporate worship. Christians would lose the opportunity to offer themselves and the work of their hands, in union with the whole congregation, to the Lord in gratitude for His mercy and grace in Christ.

The deacons collect the offerings and present them to the pastor, who gathers up the congregation's offering in his prayer of dedication.[11] His prayer will follow this basic model: "We stand now before you, Heavenly Father, to present ourselves for service in Your kingdom. Thank You for Your rich, undeserved mercy, which You have so freely bestowed upon us. In union with the perfect sacrifice

---

[11] The deacons should also bring the bread and wine for the Communion forward at this point in the service since they are also part of our "offering." As James B. Jordan notes, "Bread and wine do not drop down out of heaven. God takes our work and transforms them and gives them back to us. The Supper is not about initial justification, Christ's work apart from us. Rather, it foreshadows final justification, when our works are taken into account (Mt. 25). This is why there is judgment in the Supper. The worship service moves from initial

of Christ our Lord, receive these tithes and offerings as the token of our wholehearted dedication to Your service. Use these gifts, and our lives as well, as the means of advancing Your Gospel among Your people here and to those whom You lead us to serve both here and around the world. Receive our offering in the Name of Jesus. Amen."[12]

Choral Anthem

Since a choral anthem may be used here or almost anywhere else in the service, the function and placement of the choir calls for comment at this point. There are a number of ways in which the choir can function within the service, but the most prominent is their bolstering congregational praise. Historically choirs have stood to the side of (in a transept) or behind (in a loft) the congregation in order to sing in dialogue with the people (antiphonally, from the side) or strengthen and enable (from behind) their singing. More and more American evangelical churches are placing choirs in the front in order to "perform" and in effect "entertain" the congregation. Choir anthems and solos come across as "entertainment" not as supplementing and strengthening the congregation's praise to God. We have positioned our organ and choir in the back of the church in order to fortify the people's worship and keep the congregation's focus directed toward the Lord whom we are praising.

---

justification apart from us (the Confession and Absolution), through sanctification by the Word, to final justification as we come before God in the Offertory with our works, are judged, and enter into full Sabbath rest and festivity in the Supper" ("Four Litugical Concerns," Lecture given at *The Second Annual Pre-General Assembly Conference on Reformed Theology*, June 19, 2001 (Niceville: Biblical Horizons). For a thorough explanation of the theological and biblical reasons for this, see Peter J. Leithart, "The Way Things Really Ought to Be: Eucharist, Eschatology, and Culture," *Blessed are the Hungry* (Moscow: Canon Press).

[12] In early Reformed traditions the offertory is the place where alms for the poor are gathered along with the tithes. I owe this insight to Pastor Wesley Baker; see his lecture "The Importance of Weekly Communion" given at *The Third Annual Pre-General Assembly (PCA) Conference on Reformed Theology*, June 19, 2001 (Niceville: Biblical Horizons).

The Prayer of the Church

Having been forgiven and renewed in Christ, we now have confidence to approach God's throne of grace with some measure of boldness, as a child confidently approaches his daddy when he knows that his father is well-disposed toward him (Rom. 5:1–2; 8:12–17; Heb. 4:14–16). This portion of the service provides the opportunity for God's people to intercede for the needs of the Church, both local and universal, as well as for the world. The Church now stands before the Lord to officially intercede for the world. If we are a royal priesthood, the new Israel in Christ, then when we gather together before God, we act as representatives for all humanity. We are called, therefore, to make requests in behalf of and for the life of the world. Just as Jesus acted as our representative and gave Himself for us, so now we are called to imitate Christ and represent the world before God's throne. This is especially true when we stand to pray for the Church and the world during covenant renewal worship.[13]

Again, we approach God with our petitions *after* He has invited us. Accordingly, this movement in the liturgy, as every other, begins with the pastor, as Christ's representative, inviting the people to pray. This can be done either with a simple solicitation ("Let us pray") or by reading a portion of God's Word that appropriately calls us to prayer. Such passages as Ps. 4:3; 5:1–3; 9:10; 19:14; 34:15, 17–18; 55:22; 62:8; Jer. 29:12–13; Mt. 7:7–8; Phil. 4:6–7; Heb. 4:15–16; 1 Jn. 5:14–15, and many more have been used to invite God's people to pray.

Unfortunately, this portion of the service has often been called the "Pastoral Prayer." It may sometimes be referred to with less than affectionate overtones as "the long prayer." And you know why. First of all, the pastor is often the only one left praying at the end

---

[13] James B. Jordan explains the implications of the fact that the Church is officially the world's representative before the Father in his lecture "Covenant Renewal: Baptismal, Official, and Martial" delivered at the *Third Annual Pre-General Assembly (PCA) Conference on Reformed Liturgy*, 2002 (Biblical Horizons, P.O. Box 1096, Niceville, FL 32588).

of this prayer. Everyone else has drifted off five minutes before. They may have followed the first minute or so, but, let's face it, participating in a seven to ten minute prayer (with your eyes closed) is tough. It is especially tough when the pastor rambles—as pastors who pray extemporaneously so often do. They end up repeating the same pat phrases week after week. Or they (I guess I should say "we"!) end up not praying at all, but using the prayer as an opportunity to preach to the people indirectly. You know what I mean. The preacher ends up praying at the congregation instead of leading them in prayer before God.

The form of this prayer may vary. But the pastor ought to lead this prayer *every* Sunday. And these prayers should not be exclusively extemporaneous. He should either compose the prayer beforehand, jot down three or four important petitions to bring with him to the service, or he should use some of the many excellent model prayers found in some of the old Presbyterian, Episcopal, and Lutheran manuals of worship. This prayer may even take the form of a litany or bidding prayer. I have included an example of a bidding prayer in the model service. A litany is a responsive prayer where pastor and people alternate (modeled after Psalm 136 and others). This form of prayer is an excellent way to ensure the participation of the congregation in the prayer. At the end of each petition the congregation responds with something like "Hear us and help us, we ask you, O Lord," or "We beseech Thee to hear us, good Lord." This has the same function as a corporate "Amen."

The *Gloria Patri* ("Glory be to the Father") caps off the pastor's prayer as the people of God ascribe all glory to the Triune God— in other words, whatever riches, beauty, honor, and significance (all of which are aspects of the biblical concept of "glory") that we possess have been received by us as a gift from the Triune God of grace and will ultimately be received back by him for all eternity. The *Gloria Patri* arises from biblical texts like Romans 16:27; Ephesians 3:21; Philippians 4:20; and Revelation 1:6. The singing of the *Gloria* serves as the transition into the Lord's Supper, the third and final stage in the Lord's sacrificial work of renewing His people.

12
Communion and Benediction

The cup of blessing which we bless, is it
not a communion in the blood of Christ?
The bread which we break, is it not a
communion in the body of Christ?
—1 Corinthians 10:16

We have a standing joke in our family when we get together for meals. We come together to eat and then we talk about eating at the table. I suspect that it is not much different for most families. We congregate around food, not just for nourishment but also for social reasons. Families unite around the table. Friendships are formed and cultivated at meals. Elaborate social rituals develop to set apart common meals and to facilitate fellowship. We live to eat and eating structures our common life. This is how God has made us.[1] This is why the covenant renewal service should not end with the sermon and offering. It should never end without Communion. God has called the Church together to eat with Him. There are other times when we can gather for teaching, testimonies, praise, or whatever. On the Lord's Day God

---

[1] ". . . the whole world is presented as one all-embracing banquet table for man. And this image of the banquet remains, throughout the whole Bible, the central image of life. It is the image of life at its creation and also the image of life at its end and fulfillment: '. . . that you may eat and drink at my table in my Kingdom'"(Alexander Schmemann, *For the Life of the World* [Crestwood: St. Vladimir's Seminary Press, 1973],11).

invites us to His house for a meal. Yes, He cleanses and consecrates us, but before God sends us out to serve Him in the world He first sits us down for a common meal. He must strengthen and nourish us with bread and wine for service in His kingdom.[2] We must experience the *shalom* of God at the table. Therefore, the culmination of the covenant renewal service occurs when we sit down and eat dinner with Jesus, receiving from Him by faith His own life-giving flesh and blood.

The Lord's Supper ought to be a normal part of our weekly worship. Period. The only argument ever really raised against weekly Communion is that it might become routine. If we do it every week, it will lose its power and people will get bored with it. What shall we say in response to this? Do you hug your child once a month so that she will not become too used to it? After all, one wouldn't want such a ritual to become routine! Do you come together as a family to eat dinner once a quarter so that the children will learn how special and important the family meal is? The argument that the Lord's Supper will lose its special character if celebrated weekly is simply absurd. It is just one more example of sloppy evangelical thinking about the meaning and use of ritual. R. Scott Clark adds another telling explanation:

> Perhaps there is a more fundamental reason we are reluctant to observe the Supper more regularly. One fears that the simple gospel message of Christ offered for and to sinners is not really on the evangelical *agenda*—or *credenda* for that matter . . . . It might be that regular observance of the Supper would require a transformation of most evangelical worship services. It is difficult to imagine how a solemnly joyful service of the Supper would fit into some "seeker sensitive" services. Weekly Communion would also affect the preaching by tending to orient the service around Christ's finished work and away from the constant diet of "how to" messages. The juxtaposition of "Ten Steps to a Happy Marriage" followed by a Communion service is too jarring to contemplate. Simply considering a weekly

---

[2] For a defense of the use of alcoholic wine, rather than grape juice, see Jeffrey J. Meyers, "Concerning Wine and Beer," *Rite Reasons* 48–48 (Nov./Jan. 1997).

Communion a hypothetical possibility in our time seems to present radical challenges to evangelical piety.[3]

Falsehood and Vanity?

In addition to these problems, it appears that contemporary conservative churches do not adequately grasp the significance of the Supper. John Calvin ominously observed, "The devil, knowing that our Lord left nothing more beneficial to the Church than this holy sacrament, according to his accustomed manner, exerted himself from the beginning to contaminate it with errors and superstitions, and to corrupt and destroy its fruit, and has not ceased to pursue this course, until he has almost wholly subverted this sacrament of the Lord and converted it into falsehood and vanity."[4] I suspect that many Christian people have some idea about how the devil has converted the meaning of the Lord's Supper into "falsehood." Protestants are regularly catechized on the errors of the medieval and Roman churchs' teaching on this sacrament.[5] We have a knack for categorizing the errors of others with pithy theological terminology: transubstantiation, consubstantiation, and the so-called Zwinglian "memorial" view.

But what about Calvin's warning against turning the Supper into "vanity"? What might this be? When something is vain it is useless, empty, worthless, or without effect. How has Satan converted this sacrament into vanity? I would argue that the Lord's Supper has become a vanity wherever it is emptied of its rich meaning and significance. It becomes "vanity" to the extent that we fail to understand the rich, multi-faceted significance that this sacrament ought

---

[3] "The Evangelical Fall from the Means of Grace: The Lord's Supper," in *The Compromised Church: The Present Evangelical Crisis*, ed. by John H. Armstrong (Wheaton: Crossway Books, 1998),144.

[4] John Calvin, "Treatise on the Holy Supper of our Lord and Only Savior Jesus Christ" (1536) in *Calvin: Theological Treatises*, trans. by J.K.S. Reid, *The Library of Christian Classics* (Philadelphia: The Westminster Press, 1954),155.

[5] For an excellent, in-depth review of the eucharistic theologies of Aquinas, Luther, and Calvin, see Peter J. Leithart, "What's Wrong With Transubstantiation? An Evaluation of Theological Models," *Westminster Theological Journal* 52 (Fall 1991): 295–324.

to have in our lives. For many Protestants the mystery and power of Holy Communion have been drained from the rite. It has become something anemic and paltry.

This happens when we do the Lord's Supper badly and when we come to it in the wrong frame of mind, with the wrong attitude. If we come expecting to be emotionally stimulated and moved, we will surely be disappointed. Have you ever said or thought something like this: "Well, I didn't get much out of that Communion service today," or "The Lord's Supper just doesn't do much for me. I'm glad we don't have it very often. It is not very exciting." This kind of attitude may also be behind the practice of infrequent Communion. If we do it too often, so it is thought, it will get old. I've never quite understood this argument. Should we then not kiss our wives but once a quarter in order to keep the ritual fresh and new?

Do This As My Memorial

I am convinced that one of the fundamental problems here is that we have reduced the Lord's Supper to a means of providing mental stimulus for individual religious meditation. Communion is thought to be just another opportunity to exercise personal, private devotions at church. To some extent, the way we practice the Supper encourages this. Everyone closes their eyes, turns inward, and meditates privately. The corporate, communal dimension of the sacrament gets smothered beneath what in effect becomes an opportunity for personal quiet time in church. Such an attitude is actually a dangerous return to a pre-Reformation, medieval distortion of the sacrament. The Reformers sought to restore the *communal* dimensions of the rite thereby rescuing it from its degeneration in the medieval Roman church to an opportunity for private meditation and individual devotion.[6] There is, of course, room for silence during the rite of Communion, but there is so much more going on than individuals reflecting on Jesus' death using the visual aids of bread and wine.

---

[6] See Frank C. Senn, *Christian Liturgy: Catholic and Evangelical* (Minneapolis: Fortress Press, 1997), especially chapter 6, "Medieval Liturgical Deterioration," 211–239.

Some of this has come about because of a very feeble understanding of the words "do this in remembrance of me" (Lk. 2:19; 1 Cor. 11:24–25). The translation "do this in remembrance of me" has come to mean, "do this as a way of helping people remember me." Just as a photograph of an absent friend helps stimulate your memory, to recall to your mind what your friend was like, so the Lord's Supper functions like a picture to remind us, to aid us in remembering Jesus. We greatly impoverish the sacrament when we reduce it to such a naturalistic conception. If we restrict its meaning to the level of an illustration or picture to stimulate our memory, we have converted it into little more than a technique to arouse pious thoughts in people. The Lord's Supper is thereby stripped of any mystery and becomes a purely naturalistic stimulus to aid the religious memory, God's flannel graph for adults.

By translating the original "do this as my memorial" we are led to ask certain questions that will lead to a more satisfying understanding of this passage. Commentators have noted the oddness of Greek phrase *touto poieite eis ten 'emen 'anamnesin* (1 Cor. 11:24). The last two words literally read "my remembrance" or "my memorial"; there is no preposition "of," as in the popular translation "do this in remembrance of me." What does "do this as my memorial" mean? Many commentators have failed to take into account the liturgical context of the Old Testament and the Jewish rabbinical literature of the period when seeking an explanation for the meaning of this awkward phrase. There are a few scholars, like Gregory Dix, Louis Bouyer, and Joachim Jeremias, who have carefully investigated the proper ritual and covenantal context of these words. As Dix has aptly noted, Jesus "is not instituting a new custom, but investing a universal Jewish custom with a new and peculiar meaning."[7] These scholars present a cogent case for translating the phrase "do this as my memorial," arguing that its meaning may best be ascertained from a study of the Old Testament and Jewish use of the word in liturgical prayer. Bouyer cites example after example of

[7] Gregory Dix, *The Shape of the Liturgy* (London: A & C Black, 1945), 56.

Jewish *berakah* ("blessing") prayers that included the memorializing of the covenant to God. Here is one example, cited by Bouyer, which repeatedly uses the Hebrew *zikkaron* to describe a way of petitioning God to "remember" his covenant promises:

> Our God, and the God of our Fathers, may the remembrance of ourselves and of our fathers and the remembrance of Jerusalem, thy city, and the remembrance of the Messiah, the son of David, thy servant, and the remembrance of thy people, the whole house of Israel, arise and come, come to pass, be seen and accepted and heard, be remembered and be mentioned before thee for deliverance, for good, for grace, for lovingkindness and for mercy on this such and such a day. Remember us, JHWH, our God, on it for good and visit us on it for blessing and save us on it unto life by a word of salvation and mercy, and spare, favor, and show us mercy, for thou art a gracious and merciful God and King.[8]

Memorializing the Covenant

Translating the command as "Do this as my memorial" alerts us that there is something richer, something more profound happening in the Supper than a mnemonic technique to help us remember Jesus. First, what is the meaning of this word "memorial"? Where should one look in the Bible to find out what a memorial is? Answer: the Old Testament. The Old Testament forms the context, the background against which the New must be interpreted.

When we look at the memorials instituted by Yahweh for Israel and ask how they functioned, we discover something startling: most of them were designed to remind the Lord of His covenant! The Old Testament memorials were erected or enacted for the purpose of reminding God of His covenant with His people. Every Tribute

---

[8] Louis Bouyer, *Eucharist: Theology and Spirituality of the Eucharistic Prayer*, trans. by Charles Underhill Quinn (Notre Dame: University of Notre Dame Press, 1968), 84. For a thorough discussion of the meaning of "do this as my memorial" see Bouyer, *Eucharist*, especially chapter 5 "From the Jewish *Berakah* to the Christian Eucharist;" Joachim Jeremias, *The Eucharistic Words of Jesus* (London: SCM Press, 1966); James B. Jordan, "Doing the Lord's Supper," *Rite Reasons* 42 (Nov. 1995); and my sermon "Do this as My Memorial," 1 Corinthians 11:23–26 (Providence Reformed Presbyterian Church, September 11, 1994).

Offering (*minchah*), for example, had this covenant-memorial dimension incorporated into the ritual. Commenting on Leviticus 2:16, specifically the phrase "the salt of the covenant of your God," Kidner notes:

> It seems likely therefore that the 'memorial portion' (*'azkarah*) of the *minchah*, offered by fire with frankincense to the LORD, was to bring to God's remembrance not simply the offerers but the covenant in which they stood. And with God, as B. S. Childs has put it, "the essence of (His) remembering lies in his acting toward someone because of a previous commitment."[9]

By means of the memorial God's people dramatically rehearsed the covenant to Yahweh so that He would act to fulfill His covenant promises. The name "Yahweh" is given to Israel for this very purpose: "This is my memorial name" (Exod. 3:15). In other words, this is the name that you must use in prayer to remind me to keep my covenant; when you do so I will come to your aid. As the Psalmist says, "Some trust in chariots and some in horses but we will memorialize the Name of Yahweh our God" (Ps. 20:7). This means that when the Israelites prayed "in the Name of Yahweh" they were reminding Him of His covenant love and promises so as to move Him to answer their prayer for help. The Name of Jesus functions the same way in Christian prayer. We memorialize the person and work of Jesus before the Father when we conclude our prayers with "in the Name of Jesus. Amen."

The Passover functioned as the most prominent of all the covenant memorials in the Old Testament. It was a covenant memorial meal (Exod. 12:14). When the Lord saw the blood on the doorpost, He remembered His covenant and spared His people. Indeed, all the sacrifices made by Israel were offered as memorials directed toward God so that He would remember the covenant (Exod. 12:14; Lev. 2:2; 6:15 calls sacrifice "a memorial for the Lord").

---

[9] Derek Kidner, "Sacrifice: Metaphors and Meaning," *Tyndale Bulletin* 33 (1982): 132.

The Lord's Supper retains something of the sacrificial symbolism. Why are the bread (body) and wine (blood) separated? Why would Jesus separate the bread and wine as distinct portions in this ritual? Have you ever wondered about that? Why use wine at all? Why not just bread? If you know the Old Testament and its sacrificial system, then you know that in every animal sacrifice the blood had to be separated from the body of the sacrificial victim and poured out. Jesus' words of institution are given using sacrificial language. The body rite and the blood rite are separated as two distinct moments in the new covenantal sacrificial ritual.[10] The Lord's Supper memorializes the sacrificial death of Jesus Christ. And why is the bread broken? Again, sacrificial symbolism. In every sacrifice the body of the animal was divided. Even a small bird had to be divided; the head had to be wrung off of the body (Lev. 1:15; 5:8). Grain offerings were even divided and separated. One difference between the Old and New is that now animals are not killed, no real blood is shed, and the smell of death does not surround the ceremony. Rather, we begin with bread and wine on the table. And on that new table the body and blood are already separated. The death has already occurred. It only needs to be memorialized and the benefits enjoyed by God's people as He faithfully remembers His covenantal promises.

It is in this sense that the Lord's Supper may be properly understood as a "sacrifice." The seventeenth century French Reformed Pastor Pierre du Moulin explains "the particular reasons for calling the Eucharist a sacrifice":

> 1. Because this sacrament was instituted to proclaim the Lord's death until He come . . . . Hence the Eucharist may be called a sacrifice, since it represents the sacrifice of the Lord's death. According to the principle that signs and representations ordinarily take the name of that which they signify.

---

[10] For more reasons why the bread comes first and the wine second, see James B. Jordan, *From Bread to Wine: Toward a More Biblical Liturgical Theology*, Draft Edition 1.1 (Niceville: Biblical Horizons, 2001).

2. It may be said that in the Eucharist we offer Jesus Christ to God, insofar as we ask God to receive on our behalf the sacrifice of His death.

3. The Eucharist is a sacrifice of thanksgiving for the divine benefits and especially for the benefit of our redemption through Jesus Christ . . . . Thus, the Eucharist may be a sacrament insofar as by it God gives us and conveys His grace, and a sacrifice insofar as we offer Him our praise and thanksgiving.[11]

In the old covenantal order when the smoke of the covenant memorial sacrifice rose up to heaven, God smelled the pleasing aroma, He remembered His covenant, and He was at peace with His people. Many other passages speak of memorial objects or events as dramatic ways in which to petition God to remember His covenant (Gen. 9:8, 11–17; 8:1; Exod. 20:24; 28:12, 29; 30:16; Num. 10:10).

The New Covenant Memorial Prayers and Meal

When understood against the backdrop of these Old Testament covenant memorials, the Lord's Supper as a "memorial" is shown to be first of all a dramatized ritual prayer reminding God of His covenant.[12] The Lord's Supper is the New Covenant memorial rite. It is the fulfillment of all these older ways that the Lord instituted as the means whereby His people would call upon His Name and dramatically ask Him to remember His covenant. All the memorials of the Old Order are now fulfilled and completed (compacted) into one simple covenantal memorial meal. Jesus says, "Do this as my memorial."

This means that there are two major moments or actions in this sacrament. First, there is our memorializing the death of Jesus—our

---

[11] Quoted in Peter J. Leithart, "The Way Things Really Ought to Be: Eucharist, Eschatology, and Culture," *Blessed are the Hungry* (Moscow: Canon Press).

[12] We also find this use of the word "memorial" in the New Testament. Cornelius, the Gentile God-fearer, learns from an Angel that his "prayers and alms have ascended as a memorial before God" (Acts 10:4). God has thereby remembered him and acted graciously toward him by sending Peter.

action toward God. This is our prayer to God to remember Jesus and keep His covenant. We show forth the death of Jesus to the Father asking Him to keep His gracious promises to us in Christ. In the case of the Lord's Supper this memorializing is an act of the congregation, a pleading of the promises of God. This comes to focus in the prayers of thanksgiving (Greek: *eucharist*) and memorial before the bread and wine are distributed and eaten, but it is not limited to this. Indeed, the entire meal shows forth the death of Christ. As often as we eat and drink, we show forth the death of Christ. The "proclamation" is not limited to the prayer or the breaking of the bread, but we memorialize Christ to the Father by means of the common meal. Here is the memorial of Your Son's atoning sacrifice for us, O Lord, remember and be gracious towards us. Traditionally these prayers always included a summary of the life and work of Jesus Christ. A eucharistic memorial prayer should sound something like this:

> It is truly appropriate and right that we should at all times and in all places give thanks to You, O Lord, our heavenly Father, almighty everlasting God. But it is especially fitting that we should now, gathered around this Table, thank You for Your gracious covenant promises to us in Christ. Remember, Father, our Lord's humble birth, His holy life, His innocent sufferings and death, and His resurrection and ascension for us. Faithfully keep Your covenant with us for Jesus' sake and come now to nourish and equip us for service in Your kingdom. By Your Spirit make the body and blood of our Lord life-giving nourishment for Your people; in Jesus' Name we pray. Amen.

Louis Bouyer argues that the Jewish *berakah* (blessing) prayer said over meals helps us understand the meaning of our eucharistic prayers. The Jews understood the meaning of memorializing the Name of Yahweh. In their prayers they would ask the Lord to remember His covenant and come fulfill His promises among them, the most notable of which was the promise of the coming of the Messiah. "The memorial that this meal constituted attested to the permanent reality of the divine wonderworks for Israel as a pledge given by God of his saving and ever faithful presence. In representing it to him in their *berakah*, the Jews who were also faithful to his precept were confidently able to remind him of his promises and to ask efficaciously for their fulfillment."[13]

These prayers, then, together with the doing of the Lord's Supper "show forth the death of Jesus" (1 Cor. 11:26) to the Father. It is a dramatic prayer, a pleading of the promises of the Father by memorializing His Son's birth, life, suffering, death, and resurrection for us. Many contemporary commentators assume *katangello* ("to show, proclaim," 1 Cor. 11:26) must refer to the proclamation of the Gospel to men. This conclusion usually follows, they argue, from canvassing all the places in the New Testament where *katangello* is used. In each case it is used in connection with preaching Christ or the Gospel. This is just bad exegesis. One must look at the context and theology of the passage, not merely the words. Here, as I have argued, the Old Covenant context of covenant memorials and the entire theology of the covenant argues for a richer understanding of these words. No one would deny that the congregation does indeed hear the proclamation of Jesus' death in the prayers and ritual of the Lord's Supper. What I am arguing for is that the prayer is made to God and the death of Jesus is "showed forth" to him as the people listen and participate.[14] This, then, is the first major moment in the movement of the ritual of the Lord's Supper: the Spirit-filled church memorializes Jesus to the Father.[15]

---

[13] Louis Bouyer, *Eucharist: Theology and Spirituality of the Eucharistic Prayer,* trans. Charles Underhill Quinn (Notre Dame: University of Notre Dame Press, 1968), 464.

[14] Joachim Jeremias also argues for this "Godward" orientation of *katangello* (*The Eucharistic Words of Jesus* [London: SCM Press, 1966],252–255). See also Peter Leithart, "Showing Forth," *Rite Reasons* 50 (March 1997).

[15] This was understood by the early Church and some of the sixteenth-century Reformed churches, particularly those in France. "The Eucharist is the liturgical presentation by the Church of the sacrifice to the Father. This liturgical presentation is the action that recalls to God the Father the unique sacrifice of his Son, which is eternally actual, and implores Him by this sacrifice to grant mercy and blessings to his people" (Max Thurian, *The Mystery of the Eucharist: An Ecumenical Approach*, trans. by Emily Chisholm [Grand Rapids: Wm. B. Eerdmans, 1983], 23).

The Lord Visits His People

The second major moment in Communion is God's faithful response to our memorializing His covenant. He remembers His covenant and *comes* in blessing for His people and in judgment on His enemies. Memorializing Jesus to the Father causes Him to act, to come, to visit His people. This fits with the pattern and sequence found in 1 Corinthians 11:17–34. God's coming in blessing, however, is not highlighted in the Corinthian church; rather, because of their rebellion God *was* indeed coming, but coming in judgment (vs. 29–30).

When God visits us He does not merely give us things, but He gives Himself, specifically, the Father gives His Son as the Spirit communicates His presence and life to the congregation. The sacrament of Communion is connected not merely to the work of Christ in the past, but the Spirit communicates to us the life-giving, glorified, flesh of the resurrected and enthroned Christ in this Sacrament. How He does so is a mystery, but we receive it by faith.

The Calvinian tradition on this point is far richer than much of modern-day Calvinism. For starters, read Calvin's "Treatise on the Holy Supper of our Lord and Only Savior Jesus Christ."[16] There he argues that we miraculously receive the glorified flesh and blood of Jesus through the ministry of the Holy Spirit when we eat and drink in faith. Consider two telling quotations from Calvin on the benefits received in the Supper. The first is from his "1537 Confession," which Calvin composed free from outside influence:

> We confess that the Spiritual life that Christ bestows upon us does not consist simply in his quickening us by his Spirit, but also in his enabling us to participate in his life-giving flesh through the power of the Spirit; a participation by which we are nourished for eternal life. Therefore, when we speak

[16] "Treatise on the Holy Supper of our Lord and Only Savior Jesus Christ" (1536), in *Calvin: Theological Treatises*, trans. by J.K.S. Reid, *The Library of Christian Classics* (Philadelphia: The Westminster Press, 1954), 155.

of the communion that believers enjoy with Christ, we understand them to communicate no less in his flesh and blood than in his Spirit, so that they thus possess the whole Christ.[17]

This second quotation is from Calvin's *Petit Traicte* ("Little Tract," 1541), written, as the previous quotation, during Calvin's pleasant stay in Strasbourg:

> We must confess with one mouth, that on receiving the sacrament in faith, according to the ordinance of the Lord, we are truly made partakers in the proper substance of the body and blood of Jesus Christ. How that is done some may deduce better, and explain more clearly than the others. . . we must hold that it is made effectual by the secret and miraculous power of God, and that the Spirit of God is the bond of this participation, for which reason it is called Spiritual.[18]

We receive and eat the bread and, through the miraculous action of God's Spirit, we are as a community (re)formed as His Body (1 Cor. 10:16). We drink from the cup and we are, through the blood of the covenant shed for our forgiveness, made into living sacrifices. This is why there are two prayers, one before the bread and one before the cup. Jesus' example is clear: he prayed twice, not once (Mt. 26:26–29; Mk. 14:22–25; Lk. 22:14–23).[19] Jesus said, "Do this!" because He expects us to follow the pattern and sequence of actions He modeled for us. God is doing (at least) two things in this Sacrament. There are two distinct distributions and oral receptions. The bread strengthens us and unites us into one body. When we drink His blood we take His sacrifice into ourselves and are enabled to give ourselves joyfully for others in Christ-like ways.

Thus, the Lord's Supper is both a dramatized, ritualized prayer in which we call upon God to remember the sacrificial death of

---

[17] There are no translations in print. You can find it in *Joannis Calvini opera selecta*, eds., Peter Barth, Wilhelm Niesel, and Doris Scheuner (Munich: Chr. Kaiser Verlag, 1926–52), 1:435.

[18] Calvin, *Opera Selecta* 1:503.

[19] See James B. Jordan, *From Bread to Wine: Toward a More Biblical Liturgical Theology*, Draft Edition 1.1 (Niceville: Biblical Horizons, 2001).

Jesus Christ to keep His covenant with us, as well as the means by which our faithful, remembering God comes near to serve and nourish us with the life-giving nourishment available to us in Christ, reconstituting us as one body with His Son and transforming us individually into living sacrifices.

> In the eucharistic celebration of this memorial, the bread and the wine of our community meal, of the agape banquet, become sacrificial to the extent that they become for our faith what they represent, through the power of the divine Word and Spirit. And insofar as we ourselves, in this faith, are thus associated with the unique salvific oblation, we become one sole offering with Christ. Thus we can offer our own bodies, with His and in His, as a living and true sacrifice, giving to the Father, through the grace of the Son and in the communication of His Spirit, the "reasonable" worship which He expects from us.[20]

The Lord's Supper marks the culmination of covenant renewal worship, of our being drawn into God's presence by way of sacrifice and this closing rite, therefore, anticipates the Wedding Supper of the Lamb when the process of our being conformed to the image of Christ will be finally and comprehensively accomplished in us.

The Eucharist, finally, also teaches that our present experience of God's presence and blessing is incomplete. We have tasted that the Lord is good, sampled a bit of the heavenly gift; we have entered into the sanctuary (Heb. 6:4–6). But we are not yet filled. Like eating popcorn, the Supper just makes us want more. The taste makes us long all the more for the consummation of the promise, when we shall see God face-to-face, know even as we are known, and sit with Him at His table in the eternal kingdom of heaven.[21]

> In giving thanks with Him and through Him for His body broken and His blood shed which are given to us as the substance of the kingdom, we represent to God this mystery which has now been accomplished in our Head,

---

[20] Louis Bouyer, *Eucharist*, 465–6.
[21] Peter Leithart, *The Kingdom and the Power* (Phillipsburg: Presbyterian and Reformed, 1993), 126.

so that it may have its ultimate accomplishment in His whole body. That is to say that we give our consent to the completion in our flesh of the sufferings of Jesus for His body which is the Church, in the steadfast hope of His *Parousia* in which we shall all participate together in his resurrection. Thus we inaugurate the eternal glorification of God the creator and savior who on the last day will make the Church the *panegyria*, the festal assembly, in which all mankind will join in the heavenly worship and be brought before the Throne following the Lamb which was slain, but now lives and reigns forever.[22]

At the Table the congregation ritually anticipates the "new heavens and earth," when she will participate in the Son's eucharistic offering of the entire creation to the Father. The final chapter of Louis Bouyer's *Cosmos: The World and the Glory of God*, "The Nuptials of the Word and of Wisdom," contains this wonderful statement:

> In eternity, God's love descends from the Father into the Son and rises again in the Spirit, with the Son, toward the Father. In time, the same love, descending with the Son, returns to him in the eschatological appearance of his Bride. Thus taken up again with the Son through the Spirit, the whole of creation, the entire cosmos, is included in this eternal eucharist of the Spirit, which responds to the eternal Gospel of the Word. In the Spirit, Wisdom, the Bride of the Son, who has herself become perfectly filial, shines throughout the cosmos with the same glory that belongs to God, and to him alone, from all eternity.[23]

Departing With God's Blessing
The Song of Simeon

The first Lord's Supper was capped off with the singing of a hymn (Mt. 26:30; 14:26). One of the best ways to bring the Lord's Supper to a fitting conclusion is to sing the *Nunc Dimittis* (Lk. 2:29–32):

---

[22] Louis Bouyer, *Eucharist*, 464–5.
[23] Louis Bouyer, *Cosmos: The World and the Glory of God* (Petersham: St. Bede's Publications), 232.

Lord, now let your servant depart in peace:
According to your Word;
For my eyes have seen your salvation:
Which you have prepared before the face of all people;
A light to lighten the Gentiles:
And the glory of your people Israel.
Glory be to the Father, and to the Son, and to the Holy Spirit:
As it was in the beginning, is now, and ever shall be, age after age. Amen.[24]

The Benediction

If the whole service has been a "dress rehearsal" for life,[25] now, as the service ends, it is time to start living differently as God blesses and commissions us to go back into our families, communities, and marketplaces as the Lord's peculiar people.[26] The Benediction (or "blessing") is the final service God renders to His congregation as a whole on the Lord's Day. This is why it is ordinarily performed only by the ordained pastor, so that the congregation will be left in no doubt that it is the Lord who blesses them through His appointed representative (Lev. 9:22; Num. 6:23). Through the pastor's words the Lord assures us of His peace, promises, and His gracious presence as we leave His special presence (in the midst of His assembled human temple) to return to the world.[27]

The pastoral benediction arises both from the Lord's direction to Aaron and his sons (Num. 6:22–27), as well as from our Lord's

---

[24] The best musical arrangement of the *Nunc Dimittis*, in my opinion, is the one found in the Lutheran *Service Book and Hymnal* (1958),66–68. I have modernized the language somewhat, changing thee's and thy's to you and your.

[25] John E. Burkhart, *Worship: A Searching Examination of the Liturgical Experience* (Philadelphia: The Westminster Press, 1982), 33.

[26] Some pastors include a biblical charge to the congregation or a reading of the Great Commission at this point.

[27] "The church alternately gathers and disperses. When it assembles 'in the Spirit on the Lord's Day,' it anticipates in worship the joys of heaven but also bears the burden of a world that has not yet let itself be redeemed. When the church scatters for mission and service, it is sustained by the divine life on which it has drawn in the Bread come down from heaven and which it now offers again to the world" (Geoffrey Wainwright, "The Church as a Worshipping Community," *Pro Ecclesia* [1994]: 56–65).

practice. According to Luke 24:50, Jesus' final recorded act was a blessing pronounced upon his disciples: "He led them out as far as Bethany, and He lifted up His hands and blessed them." So also, the pastor faces the congregation, lifts up his hands, and communicates the Lord's blessing to His people. The benediction is *not* a prayer. It is a performative utterance. The congregation should not bow their heads and close their eyes, but receive the blessing facing the minister with their eyes open.

Our final response to God's gift of His peace and presence usually takes the form of solemnly singing a three-fold Amen with an awareness of the finality of the close of the service. Sometimes, however, we will respond with a counter-blessing for God by singing Psalm 72:18–19 (*Trinity Hymnal* #7) or even a blessing upon each other ("God be with you 'till we meet again").[28]

---

[28] This text by Jeremiah E. Rankin matched with Ralph Vaughan Williams's tune (RANDOLPH) offers a powerful way to end the service. This is hymn #385 in the revised *Trinity Hymnal* (1990) or hymn #328 in the Wisconsin Evangelical Lutheran Synod's *Christian Worship: A Hymnal* (Milwaukee: Northwestern Publishing House, 1993). William G. Tomer's tune (GOD BE WITH YOU), however, is much too feeble to end the service with (*Trinity Hymnal* #632).

PART III
Essays on Worship and Liturgical Theology

I am the sort of man who writes because he has made progress, and who makes progress by writing.
— Augustine, *Epistle* 143.2–3

These chapters contain a variety of essays on subjects related to worship and liturgy. I have put those that might be easier to read and more interesting to the general reader up front. Later chapters are a bit more technical and may appeal more to ministerial students and pastors. The concluding chapter is a long bibliographical essay that should help direct readers who are interested in further study in these areas.

Pastors and men in training for the ministry must begin thinking about these liturgical issues. We do not need more lay "worship committees." We need more theological thinking about biblical worship. Reformed seminaries and churches have done precious little to help prepare men in training for the pastorate to think through the biblical and theological principles of liturgy and worship. I am only one pastor with a limited amount of time and training in liturgical theology. But we all have to start somewhere. I offer these supplementary essays, in addition to what I have provided in the first two parts of this book, as "bread upon the water." Hopefully, this will help establish and enlarge some of what I have argued for in the body of this book and "after many days it will return to me" (Eccl. 11:1).

13
Whom Do We Trust: The Use of the Apostles' and Nicene Creeds in Worship

With the mouth one confesses and is saved.
—Romans 10:10b

With the rest of the country I anxiously watched the siege of the Branch Davidian compound in Waco, Texas, but there is one image that I will always remember. It is not the firefight with the ATF agents or even the apocalyptic fire that ended the assault on the compound. It was a short news clip of a woman cult member being escorted into a jailhouse with a swarm of reporters firing questions. She appealed to the camera, "How can they do this to us? We believe the Bible. Is it a crime to believe the Bible?"

Well, that depends on what you believe the Bible teaches. Everything hinges on *how* you understand the Bible and on *what* you profess as biblical truth. Jehovah's Witnesses, Mormons, Moslems, and even Branch Davidians all profess to believe the Bible. The real question is: what do they believe the Bible teaches? You see, the slogan "No creed but the Bible" is practically useless. Such a motto fails to provide an adequate means of distinguishing between cultic or heretical groups and the Church of the Lord Jesus Christ. I understand the motivation for such slogans. There is a real fear that the authority and sufficiency of the Bible itself will be suffocated by mere human creeds and confessions. That danger is very real. Nevertheless, the fact that creeds and confessions may be abused is not a strong enough argument to banish them from the worship and life of the Church altogether. They perform a necessary and beneficial service in the life of the Church.[1] The crucial service of the creeds in the life and worship of the Church is the subject of this essay.

For the sake of clarity, I should note that this essay will focus on the two ecumenical creeds that are used in the worship service—the Apostles' and Nicene Creeds. Some of my comments, especially those on the nature and necessity of creeds, might also be applied to other creedal documents (like the Westminster Confession of Faith), but my intent is to explain the Church's use of these two liturgical creeds.

The Apostles' Creed was not really written by the Apostles themselves (as legend has it), but was composed very early in the life of the post-apostolic Church. It has been used by the Western Church in one form or another at least since A.D. 150 and very possibly from the time of the apostles. It is "ecumenical" in that both the Roman Catholic and Reformation churches utilize it as a statement of faith.[2]

The Nicene Creed was composed for the ecumenical (or universal) councils of Nicea (A.D. 325) and Constantinople (A.D. 381); both of which were convened to clarify the doctrine of the deity of Christ and the Trinity. The Nicene Creed is in many ways little more

---

[1] "The Church is, indeed, not founded on symbols [creeds and confessions], but on Christ; not on any words of man, but on the Word of God; yet it is founded on Christ as confessed by men, and a creed is man's answer to Christ's question, man's acceptance and interpretation of God's word." Philip Schaff, *The Creeds of Christendom*, 3 vols. (6th ed.; Grand Rapids: Baker [1931] 1983), vol. 1, 5.

[2] The Apostles' Creed is quoted or embedded in every notable Reformation confession and catechism. It is most often explained in these Reformation documents as part of a larger structure that includes the Ten Commandments and the Lord's Prayer. See Mark A. Noll, ed., *Confessions and Catechisms of the Reformation* (Grand Rapids: Baker Book House, 1991). The origin and development of the Apostles' Creed itself is exhaustively detailed in J. N. D. Kelly, *Early Christian Creeds* (New York: David McKay, 1972),1–204.

than the Apostles' Creed enlarged to clarify the deity of the Son of God and of the Holy Spirit. With the exception of one clause, both the Eastern and Western Churches have adhered to the Nicene Creed as a preeminent summary of the Christian faith.[3]

These two ecumenical creeds have been used in the corporate worship of the Church for many centuries. The Apostles' Creed has been traditionally used for the instruction of children and new converts but was also used in liturgies that related to children and new converts (e.g. when there is a Baptism). The Nicene Creed, on the other hand, is a full confession of Christian orthodoxy and ordinarily appropriate for regular liturgical use. Should we continue this practice? What value is there in continuing to recite these ancient creeds? What are we doing when we recite these creeds in worship? These are the questions that I hope to answer.

The Necessity and Usefulness of Creeds

This may seem overly dramatic to some, but it is nevertheless true—if we are going to be faithful to the Bible itself, we *must* use "human" creeds. It is not just that creeds are permissible and biblical, but the Bible demands that we publicly express our faith in concise, accurate, and intelligible language—which is precisely what creeds attempt to do. This is an important point. When someone asks you, "What do you believe as a Christian?" you must respond with a summary of what you believe the Word of God teaches. You might say something like this: "That's a good question. If you have a few minutes I can summarize it for you. I believe the Bible teaches..." The words "I believe" (Latin = *credo*) come quite spontaneously to your lips. I am not suggesting that you simply quote the Apostles' Creed to the inquirer—though that is, of course, one

---

[3] The Eastern Orthodox churches do not include the phrase "and the Son" (Latin: *filioque*) in the third article on the Holy Spirit. Eastern texts of the Creed will also often begin with the corporate "We believe" rather than "I believe." For an excellent discussion of the origin of the Nicene Creed and an explanation of the meaning of the *filioque* clause, see Gerald Bray, *Creeds, Councils & Christ* (Leicester: Inter-Varsity Press, 1984).

acceptable way of summarizing the biblical faith—but my point is that composing creeds is inescapable. Everyone has a creed because everyone has a way of summarizing and expressing what one believes.[4]

The Bible itself demands that we make personal, public confession of our faith (Mt. 10:32–33; 16:13–17; Jn. 6:66–69; Rom. 10:9–10; 1 Tim. 6:13). Genuine faith always seeks public expression in confession and proclamation (Acts 19:18; 2 Cor. 4:13). Genuine faith that is truly a matter of the heart can never remain a secret of the heart. Our Lord said, "For out of the abundance of the heart the mouth speaks" (Lk. 6:45). The heart must speak and make public its deepest commitments. The important question is: Will your personal creed be an accurate and faithful summary of the Christian faith?

How can you ensure that your personal creed is an accurate reflection of the objective truth taught in the Bible? Keep that question in mind as we turn to the venerable Southern Presbyterian theologian Robert L. Dabney (d. 1898) for wisdom. He makes a very telling point when he reminds us that the Bible commands pastors not just to *read* the Bible, but to *explain* what it means in their own words. Consider Dabney's comments on 2 Timothy 4:2 as he marshals a telling argument for the legitimacy of creeds:

> He, as an apostle of Christ, not only permits, but commands, each uninspired pastor to give his human and uninspired expositions of what he believes to be divine truth, that is to say, his creed. If such human creeds when composed by a single teacher and delivered orally, extempore, are proper means of instruction for the church, by the stronger reason must those creeds be proper and scriptural which are the careful, mature, and joint productions of learned and godly pastors, delivered with all the accuracy

---

[4] "Indeed, a creed is quite inescapable, though some people talk as if they could have 'only the Bible' or 'no creed but Christ.' As we have seen, 'believing the Bible' involves applying it. If you cannot put the Bible into your own words (and actions), your knowledge of it is no better than a parrot's. But once you do put it down in your own words (and it is immaterial whether those words be written or spoken), you have a creed." John Frame, *The Doctrine of the Knowledge of God* (Phillipsburg, NJ: Presbyterian and Reformed, 1987), 305.

of written documents. He who would consistently banish creeds must silence all preaching and reduce the teaching of the church to the recital of
the exact words of Holy Scripture without note or comment.[5]

Every time a pastor mounts the pulpit to preach, he is explaining to the congregation what he believes the Scriptures teach. He
makes statements like, "I believe (*credo*) that this passage means..." or
"We can summarize this portion of Scripture by . . ." Should the
congregation reject his extra-biblical explanations and summaries
with the slogan "no creed but Christ, no confession but the Bible"?
No, of course not. We know the difference between the secondary
authority of the pastor's words of explanation (his *credo*) and the
primary authority of the Word of God. Similarly, but even more
powerfully, the historic creeds provide us with not just one pastor's
credo of what the Bible teaches, but the *credo* of the ancient, Medieval, and Reformation Church. How much more authority than
a single pastor's sermon does the Apostles' Creed have as a summary
of the apostolic faith.

The Authority of the Ecumenical Creeds

It follows, then, that the Nicene and Apostles' Creeds are in-
vested with all of the authority of almost two millennia of Church
history. This authority is secondary and derived, to be sure. The
Bible alone has primary and absolute authority. Nevertheless, secondary, derived authority is real authority. If a child informed his
mother, "Mom, I don't have to obey you because I know that Dad's
word is the primary authority in this house," we would not tolerate such a dismissive posture toward the mother's authority. The
father may indeed be the head of the household, and as such the
principal authority, but that does not imply that the mother has
absolutely no authority at all! You can be sure when the father
returns in the evening that he will use his principal authority to

---

[5] Robert L. Dabney, "The Doctrinal Contents of the Confession: Its Fundamental and
Regulative Ideas, and Value of Creeds" in *The Memorial Volume of the Westminster Assembly*
(Richmond: The Presbyterian Committee of Publication, 1897).

bolster the derived authority of his wife. The same holds true in any ordered society like the family. A private may not flout the authority of his sergeant with the claim that the captain is the one who is ultimately in charge. Middle management may not demand exemption from the directives of a vice president simply because he is not the president of the company. Similarly, the authority of an ecumenical creed that has been passed on to us by our forefathers in the faith, constituting as it does the universal tradition of the Church, is like the authority of a mother, a sergeant, or a vice president. It does not have the same authority as the Bible, but that does not mean it has no authority whatsoever.

Moreover, the Nicene and Apostles' Creeds have been thoroughly examined and approved by centuries of Christian reflection. The basic elements of the Apostles' Creed may even have come into existence at the same time as the apostolic Scriptures (compare the Apostles' Creed with 1 Pet. 3:18–22; Col. 2:9–15; and 1 Cor. 15:1ff). Note how closely the Apostles' Creed follows Paul's inspired summary of the Gospel:

> Moreover, brethren, I declare to you the Gospel
> which I preached to you, which also you received
> and in which you stand, by which also you are saved,
> if you hold fast that word which I preached to you—
> unless you believed in vain.
> For I delivered to you first of all that which I also received:
> that Christ died for our sins according to the Scriptures,
> and that He was buried,
> and that He rose again the third day
> according to the Scriptures . . .   (1 Cor. 15:1–4)

The apostolic Scriptures manifest on every page a common body of Christian teaching (doctrine), definite in outline and regarded by all the apostles as the possession of no individual but of the Church as a whole (1 Cor. 15:1ff; Eph. 4:5; Phil. 1:27; Titus 1:4; 2 Pet. 1:1; Jude 3). This outline bears a remarkable resemblance to the early creedal summaries of the faith. The substance of the Apostles' Creed is already found in the earliest known extra-biblical works, such as the Didache (c. A.D. 65–100) and in the writings of the first generation of post-Apostolic Fathers (for example, Justin Martyr, d. A.D. 165). Whether or not we can establish the precise dating of the origin of the Apostles' Creed, it still remains true that virtually every word and phrase of the creed is directly based on the Bible.

Even during the time of the New Testament, this body of apostolic teaching was beginning to crystallize into a set pattern and arrangement that would later form the basis for the Trinitarian baptismal creeds. The Old and New Testaments contain examples of "mini-creeds" (Exod. 20:1–3; Deut. 6:4; Mt. 16:13–18; Rom. 10:8ff; Acts 22–26; Phil. 2:11; 1 Tim. 1:15; 4:9; 2 Tim. 2:11; Heb. 13:15; 1 Jn. 4:15). Short summaries of the content of Christianity, like "Jesus is Lord" or "Jesus has come in the flesh" have their origin in the inspired Word of God. They are the forerunners of the early Church creeds that we now use. The ecumenical creeds build upon all of this biblical material and also various creedal formulations that originated just one or two generations after the apostles.

The point is that these creeds have been confessed by the universal Church (East and West), with only minor variations, for thousands of years. The lesson for us is powerful: if the Holy Spirit has consistently led the Church to make and affirm these creedal summaries of the faith, then we need to think long and hard before we reject the substance of these creeds (Jn. 16:13). When you recite the Apostles' or Nicene Creed in church on Sunday morning, you are verbally joining the venerable communion of saints, ritually confessing your solidarity with the Church of all ages.

By reciting the Apostles' and Nicene Creeds we are confessing the universal, historic faith of the Church of the Lord Jesus Christ. As one early Church Father expressed it: "In the universal Church itself, all possible care must be taken that we hold that faith which has been believed everywhere, always, by all; for that is truly and in the strictest sense 'catholic' or 'universal'" (Vincent of Lerins, d.

A.D. 450). More than any others, the Apostles' and Nicene Creeds meet these stringent requirements. C. E. B. Cranfield's comments are helpful: "What unites Christians of different traditions, languages, and nations and of different generations and centuries is a more effective and powerful vehicle of such confession than any occasional statement composed by an individual, however gifted, or by any particular denomination or group of Christians."[6]

New and Improved Creeds?

Increasingly, however, the ecumenical creeds are being omitted in evangelical worship services, or replaced with "creeds" composed by others—creeds that cannot by any stretch of the imagination claim to embody the "catholic" or "universal" faith.[7] These modern statements usually reflect some kind of agenda such as feminism or environmentalism. Sometimes they are just faddish and inferior, but they are almost always dangerous. When they are expressions of some modern social or political agenda, then they can be quite literally heretical. To alter, without biblical support, the orthodox Church's confession of God is nothing less than heresy. When a pastor or church modifies the historic Church's Scriptural confession of God in order to bring it in line with the spirit of the age, the document is idolatrous. The god confessed is only the projection of modern man's highest aspirations, not the true and living God who exists independently of fallen man's imaginary ideals.

Consider this actual example:

---

[6] C.E.B. Cranfield, *The Apostles' Creed: A Faith to Live By* (Grand Rapids: Eerdmans, 1993), 6.

[7] The temptation to despise historical creeds and confessions has dogged American Christianity with its emphasis on spontaneity, individualism, and anti-traditionalism. Consequently, sects have multiplied in America, sects which have little or no root in the historic Church of Jesus Christ. Philip Schaff's mid-nineteenth century judgment still haunts American evangelical Christianity: "Anyone who has, or fancies he has, some inward experience and a ready tongue, may persuade himself that he is called to be a reformer; and so proceed at once, in his spiritual vanity and pride, to a revolutionary rupture with the historical life of the church, to which he holds himself immeasurably superior. He builds himself in a night

We believe in God—
> who works in the hidden stillness of every dawn;
> who beckons us to visit the tomb of our fears so
> we might discover the birth of hope;
> who sends recurring dreams, fragrant flowers,
> good friends and bright angels with messages of joy and possibility.

We believe in Jesus, the risen Christ—
> who meets us on every path;
> who greets us with respect, names, and calms our fears,
> and bids us walk and talk as children of the Light;
> who is always going before us into our workplace and playspace.

We believe in the Holy Spirit—
> who gathers us into community;
> who works through the lame and the late,
> the wrinkled and the newborn, the hurting and the hopeful;
> who nudges our prayers, kindles our longings, and
> prompts our praise.

This "creed" continues with two more articles: one on the "Easter people" and another on the Church.[8] Besides the intolerable banality of the imagery and the idiotic attempt at poetic language, this creed is idolatrous, pure heresy. This new creed is not merely an attempt to update the archaic language of the old creeds or explain some of the more difficult words and phrases; nor is it even an attempt to deal with issues relevant to modern Christianity. Rather,

---

accordingly a new chapel, in which now for the first time since the age of the apostles a pure congregation is to be formed; baptizes his followers in his own name. . . rails and screams with full throat against all who refuse to do homage to his standard. . . . Thus the deceived multitude, having no power to discern spirits, is converted not to Christ and his truth, but to the arbitrary fancies and baseless opinions of an individual, who is only of yesterday. . . . Every theological vagabond and peddler may drive here his bungling trade, without passport or license, and sell his false ware at pleasure. What is to become of such confusion is not now to be seen." Philip Schaff, *The Principle of Protestantism* (Philadelphia: United Church Press, 1964 [1865]),149–50.

[8] *Sourcebook of Worship Resources* (Canton: Communication Resources, Inc., 1994),3–4.

this creed alters the *content* of the Christian faith. The God confessed has only a superficial resemblance to the biblical God, even though the Trinitarian names are retained. This creed shows no concern whatsoever to attribute to God the Father, Son, or Holy Spirit any of the attributes or activities that the Bible emphasizes. Is God creator? Is He almighty? Is Jesus God's Son? We are left to wonder. Is Jesus true man and true God? Was He really born? Did He die? Does the cross mean anything? What about man's sin? Is there forgiveness? What does it mean that He is "the risen Christ"? Did this happen in space and time ("the third day") or just in the minds of the disciples? Did He ascend to heaven? Is He coming again? Who knows? This creed certainly does not tell us! And who cares? Let's all just be happy. The god here confessed is not the Creator, Redeemer, and Sanctifier of Christianity who demands our allegiance and promises us salvation from sin in Christ; rather this god has no objective existence—he is fundamentally the projection of a modern congregation's sentimental thoughts about a higher power.

The Creeds as Doors into the Church

What standard should a church use to determine what doctrines are essential to the Christian faith? How can we know whether a person's confession is biblical? Another way to word this question is to ask what kind of personal confession of faith the leaders of the church will require of those who wish to join the church. When the elders interview a candidate for membership, what doctrines must the candidate confess? These are crucial questions today, because many churches require adherence to various idiosyncratic doctrines for membership. Even if you may not be required to confess something so outrageous as the "creed" I just quoted, nevertheless, you may not be admitted into the membership of some churches if you do not believe in a pre-tribulation rapture. You may be barred from membership in other churches because you do not agree with that denomination's mode of baptism or their particular theory of the

Lord's special presence at the Eucharist. Historically, the boundaries of the Church have not been drawn so tightly, but history often does not matter much to American Christians. The classical position is that the door into local church membership ought to be no narrower (or wider) than the door into heaven. What, then, must a person believe in order to enter into heaven? Answer: He must be able to confess honestly that he trusts "in God the Father Almighty, etc."

The Apostles' Creed embodies the common faith of Christians everywhere. It is truly an ecumenical creed, in the best sense of that word. An honest commitment to the truths outlined there ought to serve to identify true Christians. When churches and Christians abandon the ancient creeds they open a theological Pandora's box and let loose a whole host of false doctrines. Worse than that, all sorts of nonessential doctrines are often elevated as tests of orthodoxy.[9] In many independent churches that have strong personalities as leaders, the pet doctrines of the pastor himself are often made to function as boundaries for church fellowship. For example, in the past I was denied membership in a independent evangelical church simply because I did not agree with the leadership's view of the end times.

This tendency to elevate secondary, nonessential doctrines is greatly diminished in creedal churches. The ecumenical creeds do not include anything about the millennium, the rapture, or the Antichrist; in fact, they contain nothing at all about the interpretation of the book of Revelation. These doctrines are not necessary for salvation; neither should they be made necessary for church membership. The creeds set forth what is essential and abiding, not what is controversial and faddish. They deal with what God the Father, Son, and Holy Spirit have done for us in creation, redemption, and sanctification—in other words, those teachings on which

---

[9] See Gary DeMar and Peter Leithart, *The Reduction of Christianity* (Fort Worth: Dominion Press, 1988). DeMar and Leithart expose the error of many creed-less and confession-less independent churches in America that elevate pre-millennial dispensationalism such that all who reject this eschatological position are branded as unorthodox and heretical.

the Christian faith stands or falls. Other nonessential doctrines simply cannot function as barriers to true fellowship in a church that recognizes the centrality of the Apostles' Creed.

All of this comports well with the origin of the Apostles' Creed, which developed from the questions asked to church membership candidates at their Baptism. Our Lord instituted the initiatory rite of Baptism with the mandate that all be baptized "into the Name of Father, Son, and Holy Spirit" (Mt. 28:19). What does it mean to be baptized into this Name? Who are Father, Son, and Holy Spirit? What have they done for me? As a baptized Christian you bear this Name; now what does it mean to you? Your answer should be, "I trust in God the Father Almighty . . . and in Jesus Christ, his only Son, our Lord . . . and I trust in the Holy Spirit. . ."

The creeds, then, developed in the early Church as baptismal confessions. The candidate for Baptism was asked a series of three questions to which he was to respond "I believe." We have an example of how this was done in the *Apostolic Constitutions* of Hippolytus (c. A.D. 200). He has recorded for us one of the earliest examples of the creed:

> Minister: Do you believe [trust] in God, the Father Almighty?
> Candidate: **I believe**.
> Minister: Do you believe [trust] in Christ Jesus, the Son of God, who was born of the Holy Spirit of the Virgin Mary, and was crucified under Pontius Pilate, and was dead and buried, and rose again the third day, alive from the dead, and ascended into heaven, and sat at the right hand of the Father, and will come to judge the living and the dead?
> Candidate: **I believe.**
> Minister: Do you believe [trust] in the Holy Spirit, in the holy Church, and in the resurrection of the flesh?
> Candidate: **I believe.**

The Apostles' Creed, therefore, is a confession of the very Name of God into which one has been baptized. Trusting in the Name of Father, Son, and Holy Spirit cannot be compared with opinions about the time and character of the millennium or the proper form of church government. The Apostles' and Nicene Creeds embody the truths necessary for salvation. This is what defines a Christian. He or she is one who trusts in God the Father as Creator of all; God the Son, the Redeemer of God's people; and God the Holy Spirit, the Sanctifier of the Church.

In reciting these Trinitarian creeds, moreover, we learn the true meaning and importance of the doctrine of the Trinity. As baptized Christians we do not bear the generic name "God." We have not been named and claimed by a "Higher Power" or the "Unmoved Mover." Believing in "God" does not necessarily make one a Christian. God has specifically revealed His true and proper Name to us as Father, Son, and Holy Spirit. This is the only Name we confess. This is the God who has created, redeemed, and sanctified us. None other. The Triune God is the only true God.

The creeds eloquently instruct us that the origin of our doctrine of the Trinity is not to be found in idle theological speculation. Although in the history of the Church it has often been buried beneath loads of subtle metaphysical terminology, the doctrine of the Trinity is not something that ancient theologians cooked up to keep simple Christians befuddled and confused. God has revealed Himself to us in salvation history as working for us as Father, Son, and Holy Spirit. The Father is the Father because He created me and sustains me. I know that He *is* the Father because I know what He has *done* for me. The Son *is* my Lord because I know what He has *done* for me in his birth, life, death, resurrection, and ascension. The Spirit *is* the *Holy* Spirit because of what He *does* for me: He makes me holy (sanctification). There is no finer Trinitarian summary of the Apostles' Creed than Luther's brief exposition:

The First Article: Of Creation.

I believe in God the Father Almighty, Maker of heaven and earth.
What does this mean? Answer: I believe that God has made me and all creatures; that He has given me my body and soul, eyes, ears, and all my members, my reason, and all my senses, and still preserves them; also

clothing and shoes, meat and drink, house and home, wife and children, fields, cattle, and all my goods; that He richly and daily provides me with all that I need to support this body and life; that He defends me against all danger, and guards and protects me from all evil; and all this purely out of fatherly, divine goodness and mercy, without any merit or worthiness in me; for all which it is my duty to thank and praise, to serve and obey Him. This is most certainly true!

The Second Article: Of Redemption

And in Jesus Christ His only Son our Lord; who was conceived by the Holy Spirit, born of the virgin Mary, suffered under Pontius Pilate, was crucified, dead, and buried. He descended into hell. The third day He rose again from the dead. He ascended into heaven, and sitteth on the right hand of God the Father Almighty. From thence He shall come to judge the quick and the dead.
What does this mean? Answer: I believe that Jesus Christ, true God, begotten of the Father from eternity, and also true man, born of the virgin Mary, is my Lord, who has redeemed me, a lost and condemned creature, purchased and won me from all sins, from death, and from the power of the devil; not with gold or silver, but with His holy, precious blood and with His innocent suffering and death, that I may be His own and live under Him in His kingdom, and serve Him in everlasting righteousness, innocence, and blessedness, even as He is risen from the dead, lives, and reigns for all eternity. This is most certainly true!

The Third Article: Of Sanctification

I believe in the Holy Spirit, the holy Christian Church, the communion of saints, the forgiveness of sins, the resurrection of the body, and the life everlasting.
What does this mean? Answer: I believe that I cannot by my own reason or strength believe in Jesus Christ, my Lord, or come to Him; but the Holy Spirit has called me by the Gospel, enlightened me with His gifts, sanctified and kept me in the true faith; even as He calls, gathers, enlightens, and sanctifies the whole Christian Church on earth, and keeps it with Jesus Christ in the one true faith; in which Christian Church He daily and richly forgives all sins to me and all believers, and will at the Last Day raise up me and all the dead, and give unto me and all believers in Christ eternal life. This is most certainly true![10]

---

[10] *Triglot Concordia: The Symbolical Books of the Evangelical Lutheran Church* (St. Louis: Concordia Publishing House, 1921), 543–45. Luther changed "catholic" to "Christian church." A little later in this chapter I argue this is unnecessary.

In Whom Do You Trust?

During the Republican convention in Houston in 1992, the Christian Coalition sponsored a rally that featured the Vice President Dan Quayle. The crowd, packed into a hotel ballroom, went wild when Mr. Quayle appeared. "Do we trust Bill Clinton?" Mr. Quayle asked. "No!" the crowd bellowed. "Do we trust the liberal media?" "No!" the answer came again. Then Mr. Quayle asked: "Who do we trust?" The response was immediate and loud: "Jesus!" Mr. Quayle, expecting the audience to shout "George Bush," was stunned.[11]

We do this every Sunday morning. We clarify our ultimate loyalty. The pastor asks, "Christian people, in whom do you trust?" and the response comes "I believe in God the Father. . ." Reciting the creeds on Sunday morning provides us all with an opportunity for a personal, yet united profession of our faith before God and the world. Cranfield notes that before 1933, in Germany it was customary for the pastor alone to recite the creed during Sunday morning worship. With the rise of the Nazi regime that practice was altered. After 1933 the congregations began to join in the public recitation. "Church members wanted this opportunity, in the face of Nazi attacks on the church, to confess their faith personally and publicly."[12] Christians today must publicly confess their faith in the face of a new Fascism, the relentless attack on the Christian church by a sophisticated humanistic culture.[13] A vigorous and wholehearted recitation of the Apostles' Creed can serve well as a weekly reminder to the Christian community that its ultimate loyalty may never be placed in politicians, scientists, doctors, intellectuals, media personalities, or the State. Only the biblical God is Creator and Savior.

[11] Fred Barnes relates this incident in his review of Ralph Reed's *Active Faith* in the *Wall Street Journal* (June 10, 1996).

[12] Cranfield, *The Apostles' Creed*, 6.

[13] See the haunting exposé of America's growing Fascist culture by Gene Edward Veith, Jr., *Modern Fascism: Liquidating the Judeo-Christian Worldview* (St. Louis: Concordia Publishing House, 1993).

As noted before, some have criticized the Nicene and Apostles' Creeds because they do not say anything about "justification by faith."[14] This is a very weighty objection, but it arises from a fundamental misunderstanding of the language and purpose of these creeds. These creeds are not designed primarily to be a list of doctrines to which Christians give their assent. The great Dutch Reformed theologian Herman Bavink criticized the all-too-common tendency we have as Christians to reduce our faith to believing a list of ideas and doctrines: "They no longer confess their faith, but they only believe their confession." When true and lively faith wanes in a church, the creeds and confessions can easily degenerate to the level of documents to which the people give formal, intellectual assent. But the fault must not be located in the creeds and confessions themselves, but in the people.

Keeping this in mind, the Apostles' Creed is not primarily a list of ideas that we give assent to, rather it is a public, personal confession of our trust in God the Father, Son, and Holy Spirit, acknowledging God's work of creation, redemption, and sanctification for us. When you recite these creeds you are not saying something like, "I believe this about that" or "I think that these ideas and concepts are true." Some confessions and catechisms provide for this kind of thing. The Westminster Shorter Catechism is filled with abstract definitions of doctrinal terms: Q. What is justification? A. Justification is . . . There is nothing inherently wrong with this, but it is not how the Nicene and Apostles' Creeds have been written.

Since Paul considered it a safeguard to repeat himself on certain fundamental points (Phil. 3:1), I will repeat what I said in an earlier part of this book. When we say, "I believe in God the Father Almighty," we are *not* expressing what we think or what opinions

---

[14] The most notable and referenced critic of the Apostles' Creed in our circles is the Scottish Presbyterian theologian William Cunningham. After a string of criticisms, his conclusion is that "the Apostles' Creed, as it is called, is not entitled to much respect, and is not fitted to be of much use, as a summary of the leading doctrines of Christianity" (William Cunningham, *Historical Theology*, vol. 1 [Edinburgh: Banner of Truth, 1960], 90).

we hold about the deity. *Credo*—the first word in the Latin creeds—means "I believe" or "I place my trust in." *Credo* is the Latin translation of the Greek word *pisteuo*, which is precisely the word that is used for "faith" in the New Testament (Jn. 3:16, 36; Rom. 10:10). When the congregation says, "I believe [*credo, pisteuo*] in God the Father Almighty," they are not stating an opinion or even assenting to a doctrine. They are confessing their personal trust, their faith in the Father, the Son, and the Holy Spirit. "I believe [*credo, pisteuo*]" is exactly equivalent to the language of personal trust used in the New Testament: "I believe in" or "I place my faith in" or "I trust in." The creed allows the congregation to verbalize publicly their faith and trust in the God who redeems in Christ Jesus through the work of the Holy Spirit. There is no doctrine of justification by faith articulated in the creeds because the creeds express the faith of justified sinners.

Faith in Faith or Faith in God

Moreover, the faith of the justified sinner does not focus inward, but reaches out and lays hold of the one true God. After the initial "I believe" the creed is silent about the believer's subjective act of faith. The all-important thing is not the faith of the Christian, its strength or character, but the One in whom the Christian trusts. Unfortunately, these creeds are conspicuous by their absence in so many evangelical churches today. It is almost as if the experience of the people in church has become central. The focus of many contemporary church services is not so much on objectively confessing and worshipping God, but on the expression and experience of the people. The services are orchestrated and deliberately designed to produce certain desired responses in the people. Rather than providing the means whereby the congregation can offer objective worship to the God and Father of our Lord Jesus Christ in the power of the Holy Spirit, too many church services today are geared towards engineering various psychological experiences. The historical creeds serve as a healthy check on this overdose of experience so common today. They provide us with a way of moving outside of ourselves and our own experiences so that we can claim by faith for ourselves God the Father's work of creation, God the Son's work of redemption, and God the Holy Spirit's work of sanctification.

We live in an age when not many are concerned about the objective content of the faith—whether what they believe is really true or not—but are preoccupied with the Christian's own personal activity and disposition. We want to know what will uplift and help people, what will produce a certain kind of positive response in people's lives. A woman called me recently and asked me about our church. "Is it uplifting and exciting?" she asked. "Will I go away feeling good about myself every week after the service?" I told her, "Our worship is truly vigorous and joyful. We give thanks to God every week for what He has done for us in creation and redemption. But, I have to be honest with you. We meet together at God's command to glorify Him. We are not there for stimulation or excitation. We gather to confess our sins, receive forgiveness, commune with the Lord, and be instructed about sin, righteousness, and eternal life from the Word of God." After a few more minutes of conversation, it was obvious that this was not the kind of church she was looking for.[15]

In contrast to this modern experience-centered, man-oriented Christianity stands the whole undivided tradition of the Church of Jesus Christ. What is most important is not what kind of experience you have with God, but whether you trust in the true God. Now, experiences are good. When the true God works in your life, you not only know it but you feel it. Nevertheless, our faith does not rest in our own experiences, but in the gracious work of Father,

---

[15] Much more could be said about the experience-oriented tendencies of American Christianity. Emphasis on experience as foundation in the Church leads ultimately to liberalism. For an eye-opening explanation of the subtle origin and meaning of twentieth-century American Liberalism, see J. Gresham Machen's *Christianity and Liberalism*, first published in 1923, but most recently republished by Eerdmans (1985). See also Machen's "The Creeds and Doctrinal Advance" in his collection of sermons, *God Transcendent* (Edinburgh: Banner of Truth, 1982), 157–167.

Son, and Holy Spirit for us. We are not saved because we have experienced something in the past, however exciting and moving it may have been. In other words, true faith is not necessarily expressed by the statement "I believe that I am saved," but rather, "I believe in God the Father, Son, and Holy Spirit." Many people believe that they "got saved," but, unfortunately, their hope is founded on an experience they had in the past. They believe (i.e., are of the opinion that) they "got saved" even though they are not presently trusting in God the Father, Son, and Holy Spirit. Confessing the Apostles' or Nicene Creed in the worship service reminds us that we are gathered together, in opposition to the world, as those who trust in the one true God as Father, Son, and Holy Spirit.

If you have followed my arguments so far and agree with my analysis, then you should now understand the need for the public confession of the Apostles' and Nicene Creeds in Sunday worship. Furthermore, you ought to evaluate how *you* recite these creeds. If these creeds really are personal confessions of faith and trust, if they really do embody the core biblical teachings about God and His work, then you and I ought to recite these creeds wholeheartedly and energetically. When the pastor calls to the congregation, "Christians, what do you believe?" or better "Christians, in whom do you trust?" you should respond with a vigorous, loud recitation of the creed. Faithfulness to the true and living God is a life-long calling. The challenge of remaining loyal to God the Father, Son, and Holy Spirit engages the Church as her most arduous and adventurous task. G.K Chesterton called it "the romance of orthodoxy":

> This is the thrilling romance of Orthodoxy. People have fallen into a foolish habit of speaking of orthodoxy as something heavy, humdrum, and safe. There never was anything so perilous or so exciting as orthodoxy . . . . It is always easy to let the age have its head; the difficult thing is to keep one's own. It is always easy to be a modernist—as it is easy to be a snob. To have fallen into any of those open traps of error and exaggeration which fashion after fashion and sect after sect set along the historic path of Christendom— that would indeed have been simple. It is always simple to fall; there are an infinity of angles at which one falls, only one at which one stands. To have

fallen into any one of the fads from Gnosticism to Christian Science would indeed have been obvious and tame. But to have avoided them all has been one whirling adventure; and in my vision the heavenly chariot flies thundering through the ages, the dull heresies sprawling and prostrate, the wild truth reeling but erect.[16]

The Two Most Frequently Asked Questions About the Apostles' and Nicene Creed

1. What do we mean when we confess to believe in "one holy catholic and apostolic Church" (Nicene Creed) or in the "holy catholic Church" (Apostles' Creed)?

First of all, the word in this phrase that most often confounds Protestants is the adjective "catholic." What do we mean by this qualifying adjective "catholic"? The term "catholic" itself is not found in Scripture. Nevertheless, it has found its way into the ecumenical creeds because it expresses a biblical truth about the Church of the Lord Jesus Christ. The word "catholic" is derived from the Greek adverb *kath'holon* ("in reference to the whole"). The closest words we have to it are "universal," "undivided," or "whole." When we acknowledge that we believe in the "holy *catholic* Church," we are confessing our solidarity with the *whole* Church of Jesus Christ wherever and whenever she might be. The early Church bishop Ignatius of Antioch (c. A.D. 100) was the first to use the term "catholic." What he wrote is what we confess in the creed: "Where Jesus Christ is, there is the catholic Church."[17]

Now, obviously, the word "catholic" cannot refer to the *Roman* Catholic church. The very notion of a universal Roman church is a contradiction. To suggest that the Roman church is the only true church is not very catholic, but sectarian. The Church of Christ has one Head, the ascended Lord Jesus. No human pope, bishop, pastor, moderator, mentor, or anyone else, can ever claim that loyalty

---

[16] G. K. Chesterton, *Orthodoxy* (Garden City: Image Books, 1959), 101–2.
[17] Ignatius to the Smyrnaeans, 8.2 (*Early Christian Writings: The Apostolic Fathers*, trans. by Maxwell Staniforth [London: Penguin Books, 1968],103).

to him (or her) constitutes the mark of the true Church. The mark of catholicity is loyalty to Jesus Christ.[18]

The Church of the Lord Jesus Christ is catholic; therefore it is not restricted to one location or institution. We count a particular congregation as part of the catholic Church if the leaders and people confess the apostolic, orthodox faith, thereby manifesting their union with the Head of the Church, the Lord Jesus Christ. The catholic Church is the apostolic Church. Apostolic churches meet the following criteria:

1) their ministerial orders (pastors, elders, deacons) are grounded in the authoritative apostolic blueprint and provide care and discipline for members;[19]

2) they strive to maintain and guard the apostles' doctrine in their preaching and teaching; and

3) they administer the apostolic sacraments (the Lord's Supper and Baptism) regularly and faithfully. No other institutional or organizational marks are necessary. As long as they are faithful to the above three marks, they are apostolic churches, even if they are institutionally structured as independent, episcopal, congregational, or presbyterial bodies.

We dare not degenerate in our thinking to the point where we become sectarian in our conception of the local church. We may be convinced that Presbyterian government and Reformed doctrine represent the most faithful exposition of the Bible; but we must never think that because we have these commitments we are the only true church. We are catholic but not Roman, Reformed but not sectarian. In other words, the Church of Jesus Christ is larger

---

[18] Some churches have substituted the adjective "Christian" or "universal" for "catholic" in order to avoid the unfortunate Roman Catholic associations that the word has taken on since the sixteenth century.

[19] Unfortunately, various churches denominate these ministerial offices differently, which leads to much confusion. It is not my purpose here to sort out all differences in labels. I am not suggesting that only those churches that *call* their board of older wise men "elders" can qualify as apostolic churches. Nor do I mean to imply that other churches that do not use the words "Minister" or "Deacon" should be disqualified.

than our local church and denomination. It is larger than Presbyterianism, even Protestantism. The true catholic Church is also older than Presbyterianism and Protestantism. It predates the Reformation. The catholic Church is one worldwide fellowship of believing people together with the triumphant saints in heaven— both Old and New Testament saints—all united to Christ the Husband and Head. You must think of nothing less than this when you confess to believe in "one holy *catholic* and *apostolic* Church."

Secondly, what about the term "holy"? What does that mean? The Church is holy because it is united to the ascended Lord Jesus Christ. The Church is holy because it is positioned in union with Christ in the closest possible relation to our holy God. Holiness in the Bible always has spatial, even geographical connotations. This is seen most clearly when we begin with the symbolic structure of the Old Covenant. The nearer you were to God, the holier you were. In the Old Covenant there were degrees of holiness that corresponded to the degrees of nearness to the Lord's special presence in the tabernacle and temple. The land of Canaan was holy when compared to the other nations, because the Lord dwelt in the midst of His people in the land of Canaan. This was not true of other nations. The city of Jerusalem was holier still, since the temple resided within her walls. Other cities may have been holy, but not as holy as the holy city Jerusalem. All of the Israelites were constituted a holy people because they lived in the holy land and were nearer to God's special presence than the Gentile peoples. The Levites were holier still because they ministered in the tabernacle and temple area. The common Israelite was not allowed to touch or enter some parts of the tabernacle/temple complex. The priests were even one degree holier, since they were able to enter into the Holy Place to offer sacrifices. Finally, the Most Holy Place was the inner room where the Lord's special presence manifested itself over the Ark of the Covenant. Only the High Priest could enter this room. He was the most holy man in Israel. And this room was the Holy of Holies or the Most Holy Place.

The post-Pentecost situation is different. There are no more graded zones of holiness. There are only two categories—either you are holy or you are unholy. The man Jesus Christ, our great High Priest, has entered the true Holy of Holies (heaven itself) and sat down at the right hand of God. All who are united to Him ("in Christ") are holy. All who are not are not holy. The holy catholic Church consists of all believers, who in Christ are themselves "seated in the heavenly places" (Col. 3:1). This is what we mean when we confess "one *holy* catholic Church." It does not mean that everyone in the universal Church is perfectly holy in behavior. Behavioral holiness—what we call holy living—is a consequence of our positional holiness in Christ. Behavioral holiness is our duty; positional holiness is our privilege. Behavioral holiness is progressive and incremental; positional holiness admits no degrees, since one is either united with Christ by faith or not.

In the language of traditional Reformed theology we would call positional holiness "definitive sanctification"—the word "sanctification" is derived from the Latin word *sancio*, "to make holy." Our progress in behavioral holiness we would call "progressive sanctification." The catholic Church is definitively holy through its union with Christ by the Spirit, and therefore it is also being progressively sanctified by the same Spirit.[20] This is the one holy catholic and apostolic Church that we confess.

2. *What does "he descended into hell" mean in the Apostles' Creed?*

There are at least six possible interpretations of this clause:

[20] Luther highlights the Spirit's activity in this entire third section of the Apostles' Creed. He places the heading "Sanctification" over this entire article, beginning with the words "I believe in the Holy Spirit." Luther says, "If you are asked, What do you mean by these words, 'I believe in the Holy Spirit'? you can answer, 'I believe that the Holy Spirit makes me holy, as his name implies.' How does he do this? By what means? Answer: 'Through the Christian Church, the forgiveness of sins, the resurrection of the body, and the life everlasting'" (Luther's Large Catechism, II, 40–41; Tappert, trans. and ed., *The Book of Concord: Confessions of the Evangelical Lutheran Church* [Philadelphia: Fortress Press, 1959], 416).

1. It means that Jesus actually descended into hell (*gehenna*, the abode of the damned), the place of the damned, *to suffer the wrath of God.*

2. It means that Jesus actually descended into hell (*gehenna*, the abode of the damned) *to preach the Gospel* and give some residents a "second chance."

3. It means that Jesus actually descended into hell (*gehenna*, the abode of the damned) to proclaim His victory over sin, death, and the devil.

4. It does not mean that Jesus literally "descended" to hell; rather, he symbolically descended into hell, that is, He literally suffered hell for us as our substitute on the cross.

5. The phrase would be better rendered as "He descended into hades." It means that Jesus actually died, and His human soul and body were separated, His spirit leaving His body to inhabit for a time the place of the departed dead (*sheol, hades*).

6. It merely means that "He went to the dead" or "He descended to the dead" or "He descended into the grave." In other words, it means Jesus genuinely suffered *death.*

This list might seem confusing at first, but these options can be grouped according to a few common assumptions. The first four interpretations all presuppose that hell (*gehenna*) is in view, whether literally (1–3) or only symbolically (4). Option #5 suggests that "the place of the departed dead" (OT *sheol*, NT *hades*) would be a better way to render the original wording of the creed. The sixth option is a modern makeshift that only adds to the confusion, since one must then ask what this phrase adds to "He was crucified, dead, and *buried.*" Notice the very carefully ordered sequence in the creed:

who was conceived by the Holy Spirit,
born of the virgin Mary,
suffered under Pontius Pilate
was crucified, dead, and buried;
he descended into hell;
the third day he rose again from the dead;
he ascended into heaven,
and sits on the right hand of God the Father Almighty

Clearly the creed intends for the descent clause to *add* something to the affirmation that Jesus was "buried." More than that, it follows in a historical sequence of events: born, suffered, crucified, dead, buried, descended, rose again, ascended, and sits. The descent happened *before* the resurrection. The descent comes *after* his burial and *before* his resurrection. This carefully constructed historical sequence rules out the symbolic interpretation that is so common in Reformed circles (#4 above). Even though both Calvin and the Heidelberg Catechism (Q.44) explain the descent clause as another way of describing Jesus' suffering the wrath of God on the cross, this interpretation does not do justice to the placement of the clause in the historical sequence. Furthermore, we know from history that this symbolic interpretation was not the view of the early Church, which was responsible for composing the creed.

The substance of what Calvin says is true enough. Jesus did indeed suffer the wrath of God for us—that which characterizes hell. Nevertheless, this penal curse was vicariously borne by Jesus in His suffering and death on the cross (Gal. 3:13). His death marked the climax of the Father's just wrath. This rules out option #1, which understands Jesus suffering hell in some sense *after* his death and burial. There is nothing at all in the Bible to indicate that Jesus suffered any added punishment after His death on the cross. Jesus cried out "It is finished" on the cross (Jn. 19:30).

The questions therefore are: Did Jesus descend into hell or into hades? And what did He do there? Let us begin with what we *do* know. First, we know that Jesus suffered death as a human—that is, His soul and body were torn apart. That is what the Bible calls physical death. The biblical record says that when He died "He gave up His spirit" (Jn. 19:30). Luke 23:46 tells us that Jesus Himself prayed, "Father, into your hands I commit my spirit." Now, if Jesus' human "spirit" or "soul" (the two words are used interchangeably in Scripture) departed on the cross, where did it go? If Jesus' body was subsequently buried, then His soul must have gone somewhere. In other words, where was Jesus between Good Friday and Easter

Sunday morning? And what was He doing? The descent clause has an answer.

Second, before we move on, however, there is some ambiguity involved in the interpretation of this phrase. Did Jesus descend into "hell" or "hades"? Is there a difference? The Greek version of the creed has Jesus descending into *hades*. This is the general abode of the departed dead. It corresponds to *sheol* in the OT (e.g. Ps. 16:10 "for you will not abandon my soul to *sheol*"). The Latin version of the creed has Jesus *desendit ad inferna* ("descended into hell"). The Greek version, which is probably older and closer to the apostolic Church's tradition, uses the language of *hades / sheol* not *gehenna* ("hell"). We know from Peter's Pentecost sermon that Jesus did descend into *hades / sheol* and that His Father did not abandon Him there (Ps. 16:10; Acts 2:27). We have no biblical text that suggests that Jesus descended into *gehenna*/hell. It becomes complicated here because it would seem that in the Old Testament *sheol* describes the general abode of the departed dead, both righteous and damned. It would seem that with the death, descent, resurrection, and ascension of Jesus major changes happened in these realms. [21] But we need not figure out all the details of this transformation to make some headway in understanding what it meant that Jesus "descended into *hades*." [22]

Third, we know that Jesus could not have been in *hades* or hell preaching to the Old Testament dead so as to give them a "second chance." Whatever 1 Peter 3:18–20 means, it cannot mean that Jesus was preaching the Gospel to the departed dead in *hades / sheol* or to the pre-flood wicked dead in hell. The early Church father Augustine labeled this view as heretical. I do not know that I would go that far, but it certainly does not make biblical sense. The

---

[21] The very best systematic discussion of this subject is found in John W. Cooper, *Body, Soul, & Life Everlasting: Biblical Anthropology and the Monism-Dualism Debate* (Grand Rapids: Eerdmans, 1989),121–146.

[22] For a summary of what happens see James B. Jordan, *A Brief Readers Guide to Revelation* (Niceville: Transfiguration Press, 1999),28.

Reformed scholar Randall Otto summarizes the objections to this interpretation quite well: "Let it suffice to assert that any preaching to the OT saints would be superfluous, since they had already believed the Gospel and were thus justified (Rom. 4:3; Gal. 3:6–9). Moreover, preaching to the impenitent dead would be against the entire tenor of Scripture, which pronounces judgment after death (Heb. 9:27) and condemnation to the wicked dead without review as, for instance, the parable of the rich man and Lazarus indicates (Lk. 16:19–31)."[23]

Almost surely what is in view in 1 Peter 3:18–20 is a reference to the Spirit of Jesus, who inspired Noah to preach the Gospel to the pre-flood generation, the spirits who did not repent and are *now* in prison. This is Augustine's interpretation. Christ preached through the Holy Spirit using Noah during the one hundred twenty years prior to the flood. They who heard Noah's preaching are now in prison, but when Christ preached to them through Noah, they were given the opportunity to repent. This fits with the reference to the "Spirit" who strove one hundred twenty years with the generation before the flood (Gen. 6:3). Peter interprets this as the Spirit of Jesus preaching through Noah (1 Pet. 1:11). In his second epistle Peter tells us explicitly that Noah was "a preacher of righteousness" (2 Pet. 2:5; cf. Heb. 11:7).

Well, where does that leave us? If 1 Peter 3:18–20 does not help us in our understanding of the phrase "He descended into hell," are there any other Scriptures that might help? If Jesus did not descend into hell in order to suffer further punishment or to preach a second chance to the Old Covenant damned, could there be another reason for His descent into hell? Yes, in fact, there is Luther's very attractive interpretation. Luther understands the descent clause to refer to Christ's triumph over Satan and all of his hellish hosts. When Christ descended into hell it was an opportunity to proclaim

[23] Randall E. Otto, "*Descendit in Inferna*: A Reformed Review of a Creedal Conundrum," *Westminster Theological Journal* 52 (1990):143–150.

His comprehensive victory over sin, death, and the devil himself. The soul of Christ descended to hell in order to destroy it for believers, thus "redeeming them from the power of death, of the devil, and eternal damnation of hellish jaws" (*Formula of Concord, Solid Declaration* 9.4). Christ appears before Satan victoriously to announce His victory on Satan's own turf. The very kingdom of Satan has been spoiled. Jesus appears in hell as Conqueror. As *Christus Victor* Jesus descended into hell: "Having disarmed principalities and powers, he made a public spectacle of them, triumphing over them in it" (Col. 2:15).[24]

Jesus' descent into *hades* to herald His own victory seems to be the most biblical option. Since the differentiation between *hades / sheol* (the Greek and Hebrew terms for the *undifferentiated* place of the departed dead, without reference to blessedness or damnation) and hell (*gehenna*) is not always carefully distinguished in the Scriptures, this interpretation fits well with statements in the New Testament that clearly state that Jesus' soul departed for the place of the dead (*hades*) after his death. In Acts 2:27 Peter puts the words of Psalm 16:10 into the mouth of the resurrected Christ: "You will not abandon me to the place of the departed dead [*hades*]." The NIV misleadingly translates *hades* as "the grave." The soul of the man Jesus Christ was clearly separated from His body during the three days when His body rested in the tomb. His spirit/soul went to the place of the departed dead. He truly died and the evidence is that His body was buried and His soul departed for *hades / sheol* for three days until the reuniting of His soul and body at the resurrection.

Therefore, the best way to understand the biblical data about *hades / sheol* before Jesus transformed it is to think of it as the place where departed souls went after death, either to experience blessing and peace from the Lord (the paradise side of *sheol*) or to experience the Lord's wrath (the damnation side of *sheol*). We know from

---

[24] David Scaer argues quite convincingly for this interpretation in the *Journal of the Evangelical Theological Society* 35.1 (March 1992): 91–99.

Luke 23:43 that He visited the Paradise side of *hades / sheol*; and we can surmise from the passages quoted above that He also marched through hell itself (the damnation side of *hades / sheol*), announcing His victory over Satan and all his demonic legions (Eph. 4:8–10). When we recite the creed saying "He descended into hell," we are confessing that Jesus truly died and that He proclaimed His victory in the place of the departed dead, delighting the righteous and confounding Satan and the damned.

14
The Place of the Minister in the Lord's Service

Keep a close watch on yourself and on the teaching;
persevere in this, for by so doing you will save both
yourself and your hearers.
—1 Timothy 4:16

Serious biblical-theological thinking about the purpose and work of the ministry has fallen on hard times in Reformed theology. In some Presbyterian circles any attempt to restore the role of the minister to his proper, even necessary role within the worship and life of the congregation may be judged to be slippage toward Roman "sacerdotalism."[1] If I were to cite just one example of the problem, it would be the uproar that Robert S. Rayburn's lecture "The Centrality of the Christian Minister" caused at Covenant Seminary. Dr. Rayburn kicked off his lecture series with this address on October 16, 1996. He presented the men with a classical Reformed conception of the indispensability of the ministry for the spiritual welfare of the Church based on an exegesis of 1 Timothy 4:16 ("Keep a close watch on yourself and on the teaching; persevere in this, for by so doing you will save both

---

[1] I use this term according to its proper original sense as a reference to "priest craft" and not as a pejorative broadside against any theological position that affirms a "high" view of the ministry or an "instrumental" theology of the Baptism and the Lord's Supper.

yourself and your hearers"). These lectures caused such a commotion that a follow up panel discussion was necessary to assure some of the students that Dr. Rayburn was not espousing Roman Catholic priestcraft.[2]

I would argue that a "high" view of the ministry does not necessarily originate with or borrow from Roman Catholic theology. And such a view of the ministry is not inexorably tied to elitist, authoritarian forms of church government, as is often alleged. I know of Reformed seminary professors who regularly accuse men who argue for a separate office of the ministry (the so-called "three office" view of Presbyterian church government) of perpetuating the error of Diotrephes "who loves to have the preeminence" (3 Jn. 1:9). Apparently there can be no other reason to set apart the ministry as a separate office in the Church than pride and vainglory. I would like to record and explain my dissent from this popular teaching. One need not be a Romanist or a prima donna to promote a healthy view of the office of the ministry. Although it has largely disappeared from popular Presbyterian theology in America, Reformed theology itself has a surprisingly rich theological and confessional tradition that expounds and defends the distinct responsibilities and privileges of the pastor.

Bringing Balance Back

My goal here is to provide theological students, licensure and ordination candidates, as well as those who are studying to prepare for other offices within the Church of Jesus Christ, with a useful introduction to some neglected aspects of Reformed thinking on the ministry. It is not a comprehensive guide to questions about Presbyterian church government. There are other essays and books that deal with such issues. I do, however, intend to introduce the reader to a sample of biblical and theological works that discuss the office

[2] I highly recommend this lecture series (*The Joseph Ruggles Wilson Preaching Lectures*, October 16–18, 1996) which is available from Covenant Seminary Media Ministries, 12330 Conway Road, St. Louis, MO 63141 (phone: 1–800–264–8064).

of the ministry and its place in the corporate worship of the Church, a too often neglected area of Reformed ecclesiology.

Moreover, my discussion is not really very balanced at all, since I make no attempt to set out arguments for what has been called the two-office view in some Southern Presbyterian circles. Is this fair? Well, I assume that most ministerial students have been exposed to the arguments of those who advocate a two-office view. They are in the air we breathe as evangelical Presbyterians. I remember my own seminary training. In classes on church government we used Thomas Witherow, who espoused a radical two-office view in his *The Apostolic Church: Which Is It?* (Glasgow: Free Presbyterian Pub., 1983), as our plumb-line for Presbyterian church government. My use of the word "radical" is not intended as a slur, but as a reference to the fact that Witherow carries the two-office construction "to the utmost limit." He was quite consistent in the assertions he makes regarding the functional "parity" of what are now called teaching and ruling elders. Witherow, Professor of Church History at Magee College, Ireland, wrote this book in the late nineteenth century. He argued for the novel view (at the time) that the ruling elder ought to be allowed a role in ministerial ordinations, preach and teach where necessary, and dispense the Sacraments. Witherow propagated an idiosyncratic conception of the ruling elder that "took the equality theory to its eccentrically logical conclusion, arguing that the dominance of the minister in the Reformed tradition was merely an historical accident."[3]

---

[3] David Cornick, "The Reformed Elder" *Expository Times* 98 (1987): 238. The Church of Scotland had never held this view of elders; rather, the ruling elder was a lay office distinct from the ordained office of the ministry. Peter Colin Campbell wrote his *The Theory of Ruling Eldership* (1866; reprinted by Duncansville: Classic Presbyterian Government Resources, 1992) with this novel two-office view in mind. See T. F. Torrance, "Eldership in the Reformed Church," *Scottish Journal of Theology* 37 (1984):503–518 as well as the several essays in Mark Brown, ed., *Order in the Offices: Essays Defining the Roles of Church Officers* (Duncansville: Classic Presbyterian Government Resources, 1993) that examine the biblical and historical warrant for, and nature of, the office of ruling elder.

The Presbyterian Church in America (PCA), however, is not radically two-office, but rather combines elements of the older three-office theology with the "two-office" theory championed in the mid-nineteenth century by many (but not all!) Southern Presbyterian churchman. The resulting PCA form of government is much more eclectic than one might think.[4]

What I want to do is bring some balance to the discussion, and in so doing to prod the student to think about these issues more thoroughly by laying out the outlines of some of the earliest, and I believe, the best Reformed thinking on the nature of the pastoral ministry, especially its distinctive functions as a separate "office" within the body of Christ organized as a liturgical, governmental, and diaconal body in the world. I believe that ordained Christian ministers have distinct duties and therefore the ministry ought to be conceived of as a separate office from that of the "Ruling Elder" and "Deacon." This has sometimes been called a "three-office (or four-)" view of Presbyterian government—that is, minister, (doctor,) Ruling Elder, and Deacon. I will focus on books and articles that defend and explain the distinctive nature of the ministerial order, especially as it relates to the pastor's service in the corporate worship of the Church.

The Church in the Old Testament

A fundamental mistake made by so many that write on this subject involves restricting one's biblical study to the New Testament. One of the questions I often ask prospective ministers during their oral ordination examination before Presbytery is: Where are (ruling) elders first mentioned/ordained in the Bible? Where would you go to find the first examples of the office of the ministry? It is disappointing to hear most candidates answer with

---

[4] Calvin Beisner's little paper, "Evidences of an Implicit Three-Office View in the Book of Church Order of the Presbyterian Church in America" (http://capo.org/premise/98/oct/p981014.html) makes a very compelling case for this.

some reference from the New Testament. Our Reformed forefathers did not begin with the New Testament in their investigation into the biblical foundations for ecclesiastical government.

I agree with Rob Rayburn's lament: "The relationship between the polities of the Israelite and apostolic churches needs more careful delineation. Indeed, a full biblical-theological study of church polity remains to be written and is most assuredly a desideratum that is likely to throw light on a variety of vexing questions of principle and practice."[5] Even if our current understanding of the relationship between the ecclesiastical government of the Old and the New eras may not be as sophisticated as we might like, nevertheless, classical Reformed ecclesiology has affirmed that the organization of the New Covenant church was founded upon the model of the Old Testament ecclesiastical government. This is nowhere more evident than in the Westminster Assembly's *Form of Presbyterial Church-Government* (1645), a document that seems to have very little influence on modern Reformed students' conception of the ministerial office. Technically speaking, this document outlines a four-office view—pastors, teachers, other church governors (commonly called elders), and deacons.

The Westminster Assembly's *Form of Presbyterial Church-Government* provides separate discussions for each of the four offices.[6] Under the heading *Pastors*, the Westminster divines wrote:

> The pastor is an ordinary and perpetual officer in the church, prophesying of the time of the gospel. First, it belongs to his office, To pray for and with his flock, as the mouth of the people unto God, Acts 6:2–4, and 20:36, where preaching and prayer are joined as several parts of the same office. The office of the elder (that is, the pastor) is to pray for the sick, even in

---

[5] Robert S. Rayburn, "Ministers, Elders, and Deacons," in *Order in the Offices: Essays Defining the Roles of Church Officers*, ed. by Mark R. Brown (Duncansville: Classic Presbyterian Government Resources, 1993), 219–233.

[6] *The Form of Presbyterial Church-Government* (1645), 395–416 in the Free Presbyterian Publications edition (1981) of the Westminster standards.

private, to which a blessing is especially promised; much more therefore ought he to perform this in the public execution of his office as part thereof.

To read the Scriptures publicly; for the proof of which,

1. That the priests and Levites in the Jewish church were trusted with the public reading of the word is proved.

2. That the ministers of the gospel have as ample a charge and commission to dispense the word, as well as other ordinances, as the priest and Levites had under the law, proved, Isaiah 66:21, and Matthew 23:34, where our Savior entitled the officers of the New Testament, whom he will send forth, by the same names of the teachers of the Old.

Which provisions prove, that therefore (the duty of being of a moral nature) it follows by just consequence, that the public reading of the scriptures belongs to the pastor's office.

To feed the flock, by preaching of the word, according to which he is to teach, convince, reprove, exhort, and comfort.

To catechize, which is a plain laying down the first principles of the oracles of God, or of the doctrine of Christ, and is a part of preaching.

To dispense the divine mysteries (1 Cor. 4:1).

To administer the sacraments.

To bless the people from God, Numbers 6:23–26. Compared with Revelation 14:5 (where the same blessings, and persons from whom they come, are expressly mentioned,) Isaiah 66:21, where, under the names of Priests and Levites to be continued under the gospel, are meant evangelical pastors, who therefore are by office to bless the people.

To take care of the poor.

And he also has a ruling power over the flock as a pastor.

After a section on the "Teacher or Doctor" (what we might call today a seminary "professor") the FPCG includes a paragraph entitled "Other Church Governors," explaining the office of (what we would today call) ruling elder:

As there were in the Jewish church elders of the people joined with the priests and Levites in the government of the church; so Christ, who has instituted government, and governors in the church, has furnished some in his church, beside the ministers of the word, with gifts for government, and with commission to execute the same when called thereunto, who are to join with the minister in the government of the church. Which officers Reformed churches commonly call Elders.

The Westminster divines cite Romans 12:7–8 and 1 Corinthians 12:28 as evidence of a service among God's people for those who have gifts of "ruling" and "governing." It is instructive to note that passages such as 1 Timothy 3 and Titus 1 are not cited in this section, but rather are understood to be describing the qualifications for the ministry, and therefore, are cited under the previous section. That the ministers and elders work together ruling the Church is established by a reference to 2 Chronicles 19:8–10 as proof that in the Old Covenant church elders of the people were joined with the priests and Levites to adjudicate disputes within the community:

> Moreover in Jerusalem, for the judgment of Yahweh and for controversies, Jehoshaphat appointed some of the Levites and priests, and some of the chief fathers of Israel, when they returned to Jerusalem. And he commanded them, saying, "Thus you shall act in the fear of Yahweh, faithfully and with a loyal heart: Whatever case comes to you from your brethren who dwell in their cities, whether of bloodshed or offenses against law or commandment, against statutes or ordinances, you shall warn them, lest they trespass against Yahweh and wrath come upon you and your brethren. Do this, and you will not be guilty." (2 Chr. 19:8–10)

Passages like this, both in the Old and New Testaments, give rise to the Presbyterian tradition of the "parity" of ruling elder and minister. Historically, this has not meant that the two offices are leveled out and smudged together, but that when the two orders of church officers meet together for common cause in an assembly for administrative and judicial purposes they have equal rights and privileges. But this is taking us too far a field. My point is that the Westminster Assembly understood the offices and functions of ministers and ruling elders to be distinct. But our primary concern here is with the place of the minister in our Lord's Day worship.

Liturgical Leadership in the Lord's Service

What role does the minister play in the service? What role ought he to play? Can anyone in the congregation take his place? Is it okay for a laymen or ruling elder to stand in for the minister in extraordinary situations? Let's start with the last two questions. First, most Protestants, since we deny that something "ontological" happens at ordination, will acknowledge the appropriateness of lay leadership in the worship service and even at the Lord's Table in special or "emergency" situations. If the Lord's Supper is to be more than an occasional experience in a church that does not have a regular minister, then some man in the church, preferably an officer, will have to be temporarily authorized to preside at the Communion Table. Surely it is better to have one of the church's own men preside than to make the congregation wait once a month or once a quarter for Communion, only to have a strange man come in from another city or town to administer the Sacrament. This kind of setup might even encourage mistaken notions about the ontological status of ministers (i.e., that they possess some special "stuff" that the laymen does not).

That leads to a second point: the ministry is a matter of order and ritual symbolism, not of ontology. Ordination is a role, something a man does, not merely a status or "profession." It gives him the authority to *say* and *do* things in the Lord's Name. Otherwise stated, the minister has an instrumental, ritual-symbolic function in the church service. He represents the Husband to the Bride. He acts for Jesus. He speaks for Jesus. He is authorized so to act and speak. And everybody should know it. This is key. The minister is set apart to function in this capacity for the congregation. The congregation should be assured that when their minister reads, pronounces, preaches, prays, breaks, distributes, and blesses he does so speaking and acting for the Lord Himself. The congregation should have no doubts, rather they should believe that what they receive from their minister they receive from the Lord Himself.

This is why we have ministers preside and lead the service: to give God's people the assurance they need that the call to worship, the forgiveness of sins, the sermon, the bread and the wine, and the benediction are given to them by the Lord Himself. It is the Lord who serves them through His appointed servants of the Word and Sacrament. If we were to parade different men before the congregation to do these things each week, each offering his own idiosyncratic prayers or perspectives on the service of the Word and the administration of the Sacraments, we would inevitably disorient people. It would introduce uncertainty, doubt, and confusion.

This is precisely why a woman is prohibited from serving as a pastor. She cannot represent the Husband to the Bride. It is simply impossible. Period. Riesenfeld explains:

> Inasmuch as the man, as a householder, reflects Christ in His relations to the Church-Bride and to the congregation-household, it must have seemed self-evident to the early Christian mind that the officer presiding over the assembled congregation, and therefore at the Eucharist, should be a male. Even without this, ministerial duties as outlined in the New Testament could to a great extent be called masculine, particularly as regards authoritative governing and judicial functions. These, after all, are where the ministers act on Christ's behalf, and it is in full conformity with the idea of representation that the officers who founded churches and led congregations were men. Thus it is no mere chance that we find in the New Testament unanimous pronouncements as to the different functions of the two sexes and can establish that the ministers of the Church were invariably men, namely, the apostles sent forth with full authority by Christ, the missionaries who founded churches, and the heads of the local congregations. It is unlikely that the absence of female ministers should be due to any consideration paid by Christ and the early Church to the socially inferior position of the woman at that time. For one thing, there were priestesses in a number of Hellenistic cults; for another, Christianity was from the start no stranger to radical reassessments, in eluding those of a social nature, and not least as regards women's status in marriage and their equal worth as human beings.[7]

This is why the pastor who leads worship must be an ordained *man*. By virtue of his office, he must represent the Husband to the Bride. A woman cannot do so. It would upset the entire fabric of

---

[7] Harald Riesenfeld, "The Ministry in the New Testament" in *Root of the Vine: Essays in Biblical Theology* (New York: Philosophical Library, 1953),126–127.

God-ordained role relationships within the Church and home. The symbolism of male headship must be maintained in the corporate liturgy of the Church. The Church submits to her Lord as she receivers from Him the Word and Sacraments by the mouth and hands of the pastor. The pattern of male headship is rooted deeply in the created order (Gen. 2:15–24; 3:15–19; 1 Tim. 2:11–15; 1 Pet. 3:1–7) as well as in the recreated order of the Church (1 Cor. 11:3–16; 14:33–35; Eph. 5:22–33). These role relationships are nonnegotiable.[8] It is about theology not cultural imperialism. C. S. Lewis once said,

> I am crushingly aware how inadequate most of us are, in our actual and historical individualities, to fill the place prepared for us. But it is an old saying in the army that you salute the uniform not the wearer. Only one wearing the masculine uniform can (provisionally, and till the *Parousia*) represent the Lord to the Church: for we are all, corporately and individually, feminine to Him. We men make very bad priests. This is because we are insufficiently masculine. It is no cure to call in those who are not masculine at all. A given man may make a very bad husband; you cannot mend matters by trying to reverse the rolls. He may make a bad male partner in a dance. The cure for that is that men should more diligently attend dancing classes; not that the ballroom should henceforth ignore distinctions of sex and treat all dancers as neuter.[9]

This is also why ministers normally baptize babies. Not because they must do so in order for the Sacrament to be "valid," but because it is very beneficial for the Church. It is good order. It communicates the proper relation between Jesus, the Husband, and His

---

[8] See George W. Knight, *The Role Relationships of Men and Women* (Chicago: Moody Press, 1985); John Piper and Wayne Gruden, eds., *Recovering Biblical Manhood and Womanhood: A Response to Evangelical Feminism* (Wheaton: Crossway Books, 1991); Eric L. Johnson, "Playing Games and Living Metaphors: The Incarnation and the End of Gender," *Journal of the Evangelical Theological Society* 40 (June 1997):271–285; and Vern Sheridan Poythress, "Gender in Bible Translation: Exploring a Connection with Male Representatives," *Westminster Theological Journal* 60 (Fall 1998):225–53.

[9] C. S. Lewis, "Priestesses in the Church?" in *God in the Dock: Essays on Theology and Ethics* (Grand Rapids: Wm. B. Eerdmans, 1970),238–39.

Bride, the Church. The people are to think: this is the man who has been authorized by the Church (and Jesus) to perform these functions in Jesus' Name. We can be assured (as far as is humanly possible) that the child has been baptized not by Jeff Meyers, but by the Lord Himself working through the ministry that has been established precisely for this purpose. Robert S. Rayburn presses this point in his excellent lecture "Worship From the Whole Bible." Speaking of the need for the minister to baptize, Rayburn says:

> Christ will act in the body of His people through those who have been appointed to speak and act on His behalf. The reasons why no one else baptizes someone in our churches but the minister is so that it be absolutely clear that Baptism is not our act. It is Christ's act. This is the way I try to help people understand in my congregation what Baptism is and what actually happens in that moment. Suppose we were to have an infant Baptism here next Lord's Day; and suppose on this moment alone of all the moments in the history of the Church since the ascension of the Lord Jesus Christ this was a sacrament by sight and not by faith: Just as the minister was prepared to begin, with a loud, tearing sound the roof of the building parted; and lo and behold, the Lord Christ Himself descended to where I am standing right now. There were seraphim hovering above His shoulder. We were all on our faces before the glory of God, but He told us to arise. He took the baby in His arms and He pronounced the Divine Triune Name over the child and made the promise of His Gospel and covenant to this child by name and then by name summoned him or her to the life of faith and godliness and consecration. He then spoke a word to this child's parents about the sacred stewardship He was now entrusting to them and how they would answer to Him for this child's faith and this child's life on the Great Day. Then He spoke a word to this congregation about your responsibility and then a word to the minister about his. Then He blessed the child and poured water on its head and ascended back into Heaven and with a loud crash the ceiling came back to where it was before and everything was as it was.

> Let me tell you a few things that would be inevitably true. One is that that child, though he or she would be too young to have any personal recollection of that moment, would remember his Baptism forever and better than he would remember any other event in his life because scarcely a day would pass without his parents telling him what happened in the church when

he was three weeks old and what the Lord Christ said and demanded and promised. He would live as he grew up—at 3, at 4, at 6, at 8, at 12, at 18, at 26—he would live under the specter and under the mercy, the glory of Baptism. His whole life would be colored and shaped and formed by it. That's what Baptism is. That's exactly what happens in the Baptism of a child or adult when it happens in this church. The only difference is that it is by faith that you see it and not by sight. But how is it that the Lord embodies that truth and reminds us that it is so, that He is the actor in this drama? By insisting that no one has a right to perform this act except those He has set apart precisely to act on His behalf in the Church.[10]

Royal and Servant Priests

The fact that the Church as a whole is a priesthood (1 Pet. 2:5, 9) is not exactly the same thing as saying that each and every believer is his own priest, which is often what the "priesthood of all believers" is mistakenly thought to denote. Lesslie Newbigin is right about this:

> The difference between the priesthood of the one who is authorized to preside at the Eucharist and the priesthood in which all share through their incorporation into the body of Christ is not an ontological one but a relational one, not the difference between two different kinds of priesthood, but a difference of role within the ordering of the body . . . . The primary priesthood is that of Christ Himself. Into this priesthood all the baptized are incorporated by their baptism and are called to exercise it in the power of the Holy Spirit. This priesthood is exercised by the baptized in the course of their daily life in the world. The one who is described as 'a minister' is part of this same priesthood and is called to a special responsibility to cherish, nourish, and enable the priesthood of the whole body.[11]

---

[10] Robert Rayburn, "Worship from the Whole Bible," *The Second Annual Conference on Worship: The Theology and Music of Reformed Worship*, February 23–25, 1996 (Nashville: Covenant Presbyterian Church, 1996),20–21.

[11] Lesslie Newbigin,"Lay Presidency at the Eucharist," *Theology* 99 (Sept/Oct 1996): 366–370.

T. F. Torrance explains the relationship between the royal priesthood (the congregation) and the servant priesthood (the Ministry):

> In the Old Testament Church there was a twofold priesthood, the priest-
> hood of the whole body through initiation by circumcision into the royal
> priesthood, although that priesthood actually functioned through the
> firstborn. Within that royal priesthood there was given to Israel an institu-
> tional priesthood in the tribe of Levi, and within that tribe, the house of
> Aaron. The purpose of the institutional priesthood was to serve the royal
> priesthood, and the purpose of the royal priesthood, that is of Israel as a
> kingdom of priests, was to serve God's saving purpose for all nations. So with
> the Christian Church. The real priesthood is that of the whole Body, but
> within that Body there takes place a membering of the corporate priest-
> hood, for the edification of the whole Body, to serve the whole Body, in
> order that the whole Body as Christ's own Body may fulfill His ministry
> of reconciliation by proclaiming the Gospel among the nations. Within the
> corporate priesthood of the whole Body, then, there is a particular priest-
> hood set apart to minister to the edification of the Body until the Body
> reaches the fullness of Christ (Eph. 4:13). Thus in the time of the ascen-
> sion, in the eschatological reserve between the beginning of the Christian
> Church at Pentecost and what the Apocalypse calls "the Marriage-Supper
> of the Lamb" (Rev. 19:9; cf. 20:1f; 22:17), the Church is served by a
> ministry in Word and Sacrament. This ministry is as essential to the Church
> as Bible and sacramental ordinances, but like them, this order of the
> ministry will pass away at the *parousia,* when the real priesthood of the one
> Body, as distinct from the institutional priesthood, will be fully revealed.[12]

I don't have any problem at all with the fact that all the people
of God perform a general "ministry" or "service" to each other and
to the world. I simply go back to Paul's statement in
1 Corinthians11:1, "Follow my example, as I follow the example
of Christ." You can find the same kinds of exhortations all through
the NT (see the last half of Philippians 2, for example). The ministers may be the chief public servants of the flock, but they are there
to model the way that all believers should act. All the members of

---

[12] T. F. Torrance, *Royal Priesthood: A Theology of Ordained Ministry* (Scottish Journal of
Theology; Edinburgh: Oliver & Boyd, 1955), 81.

the Church don't preach, read the Scriptures publicly, lead the people in worship, preside at the Table, etc., but they all do have some priestly ministry to each other and the world to perform. Jesus is *the* Minister and Pastor. Jesus appoints pastors in His Church to minister under Him and in His Name. Moreover, all the people learning from Christ through their ministers also serve each other and the world.

There was a controversy among Lutherans in the nineteenth century that relates to this. Wilhelm Löhe taught that only the minister could declare forgiveness effectually. In the mouth of a laymen any absolving words he/she may speak to another "have only the force of consolation," not forgiveness itself. What the Lutheran Church Missouri Synod said was, no, God may and does mediate His forgiveness through the words of any of His saints. We cannot restrict the comfort of absolution to the minister. The minister's words on Sunday morning declaring the forgiveness of sins are not of an entirely different order, even if they do come with more authority and power than from a layman. Some people's faith can be restored by the words of a faithful layman, while others need more assurance, and so they rightly approach their minister for comforting words. After all, the minister has been ordained, set apart to speak for Christ to the people. So what we have is not an either/or, but a both/and answer to questions about who does ministry/service in the church, specifically the question: Through whom does God communicate the forgiveness of sins? I do, however, oppose those who would argue that the minister does not have a distinct "ministry" among God's people. I believe Ephesians 4:12 says just this. There the pastor is given to the Church to "do the work of the ministry." (For more on this, see the last section of this chapter.)

I Believe in the Holy Catholic Church

The nature of the Lord's Day service and specifically the Lord's Supper itself must be considered as well. Why is it important that the man who presides be an ordained minister? Remember that participation in the worship, especially as it is enacted at the Communion Table, is a participation in the "body of Christ." I understand this to refer not only to the local body, but also in some significant sense to the *totus Christus* (Christ, the Head + His Body, the Church). What is being done in the service and at the Table is more than a local expression of unity and more than a local participation in the local manifestation of the body of Christ. Any other conception will result in the gathering being a faction, a sect, rather than a communion of and with the Lord and His holy catholic Church. So, a proper Lord's Day service and Communion meal is one that manifests the "universalness" of the body of Christ and avoids anything that smacks of sectarianism. That being the case, I believe that it is important for a duly ordained minister to preside. Why? Because he is one who has been committed to this office not just by the local congregation but with the consent and participation of the elders and ministers representing the wider Church of Christ in the region; and, more than that, representing and acting for Christ's Church as a whole.

If ministers are not to preside and act at congregational worship and at Baptism and the Lord's Table, then what are they ordained to do? What is ordination, anyway? We believe that it is authorization to say and do what the Lord gives the minister to say and do. Without ordination no man in the church is authorized to speak and act with authority before the people of God. No man dare speak *for* the Lord in any kind of official capacity unless he is duly called and authorized by ordination. If we are not authorizing a man to do and say what he would not otherwise be authorized to do and say, then what in the world are we doing in ordination? Is it just a status thing? Admission to a certain kind of clerical professional status? Does it communicate something ontological? We should drop ordination altogether if the minister is a not called to do and say something distinctive and authoritative in the organized body of Christ, especially as the Church is assembled for corporate worship. David Cornick's article "The Reformed Elder" provides a compact summary of the development of the Reformed understanding of the lay elder. In that article he comments on the Reformed understanding of the role of the minister in the sixteenth century:

> Ministers . . . are called by God and accepted and authorized by the church, they are the means through which Christ becomes present to his people in the preaching of the Word and the administration of the Sacraments. The priesthood of all believers did not mean for the reformers what it has sometimes meant in the churches of the Reformation, an otiose Ministry and an omnicompetent laity.[13]

Bibliographical Balance

Standard bibliographies used in Reformed seminaries are typically weighted toward the two-office view, and sometimes they may not even cite any books or articles that may alert the student of another option. Here are some books and articles that will bring some balance to discussion. First, find and read Harald Riesenfeld's "The ministry in the New Testament," in *Root of the Vine: Essays in Biblical Theology* (New York: Philosophical Library, 1953).[14] This is a wonderful article that carefully and convincingly establishes the foundation of the Ministry in the New Testament as an extension of the work of Jesus for His people. I would suggest that there is more biblical theological argumentation on the origin and task of the ministry in Riesenfeld's essay than you would normally get in seminary.

John Murray was "impressed" by Riesenfeld's essay and noted that there was much of great value in it. "Riesenfeld's essay is one that challenges to careful study of the implications of the official ministry, as now exercised in the church, of those passages in which Jesus institutes a comparison between His own mission by the Father and the mission upon which He Himself sent the disciples

---

[13] David Cornick, "The Reformed Elder," The *Expository Times* 98 (May 1987):235–240.

[14] The entire article is available online at http://www.hornes.org/theologia.

as His envoys."[15] I too am particularly astonished at the way the New Testament describes the ministry (of ordained men like Paul, Apollos, Timothy, Ephradotus.) as an extension of the work of Christ. The names, titles, and descriptions of Jesus are the same ones used to describe the apostles and ministers in the New Testament (shepherd, servant, sower, gardener, architect, householder, fisher, bridegroom, rock, steward, teacher, head, husbandman, etc.). What Jesus does, they continue to do.[16] That's amazing! That's where a theology of the ministry must begin.

I was led to Riesenfeld's exposition by a footnote in William Weinrich's excellent article "Called and Ordained: Reflections on the New Testament View of the Office of the Ministry" in *Logia* 2/1 (Epiphany/January 1993): 20–27. This entire issue of the Lutheran theological journal *Logia* is dedicated to expounding the Lutheran understanding of "The Holy Ministry" and is well worth pursuing. I believe that the Reformed student can learn a great deal from a careful study of a Lutheran understanding of the biblical nature of the ministry. It may not be what you've been led to think. Having completed many years of graduate work at Concordia Seminary in St. Louis (Lutheran Church Missouri Synod), I have been pleasantly shocked to learn that the typical Reformed portrayal of Lutheranism, particularly of the Lutheran conception of the ministry, is something of a caricature. You might also consult the relevant chapters in a standard Lutheran systematic textbook, like Mueller's *Christian Dogmatics* (St. Louis: Concordia Publishing House, 1955). For a more detailed investigation that includes some

---

[15] John Murray, *The Collected Writings of John Murray*, volume 4 (Edinburgh: Banner of Truth Trust, 1982), 287.

[16] Riesenfeld concludes: "Our aim has been to show how the Ministry is part of the structure of the Church in the same way as the Messiah is indivisibly united to the structure of the People of God. With the help of those who speak and act in His name, Christ, as the Glorified Lord continues in His Church the work among mankind which He performed in word and deed during his life on earth. Though invisible, He thus still works in a visible and personal way through the Ministry which represents Him and through His power, brings the gifts of salvation within the reach of mankind" (p. 127).

very useful biblical exposition, see Kurt E. Marquart's *The Church and Her Fellowship, Ministry, and Governance*, vol. IX of *Confessional Lutheran Dogmatics*, ed. Robert D. Preus (Ft. Wayne: International Foundation for Lutheran Confessional Research, 1990); C. F. W. Walther, *Church and Ministry*, trans. by J. T. Mueller (St. Louis, MO: Concordia Publishing House, 1987 [1875]); and George A Lindbeck, "The Lutheran Doctrine of the Ministry: Catholic and Reformed," *Theological Studies* 30 (Dec. 1969): 588–612.

Every ministerial student ought to carefully study the issues surrounding the every-member-is-a-minister movement in the modern church. I would argue that the New Testament evidence indicates that there is some warrant for translating the Greek word *diakonos* sometimes as "deacon" and sometimes as "servant" and sometimes even as "minister." It may not be a "technical term" for "a professional clergyman," but the word group does seem to be used sometimes for a rather distinctive office/function fulfilled by some men and not others. Our English word "ministry" is of course the Greek *diakonia* by way of the Latin *ministerium*. But St. Paul repeatedly uses simply "minister" and "ministry" (Acts 20:24; 21:19; Rom. 11:13; 1 Cor. 3:5; 2 Cor. 4:1; 6:3–4; 11:23; Eph. 6:21; Col. 1:7; 4:7, 17; 1 Thes. 3:2; 1 Tim. 1:12; 4:6; 2 Tim. 4:5, 11) for what is elsewhere described more fully as *the* ministry or ministers "of the Word" (Acts 6:4), "the Spirit" (2 Cor. 3:8), "righteousness" (2 Cor. 3:9), "reconciliation" (2 Cor. 5:18), "the new covenant" (2 Cor. 3:6), "the Gospel" (Eph. 3:7; Col. 1:23), and "the Church" (Col. 1:25). There is one "ministry" in the New Testament Church.

The every-Christian-is-a-minister debate centers on the proper exegesis of Ephesians 4:12. Does Paul say that the Christ gave pastors "to equip the saints for the work of the ministry," as so many popular preachers suggest? Or does Paul say that some men are given to the Church as gifts of the risen Christ "for perfecting the saints, for the work of the ministry [*ergon diakonias*]?" The popular translation and interpretation has the saints doing the "work of the ministry," the traditional reading assigns this role to the pastor. Who does "the work of the ministry?" The people or the pastor?

The wording of Ephesians 4:11–12 suggests not informal arrangements, but an actual office/function that some men have been given to perform—"a good work," as Paul puts it to Timothy in 1 Timothy 3:1. Some of the references already cited touch upon this issue. Other articles that defend the traditional understanding of Ephesians 4:12 include, Mark E. Dever, "The Priesthood of All Believers: Reconsidering Every-Member Ministry" in *The Compromised Church: The Present Evangelical Crisis*, ed. by John H. Armstrong (Wheaton: Crossway books, 1998) 85–116; T. David Gordon, "Equipping Ministry in Ephesians 4?" *Journal of Evangelical Theological Society* 37 (March 1994): 69–78; Henry Hamann, "The Translation of Ephesians 4:12—A Necessary Revision," *Concordia Theological Journal* 14 (January 1988): 42–49; Andrew L. Lincoln, *Ephesians*, in vol. 42 of *Word Biblical Commentary* (Dallas: Word Books, 1990) 253–254; J. A. O. Preus, "The Holy Ministry and the Holy Priesthood: The Gospel Office and the Office of the Gospel," *Concordia Theological Journal* (1998): 36–42; David Scaer, "The Office of the Pastor and the Problem of Ordination of Women Pastors," *The Springfielder* 38 (Sept. 1974): 126–129; Herman A. Preus, "Luther on the Universal Priesthood and the Office of the Ministry, "*Concordia Theological Journal* 5 (March 1979): 55–62.

The essays in *Order in the Offices: Essays Defining the Roles of Church Officers*, ed. Mark R. Brown (Duncansville: Classic Presbyterian Government Resources, 1993) offer a Reformed perspective on the distinctive office of the ministry. You might begin with Robert S. Rayburn's essay "Ministers, Elders, and Deacons," which persuasively defends the classical three-office understanding of Presbyterian church government (see the Westminster Assembly's *The Form of Presbyterial Church-Government* [1645],395–416 in Free Presbyterian Publications edition [1981] of the Westminster standards). Charles G. Dennison's article

"Worship and Office" in *Order in the Offices* argues that the pastor has been ordained not just to preach but to lead God's people in worship. Dennison writes a fuller defense of the place of the minister in the worship service in "Report of the Committee on the Involvement of Unordained Persons in Worship Services," *Minutes of the Fifty-eighth General Assembly of the Orthodox Presbyterian Church* (1991),264–328.

Other helpful theological explanations of the ordained ministry include the following: Harry G. Goodykoontz, *The Minister in the Reformed Tradition* (Richmond: John Knox Press, 1963); J. K. S. Reid, *The Biblical Doctrine of the Ministry* (Scottish Journal of Theology Occasional Papers; Edinburgh: Oliver & Boyd, 1955); Elsie Anne McKee, *Elders and the Plural Ministry* (Geneva: Librairie Droz, 1988); Max Thurian, *Priesthood and Ministry* (London: Mowbray, 1983); T. F. Torrance, "Eldership in the Reformed Church," *Scottish Journal of Theology* 37 (1984):503–519; T. F. Torrance, *Royal Priesthood: A Theology of Ordained Ministry* (Scottish Journal of Theology; Edinburgh: Oliver & Boyd, 1955); T. F. Torrance, *The Eldership in the Reformed Church* (Edinburgh: Handsel Press, 1984); Geoffrey Thomas, "The Pastoral Ministry" in *Practical Theology and the Ministry of the Church, 1952–1984: Essays in Honor of Edmund Clowney*, ed. Harvey H. Conn (Phillipsburg: Presbyterian and Reformed, 1991); James L. Ainslie, *The Doctrine of Ministerial Order in the Reformed Churches of the 16th and 17th Centuries* (Edinburgh: T&T Clark, 1940); John B. Adger, "The First and Highest Office in the Church," *Southern Presbyterian Review* 22 (Oct. 1871); and Charles Hodge, *Discussions in Church Polity* (New York: Charles Scribner's Sons, 1878). Some of the works cited in this paragraph concern the controversy in the nineteenth century over the introduction of what many Presbyterian churchman considered a novel "two-office" theory of eldership in the Church. The works listed above, especially Brown's *Order in the Offices*, will be helpful in researching that debate.

15
On Hearing God's Voice
Extra Nos

Faith comes from hearing.
—Romans 10:17a

One does not need to read very far into Emily Dickenson's poetry to discover that her verse often captures the quintessential American religious consciousness. Consider these lines from three of Emily Dickenson's poems:

Some keep the Sabbath, going to church
I keep it, staying at home.

Of course—I prayed—
And did God care?

At least—to pray—is left—is left—
O Jesus—in the air—
I know not which thy chamber is
I'm knocking everywhere—
Thou settest Earthquake in the South—
And Maelstrom in the sea—

Say, Jesus Christ of Nazareth—
Hast thou no Arm for me?[1]

Poor Emily. She doesn't know where to go, where to find Jesus, where to find Jesus' "arm for her." "O Jesus—in the air—I know not which thy chamber is." Knocking everywhere, but nowhere in particular, Dickinson makes the shocking discovery that grace is nowhere to be found. She has no assurance that Jesus is *for her* because she doesn't know *where* He is. God's power is manifested everywhere. But how does knowledge of God's omnipotence and exhaustive control help? How can she know He loves and cares for her? The sovereign Lord is in the air and in the sea, but where is He for me?

I saw a placard on a church last year that asked passersby, "Looking for Jesus?" The answer was provided below in bold letters. "YOU WILL FIND HIM IN YOUR HEART." What does that mean? I thought. What do unbelievers think when they read that advice? Where in the Bible does it say that we should look for Jesus in our hearts or that we should turn *inward* to try to find Him? We find precisely the opposite. Jesus came down from heaven and took on our flesh (Jn. 1:14). And the true God, the God for us, is found when we learn to "come to" and "listen to" Jesus. But what does that mean for us today? While He was on earth people could literally come to Him. But now, since He has bodily ascended, where is He? Where is He to be found? How do we "come" to Jesus today? Where do we hear His voice? Did He come in the flesh and then leave this world only to leave us to our own mental or emotional inner resources?

No! Our Lord loves us so much, that He ordains that He can be found. He can still be heard. But where? Where are His hands and feet? Where is His voice heard today? Where can we find Him now that His physical body has been removed from us? He has bodily

[1] Thomas H. Johnson, ed., *The Complete Poems of Emily Dickenson* (Boston: Little, Brown, 1960), poem #324, 153–54; poem #376, 179–80; poem #502, 243–44.

ascended to heaven, to be sure, but is that all that the Bible has to say about the "body of Christ"? That it is now located in heaven? The New Testament says that the Church is the body of Christ. Jesus promised that "when two are three are gathered, there I am" (Mt. 18:20). Jesus sent the apostles to continue the mission the Father sent Him on, breathing on them so that they would possess the same Holy Spirit (Jn. 20:19–23). And, of course, Paul clearly states that the Church is the "body of Christ" (1 Cor. 12:12–14, 27). When Paul persecuted members of the Church Jesus complained to Paul, "Why are you persecuting *me*" (Acts 9:4–5).

The problem in American Christianity is that the possibility and enjoyment of a relationship with Christ has been severed from His Body, the Church, and from the ministry and sacraments of the Church. When this happens the Christian faith becomes unspecified, generalized, and abstract. Grace cannot be found here or there, or anywhere. Jesus in the air = Jesus nowhere.

Christians have an answer for Emily's dilemma. At least one-third of Calvin's *Institutes* (Book IV) is devoted to the doctrine of the Church. The doctrine of God, man, Christ, and salvation all culminate in the mystical Body of which Christ is the Head. This "high" ecclesiastical theology can be found in all of the sixteenth-century Reformers and especially in early sixteenth-century Reformed theology.[2] It is in this community of flesh and blood saints, oral speech, material rituals, and physical sacraments that God meets with us and does such wonderful things. Luther says, "The Holy Christian Church is the principal work of God, for the sake of which all things were made. In the Church, great wonders daily occur, such as the forgiveness of sins, triumph over death . . . the gift of righteousness and eternal life." [3]

[2] See the wonderful exposition of this in Geddes MacGreggor, *Corpus Christi: The Nature of the Church According to the Reformed Tradition* (Philadelphia: The Westminster Press, 1958), and also Paul D. L. Avis, *The Church in the Theology of the Reformers* (Atlanta: John Knox, 1981).

[3] Quoted in Paul Lehmann, *Ethics in a Christian Context* (New York: Harper & Row, 1975):63–64.

Luther makes it clear that it is in the community of saints gathered to hear the Word that God speaks to us:

> Some have held that God ought to deal with the individual and confer the Holy Spirit upon him by means of a special light and a secret revelation in the heart, as though the printed Word, Scripture, and the spoken Word are not needed. Therefore we should know that God has ordained that no one is to come to a knowledge of Christ . . . without external and general means. God has deposited this treasure in the spoken Word of the Ministry and does not intend to confer it privately or secretly in the heart.[4]

If this sounds odd or simply wrong to us, it is because we have been infected with a Gnostic spirituality. The Spirit speaks through the Bride (Rev. 22:17). When Jesus calls on the seven churches to hear the Spirit, He wants them to listen to the voice of their pastor as he reads the letter addressed to them (Rev. 2–3). John Calvin's first section in Book IV is on "the necessity of the Church." Speaking of the very material "body of believers" on earth, Calvin says,

> . . . because it is now our intention to discuss the visible church, let us learn from the simple title "mother" how useful, indeed how necessary, it is that we should know her. For there is no other way to enter into life unless this mother conceive us in her womb, give us birth, nourish us at her breast, and lastly, unless she keep us under her care and guidance until, putting off mortal flesh, we become like the angels. Our weakness does not allow us to be dismissed from her school until we have been pupils all our lives. Furthermore away from her bosom one cannot hope for any forgiveness of sins or any salvation (*Inst.* 4.1.4).[5]

Luther and Calvin agree. It almost seems as if Luther writes in response to Emily Dickenson's dilemma when he warns:

---

[4] Martin Luther, "Sermon Delivered at Marburg, October 5, 1529," in *What Luther Says: A Practical In-Home Anthology for the Active Christian*, ed. Ewald M. Plass (St. Louis: Concordia Publishing House, 1959),1466.

[5] John Calvin, *Institutes of the Christian Religion* (1559 Edition), ed. John T. McNeil, trans. Ford Lewis Battles, vols. 20–21 of *Library of Christian Classics* (Philadelphia: Westminster Press, 1960),1016.

Therefore, he who would find Christ must first of all find the Church. How would one know where Christ and his faith were, if one did not know where His believers are? And he who would know something of Christ, must not trust himself, or build his own bridges into heaven through his own reason, but he must go to the church, visit and ask of the same . . . for outside of the church is no truth, no Christ, no salvation.[6]

We should note that Luther and Calvin are not talking about an invisible, "spiritual" Church but the very physical community of believers who gather to serve one another and be the means by which God serves by speaking, hearing, singing, and praying for and to each other. In some sense, the Church is the preeminent ordinary means of grace.[7]

B. B. Warfield's Blunder

God's service to us on the Lord's Day is conveyed primarily by way of the Word as it is read, sung, and preached. God's service to us is found where His voice is heard. The voice of God comes from outside of us, as an *externum verbum*. We are called to "hear" the Word of God as it is read aloud, preached, prayed, and sung in the service. This is how God himself addresses us—through the voice of another. The Protestant church in America seems to have forgotten this basic biblical fact. We have a tendency to think of the means of grace in an individualistic framework. We seek the source of renewed spiritual life in private devotions or quiet times or individual reading of the Bible. For most in our culture it's "just me, God, and the Bible." We are taught to listen for some inner voice and expect the Spirit's guidance through mystical promptings and feelings. This is not the biblical way.

[6] Quoted in R. L. Greaves, "Luther's Doctrine of Grace," *Scottish Journal of Theology* 18 (1965): 393.

[7] See Peter Leithart's "Against 'Christianity': For the Church," as well as his "Sociology of Infant Baptism;" both of which are in *Biblical Horizons: Christendom Essays*, No. 100 (Dec. 1997): 29–50 and 86–106.

This is also not the Reformation way. Luther's aphorism is correct: "The church is above all a *Mundhaus* (mouthhouse) not a *Federhaus* (penhouse)."[8] It is precisely the public "reading" and the "preaching" of the Word that become "effectual means of convincing and converting sinners" (Westminster Shorter Catechism Q. #89). As Herman Hoeksema puts it in his *Reformed Dogmatics*: "Through preaching you do not hear about Christ, but you hear *him*. The difference is easily understood. When you hear about someone, he is not present. You do not hear that person's own voice, but the voice of someone else that tells you something about him. But when you hear someone, you hear his own voice. He is present with you. He is addressing you personally."[9] The first chapter of the Second Helvetic (Swiss) Confession (1566) tells us:

> *The Preaching of the Word of God Is the Word of God.* Wherefore when this Word of God is now preached in the church by preachers lawfully called, we believe that the very Word of God is proclaimed, and received by the faithful; and that neither any other Word of God is to be invented nor is to be expected from heaven: and that now the Word itself which is preached is to be regarded, not the minister that preaches; for even if he be evil and a sinner, nevertheless the Word of God remains still true and good.[10]

Apparently, in order to safeguard the sovereignty of God's work we often think that we must remove all external means, all mediation, indeed any human or created instrumentality whatsoever and confine the work of salvation and sanctification to private, unmediated operations of the Spirit on the individual soul of man.

---

[8] *D. Martin Luthers Werke: Kritische Gesamtausgabe,* Weimarer Ausgabe, (Weimar: H. Böhlaus Nachfolger, 1883–1987), *Von den Konziliis und Kirchen,* vol. 10¹, 2,41 (*Adventspostille,* 1522).

[9] Herman Hoeksema, *Reformed Dogmatics* (Grand Rapids: Reformed Free Publishing Association, 1966),637.

[10] Arthur C. Cochrane, ed., *Reformed Confessions of the 16th Century* (Philadelphia: The Westminster Press, 1966),225.

Conservative Reformed theologians and pastors are particularly susceptible to this error because of the undue influence of B. B. Warfield's little book *The Plan of Salvation*.[11] Without producing a shred of biblical evidence Warfield asserts "precisely what evangelical religion means is *immediate* dependence of the soul on God and on God alone for salvation." [12] Any theology that "separates the soul from *direct* contact with and *immediate* dependence upon God the Holy Spirit" is labeled "sacerdotalism." Warfield's work is profoundly disturbing. He subtly manages to break free of an important emphasis in the Reformation, namely the Lutheran and Calvinian insistence that God does indeed use human instrumentalities (water, bread, wine, the human voice of another, etc.) to communicate His grace to His people. Warfield's conception of a purified Calvinism as consisting of the immediacy of the Spirit's work on the soul of man was motivated more, I fear, from his own prejudice against the sacramental systems of Rome and Canterbury than by a careful reading of Holy Scripture. Warfield argues that immediacy is the essence of the Reformed faith and biblical religion come to its own.

On the contrary, I would argue that the unbiblical notion of immediacy is the Achilles' heel of so much of post-sixteenth-century Calvinism, especially in America. Why do we feel that it is unworthy of the Holy Spirit to bind Himself to such unimpressive external means as the homely words of Scripture heralded by the gravelly voice of a flesh-and-blood preacher or the bread and wine of the Supper or the water of Baptism? Is it not often because of a false spiritualism, a kind of Gnosticism that has crept into our thinking as Christians? An alien, unbiblical notion that the Spirit must operate immediately upon the soul of a man without external means or instruments? Where is this taught in the Bible?

---

[11] B. B. Warfield, *The Plan of Salvation* (Philadelphia: Presbyterian Board of Publication, 1915).

[12] Ibid., 66 (emphasis mine).

Against Protestant Gnosticism

The real essence of biblical religion is perhaps the hardest thing for us modern spiritualistic Christians to learn again. We are so accustomed to think of body and soul, flesh and spirit, physical and spiritual as opposites that we no longer understand that the whole magnitude of God's love lies in the astonishing fact that God's Son came to us *in the flesh* and that the Holy Spirit graciously binds Himself to the material means of grace. God's grace comes from outside of us (*extra nos*). We must receive it from an external source. To deny this is to slip into a form of individualistic spiritualism. Philip Lee argues persuasively that American Protestantism in particular has, perhaps unwittingly, embraced a form of Gnostic spiritualism.[13]

A kind of spiritualistic individualism has dogged Reformed theology from the start. Zwingli, in particular, inclined toward something similar to Warfield's immediacy doctrine because of his radical opposition to Roman Catholicism. If God was to have all the glory in our salvation, then nothing could be attributed to any human rite or material instrumentality. Calvin, however, rejected Zwingli's argument against an instrumental understanding of the Church's rites and rituals. In the first edition of the *Institutes* (1536) Calvin answers Zwingli's concern (that the glory and power of God will be eclipsed if we ascribe to the sacraments even secondary causality) by affirming that the material rites do indeed function as genuine instruments or means of grace: "God uses means and instruments [*mediis ac instrumentis*] which he himself sees to be expedient, that all things may serve his glory, since he is Judge and Lord of all."[14] In this paragraph Calvin says that God "distributes his blessings to us by these instruments" and "nourishes faith spiritually through the Sacraments."

---

[13] Philip J. Lee, *Against the Protestant Gnostics* (Oxford: Oxford University Press, 1987).

[14] John Calvin, *Institutes of the Christian Religion* (1536 edition), trans. and annotated by Ford Lewis Battles (Grand Rapids: Wm. B. Eerdmans, 1986), 90.

In his 1559 edition of the *Institutes*, Calvin's final answer to Zwingli's stealing-the-glory-and-power-from-God argument is even more satisfying. He refuses to rationalize, but affirms both God's sovereignty and His use of physical, outward means to accomplish His will: "God therefore truly executes whatever he promises and represents in signs; nor do the signs lack their own effect in proving their Author truthful and faithful. The only question here is whether God acts by his own intrinsic power (as they say) or resigns his office to outward symbols. But we contend that, whatever *instruments* he uses, these detract nothing from his original activity."[15]

We must, therefore, as Reformed churches embrace the rich biblical means-of-grace theology of the Bible. One of the most harmful notions ever foisted upon Reformed Christianity is this idea that God ordinarily communicates His presence immediately to the soul of man, by-passing all outward, physical means. Let me assure you that I do glory in that most Reformed of adverbs: "ordinarily." It is part of the genius of Reformed theology that the Lord is free to work outside of His constituted means in extraordinary cases. But this only means that the Lord ordinarily works just as He has promised to communicate His grace, that is through the instrumentality of the audible words of His ministers and people, through the water of Baptism, and through the bread and wine of the Lord's Supper. There are, of course, extraordinary circumstances where we would not want to limit the power and grace of the Lord. In this we differ from our brothers, the Lutherans, who often appear to bind the Lord's grace without exception to these instruments. Nevertheless—and this is the rub—as Reformed Christians we do affirm that the Lord's ordinary, normal means of delivering His gifts is indeed *through* His constituted means and not beside them or around them or without them. This is God's normal *modus operandi*. The Lord's Spirit normally works through the human and

[15] John Calvin, *Institutes of the Christian Religion* (1559 Edition) 4.14.17, ed. John T. McNeil, 1293.

physical instrumentalities that He has ordained. Otherwise, the promises that are attached to these means are misleading and even deceptive.

Recovering a Rich Instrumental Theology of Grace

As we have seen, by affirming God's use of created means, we are being very, very Calvinian (even if Calvinism has often departed from its master). To understand the Holy Spirit's promise to use the Lord's appointed means as instruments to deliver the gifts of the kingdom is the *hallmark* of Calvin's Reformed sacramental ecclesiology.[16] Why don't we believe what God has promised? Why are we offended to think that God actually delivers on His promise in Baptism? Or in the Lord's Supper? Or in the service of the Word through the men He has given the Church in the ministry? One of my professors at Concordia says it like this: "We modern people no longer find the Holy Spirit where He is to be sought . . . we no longer understand the promised bond of the Holy Spirit with the external means of grace and perhaps do not want to even hear it anymore."[17] Calvin says something similar when he comments on John 20:23 and the commissioning of the disciples as ministers of the gospel:

> We now see the reason why Christ employs such magnificent terms, to commend and adorn that ministry which he bestows and enjoins on the Apostles. It is, that believers may be *fully convinced*, that what they hear concerning the forgiveness of sins is ratified, and may not less highly value the reconciliation which is offered by the voice of men, than if God himself stretched out his hand from heaven. And the church daily receives the most abundant benefit from this doctrine, when it perceives that her pastors are divinely ordained to be sureties for eternal salvation, and that it must not go to a distance to seek the forgiveness of sins, which is committed to their trust.[18]

[16] See my extended discussion with bibliographical references in the section of chapter 22 that deals with Calvin and the Lord's Supper.

[17] Norman Nagel, "*Externum Verbum*," *Logia* 6 (Trinity 1997): 27–32.

[18] John Calvin, *Commentary on the Gospel According to John*, vol. 2, trans. by William Pringle (Grand Rapids: Baker, 1981), 272.

The foregoing discussion has been offered in support of the rich instrumental theology of the Reformation, particularly the human voice as the very physical means by which the Spirit communicates life to those who faithfully hear it. Even if God's use of human instrumentality has typically been discussed in relation to questions about the Sacraments, nevertheless, one cannot ignore that the Reformed tradition has stressed the primacy of the Word, particularly the spoken and preached Word of God. This means that the human voice has a much more foundational place as the instrument of the Holy Spirit than water, bread, or wine. The Bible calls on us to "hear" the Word. "Faith comes by hearing" (Rom. 10:17; Gal. 3:2, 5; Heb. 4:2). Private devotional reading and study are not the most fundamental ways in which God speaks to us in His Word. According to the Scriptures, the Spirit binds Himself to communicate life by means of the human voice, especially as that voice speaks Scripture or Scripture-derived wisdom to us.

We would all agree that the Spirit's work is invisible, but is it inaudible? Not according to Scripture. And is the Spirit's work private? Not primarily. The Bible does not confine the Spirit's work to an inner, isolated work in the soul of an individual. There is something ineffaceably social about the Spirit's work. He uses words. He uses human words. Words that pass between people. Words that we speak to others. Words that are spoken to us. This is so abundantly evident in the Bible that we should not even question it. You might find it interesting to search the Scriptures to see how often the presence and work of the Spirit is associated directly with the audible voice (Gen. 3:6ff; Deut. 34:9; Job 32:18; Is. 59:21; Mic. 2:7; 3:8; Mt. 3: 16–17; Lk. 1:41–42; Jn. 3:34; 6:63; Acts 2:4; 4:8, 31; 8:26ff; 10:44; 13:52–14:1; Eph. 5:18–19; 6:17; Rev. 1:10; 2:11).

Calvin even calls the Word proclaimed in a clear voice by the minister a *verbum sacramentale* ("a sacramental word;" *Inst.* 4:14:4). In his comments on John 20:22, Calvin says, "He appoints His ministers to be *organs* of His Spirit."[19] This is just standard

---

[19] Ibid., 269.

classical Reformed teaching on the ministry. The *First Book of Discipline in the Scottish Kirk* (1560) says, "For whosoever heareth Christ's ministers, heareth himself, and whosoever despiseth their ministrie and exhortation, rejecteth and despiseth Christ Jesus."[20]

Clearly, the Spirit works through human voices that communicate the *viva vox Christi*. I won't deny that the Spirit can, and sometimes does work in individuals when they are alone with themselves; but even so, even when alone, the Spirit will use the recollection—words spoken by others in the past to convict or assure or guide this man or woman in solitude. There really is no work of the Spirit apart from the community of God's people, and the ministers are the chief ordinary instruments used by the Spirit. Even insights and emotions that we might attribute to the inner working of the Spirit can almost always be traced back to words spoken to us by others in another situation.

God ordinarily speaks to us from without, through the voice of another in the Christian community. God's service to us on the Lord's Day is conveyed primarily by way of the Word as it is read, sung, and preached. The voice of God comes from outside of us (*extra nos*), as an external word (*externum verbum*). We are called to "hear" the Word of God as it is read aloud, preached, prayed, and sung in the service. This is how God Himself addresses us—*extra nos*, through the voice of another in the community of faith. This is where Jesus can be found: wherever people are gathered to hear His Word read and preached and His Sacraments administered.

* * * * * * * * * *

A Brief Excursus on John 3

According to Jesus, everyone who is born of the Spirit becomes himself a "spirit" (Jn. 3:6) whose fundamental mode of existence as "spirit" is experienced by others as "sound," or better, "voice"

---

[20] Quoted in Harry G. Goodykootz, *The Minister in the Reformed Tradition* (Richmond: John Knox, 1963), 62.

(*phone*, Jn. 3:8). Upon hearing this, Nicodemus asks Jesus, "How can these things be?" Ironically, Jesus responds by asking Nicodemus how he can be a "teacher of Israel." A teacher is one who makes his "voice" heard by others. Jesus solemnly (with a double amen) contrasts His own "speaking" with that of this Spirit-less teacher of Israel. Jesus Himself is the one preeminently born from above (*anothen*) since He Himself has come from heaven and is therefore uniquely qualified to give authoritative Spirit-voice to "heavenly things."

This is confirmed a little later on in this same chapter when Jesus responds to a disputation about the relationship between His (and His disciples) baptismal ministry and that of John the Baptizer (Jn. 3:22–36). The Nicodemian discourse and this one are connected by a set of common terms and themes: Baptism (water), teachers and teaching, eternal life, witness (or testimony), what is received from heaven, the one who comes from above (*anothen*), the Spirit, and "speaking." Here the one who comes from above (Jesus), being above all, truthfully testifies to what He has seen and heard. Jesus, as the one sent by God (the Father, v. 35), "speaks the words of God, for God gives the Spirit without measure" (v. 34).

Apparently, then, to "believe" or "reject" the Son has to do with the way a person "hears" the "words of God" given through the Spirit's unbounded overflow made audible in the voice of Jesus. If the Spirit cannot be seen, and the direction of His movement cannot be deciphered by man, nevertheless, *He can be heard*. The audibility of the Spirit's voice is the manifestation of being born anew or from above. Jesus is the paradigmatic born-from-above man. One may not be able to investigate directly His origin and destiny (where He is coming from or where He is going), but one can hear the sound or voice of the Spirit in the from-above, heavenly teaching of Jesus; so also are all who are born of the Spirit: they become the instruments by which the Spirit's voice is heard.

16
The Regulative Principle of Worship

God is Spirit and those who bow down to
Him must bow down in Spirit and truth.
—John 4:24

Confusion about corporate worship can only be overcome when the Church begins to reflect upon the centrality of the Lord's Day assembly in Scripture. Nothing else will endure but the Church assembled around the throne of God and the Lamb (Rev. 4-5). Nothing else is regulated so closely as corporate worship (Exod. 25–40; Lev. 1–27). Nothing else can call down the wrath of God like unacceptable worship (Lev. 26:30; 2 Chr. 24:18). "Worship is the supreme and only indispensable activity of the Christian Church. It alone will endure, like the love of God that it expresses, into heaven, when all other activities of the Church will have passed away. It must therefore, even more strictly than any of these less essential doings of the Church, come under the criticism and control of the revelation on which the Church is founded."[1] Given the prominent place that worship occupies in Scripture, it is imperative that Christians understand and order their activities in God's presence according to His Word.

---

[1] W. Nicholls, *Jacob's Ladder: The Meaning of Worship* (London: Lutterworth, 1958), 9.

Reformed Presbyterians have a rule called "the regulative principle of worship" that theoretically guides them in determining how to worship. Controversy continues to swirl around the precise meaning and application of this principle, but I am convinced that the regulative principle of worship simply means that the content and ritual of our Lord's Day corporate worship must be informed and regulated by the Word of God. Nothing should be added to the Church's worship without biblical warrant. The regulative principle is laid out in the Westminster Confession of Faith, chapter 21, article 1, and the Westminster Larger Catechism, Questions 108 and 109.

> *Westminster Confession of Faith* 21.1. The light of nature sheweth that there is a God, who hath lordship and sovereignty over all, is good, and doth good unto all, and is therefore to be feared, loved, praised, called upon, trusted in, and served, with all the heart, and with all the soul, and with all the might. But the acceptable way of worshipping the true God is instituted by himself, and so limited by his own revealed will, that he may not be worshipped according to the imaginations and devices of men, or the suggestions of Satan, under any visible representation, or any other way not prescribed in the holy Scripture.

> *Westminster Larger Catechism. Q. 108. What are the duties required in the second commandment?* A. The duties required in the second commandment are, the receiving, observing, and keeping pure and entire, all such religious worship and ordinances as God hath instituted in his Word; particularly prayer and thanksgiving in the name of Christ; the reading, preaching, and hearing of the Word; the administration and receiving of the sacraments; church government and discipline; the ministry and maintenance thereof; religious fasting; swearing by the name of God; and vowing unto him; as also the disapproving, detesting, opposing all false worship; and, according to each one's place and calling, removing it, and all monuments of idolatry.

> *Q. 109. What are the sins forbidden in the second commandment?* A. The sins forbidden in the second commandment are, all devising, counselling, commanding, using, and anywise approving, any religious worship not instituted by God himself; tolerating a false religion; the making any

representation of God, of all or of any of the three persons, either inwardly in our mind, or outwardly in any kind of image or likeness of any creature whatsoever; all worshipping of it, or God in it or by it; the making of any representation of feigned deities, and all worship of them, or service belonging to them, all superstitious devices, corrupting the worship of God, adding to it, or taking from it, whether invented and taken up of ourselves, or received by tradition from others, though under the title of antiquity, custom, devotion, good intent, or any other pretence whatsoever; simony; sacrilege; all neglect, contempt, hindering, and opposing the worship and ordinances which God hath appointed.

Nevertheless, questions remain. What counts as worship "instituted by God himself"? How does the Bible regulate worship? Can we look to the principles or examples in the Bible or must we have a direct command? Are we restricted to what is commanded or exemplified in the New Testament or can we also use the Old? I cannot address all of these questions in this short chapter.[2] What I propose to do here is whittle the issues down a bit by cutting off some of the more unacceptable misconstruals of the regulative principle. Unfortunately, the regulative principle of worship has too often been sloganized and applied so narrowly as to be unworkable, not to mention unbiblical. There are at least four unworkable applications of the regulative principle of worship.

Reactionary Regulations

First, the regulative principle of worship must not be defined primarily in reaction to Roman Catholic or Episcopal worship. Historical factors in our own history, particularly the life-and-death

---

[2] See James B. Jordan, *Theses on Worship: Notes Toward the Reformation of Worship* (Niceville: Transfiguration Press, 1994) and *Liturgical Nestorianism* (Niceville: Transfiguration Press, 1994). See also Peter Leithart's provocative new book on the liturgical lessons we can learn from King David's liturgical changes, *From Silence to Song: The Davidic Liturgical Revolution* (Moscow: Canon Press, 2003) and Ralph J. Gore, *Covenantal Worship: Reconsidering the Puritan Regulative Principle* (Phillipsburg, PA: Presbyterian and Reformed Publishing Company, 2002). The works of John Frame are helpful in so far as he accurately analyzes the weaknesses of the traditional formulation of the regulative principle of worship. What he offers in its place, however, is largely unsatisfactory.

struggles between the Presbyterian Scots and the Episcopal English, have led to very one-sided rules about what the Bible supposedly forbids in worship. Although it is a bit of a caricature, we often think like this: if a practice involves ceremony or ritual and Catholics and Episcopals do it, it must be unbiblical. There are, of course, very understandable historical factors behind this attitude.

The attempt to impose the Anglican Prayer Book on the Scottish church, often by violent means, did not endear the Presbyterians to the English liturgy. For just this reason, "we will not do what the Anglicans or Catholics do" is deeply embedded in the historical consciousness of many Presbyterians. If Anglicans kneel for prayer, we will not kneel (even if God's people bow down and kneel in the Bible). If the Anglicans used printed prayers, we will not (however, we will ignore the fact that God often provided His people with exemplary prayers, like the Psalms and the Lord's Prayer). Anglicans use litanies as congregational prayers; therefore litanies are works of the devil (but we'll pretend that Psalm 136 isn't in the Bible). Do the Anglicans incorporate congregational participation in the worship? This must be unbiblical. The pastor should do it all.

To our shame this is exactly what our forefathers proposed at the Savoy Conference in the mid-seventeenth century (1661). At Savoy Presbyterians opposed the *Book of Common Prayer* and asked "to omit the repetitions and responses of the clerk and people, and the alternate reading of Psalms and Hymns, which cause a confused murmur in the congregation." They went on to argue that "the minister being appointed for the people in all Public Services appertaining to God . . . the people's part in public prayer to be only silence and reverence to attend thereunto and to declare their consent in the close, by saying Amen."[3] Is *this* biblical worship? Must we ban all congregational responsive prayers, readings and tolerate no dialogue, no praying in unison of the Lord's Prayer or any other, all because

[3] See Francis Procter and Walter H. Frere, *A New History of the Book of Common Prayer* (London: MacMillan, 1908),172.

the Anglicans do it? Must the ministers do all the praying, the people following along silently? Hardly. We are no longer at war with the Episcopals. We need not react against their liturgical forms. After all, they were not the only ones who used these forms. The Reformed churches on the continent had been worshipping like this since the sixteenth century Reformation.[4]

In addition to this, in their polemic against Anglican and Roman Catholic abuses, Protestant churches accused them of imposing their liturgies. The warning against the imposition of liturgies has become a slogan. Unfortunately, on American soil the older argument against the imposition of Roman Catholic and Anglican liturgies by States on dissenting communities has been transformed into the individual's supposed right to be free from a local church's "imposition" of worship forms that he opposes. That individual Christian "consciences" should be free to decide how to and how not to worship was not the issue in historical Reformed debates. Just as a pastor has the "power" to choose a text and impose it on the congregation each week, so also a pastor and/or elders have the power to ordain a time and place for worship, choose hymns and prayers, and decide on an order of worship. If this is "imposing a liturgy" on people, then the only alternative is absolutely *free* worship. Indeed, why should I even have to gather with others only to hear them pray about and say things that I don't want to hear? There can be no genuine corporate worship without some "imposition" of liturgical content and forms.

Consider the Church year calendar, for example. Roman Catholic, Episcopal, and Lutheran churches do it, so it must be wrong. And where in the Bible are we commanded to have Advent, Christmas, Lent, and Easter? Confusion arises when statements like the following are advanced against the use of the Church year calendar: "Our heritage is rightly suspicious of the creation of ceremonies and

---

[4] See Horton Davies, *The Worship of the English Puritans* (1948; Lake Mary: Soli Deo Gloria, 1997).

rituals not authorized in Scripture."[5] The problem with this is that technically the church year does not introduce new ceremonies or rituals; rather, it organizes and directs our Scripture readings, prayers, hymns, and sermons according to the life of Christ. I don't see how a church that celebrates Christmas, remembering Christ's birth by singing, praying, and learning more about this particular event in the life of Christ is introducing new "ceremonies and rituals." Now, there are a few traditional rituals associated with Christmas and Lent, like Advent candles and ashes applied to the foreheads of worshipers; but these need not enter into the discussion at this point, since they are not part of the essence of the celebration of the Church year.

The question of liberty of conscience need not enter into the discussion at all. The members of the Church promise to submit to their leaders in the area of worship. Are pastors guilty of an "abuse of church power" when they regularly choose the hymns for the congregation, select prayers and Scripture readings, and arrange the order of their Sunday services according to their own preaching schedule? What's the difference? Do the Scriptures mandate or authorize pastors to force such an order on their congregations? Why should the congregation have to submit to worship services where the singing, praying, and Bible readings are correlated to three years of sermons through the book of Romans and yet be free to reject a year of prayers, readings, and songs organized around the life of Christ? What's the difference? One has to suspect that the real reason we rail against the Church year has to do with our passion to remain distinct from Roman Catholics and other liturgical churches and *not* because we think that such a way of ordering one's readings, hymns, and sermons is forbidden in the Bible.

---

[5] Terry L. Johnston, ed., *Leading in Worship* (Oak Ridge: The Covenant Foundation, 1996), 103.

Not Commanded—Not Allowed

The second problem with some ways of explaining the regulative principle of worship concerns a too narrowly defined principle. The regulative principle is not well formulated when we say that only that which is commanded ought to be allowed in worship. Whatever is not commanded therefore is forbidden. Why should we need only explicit "commands"? This is completely unworkable, and in practice has never been followed. It makes for great rhetoric, but lousy biblical and liturgical theology. Where does the Bible command that a "call to worship" be issued at the beginning of a service? It must be forbidden. Where are we commanded to give a benediction at the close of the worship service? Therefore it is forbidden. Where are we commanded to have choirs? Therefore they are forbidden. Where are we commanded to celebrate Baptism as part of the worship service? Where are we commanded to take vows as part of the baptismal ceremony? Where are we commanded to take an offering during the service? For that matter, where are we commanded to have a sermon each Sunday? Or meet on the first day rather than the seventh? Must all of these practices be forbidden if we cannot find a verse that *commands* us to do them? Some insist that we must actually come up with a proof text that explicitly commands a practice before we are authorized to do it in the worship of the Church.

Much better than this is the Strasbourg Reformer Martin Bucer's explanation of the regulative principle of worship: "Nothing should be introduced or performed in the churches of Christ for which no probable reason can be given from the Word of God."[6] Filling this out a little, we can state the principle like this: the Church must have biblical *warrant* for the way she worships God; such warrant can be derived from biblical commands, principles, or examples.

---

[6] Martin Bucer, *Censura*, trans. by E. C. Whitaker in *Martin Bucer and the Book of Common Prayer* (London: SPCK, 1974), 42–43.

New Testament Worship?

Thirdly, the regulative principle has often been applied in a dispensational, semi-Marcionite way. In practice, then, the regulative principle means that we only look to the New Testament for biblical warrant. Only what the New Testament expressly prescribes ought to be done. All that ceremony and ritual, that was Old Testament worship. More often than not, popular Protestant imagination inadvertently links Roman Catholic worship with Old Testament worship, as if Catholicism is somehow a throwback to Old Testament worship. The Puritans tended to make this mistake. For example, John Owen (an independent Puritan) does not like the Lord's Prayer. Why? Because it was part of Old Testament worship structures:

> Our Savior at that time was minister of the Circumcision, and taught the doctrine of the gospel under and with the observation of all the worship of the Judaical church. He was not yet glorified, and so the Spirit was not as yet given; I mean that Spirit which he promised unto his disciples to enable them to perform all the worship of God by him required at their hands, whereof we have before spoken. That, then, which the Lord Jesus prescribed unto his disciples, for their present practice in the worship of God, seems to have belonged unto the economy of the Old Testament. Now to argue from the prescription of, and outward helps for, the performance of the worship of God under the Old Testament, unto a necessity of the like or the same under the New, is upon the matter to deny that Christ is ascended on high, and to have given spiritual gifts unto men eminently distinct from and above those given out by him under the Judaical pedagogy. (Owen, *Works*, vol. 15, 14)

Frank J. Smith asserts "Romanism . . . retained much of the Old Covenant sacrificial system."[7] What exactly does this mean? How can Roman Catholicism be said to have "retained" Old Covenant sacrificial practices? Did the error of the Mass develop because the

---

[7] *Worship in the Presence of God*, eds. Frank J. Smith and David C. Lachman (Greenville: Greenville Seminary Press, 1992), 11.

church returned to the liturgical elements of the Old Testament ceremonial system? Or did it develop as a result of the influence of alien philosophical (Aristotelian) categories on biblical teaching? Does Frank Smith want to suggest that the God-given sacrificial system was Romanist? Are we to believe that the corruption of the medieval church came about because of the influence of the Old Testament on the church's liturgy? This kind of argument is historically and theologically erroneous.

There is a disconcerting penchant among Reformed theologians, from the Reformation on, for disparaging Old Covenant sacrificial ritual by identifying it too closely with Roman Catholic errors. This erroneous identification became more and more prominent in the seventeenth and eighteenth centuries. Even though it is not about worship per se, I highly recommend Henning Graf Reventlow's *The Authority of the Bible and the Rise of the Modern World* (Philadelphia: Fortress Press, 1985). Reventlow chronicles the rise of Deism in England and Germany as the precursor to higher criticism. In the process of his research he shows how English Protestants, particularly the Puritans, displayed a deep-seated hostility to anything that smacked of material ceremony and ritual and that they read the Old Testament with these colored lenses such that they tended to interpret Old Testament religion as a kind of Catholicism before Rome. Furthermore, this moralistic, anti-ceremonial bias fed right into (or possibly even "caused") the rising humanistic antipathy to revealed religion, particularly that of the Old Testament, leading to the rise of higher critical methodologies that deconstruct the first four-fifths of the Bible. At any rate, Reventlow's research on the anti-ritual "spiritualism" of the English post-Reformation theologians is extremely troubling. This work reveals something of the shortcomings of our own anti-liturgical, spiritualistic heritage.

Another odd characteristic of much of Reformed polemics on the regulative principle has been the appeal to synagogue worship over against the Old Testament biblical regulations regarding the temple liturgy. I say it is odd because there are no explicit biblical regulations concerning synagogue worship. We know that the people of Israel worshipped weekly in local assemblies since a Sabbath day "holy convocation" or "assembly" was commanded by Yahweh in Leviticus 23:3: "Six days shall work be done, but the seventh day is a Sabbath of solemn rest, a holy convocation. You shall do no work. It is a Sabbath to Yahweh in all your dwelling places." Now, it is true that the local Sabbath worship was not explicitly regulated. That is, God did not lay out a how-to list like he does in Leviticus. But that doesn't mean that wise Levites and elders in the local towns would not understand that the regulations of the temple and sacrificial system applied *mutatis mutandis* to the local services over which they presided. We have a great deal of evidence to suggest that this is exactly what synagogue worship became: sacrificial worship without the animal sacrifices. Synagogue practice was modeled on the temple (e.g., prayers were described as "sacrifices," similar to the New Testament and the synagogue itself was considered holy space).[8] Although a staple of much Reformed antiliturgical polemics, the notion that synagogue worship was "simple" and a-liturgical and therefore must function as a model for "simple" New Testament worship lacks credible support.

Worship In Spirit and Truth

A New-Testament-only approach to the regulative principle invariably ends up advocating an overly inward, rationalistic approach to worship. The inward, spiritual, non-material movement of the mind is more important than the movement of the body (tongue or knees or hands) in worship. So anything material detracts from the true "spiritual" worship of the New Testament. A seminary

---

[8] See Peter J. Leithart, "Synagogue or Temple? Models for Christian Worship," *Westminster Theological Journal* 64 (2002): 119–33; Leithart, *From Silence to Song*, chapter 6, op. cit.; John W. Kleinig, *The Lord's Song: The Basis, Function and Significance of Choral Music in Chronicles* (JSOT Supplement #156; Sheffield: JSOT Press, 1993); and Donald D. Binder, *Into the Temple Courts: The Place of the Synagogue in the Second Temple Period* (SBL Dissertation Series 169; Atlanta: Society of Biblical Literature, 1997).

professor of mine, after participating in worship at our church, once commented how much he appreciated the *times of silence*. "*That* was true spiritual worship!" he said. Now, I think times of silence in the worship service are fine, but they are definitely not more "spiritual" than when the congregation is belting out a vigorous hymn or Psalm. In the Bible the adjective "spiritual" means "of the Holy Spirit" not something non-material or inward or mental as opposed to the material, physical, and outward.[9]

This "spiritualizing" tendency is the fourth distortion to analyze. It is often justified by a misreading of Jesus' discussion with the Samaritan woman in John 4. Jesus' assertion in John 4:24 is often lifted from its context and dangerously misconstrued to function as a warning against all "outward" and "external" liturgical worship. A more literal translation, however, will help us understand what Jesus means by worshipping in "Spirit and truth":

> The [Samaritan] woman said to him, "Sir, I perceive that you are a prophet. Our Fathers bowed down [*proskuneo*] on this mountain, but you say that in Jerusalem is the place where people ought to bow down." Jesus said to her, "Woman, believe me, the hour is coming when neither on this mountain nor in Jerusalem will your people bow down to the Father. Your people bow down to what you do not know; we bow down to the one we know, for salvation is from the Jews. But the hour is coming and is now here, when true worshipers will bow down to the Father in Spirit and truth, for the Father is seeking such people to bow down to Him. God is Spirit, and those who bow down to Him must bow down in Spirit and truth." (Jn. 4:19-24)

Jesus is not saying that God is non-material, so therefore His worshipers must unite with Him by means of their spirits or souls. The NIV study Bible is quite wrong in its explanatory note: "The place

---

[9] For more criticism of dispensational tendencies in our own tradition's understanding and practice of worship, listen to the lecture tapes or read the transcribed manuscripts of Robert S. Rayburn's lecture "Worship from the Whole Bible" given at *The Second Annual Conference on Worship*, February 23–25, 1996 (Nashville: Covenant Presbyterian Church, 1996) and Jeffrey J. Meyers, "Ritual and Redemptive History" (Biblical Horizons 1993 Bible Conference).

of worship is irrelevant, because true worship must be in keeping with God's nature, which is spirit." Jesus is not restricting genuine worship to inward, sincere worship. This follows from two considerations: 1) the meaning of the word *proskuneo*, often translated "to worship," and 2) the redemptive-historical context of Jesus' remarks.

First, the Greek verb *proskuneo* (used nine times in six verses in Jn. 4:20–26) means "to bow down," "to kneel," or "prostrate oneself." Even though my translation of this passage is awkward, I have tried to bring out the ritual dimensions of the conversation by consistently translating *proskuneo* as "bow down." One must remember the very concrete meaning of *proskuneo* in the ancient world. Doing "obeisance" means bending your body and placing yourself "under" another. When you *proskuneo-ed* before someone, you bowed down in their presence, even at their feet.

The English word "worship," especially as it is used in modern times, is not a very helpful translation. One of the problems with our word "worship" is that it now refers to all sorts of activities, both physical and mental. In fact, a recent fad is to stress that all of life is "worship." In some sense this is true, but only in a very loose sense. When used in this sense "woship" denotes a mental disposition. But this is not the sense in which this word *proskuneo* or "bowing down" is ordinarily used in the Scriptures. If you want to say that all of life is "bowing down," that is fine; but this can only be so in a very abstract or metaphorical way. If you are working hard on a painting job, for example, you may, indeed you should mentally give thanks and praise to God while you do so, but . . . you are not bowing down at that time with others who reverence the same God.

The woman and Jesus are not talking about this kind of mental attitude. Jesus is addressing the question of where one should bow down to the Father. He is talking about the ritual act of bowing down or kneeling before God in order to honor Him and express one's proper devotion. This woman asks in effect, "Where is the place, the location, where we should bow down to God?" We will see how Jesus answers that question in a moment, but for now simply attend to the kind of devotion in question. The activity in view here is what we might call "special" as opposed to "general" devotion. It is special in the sense that it happens at a known location and it involves the people of God in acts of ritual devotion before God. Furthermore, the bowing down in question has to do with corporate or public worship, not private worship.

Bowing down, then, is a kind of synecdoche for everything the people of God *do* when they gather together in corporate worship. It simply has to be this. Everyone, both Jews and Samaritans knew that one could pray and praise and petition God, one could even get down on one's knees anytime or place. Individual bowing down was never restricted to the temple or Jerusalem or in Samaria, to Mt. Gerizim. Please, pay careful attention to this point. The big point being made by Jesus in this passage *cannot* be that now in the New Testament individuals can bow down, pray to, or mentally worship God wherever they want. This has always been the case. The controversy here is about where the people of Samaria should gather to bow down in special corporate worship. All special, corporate worship in the Bible is external and bodily and involves the biblical ritual (among others) of kneeling or bowing down.

Therefore, Jesus' words, "worship in Spirit and truth," must be understood according to the context of Jesus' discussion with the Samaritan woman. She had asked *where* the proper place of worship should be—Mt. Gerizim in Samaria or Mt. Zion in Jerusalem? Jesus responds with a prophetic statement, an utterance about something that will soon be in effect. At the time Jesus spoke to the woman, Jerusalem was the place where God had placed His Name. The Spirit descended in glory upon the tabernacle and temple. If you wanted to be faithful to the truth and enter into the environment of the Spirit, you went to Jerusalem with the people of God. The Samaritans worshipped in ignorance. They bowed down as a people in the wrong place. There was no guarantee of the Spirit's presence on Mt. Gerizim. Jesus makes this clear. They were wrong to worship God on the mountain of their own choice.

But a time was coming—indeed, it was being inaugurated in Jesus' own ministry—when bowing down "faithfully" and "in the Spirit" could be done by God's people anywhere, not merely in Jerusalem. The post-Pentecost situation would radically decentralize corporate worship. Not individual worship. That had always been decentralized. The big change now would be that no longer would worshipers gather together only at Jerusalem, but the Spirit would be present wherever the Church assembled in the Name of Jesus.

> Today most exegetes agree that in proclaiming worship in Spirit and truth, Jesus is not contrasting external worship with internal worship. His statement has nothing to do with worshipping God in the inner resources of one's own spirit; for the Spirit is the Spirit of God, not the spirit of man, as verse 24 makes clear. . . . Jesus is speaking of the eschatological replacement of temporal institutions like the temple, resuming the theme of 2:13-22. In 2:21 it was Jesus Himself who was to take the place of the temple, and here it is the Spirit given by Jesus that is to animate the worship that replaces worship at the temple.[10]

In John 4:24, therefore, Jesus is not emphasizing the importance of one's inner emotional experience. Jesus is not saying if you want to have genuine worship you must participate with your innermost spirit. There's nothing new about such an admonition. It was true in the Old Testament. If worship "in spirit" only meant that individuals should worship sincerely, honestly, with one's heart and soul, such an assertion could not have answered the Samaritan woman's question. "Spirit" is not a description of God's non-material nature. We should not read it like this: God is a spirit. That is, God is in the category of what we call "spiritual beings." That is not John's concern. The "S" should be capitalized. God is Spirit. This is not a statement about the "nature" of God, but of the way in which God is present to human beings, His dynamic relations with humanity.

---

[10] Raymond E. Brown, *The Gospel According to John, I-XII* in *The Anchor Bible* (New York: Doubleday, 1966), 180.

The Father gives the Spirit (Jn. 14:1) and the Holy Spirit is the medium of His relationship with us.

Compare this with 1 John 1:5 ("God is light") and 1 John 4:8 ("God is love"). These statements do not describe God's "nature," but His relational being. To say that "God is Spirit" in the context of a discussion about the place where one should bow down means that God will be properly worshipped wherever His Spirit is. We must be "in the Spirit" if we are to be in God's presence, the place where He is. This is similar to Jesus saying that one must be "born from above" and "born of water and Spirit" (Jn. 3:3–8). The Spirit connects us with heaven, with the Father. If you want to worship the Father, you will be where the Spirit of Truth is. Once again, I am not denying we can worship individually anywhere and anytime, and by the Spirit. That was true in Old Testament times as well. But there is a more specific sense of "in Spirit," which is in the community of believers gathered at a specific place for special worship. The context makes it clear that Jesus is speaking in this specific sense.

In the context of the Old Testament "bowing down in Spirit" meant gathering with the people of God for corporate, sacrificial worship wherever the tabernacle was pitched or at the site of the temple in Jerusalem. But not any more. The Spirit that descended and filled the old tabernacle and temple is the same Spirit that descended and remained upon Jesus, the true and final temple. The place where God and man are united is in the flesh of Jesus. He is the new temple (Jn. 2:19–22). Jesus will ascend to heaven shortly, but He promised to send the Spirit to indwell and empower His Body, the Church (Jn. 14–16; Acts 1:8; 2:1–4). When the Church gathers, the Spirit is there. Where the Spirit gathers the Church, there is Christ. She is the temple of the Holy Spirit (1 Cor. 3:16; Eph. 2:21). And so worship to the Father occurs through Jesus and in the Spirit where the earthly temple of living stones is gathered (1 Pet. 2:5). Thus, in the New Testament, people who worship "in Spirit and truth" will gather with the body of Christ to participate in Spiritual worship of the Father (1 Cor. 12:12–14).

Some have even used Jesus' statement to argue that he was condemning all kinds of external and material worship—rituals, corporeal objects, and the rest. That doesn't work. Jesus is not speaking here about individual in-your-thoughts worship. But about people and what they do. The Samaritan woman asked where one should "worship," that is, where is the proper place to *bow down* before God. In the New Covenant God has not suddenly become available only to individuals who turn inward or seek some immaterial/spiritual means of communion. Nor has He become a "vagabond God" (Luther's phrase), wandering here and there apart from any place. Rather just as God limited and bound Himself to specified places and times and people in the Old Testament, so also in the New. This has not changed in the New Testament. We have not become disembodied spirit beings. We have no independent, immaterial access to God in the New Covenant. What we have is a different set of physical means appropriate to the change made in the resurrection and ascension of Jesus.

In the Old Covenant it was *one* place and people—the tabernacle, the temple, the ark of the covenant, the altar, and the physical rituals of sacrifice that were performed at these centralized sites. We Christians, however, unlike the believers in the Old Testament, are no longer bound to one geographical location, to one physical temple at the center of the world. We no longer go to one nation that has been given the ministry of priestly intercession and ministry. The Spirit no longer binds Himself to one location or one people. This is evident even in this passage. The living water that the woman receives (i.e., the Holy Spirit) wells up in her such that when her fellow towns people hear her witness, they too receive the living-water Spirit and believe (Jn. 4:28–30, 39–42).

What Jerusalem and the Jews were to the Old Testament—the place and ministers by which God met with men and women—Christ and His Body, the Church, are today. Jesus' humanity is the place to which God summons us. Christ alone is the new sanctuary, the mercy seat, and the high priest through whom we must draw near to God. And Christ has given the Spirit to fill His Body, the Church, on earth so that she might be the place where humanity finds God. She is the New Jerusalem. If we wish to worship God in Spirit and truth, we will seek God among His people, where the Word is audibly read and preached, where the physical sacraments are given and received. He still embodies His presence by the Spirit, but it is no longer a centralized, geographically limited embodiment.

The Spirit is given by Jesus (as Jn. 14–17 will make clear). He is the proper environment of worship. And the Spirit brings men and women together in various places by the Spirit in order that they might worship God through the Messiah. In union with the humanity of Jesus, we have access to the Father through the Spirit. We bow before God in Christ in the environment of the Spirit. Luther reminds us that the ministry of the Holy Spirit "is thoroughly external and completely available to our sense . . . we see and hear the Holy Spirit in the dove, in tongues of fire, in baptism, and in a human voice."[11] Paul Althaus summarizes it well:

> Christ is present to us in very earthly ways. Everywhere in the history of revelation God embodies Himself for us. His Spirit came in the form of a dove and the fiery tongues of Pentecost. And God still embodies himself for us. The Holy Spirit comes to us and brings Christ to us through the external, physical, sensible means of the Word, of the human voice, and of the Sacraments.[12]

God meets with us at trysting places (Luther's evocative terminology). Where the people of God are gathered as the Church and there is Baptism, the Lord's Supper, and the Word of God on the lips of His ministers and all His believers—that is where God is. That is where we bow down in Spirit and truth.

---

[11] *WA 391*, 217 (cited in Paul Althaus, *The Theology of Martin Luther* [Philadelphia: Fortress Press, 1966],21).

[12] Ibid.,22–23.

Conclusion

I reject all four of these deformations of the Reformed regulative principle of worship. Much better is A. A. Hodge's simple comments on the Westminster Confession of Faith 21.1. According to Hodge, this section teaches, "That God in His Word has prescribed for us how we may worship Him acceptably; and that it is an offense to Him and a sin in us either to neglect to worship and serve Him in the way prescribed, or to attempt to serve Him in any way not prescribed."[13] This is a very proper summary of the regulative principle. It avoids the dangers of an unworkable, overly strict formulation (like "whatever is not commanded is forbidden"). It does not, of course, answer all of our questions in advance. We must still do the hard work of biblical exegesis to determine precisely how God regulates worship. We can be confident, however, that God has prescribed for us in His Word how we may worship Him acceptably. This authoritative prescription comes by way of command, principle, and example from both the Old and New Testaments.

---

[13] A. A. Hodge, *The Confession of Faith* (Edinburgh: Banner of Truth, 1958 [1869]), 270.

17
Using the Traditional Liturgies

Do not move the ancient landmark that your fathers have set.
—Proverbs 22:28

The traditional liturgy of the Church has been shaped by the sacrificial, covenantal pattern such that the order of most Christian liturgies moves from confession and forgiveness, then to the service of the Word, and finally culminates with Communion. This consistent tradition of the Church confirms that we are on the right track in our analysis of the biblical data. It also raises suspicions about popular American attempts to replace the historic order of worship with creative sequences. John Frame, for example, thinks that a church that does not follow an "historical" order of worship should not worry too much about the question: "Why shouldn't our worship services have a more historical character?" He seems to think that the one who asks such a question is at best misguided as to the real issues in worship.[1]

Nevertheless, this is a legitimate question after all. One surely ought to be suspicious—at least curious—at the radical break

[1] Frame's thoughts on the value of the historic liturgy of the Church can be found in various places in his writings. See especially his *Worship in Spirit and Truth* (Phillipsburg: Presbyterian and Reformed, 1996), *Contemporary Worship Music* (Phillipsburg: Presbyterian & Reformed, 1997), "Some Questions About the Regulative Principle,"

made with liturgical tradition in the twentieth-century American evangelical church. We might safely assume that the historical Church has accumulated much wisdom concerning how to worship the Lord after twenty centuries of experience. And surely it is not without reason that the historical Church has, throughout its entire history, manifested remarkable unity concerning the proper manner in which to approach God in corporate, Lord's Day worship—a unity of approach that includes both order and content. To abandon this accumulated tradition does not seem wise to me. Of course, neither would it be wise to venerate every detail of this tradition as something untouchable.[2]

And I should be quick to point out that "traditional" Presbyterian worship is not exactly what I am advocating as liturgical worship. Part of the problem is trying to figure out what "traditional" means. Does it mean worship as it was done in conservative churches in the 1960's? The 1940's? Or maybe the 1850's? In Northern or Southern Presbyterian churches? I have been dismayed to discover that what passes for "traditional" worship in many older Presbyterian churches is quite minimalistic. The pastor has the secretary fill in the variable slots in a bare-bones order of service, rotating the ten commandments, the Lord's Prayer, and the Apostles' Creed in a three-week recurring cycle. The people's part consists of singing three hymns, reciting one of the three items mentioned above, trying to follow a long pastoral prayer, listening to a forty-five-minute sermon, and receiving Communion once a quarter. If you have persevered through this book, you know I am arguing for something quite different than simply "old" Presbyterian worship.

Westminster Theological Journal 54 (1992): 357–366, "In Defense of Something Close to Biblicism," *Westminster Theological Journal* 59 (Fall, 1997): 269–318, and his unpublished essays "The Lordship of Christ and the Regulative Principle of Worship" and "Traditionalism."

[2] See Hughes Oliphant Old's helpful discussion in *Guides to the Reformed Tradition: Worship* (Atlanta: John Knox Press, 1984), chapter 10, "Tradition and Practice," 157–77.

Giving Our Ancestors a Vote

The bigger question is the wisdom of jettisoning the mind of the Spirit revealed in the worship tradition of the Church. Chesterton once defined tradition as "an extension of the franchise":

> Tradition means giving votes to the most obscure of all classes, our ancestors. It is the democracy of the dead. Tradition refuses to submit to the small and arrogant oligarchy of those who merely happen to be walking about . . . . Tradition asks us not to neglect a good man's opinion, even if he is our father.[3]

After all, cultural considerations aside, some "Christian" churches today "worship" in a manner that would be hardly recognizable as *Christian* worship by our ancestors in the faith. Of course, these churches may sing, read the Bible, preach, and pray, as John Frame notes; but the context and the manner, to say nothing of the order in which these things are done is often not that of classical Christian worship. The modern context is often therapeutic, entertaining, or scholastic, but the context is all-important. The order often shows little or no resemblance to the biblical protocols so important for approaching God. Context and order determine what the congregation thinks they are really doing on Sunday morning. If the Church fathers of the fourth century were correct and "public doxology" is practically "a test of faith," how would the American evangelical church at the turn of the twenty-first century score?[4]

For example, in order to make people feel more comfortable and ensure that they will come back next week, the atmosphere of a typical American evangelical service has become entertainment-oriented (TV-like or concert hall-like) because that's what people in our culture (supposedly) relate to. The people are conceived of as religious consumers. The role of the pastor in this new context is that of a businessman, a talk show host (always smiling!), or a

---

[3] G. K. Chesterton, *Orthodoxy* (Garden City: Image Books, 1959), 48.
[4] John Henry Newman, *The Arians of the Fourth Century*, 3rd ed. (London: E Lumley, 1871), 298.

psychologist, all of which explains the businessman costume of most evangelical preachers, the TV set appearance of the inside of their churches (auditoria), and the "help" oriented therapy ("how to do this" and "three ways to succeed in that") into which most of their sermons have degenerated.

I am reminded of something G. K. Chesterton said in his book *What's Wrong with the World?* "It ought to be the oldest things that are taught to the youngest people," Chesterton wrote in 1910. The child, he complained, is oftentimes older than the theory he is taught, so that "the flopping infant of four actually has more experience . . . than the dogma to which he is made to submit."[5] "Cranks and experiments," said Chesterton, "go straight to the school room when they have never passed through the parliament, the public house, the private home, the church, or the market place."

Chesterton was complaining about twentieth-century man's intoxication with the newest intellectual fads and fashions in education, economics, politics, and religion. "In the modern world we are primarily confronted with the extraordinary spectacle of people turning to new ideas because they have not tried the old" (p. 65). Words like new, emergent, innovative, and revolutionary function like magic words used to function in earlier societies. Call a theory innovative or new and eyes light up, bells ring, and money changes hands. Conversely, there are bad magic words. If an idea or theory or teaching is old and historic then we have all sorts of evil sounding adjectives like "antiquated" and "rigid" or "traditional." Something that is "traditional" surely must be classified with something evil, associated with the vicious powers of darkness that hold us down.

This equating of the new with the good is nowhere more evident than in American Christianity. Today, whatever is contemporary is good. Nowadays, it seems, the most recent developments in biblical criticism, the latest speculations of religious philosophers in

[5] G.K. Chesterton, *The Collected Works of G.K. Chesterton*, vol. 4 (San Francisco: Ignatius Press, 1987), 65.

German Universities, whatever psychological recovery fad seems to be the most popular, the gaudiest programs and marketing strategies emerging in corporate America—these go straight into the pastor's office, into his sermons, or worse, straight into the Sunday School curriculum without ever having to pass through the real world or pass the test of the authority of the Scripture and the wisdom of Christian tradition. For American Christendom, the first commandment with a promise is "Honor the latest fad in psychology, sociology, and education and you will grow big and be prosperous."

Frank Senn has warned of the danger of simply abandoning the historic liturgy of the Church with its carefully sequenced Trinitarian order of service:

> This historic order can no longer be presumed to be intact in the churches of the Reformation (except in the Episcopal/Anglican Churches in which the use of the prayer book is required by canon law). The pressure is great for these churches to devise "alternative" or "creative" liturgies that will be "seeker friendly." What these well-intentioned efforts run the risk of doing, however, is undermining *orthodoxia* the "right praise" of Trinitarian worship that is expressed in the texts of the historic order of service. The "glory and praise" choruses and Jesus-songs in neo-evangelical worship (usually called "celebrations") do not offer the same sturdy articulations of the Trinitarian faith expressed in the texts of either the Latin chants or the chorales of the German Lutheran song mass (*Lied Messe*). No matter how conducive to engendering liturgical enthusiasm the "glory and praise" choruses might be, they are theologically unequal to the *Gloria in excelsis Deo* or *Allein Gott in der Huh sei ehr.* The experience of the Reformation teaches us that the forms of public worship are not matters of indifference (*adiaphora*) because prayer (especially sung prayer and praise) forms belief; or, as the church fathers would have said, the *lex orandi* establishes the *lex credendi.* It is not adequate to claim the evangelical freedom to change forms of worship if those changes diminish expressions of the ecumenical dogmas of God the Holy Trinity and the two natures of Christ on which Luther, Zwingli, Calvin, Cranmer, and the Council of Trent were not in disagreement. The catholic faith requires catholic worship.[6]

[6] Frank Senn, "The Reform of the Mass: Evangelical, but Still Catholic" *The Catholicity of the Reformation*, ed. Carl E. Braaten and Robert W. Jenson (Grand Rapids: Eerdmans, 1996), 51.

Proper Uses for Historical Liturgies

I will begin with a rather modest thesis: it seems to me that a right use of the knowledge of historical forms of Christian worship could assist us in the twentieth-century American church by helping us to break free from bondage to our own culture. I recall that being one of the proper uses of the knowledge of history. Even though the desire for historicity is a valid one, it ought not to be an end in itself. We are motivated to examine the liturgical history of the Church in order to use what we learn as a resource in the renewal of the contemporary church. Professor Frame, for example, prejudices the case against traditional liturgical worship by characterizing its genius as that of "seeking historicity in worship." This is not a major motive. To seek historicity for historicity's sake would be at best superficial, and at worst stupid. In fact, no liturgical scholar worth his salt claims that the mere presence of the historical (whatever that means) in a modern worship service improves the quality of the service.

Second, Frame sets up a false dilemma when he suggests that the best way to recover the historical dimension is not to "imitate the practice of nine hundred years ago, but to seek to bring the true Word of God to bear with force and power on our contemporary situation." First of all, as I will restate below, no competent liturgical scholar or reformer wishes merely to "imitate" the liturgy of any period of the historic Church. This is not what most scholars want when they push for a greater sensitivity to the historic forms and content of worship. It is certainly not what I am advocating.

Furthermore, I fail to see how Frame's alternative to this caricature (a radical biblicism, as he puts it) fulfills the mandate to recover the historical dimension. Without doubt, we need to bring God's Word to bear on our own culture, but the issue is: What does the historic Church have to teach us in this matter? Can we learn anything from them? How did they bring the Word to bear upon their culture? And especially, what was the role of worship and liturgy in this endeavor? I'm not sure Frame grasps the chief motives of those of us who have an interest in reforming contemporary evangelical worship. To be fair, neither his essays nor his book really deal with this in any depth, but there does seem to me to be a fundamental misunderstanding as to what liturgical reformers want and why they want it. I know, of course, that he cannot be expected to know everything about everything.

Even so, the desire to avoid "superficiality by using ancient liturgies" is not a major motive in the liturgical renewal movement. Nor is it to give a "greater sense of unity with the church of all ages." Surely, these are important concerns, but not primary. They ought not to be central reasons for making use of the riches of ancient or Reformation liturgies. And the best liturgical scholars would be quick to point this out. Frame seems to imply that it is primarily a concern for the "historical" that leads some to incorporate traditional liturgical forms in contemporary worship. But surely there is a difference between using the historical and the desire to be faithful to history, or between reviving the historical for the sake of being historical and the use of the historical for the sake of depth or beauty or meaningfulness or whatever. The former is artificial and romantic, the latter seems to be a legitimate way to enrich our worship. Pastors and churches are returning to liturgies modeled on historic Christian worship because they see how biblical these services are and how effective they can be in forming the prayer and praise of the Christian community.

> As far as meaning is concerned, Joseph Jungmann taught that "Mass properly celebrated is itself the best catechesis." The liturgy has served for centuries as the "school of the church" in which one learns the faith by gathering with the community of faith to praise the Creator, by attending to the proclamation and exposition of the Word of God in Scripture, by professing one's faith in public and praying for the needs of the world, by offering the world to God in a sacrifice of praise and thanksgiving and by receiving the gifts of creation—bread and wine—as the means of Communion with Christ. Only if these ritual acts are intact can there be adequate catechesis or teaching based on them.[7]

[7] Senn, "The Reform of the Mass," 52.

As I mentioned previously in this chapter, the attempt to "imitate the practices of nine hundred years ago" is liturgical romanticism and has no place in a genuine liturgical renewal. Frame should know better. This is a straw man. This is not what authentic worship renewal is all about. This is what the liturgical scholar Louis Bouyer calls "archaeologism." According to Bouyer, such romanticism constitutes "one of the fundamental problems of the liturgical movement. For no reconstructions of the past—however excellent the period one chooses to try to bring to life—can be achieved without a large admixture of the products of one's own fancy; and such reconstructions are likely to raise more problems than they can solve."[8] As Bouyer warns us in another place, there is always the danger for those interested in liturgical renewal to become possessed by the "spirit of bogus archaeological restoration." And again: "For if the stubborn rejection of the Church and the world as they are today were held to be the necessary preliminary to any authentic liturgical renaissance, this fact in itself would certainly constitute the most perfect condemnation of that renaissance."

Every generation must submit to and appropriate the liturgical tradition of the Church in responsible, creative ways. Goethe's words are apropos: "What you receive from your father, earn it anew before you call it your own."[9] The result should then be something described by Augustine's vision: "beauty ever ancient, ever new."[10]

Intelligibility or Acceptability?

This leads to another problem with Frame's discussion. Why must he repeatedly pit the "historical" against the "intelligible"? It is hard to respond to this because I'm not sure what "historical forms" Frame is thinking of when he warns against their unintelligibility.

---

[8] Louis Bouyer, *Liturgical Piety* (Notre Dame: University of Notre Dame Press, 1954), 12.

[9] Johann Wolfgang von Goethe, *Faust*, 682–3.

[10] Augustine, *Confessions*, 9.27.38 (cited by Jaroslav Pelikan in *The Vindication of Tradition* [New Haven: Yale University Press, 1984], 8).

Just how are sung responses, say, unintelligible to modern people? And what about responsive readings (since he mentions these)? Are they unintelligible to modern man or simply unfamiliar? Is kneeling unintelligible or unfamiliar? Are printed confessions of sins and litanies unintelligible or unfamiliar? Is a theologically and biblically sound order of worship unintelligible or just plain unfamiliar? Are symbolic gestures and actions unintelligible or unfamiliar? Surely they can be learned and appreciated by modern people as they participate in a liturgical community. It doesn't seem to me that unintelligibility is the real issue. It may take some work to understand these liturgical practices, but they are not unintelligible. The fact that they have been used for almost two thousand years in hundreds of disparate cultures to the benefit of millions of Christians means that they are not inherently incomprehensible. They may be just plain strange to the American man on the street, but they are surely not indecipherable. He may be unaccustomed to joining his voice with others in reciting a creed or Psalm, but he can surely understand the words and rituals over time.

Must everything in Christian worship be readily intelligible to the man on the street? Must everything be pitched to the unbeliever? Is that what 1 Corinthians 14 really means? Is that why American evangelical services conform more to the pattern of the entertainment industry rather than to the pattern of traditional worship of the historic Church? Does biblical worship come naturally and easily to the unbeliever? Should an unbeliever be able to walk into a Christian service and participate without any training or explanation? I think an *a priori* case can be made for the idea that biblical worship will appear strange to the modern American pagan. Surely someone unfamiliar with the Bible and the Christian faith will need to be trained in biblical worship. He or she will need to learn how to approach God. Is it not reasonable to assume that some of what Christians do in worship will actually run against the cultural grain such that what Christians say and do in worship may be profoundly unfamiliar, even odd to American "consumers"? Are forms such as responsive readings and kneeling in church really unintelligible to modern men? Isn't it rather a matter of familiarity and receptivity? And speaking of familiarity, surely this is one of the problems in "contemporary" worship: it breeds over familiarity with God. When we adapt our worship to the prevailing cultural forms of the day are people really being trained in biblical worship? As Bouyer again puts it: "We must not try to provide an artificial congregation to take part in an antiquarian liturgy, but rather to prepare the actual congregations of the Church today to take part in the truly traditional liturgy rightly understood."[11] This will train people in the biblical forms of worship.

I have often called on visitors who were not raised in the church, any church. I recall one recent case. She was what some would call a "seeker," someone looking for a church. During my visitation she told me that she was having a difficult time with our liturgy. She had attended our worship service twice. "It takes a lot of work to know where we are and why we are doing what we are doing," she confided. I was about to "apologize" for our worship and encourage her, when she made a remarkable confession. She said, "You know, Pastor, I realize that I am a very new Christian. I know that I don't know my Bible. I don't know very many of the hymns that you sing. The music is not familiar to me, since I didn't grow up in a church. But that doesn't bother me, because I also know that I have a lot to learn. I shouldn't expect to know how to worship God after two weeks of church, should I? I look at all the children in your church and I weep. They know the hymns. They know where to turn in their Bibles. I want to learn all of that, too. I wasn't raised that way. I need to learn how to worship God. Will you be patient with me and help me? It's hard." Now, that's only a summary of what she said. It almost made me weep right there on the spot. Tears did come to my eyes in the car driving home. It was not so much

---

[11] Louis Bouyer, *Liturgical Piety*, 15.

that the service was "unintelligible" to her; it was just unfamiliar. She simply had to *learn* how to worship God.

As a pastor I have called on scores of visitors like this. I have never yet talked to people with "intelligibility" problems who were new Christians or unchurched people. They know that they don't know much about Christian worship. They are often willing to learn. But I have almost always had problems with evangelical Christians who come to our service with all kinds of preconceived notions about their own preferences for worship. Yes, our worship is unfamiliar to the unbeliever. So what? Is worship supposed to come naturally to people outside of the Church who don't know the Bible? Who have not experienced worship in the Christian community?

A few years ago, I had a visiting young couple sit a few rows from the front of the church and snicker and jeer at the prayers, the hymns—the entire liturgy—throughout the whole service. It was obvious to me. They were so irreverent that it made me burning mad while I was leading the service. I wanted to halt the service and call them to repentance right there on the spot. I didn't. I didn't know them from Adam and Eve. The Spirit said, "Patience, Meyers!" After the service, I found out that they had just moved in town and were members of an evangelical Presbyterian church in their former residence. Our people showered them with greetings, handshakes, and welcomes. They never came back. This kind of thing has happened to me over and over again. It has nothing to do with intelligibility; it has everything to do with preference and style and sometimes arrogance. Unfortunately, our worship service is just plain "unacceptable" to many prior-churched evangelical people. This is the real issue. Not unintelligibility.

Doing the Liturgy Well: An Admonition to Ministers

One last comment for ministers and ministerial students: a liturgy that partakes of the best of the historic Church's worship must be "performed" correctly. One of the reasons why people don't like "traditional" liturgies and services is because they are often executed sloppily and slowly.

A Reformed pastor will typically have to learn how to lead worship. This does not come naturally either. It must be carefully learned. It has been distressing for me to visit churches with more or less historic liturgies where the pastor and people plod through the service as if it were merely a task to complete. People mumble the responses. The pastor reads his part without looking up at the congregation. Organists and pianists play hymns and songs much too slowly. No wonder people think that traditional liturgies won't connect with modern people.

> The experience of the Reformation also teaches us that when liturgy goes awry the problem may be less with its form and content than with the way in which it is celebrated and interpreted. Today historic forms of worship are being jettisoned in favor of "alternative liturgies" that employ popular-type songs and dramas with the argument that traditional liturgy is boring or meaningless to occasional (and sometimes even to regular) worshipers. Almost invariably this argument is put forward by pastors who have little competence in presiding at the liturgy in a knowledgeable or compelling way and who may even be insecure in the role of presiding minister. This ritual incompetence includes not only poor public performances by ministers, musicians, and congregations but also poor judgment on the part of worship planners in deciding what to add to or subtract from the orders provided in the authorized worship books. Many liturgies get bogged down in extraneous details not specified by the order, or go in uncertain directions ritually and therefore also theologically. It is little wonder that they fail to engage contemporary worshipers. As to the argument that the liturgy is boring, the historic Western liturgy does not suffer from a monotonous sameness; it has a built-in principle of variation in the rites, customs, and textual and musical options of the Church year.[12]

Ministers must learn that the liturgy of the Father's drawing us to Himself in His Son and by the Spirit should be dramatic. If the pastor and people participate enthusiastically with vigorous reading

---

[12] Senn, "The Reform of the Mass," 51–52.

and singing, the service will engage the worshipers and proclaim the vitality of our faith to the watching world.

But whatever the reasons for Presbyterian evangelicals' suspicion of all things liturgical, our Presbyterian brothers and sisters in Christ will never enthusiastically embrace such liturgical worship without an enthusiastic pastoral leadership that is not only able to *explain* its biblical and theological rationale in lessons and sermons, but maybe more fundamental even than didactic expertise, ministers must also be able to lead such worship with pastoral expertise and sensitivity.[13] I believe that too many Presbyterians congregations have not experienced the benefits of a liturgical service and this is because our ministers themselves have not experienced anything like the kind of lively, engaging, biblical liturgy of which I write, and they have not been sufficiently trained in liturgical leadership.

Presbyterian congregations don't like liturgy because their ministers don't know how to lead such worship. They don't have the competence to officiate in a liturgical worship. Consequently, since they have had no definitive training, pastors either casually and often rather apologetically and bashfully "lead" worship services without much confidence in their official station as ordained ministers or they abdicate leadership entirely to "worship committees" and "worship teams." There are all sorts of "performance" issues that obstruct proper appreciation of liturgical worship. Some "traditional" services are performed so slowly and deliberately that they lack the life and drama that ought to characterize liturgical worship. The minister's portion of the service may be conducted with such tediousness that no one is inspired to respond with heart-felt words of confession or praise. Hymns may be sung at such a ponderous tempo that many in the congregation look forward to the final stanza. Even if the proper order of approach to God is observed,

---

[13] Every ministerial candidate who has some interest in liturgy, before he takes a call to a church, ought to listen to Robert S. Rayburn's telling lecture "Roadblocks to Liturgical Reformation" presented at *The Second Annual Pre-General Assembly (PCA) Conference on Reformed Liturgy*, June 19, 2001 (Available from Biblical Horizons, P.O. Box 1096, Niceville, FL 32588).

the leadership can so obscure the order that people fail to appreciate what God is doing for them at any given point in the service. A minister (or lay leader) may be too wordy or flippant or casual such that he calls attention to himself rather than functioning as the instrument of God in service to the people. Ministers or lay readers that fail to adequately prepare before the service can divert the congregation's attention from the Lord's service to them and their grateful response so that they feel sorry for the man who cannot seem to find his place or the right words to say at any given point in the service. Arguably one of the worst hindrances to worship is ministerial leadership that is not sensitive to the solemnity of the situation and does not therefore carefully serve God's people in the service. If this is what it means to do traditional worship, our people think, then by all means bring on the spontaneous, congregation-initiated praise.

Without being overly critical, one can learn even from the mistakes of others. Once I worshipped with my family in another evangelical Presbyterian church. The pastor was quite casual and cheeky during the entire service. A number of Baptisms were scheduled for that morning. When the parents of the infants brought their children forward for Baptism, the pastor joined them at the font but was visibly discombobulated. He had not memorized the names of the covenant children and he had no printed resource at hand.

In order to cover his mistake, he told a few jokes about remembering names and then asked the three sets of parents the names of the children. (To be clear, this was *not* done according to the traditional ritual of some churches where the minister asks, "What is the name of this child" immediately before the administration of the Sacrament.) He then called three elders up front (before the Baptism), had them take the children, and parade them around the sanctuary while he was making comments about how cute and sweet they were. After the children were brought back up onto the stage, he baptized each of the children, having again to ask each set of parents the name of their child. After he had baptized them (without using the traditional formula, I might add) he bellowed out a hearty laugh and said,

"Oh my, I guess we forgot to have the parents take vows. Well, in case there are any Presbyterian sticklers here who might bring charges against me —chuckle, chuckle—I guess we should ask the parents some questions. But, whoops, I don't seem to have a copy of the vows, so I'll just wing it. Parents, do you all love the Lord?

"Yes," they say.

"Good. Will you promise to bring your children up faithfully?

"Yes," again.

"Amen! Well, that about does it. Time to sing a hymn." At which point he sat down with the congregation and the worship team led the congregation in singing "Go tell it on the mountain."

Now, the reader may think that this is an extreme example, but I've been around enough to know better. When our family was home after that service and eating lunch together, even though I have a strict rule not to critique sermons, services, or churches on the Lord's Day, especially in the service itself, my older daughters asked me, "Dad, what did you think of the service?" I answered something like, "Well, it was not like ours. Was it?" "No, it wasn't," they said. My oldest then felt compelled to say, "You know, if I was one of those three families, I think I would have my baby re-baptized!" With that I broke my rule and had a very productive conversation with my children about liturgical protocols and the valuable service it renders to God's people. As Paul says to Timothy, "Watch yourself and teach carefully. Persevere in them, because if you do, you will save both yourself and your hearers" (1 Tim. 4:16).

Liturgy is not something you can just read about in a book and go do. The one who would lead people into God's magestic presence needs mature direction and a great deal of guided experience under someone skilled in the art of liturgical leadership. Some of us who have been raised in liturgical churches have a distinct advantage. Others, aware of their own deficiencies, have deliberately attached themselves to qualified pastors for mentoring during their seminary training or internship. If you are already in the pastorate, however, there are ways to acquire adequate competence. I suggest that you use every opportunity when you are not officiating at your own congregations to visit, worship, and carefully observe qualified ministers in more liturgical communions. To this day, I continue to visit orthodox Lutheran and Episcopal churches when I am on vacation, watching, observing, learning, and critiquing their liturgical craft. And if you do have some competence in these matters, spend time with ministerial candidates in your church, teaching, training, and guiding them in the fundamentals of liturgical leadership.

18
A Parking Lot Parable:
Is the Church Year Biblical?

Redeeming the time, because the days are evil.
—Ephesians 5:16

Once upon a time, Jeff Meyers and Tony Rollins—old friends who had not seen each other for a few years—met in the parking lot of a neighborhood church. They were dropping off their preschool children at the church for Mother's Day Out. (They were such conscientious and helpful fathers.) As they were walking into the church, Tony pointed at the church's sign with a grimace and a confident wag of his head: "Is that biblical?"

"What?" Jeff asked. "The sign?"

"No," Tony replied. "The sign says that this church has Lenten services every Wednesday evening. Is *that* biblical?"

It was early in the day and Jeff was feeling frisky, so he answered with a few of his own questions. Somewhere in the middle of this conversation, the two conscientious fathers remembered to sign their children in. They continued their friendly discussion once they were outside again.

JM: Is there something unbiblical about having church services on Wednesday?

TR: No, no, that's not what I mean. I mean Lenten services. Is that biblical?

JM: What makes meeting on Wednesday evenings for a month or so to commemorate the sufferings of Jesus unbiblical?

TR: It's not the Wednesday meetings that I'm concerned about. Let's leave that out of it. It's the celebration of the season of Lent. The Bible says nothing about such annual events. Presumably this church celebrates Lent for a period of time on Sunday, too. And they probably also observe Advent, Christmas, Easter, and all of those other man-made seasons. Right?

JM: Sure. So, let me get this straight. Because the Bible doesn't explicitly say anything about a yearly observance of Lent (that is, meeting together to commemorate Jesus' suffering and death), it is therefore unbiblical? Furthermore, the Bible doesn't command us to reflect upon the birth of Christ in corporate worship, therefore Advent and Christmas are unbiblical and forbidden as well. Is that what you mean?

TR: Yeah, that's what I mean. The Bible does not command that kind of worship. It's unbiblical for a church to think it is pleasing God by observing Lent, or for that matter, Advent, Christmas, or Easter services. God has commanded no such thing.

JM: Wait a minute, let's not muddy the waters. It's not the "kind of worship" that is under discussion, but the time and theme of worship. This church does not get together on Lent to engage in a different kind of worship. Rather, the people gather to hear the Word, meditate, pray, sing—all the normal activities of worship. Lent does not actually change the worship, but the theme of the worship, especially the Scriptures that are read, the psalms and hymns that are sung, the content of the prayers that are offered up, and the subject matter of the sermons.

TR: That may be true. I don't have a lot of experience with these kinds of worship services.

JM: Well, let's assume for the sake of the discussion that no new elements of worship are introduced. What if I frame the issue this way: during Lent some Christians focus their meditations, Scripture readings, and prayers on the sufferings and death of Jesus. Is *that* unbiblical?

TR: But that's the problem—the Bible does not command the church to celebrate a season of Lent.

JM: Granted. But does that make it wrong to observe such a season? Is it dangerous and unbiblical for the Christian community to set aside a particular time to read, meditate, sing, and pray about Jesus' sufferings and death?

TR: Yes. When it comes to worship, whatever is not commanded in Scripture is forbidden. Lent and Advent are not commanded, therefore they are forbidden. When church leaders invent man-made seasons like this and impose them on congregations, they are binding their people's consciences where God has not bound them.

JM: That's interesting. Tell me about your church, won't you? What has your pastor been preaching about?

TR: I'm a member of Calvin Reformed Memorial Church. My pastor is Rev. Regulative. He's been preaching through the book of Romans for quite some time. We've been in chapter nine for a few months.

JM: How long has he been preaching from Romans?

TR: For about three years now. We believe in preaching straight through books of the Bible.

JM: Wow! How much longer till he finishes Romans?

TR: He estimates that it will take him about two more years— five years total.

JM: Does the pastor choose hymns and compose his prayers each Sunday such that they support whatever theme he is preaching from Romans?

TR: Yes, that's the general practice.

JM: Is *that* biblical? Where in the Bible has God commanded that pastors preach through entire books of the Bible like that?

Where has God commanded that a pastor select hymns and readings based on his own man-made preaching scheme and then impose them upon the consciences of worshipers gathered on the Lord's Day for church?

TR: Oh, I see! You were trying to set me up, weren't you?

JM: I confess. You caught me. But, let's not get sidetracked. I asked you whether your church's way of ordering its worship was biblical. I am referring to the time and themes of your services. Where does God command that the pastor order the Scripture readings, sermons, hymns, and prayers according to this method of continuous preaching?

TR: Off the top of my head, I don't know. But this has been the Reformed way since the Reformation. Our church is being true to a venerable Reformed legacy when we follow the *lectio continua* ("continuous reading") method of preaching.

JM: A venerable legacy, huh? Isn't that kind of like an "old tradition"?

TR: It's more than just a tradition. We believe that it's the best way of teaching people the Bible.

JM: Maybe so, but my point is that it is nowhere *commanded* in the Scriptures. Is it? You say it's the best way, but I ask: Is it the biblical way? There is absolutely no evidence to suggest that either Peter or Paul preached verse by verse through entire Old Testament books. The Bible does not command pastors to select themes for their worship services—readings, prayers, and hymns—according to this method of preaching, does it? My bottom-line question to you is: What really differentiates your church's way of ordering Scripture readings, hymns, and prayers from one that uses the traditional Church year? Your pastor "forces" five years of Romans on his congregation's worship and this other church's pastor "forces" a year of the life of Christ on his. What's the essential difference?

TR: When you put it like that, you make it sound like the Church year is primarily a way for the church to order its readings, prayers, and hymns over time. Are you suggesting that it's not all that different from what Reformed pastors do when they choose themes for their worship service based on their preaching texts?

JM: Exactly. The church is free to order her readings, prayers, and hymns according to the preaching texts chosen by the pastor and she is also free to order its readings, prayers, and hymns according to the life of Christ as embodied in the traditional Church year. If your church can emphasize the truth of God's election (Romans 9) in a worship service with preaching, prayers, readings, psalms, and hymns appropriate to such an emphasis, then this church can also choose to commemorate the Lord's birth (Luke 2) and adorn the celebration with appropriate preaching, hymns, readings, and prayers. What's the difference?

TR: I guess that makes sense to me, but I'm not so sure that you haven't tricked me somehow. I've always been suspicious of the Church year because Catholics and Episcopalians do it. Don't they force the churches to keep the Church calendar? I don't think I would appreciate being mandated to celebrate something that the Bible doesn't command.

JM: Whoa, do we have to go through the Bible-doesn't-command-it routine again?

TR: No, I don't think so. But I am concerned about binding people's consciences with extra-biblical requirements.

JM: You mean like imposing the epistle of Romans on people for five years?

TR: Ha, ha. Very funny.

JM: I'm serious. Why do you submit to such an imposition on your conscience? The Bible does not command pastors to preach through Romans for five years. Your pastor has chosen to order your church's services according to a man-made, extra-biblical scheme. The people are subjected to a five-year diet of Romans. Is that biblical? What makes this scheme more biblical than Lent or Advent? Why couldn't your pastor choose to preach through the life of Christ in a year and lead the congregation through meditations, Scripture readings, and prayers keyed into the life of Christ? That's precisely what the Church year is designed to do. Why do you object to Lent and not to Romans? What's the difference?

TR: Hey, aren't you doing graduate work at that Lutheran seminary?

JM: You mean Concordia? Yeah, why?

TR: That's where you're getting all of these liturgical ideas. They'd never teach this kind of thing at a Reformed seminary, would they?

JM: Look, Tony, sometimes you need to step outside of your own tradition so that you can think objectively about it. Besides, why do you think Reformed Christians have such divergent liturgical practices? It may have something to do with the fact that Reformed seminaries don't teach students to think about worship and liturgy at all. I don't need to convert to Lutheranism to appreciate many of their insights into corporate worship. We seem to have forgotten that the Reformation itself was a liturgical renewal as much as anything else. By the way, I am not suggesting that the received Church year is flawless; but I do believe that the Bible gives churches the freedom to use it if they so choose.

TR: Goodness, time has gotten away from me. I've got to run. My wife is helping to plan our church's Vacation Bible School today, and I promised to help.

JM: Is that biblical?

TR: What? Me helping my wife?

JM: No. VBS. Is Vacation Bible School biblical?

TR: Yikes!

JM: Well . . . where is VBS commanded in the Bible?

TR: You are ruthless!

JM: See you later, Tony. Go help your wife!

TR: Thanks. Let's talk about this again sometime soon.

JM: Sure.

19
A Ministerial
Robe and Collar

For Aaron's sons you shall make tunics and sashes and
headbands; you shall make them for glory and beauty.
                                        —Exodus 28:40

The minister officiating at the Lord's Service ought to be dressed
in a way that identifies him as the representative and spokesman
of Jesus Christ. This is his calling and the congregation should
be visually reminded of his responsibilities and place in the Divine Service. Traditionally, the minister wears a white tunic or
robe. All sorts of questions may surface at this point in a reader's
mind. Is this biblical? Or is this something that has just always
been done that way? Isn't this too "Catholic"? Does the robe
mean that the pastor is better than me? Closer to God than I am?
Is he a priest? Why does the pastor lead the entire worship service anyway? These are the kinds of questions that I will attempt
to answer in this chapter.

Office Over Personality

First, the robe, among other things, helps emphasize the office of the pastor and de-emphasize the personality of the man
in the pulpit. Sometimes it is hard to be led in worship by an

elder or pastor who is a good friend or a peer or even (especially) one
who is younger. To help us get over this feeling, the Church in general, and the Reformed church in particular, has historically placed
special robes on her ministers when they conduct worship. This
helps the people remember that it is not just good old Jeff Meyers
up there; rather, this is the Lord's ordained minister leading us into
God's presence and speaking God's Word to us. Strictly speaking,
the worship service is *not* conducted by Jeff Meyers anyway, but by
the robe of office that Jeff Meyers happens to be filling at the
current time. We submit to the *office*, not to the man, during worship.
(The concept of submission to church office is eminently biblical:
Acts 20:17, 28–35; 1 Cor. 12:28; 16:16; Eph. 4:11–16; 1 Thes.
5:12–13; 1 Tim. 3:1ff; 4:14; 5:17; Heb. 13:7, 17; 1 Pet. 5:1–7.)

These truths are reinforced when the pastor wears something that
reminds the people of his special calling on the Lord's Day. In the
Bible clothing and calling are often connected; a person's calling or
office, together with whatever authority is connected with the office, is often visually symbolized by the clothing the man wears
(Gen. 9:20–27; 39:1–13; 37: 3–11, 23; 41:1–44; all of the references to the clothing of the priests in Exodus and Leviticus; 1 Sam.
2:19; 15:27; 18:4; 24:4–5, 11, 14; Ezra 9:3–5; Est. 8:15; Is. 22:21; Jn.
3:6; Mt. 22:11ff; 27:31; Mk. 16:5; Lk. 15:22; Rev. 1:13; 4:4; 6:11;
19:13, 16). The purpose of the robe is to cover the man and accent
his God-ordained office or calling.

From the Reformation until comparatively recently Presbyterian ministers
wore robes or some dress of office when serving in the sanctuary. The biblical support for this is straightforward enough:

A. "And you shall make holy garments for Aaron your brother, for glory
and for beauty" (Exod. 28:2). This is the only rationale ever provided (i.e.,
these are not vestments in the traditional sense). Would you want the contrary: your minister, as he is leading worship and preaching God's Word,
to be without dignity and honor (again v. 40)?

B. When is it worn? See Exodus 35:19 and 39:1.

C. These are timeless considerations and have usually been thought to be so in the history of the church.[1]

Putting the Minister in His Place

Second, the minister who leads the worship plays a symbolic role during worship. When he leads the congregation in prayer before God, he symbolizes Christ leading the Church in prayer before the Father. When he reads and preaches the Word, he symbolizes Christ, the Husband, speaking to His holy Bride (which is, by the way, one of the main reasons why women cannot be pastors: they cannot publicly symbolize Christ the Husband to His Bride, the Church, 1 Cor. 11:2–10; 14:33–38; Eph. 5:22–33; 1 Tim. 2:11–15). When the minister baptizes he symbolizes and represents Jesus who baptizes by the Holy Spirit (Mt. 3:11; Jn. 1:33; 1 Cor. 12:13). When the pastor stands behind the Lord's Table he serves bread and wine on behalf of Christ (Lk. 22:26–27; Jn. 13:15; Rev. 3:20). Of course, we might reverse this way of speaking and say that Jesus speaks, baptizes, and serves at the table by means of His ordained ministry.

The symbolic, representative role of the pastor in corporate worship is crucial. The pastor acts and speaks for Christ to His Church. When this symbolic dimension of the pastoral office is lost, strange conceptions take its place. Without this understanding the reasons for differentiating the minister from the people may become bizarre. One minister recently told his congregation that the only reason he was up front and leading the congregation on Sunday morning is because "he was farther along in his walk with Jesus" than they were. Oh, really? How does one gauge who is walking closest to Jesus? It seems rather presumptuous for a forty-year old man to claim spiritual superiority over the grandmothers and grandfathers in his congregation. Furthermore, if liturgical leadership is

---

[1] Robert S. Rayburn, "Worship From the Whole Bible," in *The Second Annual Conference on Worship: The Theology and Music of Reformed Worship,* February 23–25, 1996 (Nashville: Covenant Presbyterian Church, 1996), 25.

tied to subjective spirituality, then it may be appropriate to have a different man or woman lead worship every week. After all, someone may have raced past the pastor during the week. How does one measure and determine which member is farthest along and therefore qualified to be up front each week?

In contrast to this ridiculous notion, the Church has ordained men to speak and act for Jesus Christ in an official capacity. To be sure, they ought to be men of mature spirituality, but their ministry is not entirely based on this. Many members of the congregation are often older, wiser, and more mature than their pastor. Nevertheless, he is called to serve them as the representative of Jesus Christ. The robe need not set him *above* the congregation, but only *apart* from them because of his unique office as pastor during the Lord's Day worship service. Here is what the French Calvinist theologian Richard Paquier says about this:

> It is natural that the man who officiates in the worship of the Church be clothed in a manner corresponding to the task assigned to him and expressing visibly what he does. Moreover, whoever leads in the act of worship does not perform as a private party but as a minister of the church; he is the representative of the community and the spokesman of the Lord. Hence, an especially prescribed robe, a sort of ecclesiastical "uniform," is useful for reminding both the faithful and himself that in this act he is not Mr. So-and-so, but a minister of the church in the midst of a multitude of others.[2]

Paquier goes on to insist that the minister wear a white, not black robe. The traditional black Genevan gown worn by so many traditional Presbyterians is an academic gown. Today it is even worn by secular judges. The minister, however, does not demand respect or a hearing because of his academic credentials. Furthermore, the corporate worship of God's people is not the place for pastors to show off their academic achievements by wearing doctoral chevrons on their Genevan Gowns. A simple white robe is sufficient. After

---

[2] Richard Paquier, *Dynamics of Worship: Foundations and Uses of Liturgy* (Fortress Press, 1967), 138.

all, the Bible says, "Let your garments be always white" (Eccl. 9:8). Here are Paquier's strong words:

> The Genevan gown, this anti-liturgical, secular vestment, which appears in the color of the shades of darkness, this clothing which is comparable to the sack cloth and ashes of mourning in the old covenant, is the negation of the right of the church to rejoice and be consoled in the presence of the heavenly Bridegroom. Perhaps for the synagogue, in its tribulation, to wear such a vestment would be the normal thing. But in modern Protestantism it is a depressing sign that we are not more aware of the nuptial joy of the Eucharist and that we do not believe in the victorious struggle Christ led against the world.[3]

Businessman or Minister of the Word?

Third, think about who the pastor is and what he is doing. The pastor is not a businessman. He is not the CEO of the ecclesiastical corporation. I always feel a little uncomfortable in a starched shirt, suit and tie. It tends to contribute toward a very real problem in our Presbyterian churches—we tend to attract upper-middle class people. Upper-middle class people are comfortable around a pastor whose uniform is a suit and tie. People in other economic strata, however, sometimes find it hard to relate to a pastor who dresses like and acts like a country club capitalist. When I dress like this I often sense that what I wear erects unfortunate barriers in certain situations.

Just because a congregation doesn't have its pastor wear a robe doesn't mean that they escape the idea of a uniform. In most American Protestant churches, for example, there is an expectation that the pastor dress conservatively, with a black or dark suit, a white starched shirt, a conservative necktie (no Mickey Mouse ties!), etc. In our culture this is the weekday uniform of a lawyer or middle to upper management businessman. This has become *de facto* the American Evangelical clerical garb. I think this "uniform" often communicates precisely the wrong message in our churches and the

[3] Ibid., 142.

communities in which we minister. Our pastors too often seek to conform to the patterns and symbols of authority prevalent in American culture. It is simply not possible to escape the symbolism of clothing. When the minister of the Word wears a robe, it helps to focus the congregation on the work of Christ and the apostles, because the minister has no authority outside of his connection to them.

Reactionary Reasons

I should answer some possible objections. Some might think that this smacks too much of Roman Catholicism. First of all, we are not talking about a collar, but a robe. But even here we have to be circumspect. The Roman Catholics are wrong in many areas, but we need to be careful not to throw out the baby with the bath water. Just because Roman Catholics do something, that does not automatically make it wrong or undesirable. Besides, if you would care to check it out, Reformed pastors in the past actually wore uniforms of some kind not just in worship, but during the week as well. That holds true for continental Reformed churches and even for many of the Puritans. Pictures and portraits that we have of these pastors show them in clerical or academic garb.

Take for example the painting on the cover of James Bannerman's *The Church of Christ* (Edinburgh: Banner of Truth, 1974). James Bannerman was one of the most respected Scottish apologists for the Presbyterian form of government. You might call him a super-Presbyterian. The painting on the cover of this volume is by John Lorimer, and it is called "The Ordination of Elders." The minister in the picture is wearing a black gown, and he also has a peculiar collar—you've probably seen pictures of these before—with two white tabs sticking out from it. No one else is dressed that way in the service. Scottish Presbyterian ministers, who traditionally have been fiercely anti-Catholic, have historically worn clerical uniforms. There is nothing characteristically Roman Catholic about pastors wearing distinctive clothing during the worship service.

Finally, in response to the objection that the robe is somehow Roman Catholic or Episcopalian, I append below a portion of Horton Davies' *The Worship of the English Puritans.*[4] This section comes near the end of chapter four, in which Davies discusses how Puritan liturgical practice in England and Scotland departed from the continental Reformed tradition. Davies quotes from John Durel's work, *A View of the Government and Publick Worship of God in the Reformed Churches Beyond the Sea* (London, 1662). Durel was a minister of the French Reformed Church, and his book is an attempt to confute the claim that the radical Puritans were necessarily closer disciples of the Reformed churches than were the Anglicans when it came to ceremonies in worship. At one point he asserts that some of the Westminster Divines held conceptions of the continental Reformed Churches that "were mere Chimeras and Ideas; which, like the *Utopia* of Sir Thomas More, never existed but in their brain."[5] Here is what Davies writes about distinctive ministerial clothing:

> Finally, there remains to be considered the Puritan attitude to ecclesiastical vestments, compared with the view of the Reformed churches. Durel asserts that it is the custom of the Reformed ministers to wear ecclesiastical vestments both during the divine service and out of doors: "The ministers of France, in the towns where the greatest part are Protestant, and where they may freely appear for what they are . . . never go out of their houses into the open street without a long *Cassock* or narrow coat down to the very ground, and a *Gown* over it, with a *Girdle* upon the *Coat*: And it would be taken very ill if they should appear without this decent apparel." He also informs us that the ministers of Hungary and Transylvania wear a long cloak and cassock when they go out of doors, whilst long cloaks are worn by German pastors, or "a Gown and a long cap, as at Basil." It is fairly certain that in the Genevan Church the ministers wore the priest's outdoor habit, consisting of cassock, bands, black gown, scarf or tippet, and cap. This is corroborated by a letter of Calvin's in which he tells how he confuted a woman who claimed that the "long habits" (presumably cassocks) worn by the

[4] Horton Davies, *The Worship of the English Puritans,* (1948; Lake Mary: Soli Deo Gloria, 1997).

[5] Cited by Davies, 35.

Genevan ministers were disobeying our Lord's command to "beware of the Scribes, which desire to walk in long robes" (Lk. 20:46). Calvin did not deny that the ministers wore long robes, but he told her that her faulty exegesis was derived from the "Gospel of the Manichaeans."

The English Puritans, however, objected strenuously to all vestments. In 1562 a request was made to Convocation to do away with copes and surplices "so that all ministers in their ministry use a grave, comely, and side-garment, as they commonly do in preaching," whilst it petitioned "that the ministers of the Word and Sacraments be not compelled to wear such gowns and caps, as the enemies of Christ's gospel have chosen to be the special array of their priesthood." Six years later the Puritans appealed to Beza, Calvin's successor at Geneva, to know his opinion of their being coerced into wearing gowns and vestments in England. Beza expressed regret at hearing that the vestments [not the gowns] had been restored, "yet since they are not of the nature of those things which are themselves ungodly, we think them not of so great moment, that therefore either the pastors should leave their ministry or that the flock should neglect their public food, rather than hear pastors so habited."

In Scotland it appears to have been the regular custom for ministers to wear a gown when conducting divine service. The cassock also was in frequent use, but this is not surprising since it was not a liturgical vestment, but the usual out-of-doors dress of the Ministry. In England, however, the Puritans appear to have discarded the cassock, whilst there is little evidence to show that the early Puritans wore gowns . . . . In this disapproval of any distinctive dress for the clergy, the English Puritans departed from the Reformed tradition.[6]

Formality in Worship

A second objection: the formality will turn people off. Years ago, before I began wearing a robe, a visitor to our church (from another denomination) commented on the beauty and solemnity of the service, but then asked why the pastor was wearing a suit and tie rather than a robe. She said that looking at the pastor in his own suit and tie was awkward and distracting. It seemed too casual. Why didn't he wear something appropriate to his calling and duties on Sunday

[6] Ibid., 46–48.

morning? she asked. Many mistakenly think that avoiding formality and ceremony is evidence of simple faith and humility. C. S. Lewis said, "The modern habit of doing ceremonial things unceremoniously is no proof of humility; rather it proves the worshiper's inability to forget *himself* in the rite, and his readiness to spoil for everyone else the proper place of ritual." [7]

Since for Americans there is often an in-built negative reaction to any mention of formality in worship, proper attention should be paid to passages like Hebrews 13 and Revelation 4–5. Hebrews 13:22–24 describes a New Covenant corporate, Lord's Day worship service (contrasted with the Old Covenant worship of verses 18–21). When the Church gathers on the Lord's Day she enters into heaven (by faith) to worship God with all of the angelic host and departed saints. It is as if the roof of the church building is torn off when the pastor calls the people to worship. Notice that the worshipers are all organized around the throne of God. The worship service does not merely provide an opportunity for private devotional experiences. The Church is a "city" and a "joyous assembly" or "festal array" (v. 22). The word translated "festal assembly" denotes an assembly of people gathered for a formal celebration or festival.

Later, when we are privileged with the apostle John in the book of Revelation to peek into heaven, how is the worship conducted? What kind of worship is modeled for us in heaven? There are all kinds of liturgical lessons to be learned here. I only wish to highlight one aspect: the heavenly service is liturgical and formal. According to Revelation 4–5, heavenly worship is a formal, coordinated activity. There are cooperative, formal responses by groups of worshipers. Everybody responds together with the same words. There are no individual displays of spirituality. Angels, elders, and creatures respond antiphonally with responses that must have been learned. They have been trained. There is a pre-arranged

[7] C. S. Lewis, *Preface to Paradise Lost* (Oxford: Oxford University Press, 1942),52.

form to the worship. They have rehearsed this event, and they are dressed accordingly (Rev. 4:4). In other words, heavenly, Spirit-guided worship is liturgical and formal (1 Cor. 14:26–33).

There is more than a little bit of irony in the fact that American Christians love the formality of weddings, but want informal cheeky weekly worship services. It seems we want to honor our sons and daughters with a beautiful service, but when it comes to the fore-taste of the Marriage Supper of the Lamb and the honor of the Bride of Christ we have little interest. Why is it that pastors wear robes during wedding services and not during Lord's Day worship services? At weddings the robe adds to the solemnity and glory of the event. The same ought to be true on the Lord's Day. Are wedding services more important than Sunday services? No, just the opposite. The Lord's Day worship service ought to be just as (or more) glorious and formal as a wedding. The robe adds dignity and reverence to our services; it glorifies and beautifies the representative of Christ (Exod. 28:1).

Is the Robe a Barrier or Bridge?

Others object that the robe will make the pastor unapproachable. Not so. It makes him more approachable in his capacity as pastor. It forces "Jeff Meyers" to recede and brings forward the office of pastor. The robe will highlight the pastor's office and role. In fact, people may be more apt to address the pastor with spiritual questions and concerns. They will be reminded that Jeff is their pastor, the one whom Christ has given them as a gift (Eph. 4:8–13).

After all, people want to be able to trust their pastors. They want their pastors to be different. People need to be able to place some kind of secondary confidence in the office of the pastor and elder (our primary confidence, of course, is in God's Word.). An outward sign of that office helps people. This is not too difficult to prove. Think about doctors, nurses, judges, and policemen. People want them to wear something distinctive that reminds them of their expertise or calling. We are helped when our doctor wears a white uniform. The uniform assists us in remembering that we can place some confidence in him. This is his calling. The uniform reminds us of his training and commitment. The same ought to be true with our pastors.

Biblical teaching as a whole links clothing and calling. You are what you wear or you wear what you are. Just as judges, physicians, policemen, and auto mechanics wear clothing that befits their calling, so should the pastor, especially when he is performing the specific duties of his office during the Lord's Day worship service. Again, Rayburn's comments are helpful: "We do not obey them or listen to them [judges, mayors, congressmen, or policemen] as individuals, or because of their personal virtue or opinions. But because they hold office. The judge speaks for the law and the minister speaks for God. The man himself should fade into the background and the office come to the fore. What has happened over the last generation has been the reverse. The man has come to the fore and the office has been in full retreat from the view of the congregation."[8]

In Christian worship, biblically and historically, the ministers wear distinctive garments to testify to their office as representatives of Christ. The robe serves to hide the personality of the man and highlight his special calling. The pastor represents Christ, the Husband, to the Church, His Bride. When the pastor leads worship, the robe helps remind us that it is not "my friend Jeff" up front. God in Christ calls us to worship, to confess, to hear His Word, to give, etc., and He does so by means of His ordained servant. The pastor does not act for himself, but for Christ. A judge or a policeman wears a uniform because he does not act for himself.

The pastor's authority, therefore, does not derive from his economic or social status (expensive suits and starched shirts). It does not derive from his natural charisma (impressive hair or flashing dark eyes). It most certainly does not derive from the fact that he looks

---

[8] Robert S. Rayburn, "Worship From the Whole Bible," 26.

and acts like other leaders in the world (business suits), even though this is what happens too often in America. Therefore, by placing a robe on the minister during the Divine Service we are 1) taking a stand against the current American evangelical church's tendency to transform the Pastorate into something like an executive position (the CEO of the church) by mimicking American corporate big business, and 2) seeking to bring our practice in line with what the Bible implies, back in line with what the historic Church has practiced, and in line with what other Reformed churches do worldwide.

A Collar During the Week

A few years ago I began to wear a recognized uniform of my calling—the white tab-collared shirt—during the week. The collar is for my week-day ministry. It serves to identify me as a minister in the community. For me there is one overriding reason for wearing a collar: it will open doors for evangelism and ministry in the community that I would otherwise miss.

"Hold your horses," someone may say. "If you need a collar to do ministry then you've got a problem. You should be identified as a Christian minister simply by your life and words." I've actually had someone (not a member of my congregation) say this to me. I do think that there is more than a little truth in such a statement. Surely a collar alone does not make one a minister. But I don't think it is really that simple. The real question is not whether I need one, but will wearing a uniform help me better perform my ministry in the community. I certainly don't need a collar to do ministry. I will never claim that it is necessary. Rather, I think it is beneficial. The same holds true for other professions. A waiter or EMT specialist doesn't need a uniform, but it sure helps. And if it is helpful for waiters, policeman, doctors, even UPS drivers to be readily identifiable by their uniform, shouldn't the same hold true for pastors?

Furthermore, I don't deny that a collar alone is worthless. There must be godly living and speaking if there is to be any real ministerial service to others. To be sure, some ministers may wear a collar out of haughtiness and self-promotion. Some may even mis-interpret my decision to wear the pastoral collar as arrogance—a kind of spiritual one-up-manship. I'm a minister and you're not. Look at me. But I know my own motivations. I fully expect that a few will call me pompous and elitist. But that is not the effect that wearing the uniform of a pastor has on me. It affects me in just the opposite way. The actor Laurence Olivier once said that he could not become a character until he had decided upon the right nose. Clothes do the same thing for us. A moment's reflection will show that the kind of clothes you wear affects the way you behave. Ray Bradbury wrote a powerful short story called "The Wonderful Ice Cream Suit" in which six down-and-out men experience a miracu-lous transformation in their attitude and behavior when they wear a brand-new white suit around town for an evening.

When I wear a collar I am continually reminded of my account-ability as a minister of the Gospel. In a word, I speak and behave differently. I have a constant reminder that I am a slave of Jesus Christ. With all due respect to those ministers who don't wear a collar, I find dressing like a West County banker or lawyer to be a much greater temptation. Why should I pretend to be someone I'm not? Why should I wear clothes that affect me in ways that do not contribute to my ministry? I think the offense of the collar is of-ten determined in large part by the man wearing it. If he is a smart aleck with a haughty attitude, he'll probably come off as a high-church upstart. This is a real temptation. Nevertheless, I think wear-ing the collar has actually served to curb this temptation for me. It constantly reminds me of my calling, of how I should speak and act before the world a representative of Jesus Christ and His Church.

Moreover, when I wear a uniform, I can no longer travel around town incognito. What I say and do is evaluated differently by everyone who sees and hears me. Wearing the collar is an act of self-denial, a helpful means of rectifying my own sinful tendency to hide my calling. That white tab over my voice box constantly reminds me of the need for sanctified, life-giving speech. While I'm out in the community, I must take Paul's charge to "Pastor" Timothy with the utmost seriousness: "Watch your life and doctrine closely. Persevere in them, because if you do, you will save both yourself and your hearers" (1 Tim. 4:6).

When a pastor wears distinctive garments around town it testifies to his office as a special servant of Christ. The white collar has been associated with the iron collar of a slave. The minister is the bondslave of Jesus Christ. The symbolic clothing serves to hide the personality, social class, or economic status of the man and highlight his special calling. The pastor represents and ministers Christ to the world. The pastor does not act for himself, but for Jesus Christ. Judges, policemen, and military personnel wear uniforms precisely because they do not act for themselves. They are *under orders*. They represent the law and government of the county, city, or state which they serve. In the same way, a minister represents the law and government of another kingdom—the clothing he wears testifies to this. He also is under orders, as Paul reminds young "Pastor" Timothy:

> You therefore must endure hardship as a good soldier of Jesus Christ. No one engaged in warfare entangles himself with the affairs of this life, that he may please him who enlisted him as a soldier. And also if anyone competes in athletics, he is not crowned unless he competes according to the rules. The hard-working farmer must be first to partake of the crops. Consider what I say, and may the Lord give you understanding in all things." (2 Tim. 2:3–7)

As I said above in arguing for the ministerial robe, the pastor's authority does not derive from his economic or social status, his natural charisma, his educational accomplishments, or from the fact that he looks and acts like other leaders in the world (business suits). Just as the church building with its steeple and cross symbolize the presence of a congregation of believers in the community, so also the visible presence of the pastor in his "uniform" at the grocery store, post office, cleaners, mall, or bookstore, makes the ministry visible and more readily available to those outside of the Church. It creates opportunities to speak to and serve people in the community.

Many of our Christian forefathers would not have understood the need for such an essay as this. Before the democratization of American culture, ministers commonly wore uniforms that set them apart from other callings.[9] This was the accepted practice. In many parts of the world, this is still true. There is no need to explain why a minister should wear his uniform around town. Since the time of the Reformation there were, of course, questions about exactly what kind of clothing Protestant ministers should wear, but there was not a great deal of controversy about the fact that they should wear something visibly different.

Puritan ministers objected to Episcopal vestments in the sanctuary, for example. But even they themselves wore some sort of robe to lead in the assembly on Sunday and many of them also wore clerical clothing during the week around town to identify them as pastors. It may have been something as simple as the "Geneva bands." If you've seen portraits of seventeenth- and eighteenth-century ministers (like George Whitefield or Jonathan Edwards), then you've seen the two strips of white cloth that hang from the front of the collar. It seems like every other *Banner of Truth* magazine displays on its cover a portrait of a seventeenth-, eighteenth-, or nineteenth-century minister wearing pastoral tabs. It is clear from paintings of Presbyterian clergy of an earlier era (e.g. John Witherspoon in the late 1700's or Archibald Alexander Hodge in the mid-1800's) that clerical garb was considered normal.

At one point in a recent adult Sunday School class in our church on American Presbyterian history, Dr. David Calhoun, professor of Church history at Covenant Theological Seminary, after he had been displaying various pictures of eighteenth-century Presbyterian ministers on the overhead projector, was asked by someone in the congregation, "I can't help but notice that all of these Presbyterian

---

[9] I am using "democratization" in a negative sense. American culture was radically affected by egalitarian socio-political movements at the opening of the nineteenth century. Traditional notions of authority and leadership in society and church were attacked as "undemocratic." One of the most fascinating and instructive accounts of this period is Nathan O. Hatch's *The Democratization of American Christianity* (New Haven: Yale University Press, 1989).

ministers wore some sort of distinctive clothing. Did Presbyterian pastors wear ministerial clothing and collars back then? If so, when did this practice change and why?" Dr. Calhoun answered the question in the affirmative and briefly explained that the practice of wearing pastoral uniforms became problematic in the nineteenth century with the increasing democratization of the American church. Of course, Protestant ministers did, over time, choose clothing that distinguished them from Roman Catholic priests. In our context, I think this may mean avoiding the black and white-collared shirt. A minister who wears either a white, blue, or gray colored shirt with a small white tab over the front of his throat is hardly likely to be misidentified as a Roman Catholic priest.

The objection cited at the beginning of this essay implied that it was unnatural for a minister to be identified in any other way than by his life and speech. Is this helpful? How a minister is identified is a little more complex than how Christians with other callings are known to be believers. Around my neighborhood, people know that I'm the pastor of the Presbyterian church that meets at the corner of Sappington and Eddie & Park roads. I have had a few opportunities to talk with people based on that general knowledge. They came to me with questions or favors. They did so because they knew I was a minister. A similar kind of thing ought to happen to all Christians in their neighborhoods. People should know that you are a believer. But you will have to tell them. They will not be able to discern that you are a genuine believer in the Lord Jesus Christ by observing your activities around your home. Even if you offer your help and service to various neighbors, you are nothing more than a nice guy (or maybe even a Mormon!) unless you make it known somehow that you are a Christian. With those we have contact with on a regular basis this works just fine. We will have opportunities to share Christ with our relatives, our neighbors, and our workmates if they know we are Christians and see that we live according to the example of Jesus Christ.

There are, however, people at the post office, the restaurant, the bank, the video store, Barnes & Noble, that will never be able to guess that a man is a Christian minister by the way he acts or talks. Not unless he is obnoxiously going around announcing the fact to everyone he meets. But if a man wears a collar, then everyone who sees him knows that he is a pastor. They may not discern what kind of minister he is, whether liberal or conservative, Lutheran or Reformed, but they can recognize the distinctively Christian clothing of a pastor. But what, you may ask, will that accomplish? Well, with some people it may mean nothing. For others it will evoke hatred and spite. But there are those who may be curious and want to ask the pastor about his church or ministry. Other people who are in need may ask for help. Some may have questions about difficult situations they are facing. The pastor who wears a collar during the week should anticipate one day walking into the local grocery store or community center and having people actually recognize him. "That's the pastor of such-and-such church down the road." That kind of visibility and familiarity cannot hurt the church, can it? I suspect that it will greatly increase her ability to evangelize and serve to people in the community.

20
The Ascension
Offering Examined

Who shall ascend the hill of Yahweh?
—Psalm 24:3a

The basic outline of the order or sequence of God's drawing us to Himself symbolized in the sacrificial system has already been laid out in chapter four. The simple order is cleansing, consecration, and communion. As I argued earlier, this sequential way of God's drawing men near can be seen both by observing the order in which the three major offerings are made (Purification Offering first, Ascension Offering second, and Fellowship Offering last, as in Lev. 9) and by examining details of the individual offerings themselves. In the latter, the pathway the animal/worshiper follows as the sacrificial operations are performed on it/him gives us the same sequence: death/confession, ascension/consecration, and transformation/communion.

Examining the "Ascension Offering" (Lev. 1:3ff) in more detail will provide an example of how this is fleshed out. The sacrificial animal was both a vicarious substitute as well as a representative of the worshiper and worshipping community. As a substitute the animal was executed, but as a representative the animal was drawn up to God. Interpreting this correctly helps us understand how Jesus is both our substitute (on the cross) as well as our kingly representative (as He rises again and ascends into heaven for us). The priest that assists the worshiper and enables the animal to ascend is a type of the Holy Spirit. This entire movement from death to fellowship with God is typologically symbolized in the sacrifices, particularly the "Ascension Offering." We ascend to the Father in the Son and by (or with the help of) the Spirit. And, of course, this process is repeated every week when the Lord renews His covenant with His people, using the Spirit to draw them near to Himself in Christ as living sacrifices.

Before beginning a verse-by-verse exposition, an accurate translation of Leviticus 1:1–9 will help us get the overall flow of the passage:

> Yahweh called to Moses and spoke to him from the Tent of Meeting, saying, "Speak to the sons of Israel and say to them, When a man draws near [*qrb*] with an offering [*qorban*] to Yahweh, you shall draw near [*qrb*] with your offering [*qorban*] from the herd or from the flock. If his offering is an Ascension [*'olah*] of the herd, let him draw near with a male without blemish; he shall cause it to draw near at the entrance of the Tent of Meeting that he may find favor before the face of Yahweh. Then he shall lay his hand on the head of the Ascension, and it will be accepted on his behalf to make atonement for him. And he is to slaughter the son of the herd [*ben habaqar*] before Yahweh, and then Aaron's sons the priests shall cause the blood to draw near [*qrb*] and dash it against the altar on all sides at the entrance to the Tent of Meeting. And he is to skin the Ascension and cut it into pieces. And the sons of Aaron the priest shall put fire on the altar, and lay the wood in order on the fire. Then the priests, the sons of Aaron, shall lay the parts, the head, and the fat in order on the wood that is on the fire upon the altar; but he shall wash its entrails and its legs with water. And the priest shall cause it all to turn into smoke [*qtr*] on the altar as an Ascension, a food offering [*'isheh*], a sweet aroma to Yahweh.

Leviticus 1:1–2, *Yahweh called to Moses and spoke to him from the Tent of Meeting, saying, "Speak to the sons of Israel and say to them, When a man draws near* [qrb] *with an offering* [qorban] *to Yahweh, you shall draw near* [qrb] *with your offering* [qorban] *from the herd or from the flock."*

The Hebrew name of this sacrifice is *'olah*. It means "ascension" not "whole burnt offering."[1] The noun is related to the verb *'alah*, which means "to go up, to ascend." This sacrifice, therefore, highlights the fact that the whole animal is burned up on the altar and ascends into God's presence as smoke. Peter Leithart explains,

> The normal word (*'olah*) that is translated as "burnt offering" and "whole burnt offering" has nothing to do with either burning or wholeness. It is the noun form of a verb meaning "to go up, to ascend, to climb." The reason for translating it as "burnt offering" is not difficult to see. After all, the burnt offering was the only offering wholly consumed in the altar fire. Yet, the names of the other offerings have nothing to do with the disposition of the animal's flesh or blood. The "sin offering" is not called the "sprinkling offering," though the sprinkling of blood is highlighted in the rite of the sin offering (Lev. 4). The peace offering is not called the "partly eaten" offering, though the communion meal is highlighted (Lev. 3). Instead, the names of the other offerings tell us something about the *meaning* of the offering, not something about the rite, and it is only reasonable to conclude that the name of the burnt offering does the same.[2]

Yahweh invites the worshiper to "draw near" (*qrb*) with an offering (*qorban*). The offerings are called *qorban*, "that which is brought near" (Lev. 1:2; 2:1; 3:1–2; 4:23; 5:11; 7:38). The worshiper draws near as the *qorban* approaches the altar and then ascends into God's presence. The only part of the animal that does not ascend is the old "skin" which the priest keeps. This means that the animal must be

---

[1] According to Jacob Milgrom, "*'olah* literally means 'that which ascends,' which implies that the offering is entirely turned into smoke" (*Leviticus 1–16*, vol. 3 in *The Anchor Bible* [New York: Doubleday, 1991], 172). George Bush explains, "The original term for burnt-offering, (*'olah*), comes from the root *'lh*, "to ascend." It is so called, because it was laid whole on the altar, and then, with the exception of the skin, being consumed by fire, the greatest part of it *ascended toward heaven*" (*The Book of Leviticus* [New York: Newman & Ivison, 1952], 9). See also S. R. Hirsch, *The Pentateuch* [Gateshead: Judaica Press, 1989], vol. III, 10–11; Baruch A. Levine, *Leviticus* [Philadelphia: Jewish Publication Society, 1989], 5–6; and James B. Jordan, "The Whole Burnt Sacrifice: Its Liturgy and Meaning," Biblical Horizons Occasional Paper No. 11 (Niceville: Biblical Horizons, 1991).

[2] Peter Leithart, "Skinned and Cut," *Rite Reasons* 35 (March 1992).

given a new skin/clothing fit for the presence of God. In fact, he is clothed in the garment of the selfsame glory cloud with which God wraps Himself (Job 38:9; Ps. 18:11; 97:2; 104:2). Remember, the earthen altar is a miniature holy mountain, a portable Mt. Sinai, with three main areas that correspond to the three zones on Mt. Sinai and the tabernacle (Exod. 20:18–26).[3] The animal's entrance into the fire and its transformation into smoke represents the worshiper's entrance into the Most Holy Place and his incorporation into the glory cloud of God's presence.

Leviticus 1:3–4, *If his offering is an Ascension* ['olah] *of the herd, let him draw near with a male without blemish; he shall cause it to draw near at the entrance of the Tent of Meeting that he may find favor before the face of Yahweh. Then he shall lay his hand on the head of the Ascension, and it will be accepted on his behalf to make a covering for him.*

The sacrifice must be "a male without defect" or "blemish" (1:3, 10). This is the language of the requirements of priestly service in God's presence (Lev. 21:17–23). Priests had to be "without blemish" to represent Israel before Yahweh in the service of the tabernacle. The implication, then, is that the animal is selected as a representative for the worshiper. The laying on of hands ordains the animal to represent the worshiper. This is ordination language. A male animal is brought before the tabernacle and then hands are laid upon it. The worshiper is "to lay his hand on the head of the Ascension Offering" (1:4). The laying on of hands does two things: it imparts

---

[3] The two are visually correlated in Exodus 20:22–24. The fire and smoke on the top of Mt. Sinai was symbolically reproduced on the earthen altar. On top of that mini holy mountain the fire and smoke of God's presence rested. Animals ascending the altar are equivalent to Moses' ascent as a mediator (Exod. 20:21). "The equivalence of the Tabernacle to Sinai is an essential, indeed indispensable, axiom . . . The Tabernacle, in effect, becomes a portable Mt. Sinai, an assurance of the permanent presence of the deity in Israel's midst" Jacob Milgrom, *Leviticus 1–16*, vol. 3 in *The Anchor Bible* (New York: Doubleday, 1991), 574; see also 134ff). See also Mary Douglas, "The Eucharist: Its Continuity with the Bread

something from the worshiper to the sacrificial animal and it appoints the animal as the worshiper's substitute/representative.

First, as the worshiper's substitute, the animal is executed. Hands are laid upon the animal to symbolize the transfer of the curse of death. What is imputed to the animal (as also to Christ, the antitype) is the judgment of death against the worshiper. The pressing of the hand upon the head (Lev. 1:4) was almost surely accompanied by a confession by the worshiper. But even if he may not have verbally expressed it in a prayer, the ritual action says it all. "I am worthy to die, but this animal will now take my place." The ritual itself functions as a dramatic prayer. "I cannot enter into Yahweh's presence myself, but I must do so by means of a representative animal. By faith I reckon that God is drawing me into His presence through the performance of this ritual action." In other words, the animal dies and the worshiper lives. The animal stands in for the human worshiper. This is the great scandal of animal sacrifice. Every animal sacrifice is a human sacrifice.

The great scandal of orthodox, biblical Christianity is that it is all about human sacrifice. Every one who desires to draw near to God must do so by means of a vicarious sacrifice. If you dare to draw near into God's presence without a vicarious sacrifice, you are as good as dead. You either die "with" the substitute or you die yourself. Either way there must be death. The animals represented human beings all along (the ram is given in place of Isaac in Genesis 22:13). They were symbolically human sacrifices. God requires the life of man for his sin. The wages of man's sin is his death. The animals symbolized the human being executed for his rebellion

---

Sacrifice of Leviticus," *Modern Theology* 15 (April 1999): 220–1. The animal's entrance into the fire and its transformation into smoke represents the worshiper's entrance into the Holy of Holies and his incorporation into the glory cloud of God's presence. The symbolic parallels between Sinai, the tabernacle, and the altar are fully explained in the taped lectures from two conferences: *Worship & Sacrifice* (Biblical Horizons Bible Conference, August 17–21, 1992) and *Temple & Priesthood* (Biblical Horizons Bible Conference, July 12–16, 1993). I highly recommend these lectures.

against God's sovereign majesty. The only way for sinners to approach God is by means of a penal substitutionary sacrifice. It was true millennia ago when God spoke to the Israelites in the wilderness. It is true today in the twenty-first century. The death of Jesus Christ on the cross, "the lamb of God who takes away the sin of the world," was *the* human sacrifice to which all of the animal sacrifices in the Old Testament pointed.

Moreover, secondly, the animal was not only a substitute, but also a representative. Hands were laid upon the animal to commission it as the worshiper's priest. Israel laid hands upon the Levites too as their substitutes/representatives (Num. 8:10). The laying on of hands implies appointment to a special office/function (Num. 27:18–20). The animal will go where the lay Israelite worshiper may not—into the holy presence of God. He will be ritually executed and then symbolically made fit for God's presence by being chopped up and reconstituted on the altar fire of God's presence. The animal will symbolically ascend into God's presence.

Leviticus 1:4 continues, "and it will be accepted on his behalf to make atonement for him." The worshiper and the animal are identified, as we've noted. But here comes the important point. There is a double identification. The identification is both negative (death) as well as positive (ascension and acceptance by God). As his substitute the animal dies for the man. The judgment is taken by the animal substitute. This looks forward to the death of Christ on the cross, suffering the penalty for our sin.

But there is more. This is crucial. A sacrifice did not merely result in the animal's death. The fact that the animal is not discarded immediately after its death symbolizes the worshiper's survival through death and his subsequent entrance into God's life-giving presence by means of the transformation by fire. As the worshiper's representative the animal has more operations performed on him to prepare him for ascension into God's presence. As his representative the animal is accepted by God, a sign that the worshiper himself has been accepted by God. More is done to the animal, as we shall see, than just his ritual execution. The animal is processed, ascends the altar, and having been transformed into smoke, is incorporated into God's presence. The Lord is pleased. God, in the language of the Old Testament, "eats" the sacrifice, thereby incorporating it into Himself—a sign that the worshiper is accepted and united with God (Lev. 3:11; 3:16; 21:17–25).

Without both dimensions (death and transformation) there would be no "covering" (*kaphar*) for the animal/worshiper. The book of Leviticus has a great deal to say about "coverings." Some form of the Hebrew *kphr* occurs almost fifty times in the book. There is some controversy about how these words should be translated, as "atonement" or "covering." The word itself, however, means "covering," and if one choose the more metaphorical translation "atonement," then one should not forget that the root idea is "to cover." Before one can be received into God's presence, one has to be properly clothed or covered. When Adam sinned, God graciously clothed him (Gen. 3:21). That which is defiled must be covered before it is permitted to draw near to God. The word atonement covers the entire process of making "one" (at-*one*-ment) God and the worshiper; that is, bringing them back into a right relationship by satisfying God's judicial sentence (death), *and* by consecration/transformation (cutting, washing, and burning) so that the animal/worshiper can enjoy full fellowship within the glory-cloud presence of God. Remembering that the root idea in the Hebrew word we translate "atonement" has to do with "covering," we remember that unless we are clothed in Christ we cannot ascend into God's presence safely (2 Cor. 5:3; Gal. 3:25).

Leviticus 1:5, *He is to slaughter a son of the herd* [ben habaqar] *before Yahweh, and then Aaron's sons the priests shall cause the blood to draw near* [qrb] *and dash it against the altar on all sides at the entrance to the Tent of Meeting.*

The *qorban* is now called "a son of the herd" (*ben habaqar*). Alert readers will no doubt link this with the "sons of Israel" (1:2) and the "sons of Aaron" (1:7-8). Theologically this reminds us that the sacrifice represents "the sons of Israel." The fact that the animal is designated a "son" looks back to Adam and forward to Christ. Jesus will be the true "son of Adam" and the fulfillment of all the "sons of the herd" offered on Israelite altars. He will die and rise again, accomplishing atonement for His people. Thus, the Ascension Offering is the typological answer to the sin of Adam because it looks forward to the eschatological Son of Adam's self-offering and ascension to the Father.

The Israelite worshiper himself, not the priest, slaughters the "son of the herd." The two ritual actions of laying on of hands and slaying manifest the intensely personal character of this entire ritual. The ritual itself works against the danger of worshipers performing these actions in a perfunctory way. Another important point that is often missed: the sacrificial knife executes the animal, not the fire on the altar. Note that it is only when the animal/worshiper goes through "the knife and the fire" that he enters into God's presence. This is the only way back into the Garden Paradise of God (Gen. 3:24).

As we shall see, something else happens on the altar itself. The animal must be put to death first before he ascends the altar. This execution by the knife is the punishment for sin, as we have seen. Since the way into God's presence for sinful man is the way of death and the altar is the worshiper/animal's pathway into the presence of God, the blood must be publicly "offered" before the Lord and then splashed on the altar before the animal makes his ascent. Putting the blood on the altar is a display of evidence that the man has been executed for his sin (of course, the animal substitute has been slain). This display of blood propitiates the anger and wrath of God; it turns the judicial sentence of God from man onto the animal (which, of course, is a type of Christ, the sinless human sacrifice for sin). Remember the Passover. The lamb was killed (as a substitute for the firstborn of the household) and the blood was smeared on the doorpost of each house. The Messenger of Death, then, passed over them when he saw the evidence of the blood.

Leviticus 1:6, *He* [the worshiper] *is to skin the Ascension and cut it into pieces.*

After the death of the animal, we are reminded again in this verse of the name of the sacrifice—the Ascension Offering—because now the animal is being prepared to make his ascent. Once the blood is splashed on the altar, the way is cleared for the worshiper to ascend the altar in the person of the substitute animal. Now begins what we might call the *positive* side of the animal's representation of the worshiper in this sacrificial ritual. The animal now ascends into God's presence, symbolizing the ascension of the worshiper into God's presence. But before the animal/worshiper can ascend, he needs more than the penalty for sin taken away, he must also be positively prepared. "Without holiness no one will see the Lord" (Heb. 12:14). Speaking of the operations performed on the animal immediately preceding its being turned into smoke, Derek Kidner explains, "The whole procedure was such as to impress on any thoughtful worshiper the high demand of God for a devotion that was total, pure and disciplined, worked out to the last detail, yet only acceptable through atoning blood and priestly mediation."[4] So what is pictured next in the ritual of sacrifice is the consecration, the sanctification of the worshiper. The images that follow become key for the New Testament's conception of the Christian life.

First, the worshiper skins the animal. The old skin must be removed, and the new skin put on. Skin and clothing are analogous to one another (Lev. 13:22, 47–51). The priest had to wear undefiled garments (Exod. 28; Zech. 3:4), and he was barred from priestly service if he had unclean skin (Lev. 21:20). The same word is used in Leviticus for "skinning" an animal and for "stripping off"

---

[4] Derek Kidner, "Sacrifice: Metaphors and Meaning," *Tyndale Bulletin* 33 (1982): 132.

the clothes of a man (Lev. 1:6; 16:23). When Adam and Eve sinned, they needed new clothes to be fit for God's presence (Gen. 3:21). This connects with the language of "taking off and putting on" in the New Testament and describes the sanctification of the Christian (Eph. 4:22; Col. 3:9).

Second, the worshiper cuts up the animal. We get clues, inspired clues I might add, when we discover the New Testament using this sacrificial ritual terminology to describe New Covenant realities. Remember Hebrews 9:9, all these sacrificial rituals are "symbolic of the present time," that is, of course, the time of the New Covenant. It is instructive, then, that the New Testament uses this language to refer to the positive work of the Word of God on the believer. Hebrews 4:12, "For the Word of God is living and powerful, and sharper than any two-edged sword, piercing even to the division of soul and spirit, and of joints and marrow, and is a discerner of the thoughts and intents of the heart." The Word of God chops us up and makes us fit for God's holy presence.[5]

Leviticus 1:7–9, *The sons of Aaron the priest shall put fire on the altar, and lay the wood in order on the fire. Then the priests, the sons of Aaron, shall lay the parts, the head, and the fat in order on the wood that is on the fire upon the altar; but he shall wash its entrails and its legs with water. And the priest shall cause it all to turn into smoke* [qtr] *on the altar as an Ascension, a food offering* ['isheh]*, a sweet aroma to Yahweh.*

The fire was originally lit by God on this altar, but it was kept burning by the priests (Lev. 6:13). At this point in the ritual they would stoke it up by bringing wood and laying it on the fire. This is the fire of God's presence. It will burn up the sacrifice as food for God. That's the language of the Bible (Lev. 3:11; 3:16; 21:17–25). This is *not* the fire of destruction and wrath. The burning on the altar is not the judgment against sin, but rather it represents the

---

[5] See Leithart, "Skinned and Cut."

purifying and transfiguration of the sacrifice into smoke that ascends into the presence of God. It is *sanctifying* fire. This is too often missed. God is a consuming fire. But the "fire" of God's presence may have one of two effects. It may consume by utterly destroying (Lev. 10:1–2) or it may consume the dross and purify in a positive way (Is. 1:25; 4:4; Zech. 13:9; Mal. 3:2). Hell represents an instance of the first, but the fire on the altar is an example of the second. The altar fire purifies and transfigures the animal into smoke.

Notice how the parts of the animal are treated here at the climax of this ritual. The head and choice inner parts ("fat") are taken by the priests and laid on the altar without being washed. We are specifically told that the head and the choice inward parts are not washed. They are already clean. Notice also that the *priest* puts the head and choice inward parts into the fire first. By doing this the priest is identified with them. Could it be that the head and choicest fat represent the true priest Christ, the head, the pioneer and forerunner of our faith? We follow as sacrifices in Him. Second, the *layman* ("he") washes the remaining two parts of the sacrifice, the entrails and the legs. Thus the worshiper is identified with these parts. The priest brings him water from the laver and he baptizes them. These parts are unclean and need to be washed before they ascend. Therefore, if the head and fat (the choicest part which does not need to be washed because it is clean) represent Christ, then He is offered first. He is *the* offering. But then the rest of the sacrifice is washed (which represents us) and is placed on the altar as well. So the whole of it is burned up and ascends into God's presence and is a sweet smelling aroma to Him. Remember what Paul says in 2 Corinthians 2:15–16, "For we are to God the fragrance of Christ." An aroma of life unto life. This last great event on the altar represents the ultimate glorification of the believer, his incorporation into God's glory cloud. It is "turned into smoke" and ascends into God's presence. The worshiper now has union and communion with his Lord. In the language of the New Covenant, his life and work have been accepted "in the Beloved" (Eph. 1:6).

21
We All Partake of One Loaf: Restoring Our Children to the Lord's Table

Let the little children come to me; do not hinder them, for to such belongs the kingdom of God.
—Mark 10:14

Have you ever heard (or engaged in!) a conversation during the Lord's Supper that went something like this:

> "Mommy, why can't I eat and drink?" the child asks. "Everyone else is!"
> Mother: "You will have to wait until you're older, son."
> "Does Jesus still love me?"
> "Yes, of course he loves you, son."
> "Then why can't I eat dinner with him, Mommy?"
> "Because you have to wait. Now stop asking questions, I'm trying to concentrate."
> "But what am I supposed to do, Mommy?"
> "Just be quiet . . . Here, you can draw. We're almost done."

Or what about this hypothetical conversation (one that uncovers what is assumed in most Reformed theological discussions about children at the Table):

Johnny whispers, "Daddy, why can't I eat some bread?"

Dad says, "Shhh. You're not ready yet, son?"

"What do I have to *do* to get ready, Dad?"

"Well, you have to be able to examine yourself. Can you do that?"

"What's that mean, Daddy? I believe in Jesus. Is that what you mean?"

"Not exactly. You have to know what's going on right now. I mean, you have to be able to explain what the Lord's Supper means, what everything symbolizes and stands for. You have to be able to 'discern the Lord's body and blood.'"

"Oh. How can I find out about that? Do I have to wait until I'm older?"

"Yes. In a few years you can take a new members class and learn about the Lord's Supper. Then you can be examined by the elders to see if you are ready."

"A new member's class? I thought I was already a member of the church?"

"Shhh, please. That's enough questions for now, Johnny. The bread is coming down the aisle and I have to concentrate."

Protestant theologians and pastors traditionally cite 1 Corinthians 11:28 as *the* argument against those who want to restore our young covenant children to the Lord's Table: "A man ought to examine himself before he eats of the bread and drinks of the cup" (NIV). They suppose that this text demands a certain level of intellectual competence as well as a capacity to engage in self-conscious introspection, both of which, we are told, small children do not possess. Children must be able to "examine themselves" before they are allowed to come to the Table. Young children simply are not able to fulfill the requirement of "self-examination" mandated in 1 Corinthians 11. If they are permitted to eat from the Lord's Table too soon and they don't understand what is going on in the sacrament, they will "eat and drink judgment upon themselves" (1 Cor. 11:29). John Calvin's argument against communing young children stands or falls with this argument:

> "[The Lord] does not . . . hold forth the Supper for all to partake of, but only for those who are capable of discerning the body and blood of the Lord, of examining their own conscience, of proclaiming the Lord's death, and of considering its power. Do we wish anything plainer than the apostle's teaching when he exhorts each man to prove and search himself, then to

eat of this bread and drink of this cup? A self-examination, therefore ought to come first, and it is vain to expect this of infants . . . why should we offer poison instead of life-giving food to our tender children?" (*Institutes* 4.16.30)

This line of reasoning has been repeated over and over again in churches that are part of the Reformation tradition. It has attained the status of "common sense" in modern conservative Presbyterian circles. But does 1 Corinthians 11:28 really require the kind of self-examination that Calvin and Presbyterians have traditionally thought? To whom does Paul address this admonition? What does the verb "examine" mean in the context of 1 Corinthians 11? Does it actually require an ability to perform internal soul-searching and deep personal introspection before one can be judged worthy of participation at the Lord's Table? I am convinced that this text has been made to serve a function in traditional discussions about the admission requirements for Holy Communion that goes well beyond Paul's solution for the problem in the Corinthian church's practice of the Supper. More ominously, I am convinced that this text properly understood actually stands *against* the traditional Presbyterian practice of excluding young children from the Table. Those who fail to commune the body's youngest, weakest members are not "discerning the body" and are therefore eating the Lord's Supper in an unworthy manner. Traditional Presbyterian theologians and pastors need to examine themselves. Permit me to explain.

Each Man Must Prove Himself

Let us begin with the command in 1 Corinthians 11:28. The Greek verb Paul uses here is *dokimazo*, which means "to prove, approve, or test." To bring out the meaning of this word in context, it is best to translate 1 Corinthians 11:28 as follows: "Let a man prove himself and so eat of the bread and drink of the cup." This is how *dokimazo* is normally used in Paul's writings (see, for example, 1 Cor. 3:13; 2 Cor. 13:5). It does not normally refer to a self-reflexive internal act of evaluation; rather, it has to do with "proving" or "approving" something or someone, often publicly or at least in relation to others. Consider, for example, Paul's warning to ministers: "each one's work will become manifest, for the Day will disclose it, because it will be revealed by fire, and the fire will prove [*dokimazo*] what sort of work each one has done" (1 Cor. 3:13; see also 1 Thes. 2:4; 1 Pet. 1:7). And again, his instructions at the end of his epistle: "And when I arrive, I will send those whom you accredit [*dokimazo*] by letter to carry your gift to Jerusalem" (1 Cor. 16:3 [ESV]; see also 2 Cor. 8:8, 22). How then does a man "prove" himself?

I am convinced that in this context (1 Cor. 10–12) the "proof" that a Christian must display is his or her behavior with respect to the unity of the body of Christ and *not* the performance of introspective self-examination. A man "proves himself" by *how* he eats, not how much he understands or how thoroughly he searches his heart. There are those in the Corinthian church whose behavior in the church and especially at the Lord's Table manifests selfish pride and therefore divisiveness. They are *doing* the Lord's Supper in a way that visibly violates one of its defining purposes. The Table ought to constitute the people of God as one. As Paul said earlier: one loaf = one body (1 Cor. 10:17). A Christian "proves himself" when he behaves as a loving member of the body of Christ, avoiding divisive and schismatic behavior, especially at the Communion [*koinonia*] Table. This is precisely what the Corinthian Christians were *not* doing; they refused to wait for one another at the Lord's Supper, even going so far as to eat their own private family or cliquish meals (1 Cor. 11:20–22, 33–34). This way of eating the Lord's Supper had the effect of dividing the body, and since the rich were using the Table as an occasion for a feast with their rich friends, the weaker, poorer members of the body were being treated as second-class Christians at the meal. "Do you despise the Church of God and humiliate those who have nothing?" (1 Cor. 11:22)

The Immediate Context—Their Misbehavior at the Table

That Paul admonishes each of them to prove, by their behavior at the Table, their unity with Christ and with one another fits perfectly with the thrust of his entire letter, as we shall see. But it is particularly fitting in this smaller section of 1 Corinthians. The overarching context of Paul's admonition in 1 Corinthians 10–11 has to do with the unity of the church, the body of Christ. All Christians "participate in the body of Christ," and "because there is one loaf, we, who are many, are one body, for we all partake of the one loaf" (1 Cor. 10:16b–17). That unity or participation [*koinonia*] in the body of Christ must be manifest at the Lord's Table when the entire Church eats *together* from the *one* loaf. The problem in the Corinthian church was that people were misbehaving in the church at large and especially at the Supper—they were both acting and eating in a manner that contradicted the reality of their corporate (*corpus* is Latin for "body") unity in Christ. They were *divided* in their relations with one another, and, not surprisingly, their divisive spirit manifested itself at the Table. Paul begins and ends his admonition concerning the Lord's Supper with this problem:

> In the following instructions I do not commend you, because when you come together it is not for the better but for the worse. For, in the first, place, when you come together as a church, I hear that there are divisions among you. And I believe it in part, since [as you think] there must be divisions among you in order that the proven ones [*oi dokimoi*] might be manifest. When you come together it is not the Lord's Supper that you eat; for as you eat, each of you goes ahead without waiting for anybody else—one goes hungry and another gets drunk. What! Do you not have houses to eat and drink in? Or do you despise the Church of God and humiliate those who have nothing? What shall I say to you? Shall I commend you in this? No, I will not. (1 Cor. 11:17–22)
>
> . . . .
>
> So then, my brothers, when you come together to eat, wait for one another—if anyone is hungry, let him eat at home—so that when you come together it will not be for judgment. (1 Cor. 11:33–34b)

Between these bookend references to their discordant behavior at the Table we find Paul's specific admonitions concerning how they ought to act during Communion—they need to "prove" themselves and "discern the body" (1 Cor. 11:28–29). Reading these exhortations in context yields something different than what is commonly thought. The idea is that the delinquent Corinthian Christians need to "prove" their unity with one another and thereby show that they truly "discern" or "judge" the unity of the body of Christ. The proof that they discern or judge the Body properly will be their eating the Supper in a manner worthy of that meal's meaning and significance.

One ought not read the exhortations sandwiched between these two references to behavior that befits our unity as a body as if they are some sort of free-floating, context-less instructions about admission to the Lord's Table. In other words, 1 Corinthians 11:23–32 must not be yanked out of the context of the specific troubles in the Corinthian church. Unfortunately, that is exactly how they have been read and used in our "church orders" and even in the liturgical reading of these texts during the celebration of the Lord's Supper. If anything from 1 Corinthians 11 is read before the administration of this sacrament it is typically only verses 23–32. Verses 17–22 and 33–34 are hardly ever read. By so doing, we have lost the original context, and I will argue, therefore, the genuine significance of the words "prove oneself" and "discern the Body." They have been used to address foreign concerns. Christians who think that they are not "worthy" to come to the Table because they have not sufficiently plumbed the depths of their soul, searching for sinful attitudes and thoughts, have misunderstood Paul's call to "examine/prove oneself." Elders and pastors who refuse to admit children and adults to the Table until they can *understand* and *articulate* the Reformed understanding of the locus of the Lord's glorified human nature over against rival Baptist, Lutheran, and Roman Catholic theories have missed Paul's point entirely. This sort of theological pin-the-tail-on-the-body-of-Christ contest has nothing to do with his exhortation to "judge the Body."

Holy Food for Holy People

Moreover, Paul's concern for unity in the church at Corinth dominates the letter as a whole. A great deal of this first epistle to the Corinthian church attempts to deal with just this problem. Even his salutation and initial prayer set the stage for the solution to the problem of their disunity:

> To the church of God that is in Corinth, to those made holy [or "sanctified," *hagiazo*] in Christ Jesus, called to be holy ones [or "saints," *oi hagioi*] in union with all those who in every place call upon the name of our Lord Jesus Christ, both their Lord and ours. (1 Cor. 1:2)

> ... God is faithful, by whom you were called into the fellowship [*koinonia*] of His Son, Jesus Christ our Lord. (1 Cor. 1:9)

Every baptized member of the church at Corinth is "holy" in Christ and for that reason they all share a common fellowship as the body of Christ. It should be noted here that Paul's introductory salutation and prayer embrace the children of believers since they are explicitly said to be "holy" in 1 Corinthians 7:14. Later in his epistle Paul will argue that even though they may be "weaker" members of the Body they are to be given more honor by other "stronger" members of the Body (1 Cor. 12:22–25). How then can a church faithfully eat the Sacrament that symbolizes and seals the unity of the body of Christ while systematically excluding the weakest members of the Body? Is the Table only for the strong and intelligent? Are our children not "holy"? Are not all the baptized of the Church "members of the Body" (1 Cor. 12:12). If so, do we rightly "discern" or "judge" the body of Christ when we exclude certain baptized members of his Body because they are smaller or weaker or less intelligent? If the meal is *Holy* Communion, and eating at this Table is one of the definitive ways in which God's Holy people are set apart from the world, then all those that are holy ought to be included in the meal—including our children!

Early Church pastors often called out "holy food for the holy people of God" when they were distributing the bread and wine. The holiness of the family of God is ritually constituted by Baptism and maintained by participation in the holy meal. If our children are part of the holy family by Baptism, sanctified by the Spirit in Christ, then they ought to be at the Table. Unless, of course, we want to make the Table more restrictive than Paul, who says that the oneness of the body of Christ is manifest by those who eat of the one loaf (1 Cor. 10:17). All those who eat of the one loaf are part of the body of Christ; those who do not are outside of the covenant and Church.

Eating at Yahweh's Table

Including covenant children in the fellowship meal has always been God's arrangement. Throughout the Old Testament Israelite children were considered full members of the covenant and therefore participants in the covenant meals. One of the highlights of most of the Old Testament feasts and sacrificial rituals was the covenantal meal shared by the whole community. The primary food for these covenantal meals—the meat—was taken from the Fellowship or Peace Offerings sacrificially slain by the worshiper and offered on the altar by the priests. After the fellowship offering had been made the priests took the cooked meat and gave it back to the worshiper to eat with his family or in the case of a major feast he distributed it to the people gathered in households to eat. The Passover meal was simply the most prominent Fellowship Offering and Meal.

In the Old Testament small children participated with the household in these Sacraments. The nourishing Sacraments of the Old Testament were many and varied, but they are all fulfilled in the Lord's Supper.[1] The basic argument is as follows: If all the covenantal

---

[1] This argument builds upon two Reformed biblical-theological presuppositions: 1–The essential unity of the Old and New Covenant with respect to salvation and sanctification (Gen. 15:6; Rom. 4:13; Rom. 2:25–29; Gal. 3:6–18; WCF 7:5 & 6); and 2–the essential unity of the Old and New Covenant with respect to the Sacraments (1 Cor. 10:1–5;

meals of the Old Covenant are fulfilled in the one covenantal meal of the New Covenant, the Lord's Supper, and if children partook in the Old Covenant communion meals, therefore, unless there is some explicit New Testament statement to the contrary, children in the New Covenant ought also to eat with the family at the New Covenant feast, the Lord's Supper.

First, consider the sacrificial-covenantal meals that the entire "household" ate when the family offered a Fellowship (or "Peace") Offering (Lev. 3). Deuteronomy 12:7 states that when the one place of worship is established (Jerusalem, as we later discover) "there you shall eat before the Lord your God, and you shall rejoice in all to which you have put your hand, you and your households, in which the Lord your God has blessed you." Clearly, a household means all the members of the family—adults, children, and in the Old Testament, servants as well. It is simply incredible to believe that when a family made that rare trip up to Jerusalem to offer a fellowship offering and to eat a rich covenantal meal in God's presence (Israelites did not usually eat this well) that only the mature adults would be able to participate in the dinner. It is hardly conceivable that the children would not have been able to eat with the rest of the family. Where is the evidence that they were excluded from the Old Covenant sacramental meals? The *burden of proof* lies with those who think that children were excluded from these meals. Where is the Old Testament command or the illustration that indicates that children were barred from these communion meals?

Secondly, biblical evidence for young child Communion can be found in the presence of small children at the major feasts of Israel—feasts where the Israelites ate sacrificial covenant meals with their families and each other. The worship services of the Church are not for "adults only," but must included infants and small

---

Col. 2:11–12). According to *Westminster Confession of Faith* 27:5, "the sacraments of the Old Testament, in regard of the spiritual things thereby signified and exhibited, were, for substance, the same with those of the New."

children. The Old Covenant worship gatherings included children. God commanded them to bring their little ones. When Joshua recited the whole of the Law of Moses to the people, "the entire congregation, with the women, the little ones, and the strangers" gathered and stood to hear the Word of God (Josh. 8:35). These kind of covenantal gatherings occurred throughout the history of Israel, and even though children are not always explicitly mentioned, nevertheless, they are often present at these feasts (2 Chr. 20:13; Ezra 8:21; Joel 2:15–16). There is certainly no good reason to believe that they were not present.

1 Samuel 1:1–8 provides us with a specific instance of a family—a man, his wife, and his children—partaking of the sacramental food of a Fellowship Offering at one of the major feasts of Israel. Here Elkanah as the godly covenantal head of his family takes his entire family up for the yearly feasts and sacrifices (Deut. 16:6). The feast could very well have been the Passover. According to verse 4, "Whenever the time came for Elkanah to make an offering, he would give portions to Peninah his wife and to all her sons and daughters." Note the word "all." No ages are given. All the sons and daughters partook. The normal practice would be for the whole family to participate in these sacrificial Sacraments. Remember, the food taken from the sacrificial altar and eaten by the worshipers in the Old Covenant is equivalent to the food taken from the final sacrifice and distributed to the New Covenant people of God. The *Westminster Confession of Faith* 27.5 reminds us that "the sacraments of the Old Testament, in regard to spiritual things thereby signified and exhibited, were, for substance, the same with those of the New."

Men, women and children, according to Nehemiah 12:43, participated in a great sacrificial feast convoked to celebrate the dedication and purification of the new walls of Jerusalem: "Also that day they offered great sacrifices and rejoiced, for God had made them rejoice with great joy; the wives also and the children, so that the joy of Jerusalem was heard afar off." The great sacrifices refer to the large number of animals killed and cooked; the rejoicing of the people would have consisted primarily in eating such a sumptuous meal while praising God for His gracious provisions. Would the children have had to eat something else? Would they have been purposefully excluded from these covenant meals because they were not old enough? Do we find any evidence that this ever happened?

Some think that the Passover meal, a particularly solemn example of a Fellowship (Peace) Offering, provides proof that little children did not eat at these sacrificial meals. The regulations and explanation of the Passover meal, however, offer no positive proof for this. In fact, the Passover meal will provide us with a third argument from the Old Testament for admitting young children to the Communion Table. The controversy centers on Exodus 12:26:

> And it shall be when your children say to you, "What do you mean by this service?" that you shall say, "It is the Passover sacrifice of the Lord, who passed over the houses of the children of Israel in Egypt when He struck the Egyptians and delivered our households."

This passage does not establish that such "question asking" by the child was the *prerequisite* for *participating* in the meal. The very idea that the child must first ask this question before he is allowed to eat must be read into the passage. Neither does this passage mandate some kind of ceremony before which the child would not be allowed to share in the sacrificial meal. Nor is there any evidence that ancient Israel practiced such a ceremony as the Jews today call *bar mitzvah*. The rite of *bar mitzvah* is a post-New Testament development and may not be read back into the Old Testament. It has no bearing whatsoever on the question of young child Communion.

The myth that children did not eat the Passover meal until they were thirteen is very widespread in Reformed churches. Often this myth is based on the supposed practice of the Jews—the rite of *bar mitzvah*. Even if *bar mitzvah* functioned as a rite of admission to the Passover Table in Modern Jewish religion (as we shall see, it does *not*), the ritual practices of the Jews today do not necessarily help us understand Old Testament rites. There is absolutely no evidence that the Old Testament Jews practiced *bar mitzvah*. To read back into the Old Testament the practices of post-New Testament Judaism is always dangerous—so much of the customs, theology, and ceremony of post-A.D. 70 Judaism was developed in reaction to Christianity and also betrays the influence of alien Hellenistic and pagan ideas and practices that infiltrated Judaism as a result of the dispersion of the Jews from Jerusalem after the destruction of the temple. After the believing Jews were harvested into the Church during the Apostolic age, and the city of Jerusalem was judged and destroyed by God, the Jews hardened in their opposition to the Christian Church. Much of what we call "Judaism" today has little or nothing to do with genuine Old Testament Israelite religion. This includes the *bar mitzvah* ritual.

The most natural way to understand Exodus 12:26–27 is that when the children ask the parents why *the family is eating* such an extraordinary meal, the parents would then explain the significance to them in the context of the dinner. Exodus 12:3 confirms this. Here it is clearly stated "every man shall take for himself a lamb, according to the house of their fathers, a lamb for a family." Exodus 12:4, therefore, requires that every man, acting as the covenantal head of the family, estimate the size of his family (including wife, children, and servants, etc.) to determine the appropriate size of the dinner lamb. He is to take a lamb "according to the number of souls" in his household (KJV). This was a family meal. As if to emphasize this, God commands in Deuteronomy 12:7 that the households shall celebrate by eating together the sacrificial meals. The entire family or household was to eat the roasted lamb together.

Further evidence that children were not excluded from the Passover meal can be found in Exodus 12:43–49. There God specifically lists those who would not be allowed to participate in the Passover. The distinguishing characteristic that forbade participation was *not being circumcised*. Circumcision was a sign of being in covenant with God, it was the sign of the righteousness that the

Israel possessed by faith (Rom. 4:11). The small children of Israel were in covenant with God. They had the right to enjoy the salvation and fellowship of the Savior and covenant Lord. To imagine that the rest of the family ate something else or just watched while the adult men ate the Passover is ludicrous considering the familial, covenantal assumptions of the Old Testament (Francis N. Lee and Roger Bacon both argue that neither women or children partook of the Passover, but merely watched the adult men eat!).

Remember 1 Samuel 1:1–8, where Elkanah travels yearly to Shiloh for the annual festivals. He takes his family and the entire family partakes of the sacrificial food (1 Sam. 1:4). This was most likely a Passover meal. The entire family rejoiced together in their covenant meal with the Lord (Deut. 12:7).

The Passover is one of the primary typological forerunners to the sacrament of the Lord's Supper; and *there is no evidence in the Old Testament that children were excluded from the Passover meal.* After all, what else was there to eat? To even suggest that the children sat there and watched as the parents ate strikes at the heart of God's covenantal familial relations with His people. The same applies today. Adults eat dinner with Jesus and the children watch. The adults and parents of the congregation are again assured of their place in the family of God during the Communion meal, but the children are excluded.

A fourth argument from the Old Testament for young child Communion arises out of a thoughtful consideration of 1 Corinthians 10:1–5. Consider the manna that Israel ate in the wilderness. In 1 Corinthians 10:1–5 Paul reminds the Corinthian church that Old Covenant Israel experienced the Sacraments typologically and that this means we can learn something from these Old Covenant stories about the New Covenant church, and specifically, how we are to behave with reference to the New Covenant Sacraments. Paul refers to the crossing of the Red Sea as Israel's *baptism* and their eating the manna in the wilderness as their *Communion* meal with Christ, thereby drawing a direct parallel between the spiritual food (food in which the Holy Spirit is present to give life to those who eat) of the Old Covenant (manna and water) and the Spiritual food of the New Covenant (bread and wine). "All were baptized into Moses in the cloud and in the sea," Paul explains, "all ate the same spiritual food, and all drank the same spiritual drink" (1 Cor. 10:2–3). Jesus makes this point also in John 6:31–65. Now, the question is this: Who partook of these Old Covenant Communion meals? The answer is that "all" did—adults and children. What else was there to eat in the wilderness but the manna and water that God provided? The burden of proof lies on the one who would deny that children ate these covenantal meals.

Finally, remembering that Jesus lived during the Old Covenant era, there are all those passages in the New Testament where Jesus invites the little children to come to Him, even to be carried to Him. Jesus also warns the disciples of the terrible curse on those who "hinder" or "do not permit" little children to come to Him (see Mt. 18:1–6; 19:13–15; Mk. 9:33–37; 10:13–16; Lk. 9:46–48; 18:15–16).

How strange it would be if we would gather around the family table to eat and yet exclude our young children from eating dinner. If the Lord's dinner table serves the family of God, why then are the little ones not also served? Are they not to be fed at God's family dinner table? Does Jesus only want to feed and nourish the adults?

Although the evidence presented here has been suggestive rather than exhaustive; nevertheless, we can be assured that the Old Testament presupposes the presence of children at the Communion meals. To suggest otherwise places the burden of proof on those who would keep children from the table. If we could be careful not to let our *traditions* obscure the evidence, the biblical facts are obvious. The Israelites' "little ones" were delivered from Egypt, included in the covenant God made with Israel on Mt. Sinai, and participated in all of the benefits and responsibilities of the covenant (Baptisms, circumcision, Passover, water from the rock, manna, the sacrifices, etc.). The children of Old Covenant believers were baptized (Gen. 17:7–12; Exod. 24:6–8; 1 Cor. 10:1–2; Col. 2:11–12), and God entered into covenant with them (Deut. 29:10–12). They also participated in the Sacraments of nourishment and Communion as well (Exod. 12:3; 1 Sam. 1:1–8; 2 Chr. 20:13; 1 Cor. 10:1–4). There is nothing to suggest that they were excluded until they reached a certain age or attained a certain level of knowledge.

The Big Problem in the Church at Corinth

With that Old Testament background before us, we return to Paul's emphasis on unity in 1 Corinthians 10–11. Throughout this epistle Paul is concerned with the divisive self-centeredness for which so many in the congregation have become so well known. His opening *salvo* is aimed at this very problem:

> I appeal to you, brothers, by the name of our Lord Jesus Christ, that all of you agree and that there be no divisions among you, but that you be united in the same mind and the same judgment. For it has been reported to me by Chloe's people that there is quarreling among you, my brothers. What I mean is that each one of you says "I follow Paul," or "I follow Apollos," or "I follow Cephas," or "I follow Christ." Is Christ divided? Was Paul crucified for you? Or were you baptized into the name of Paul? . . . . Let the one who boasts, boast in the Lord." (1 Cor. 1:10–13, 31)

It appears that all of the problems in the church at Corinth, as numerous and notorious as they were, can be traced back to the lack of love and self-effacing service that are needed for the maintenance of genuine ecclesiastical fellowship and unity. Consider how often Paul returns to this problem:

> But I, brothers, could not address you as spiritual people, but as people of the flesh, as infants in Christ. . . . For while there is jealously and strife among you, are you not of the flesh and behaving only in a human way? For when one says, "I follow Paul," and another, "I follow Apollos," are you not being merely human? (1 Cor. 3:1, 3–4)

I have applied all these things to myself and Apollos for your benefit, brothers, that you may learn by us not to go beyond what is written, that none of you may be puffed up in favor of one against another. For who makes you to differ? What do you have that you have not received, and if you received it, why do you boast as if you did not receive it? (1 Cor. 4:6–7)

When one of you has a grievance against another, does he dare go to the law before the unrighteous instead of the saints. . . . Brother goes to law against brother, and that before unbelievers! To have lawsuits at all with one another is already a defeat for you. Why not rather suffer wrong? Why not rather be defrauded? But you yourselves wrong and defraud—even your own brothers! (1 Cor. 6:1, 6–7)

Knowledge puffs up, but love edifies. . . . Take care that this knowledge of yours does not somehow become a stumbling block to the weak. For if someone sees you who have knowledge eating in an idol's temple, will he not be encouraged, if his conscience is weak, to eat food offered to idols? And so by your knowledge this weak person is destroyed, the brother for whom Christ died. Thus, sinning against your brothers and wounding their conscience when it is weak, you sin against Christ. (1 Cor. 8:1, 9–12)

For though I am free from all, I have made myself a servant to all, that I might win more of them . . . . To the weak I become weak, that I might win the weak. I have become all things to all people that by all means I might save some. (1 Cor. 9:19, 22)

I want you to know, brothers, that our fathers were all under the cloud, and all passed through the sea, and all were baptized into Moses in the cloud and in the sea, and all ate the same Spiritual food, and all drank the same Spiritual drink. For they drank from the spiritual Rock that followed them, and that Rock was Christ. Nevertheless, with most of them God was not pleased, for they were overthrown in the wilderness . . . . Therefore, my beloved, flee from idolatry. I speak as to sensible people: judge for yourselves what I say. The cup of blessing which we bless, is it not a participation [*koinonia*] in the blood of Christ? The bread we break, is it not a participation [*koinonia*] in the body of Christ. Because there is one bread, we who are many are one body, for we all partake of one bread. Consider the people of Israel: are not those who eat the sacrifices participants [*koinonos*] in the altar? (1 Cor. 10:1–5, 14–18)

This is only a sampling of the texts that deal with the problem of pride and disunity in the Corinthian church. It brings us up to chapter eleven and Paul's admonitions about the proper way to eat the Lord's Supper. Of course, we could go on with chapters twelve and following to show how the whole "spiritual gifts" fiasco in the Corinthian church centered on their prideful elevation of certain showy sign gifts. Not only does Paul explain at great length the Spirit's work in the whole body of Christ (12:1–31), but he finally offers them a better way: love. It should be emphasized that Paul is concerned in these chapters that deal with "spiritual gifts" to elevate and honor the members of the Body that the Corinthians think are weak and insignificant.

> For just as the body is one and has many members, and all the members of the body, though many, are one body, so it is with Christ. For by one Spirit we were all baptized into one body—Jews or Greeks, slaves or free—we were all drenched with one Spirit. For the body does not consist of one member, but many . . . . God has arranged the members in the Body, each one of them, as He chose. If all were a single member, where would the body be? As it is, there are many parts, one body. The eye cannot say to the hand, "I have no need of you," nor again the head to the feet, "I have no need of you." On the contrary, the parts of the body that seem to be weaker are indispensable, and on those parts of the body that we think less honorable we bestow the greater honor, and our unpresentable parts are treated with greater modesty, which our more presentable parts do not require. But God has so composed the body, giving greater honor to the part that lacked it, that there may be no division in the body, but that the members have the same care for one another. If one member suffers, all suffer together; if one member is honored, all rejoice together. Now we are the body of Christ and individually members of it. (1 Cor. 12:12–14, 21–27)

Once again, Paul says that there should be "no division in the Body" (10:25). That we are *all* "the body of Christ" because of our common Baptism (12:12) is the same language used to describe what is symbolized and enacted at the Lord's Supper (1 Cor. 10:16–17). Surely it is not too difficult to see how we have excluded the weakest baptized members of the body of Christ from the Lord's Table and so violate Paul's admonition here. Even though Paul says that our children are "holy" (1 Cor. 7:14) and that they are baptized members of the body of Christ (1 Cor. 12:12), yet in our tradition they are not allowed to fellowship [*koinonia*] with the rest of the Body at the Sacrament that is designed to signify and seal the unity of the entire body of Christ over against the world. The whole body of Christ is holy, that is, set apart from the world as being united to and belonging to Him, not simply the mature and intelligent parts. Theologians and pastors in our churches that perpetuate traditions that exclude weaker members of the body of Christ from the Table ought to be ashamed of their arrogance. Not only are our youngest children excluded, but in my experience many Reformation churches also exclude the mentally handicapped members of the covenant as well. Baptized autistic children and others are not permitted to come to the Table because they cannot complete the class work and/or successfully articulate their faith to a room full of blue-suited elders. We may not say this out loud to them, but we have ordered our Communion meals such that they communicate to the weak and handicapped: "You are not really a part of this Body" and even "We're not sure that you can ever be." For those younger and weaker members of the body of Christ that cannot and may never be able to benefit from the highly intellectual and discursive forms of communication in our churches, barring them from the Table removes from them one of the only means of communication they "understand." Truly the head has said to the feet, "I have no need for you."

1 Corinthians 11:28—Examine or Prove?

The admonition, "let a man prove himself" (1 Cor. 11:28) means: let a man *show* that he rightly judges the unity of the body of Christ as he comes to the Table. Let his actions demonstrate to all (especially to the elders) that he is one who lives in a manner that manifests his unity with the brethren. The evidence of this "self-demonstration" would be the manner in which he treats his brothers in Christ, especially when he partakes of the Sacrament—eating in a manner that exhibits his unity with the body of Christ in the local church. This understanding of the verb "to prove" (*dokimazo*) can be established from the immediate context. Paul says in 1 Corinthians 11:19, "No doubt there have to be divisions among you in order that the proven ones (*oi dokimoi*) may be made manifest." This is a difficult sentence. Commentators are divided over its meaning. But it uses the noun form of *dokimazo* and so should help illumine Paul's use of that verb a few verses later.

Unfortunately, verse nineteen has often been cited as a proof text to establish that God wills divisions in the Church in order that the "proven ones" will be evident to all. That is one way to understand it. The "proven ones" of 1 Corinthians 11:19 would then be those who have "proved themselves" in 1 Corinthians 11:28. But in the context of 1 Corinthians 11, not to mention the entire letter, such an interpretation makes little sense. It actually undercuts Paul's polemic against the dangerous *divisiveness* of the Corinthian church and seems to give divine sanction to it. Does God really will that there be factions in the Church? Considering what we have discovered so far from our analysis of Paul's letter, it hardly seems consistent with Paul's drumbeat for unity in the Church. Moreover, verse nineteen is immediately followed in verse twenty with a "therefore" (*oun*) by which Paul nullifies this saying. Many translations leave it out because it doesn't seem to fit the flow, especially if verse nineteen is understood as validating some sort of "useful necessity" for the presence of factions.

The best way to understand verse nineteen, however, is as Paul's sarcastic reference to a despicable Corinthian attitude. He may even be alluding to one of their own slogans. Paul mocks their own attitudes and spiritual aphorisms quite often in this epistle. Sometimes he even quotes their own slogans in order to ridicule and dismantle them. Commentators often miss Paul's devastating sarcasm. But Paul's use of irony is powerful and often quite derisive. For example, when Paul says, "I thank God that I baptized none

of you . . . for Christ did not send me to baptize," he is mocking
their distorted understanding of Baptism (see 1 Cor. 12:12ff). Paul
is not really giving thanks that he didn't baptize anyone, as if whenever someone baptizes someone else, he risks contributing toward
schism. Surely Paul knows and submits to Jesus' mandate to
baptize (Mt. 28:18–20). Rather, Paul is using his rhetorical skills to
express his contempt for the Corinthian understanding of ministers and their role in Baptism.

Consider another example. In 1 Corinthians 4:6–7 Paul continues
to deride their distorted perspective on the ministry: "I have applied
these things to myself and Apollos for your benefit, brothers, that
you may learn not to go beyond what is written, that none of you
may be puffed up in favor of one against another. For who sees anything different in you? What do you have that you have not received?
If then you received it, why do you boast as if you did not receive
it?" Again Paul turns to biting irony and sarcasm to topple them
from their supposedly exalted status. The New American Standard
translates the first question in verse seven as "Who regards you as
superior?" The Jeff Meyers Version (JMV) would say either, "Who
in the world do you think you are?" or "Who died and made you
kings?" But the point is clear. They are walking around with their
heads puffed up and Paul uses rhetoric like a needle to burst their
inflated egos.

Much more like the passage we are considering are those places
where Paul quotes the Corinthian "wisdom" in order to ridicule it.
"All things are lawful for me" is a Corinthian slogan, *not* an apostolic
maxim. Paul dismantles this stupid saying in 1 Corinthians 6:12ff
and 10:23ff. I am pleased that the new English Standard Version
(ESV) uses quotation marks in 1 Corinthians 7:1 to set apart what
the Corinthian leaders were saying: "Now concerning the matters
about which you wrote: 'It is good for a man not to have sexual
relations with [lit. *touch*] a woman.' It is, however, the Corinthian
rule that is most certainly not "good" and Paul goes on to show
what kind of foolishness and problems this super-spiritual

sounding prohibition leads to. Then there is 1 Corinthians 12:31, where Paul almost surely either quotes the Corinthian "wisdom" about spiritual gifts ("Earnestly desire the higher gifts") or sarcastically derides their own way of elevating the sign gifts ("But *you* earnestly desire the higher gifts"). What Paul does is show them "a more excellent way" as well as what the true "higher" gift is—love (1 Cor. 13:1ff).

With that background, therefore, we return to Paul's strange words in 1 Corinthians 11:19. This, I believe, is what Paul is saying:

> For in the first place [or most prominently], when you come together as a church, I hear that there are divisions [*schismata*] among you. And I believe it in part, for [according to your own foolish wisdom] "there must be factions" among you "in order that the proven ones [*oi dokimoi*] may be recognized." On the contrary! If that is your attitude, then when you come together, it is *not* the *Lord's* Supper you eat. (1 Cor. 11:18–20)

The Corinthians believed that the presence of "factions" in their church was "necessary" in order to show those who are "approved." If you were a member of the "approved ones" (the *oi dokimoi*), then you could look down on the weaker and poorer members of the church. Some in the church, almost surely the leadership, were willing to sacrifice the unity of the church in order to promote themselves. Just as in any cesspool the larger chunks rise to the top, so the "approved ones" loved setting themselves over against the rest of the church in order to promote their own spirituality and status. I have already quoted numerous passages from Paul's letter to establish this as a major problem in the church at Corinth. A very large part of Paul's second letter to this church concerns those who "commend themselves as approved" but, in fact, have no such divine approval (see 2 Cor. 5:12; 10:18; 13:7).

What this means for our present inquiry is that the Corinthian Christians were not "coming together" as a unified body of Christ when they "came together as the church." Some were even glorying

and boasting in their divisions. Paul says that they should not call
what they were doing at their separate tables the *Lord's* Supper because they were all eating as factions, not as the body of Christ. Each
group had their own meal. No one waited for anyone else. No one
served the others. It is as if before the Supper began someone stood
up and announced, "Listen up! All the 'approved ones' sit here and
the rest of you who can't cut the mustard, sit over there at a separate Table. And don't bother us!"

Of course, they were probably not so crass about it; but their actions communicated just such an attitude. They were making a
mockery of the unity that ought to be manifest at the Table of the
Lord (1 Cor. 10:16–17). When Paul sarcastically asks "What? Do
you not have houses to eat and drink in?" he is reminding the
church that the Lord's Supper is a *ritual* meal, not simply a meal.
In partaking of the Lord's Meal the Church ought to be constituted
as the body of Christ because they all eat from a common loaf. By
using the Lord's Supper as an opportunity to have their own private parties, the rich are "despising the Church of God" and "hu-
miliating those who have nothing" (11:22). Once again, Paul
defends the cause of the poor and weaker members of the body of
Christ. To divide the body of Christ—the rich at one table with
their own sumptuous food and drink and the poor at another with
little if anything—is despicable. Those who eat *in such a way* are not
properly "discerning" or "judging the Body." They are eating in an
unworthy manner (11:27)

Thus Paul indicts the church for eating and drinking "unworthily" (1 Cor. 11:27). "Unworthily" (*anaxios*) is an adverb that
modifies the verb "eat." Paul is not talking about checking to see if
you are a worthy *person* before you come to the Table. He is talking about *how* you partake of the Supper. The ESV translates it like
this: "Whoever, therefore, eats the bread and drinks the cup of the
Lord in an unworthy manner will be guilty of profaning the body
and blood of the Lord." Eating "in an unworthy manner" refers to
one's *behavior* at the Table. The Corinthian church's conduct at the

Table is in view here. They were conducting the meal in a way that did not evidence the unity of the body of Christ. Therefore, "let a man prove himself" refers to his *manner* of participation at the Table, or more broadly, to his relationship with the local body of Christ. There is nothing here about individuals deciding for themselves if they are worthy to come to the Table based on the performance of some introspective self-examination. I don't believe that this passage requires an inward act of contemplating and evaluating one's sins. "Proving oneself" and "discerning the body" do not refer to internal, subjective acts of self-examination or theological accuracy. Christ's Table should be approached with demonstration of faithfulness, ecclesiastical faithfulness. It is not so much that subjective contemplation and self-examination are bad; rather, they are simply not in view in this passage. Paul highlights the need for an objective demonstration of one's behavior with respect to the Body when one partakes of the Sacrament of unity. These commands cannot be used to exclude our children, some of the weakest members of the body of Christ, from the Holy Communion Table. As we shall see, they actually cut the other way. Those that refuse to commune children are in danger of failing to judge the unity of the body of Christ.

Discerning the Body

So what does Paul mean in 11:29 when he says, "For anyone who eats and drinks without discerning the Body eats and drinks judgment on himself"? What does "discerning" or "judging (*diakrino*) the Body" mean?

This answers the question, "How should one prove oneself?" The correct response is that one should "judge the Body" rightly. Again, according to the context, this most naturally means "to take cognizance of the whole Church that is seated as one Body at this meal" (Gordon Fee). The point is that we dare not forget whose "Body" the Church is and who is included in that Body. We dare not stretch out our hand to receive the sacramental body when we are the cause of schism and division in the corporate Body. Remember, the Corinthian church came to the "common" Table in groups or parties (1 Cor. 11:21–22). The rich were over here with the best food and wine, and the poor where over there with whatever they happened to be able to bring. They were eating the Lord's Supper as a divided church! They failed to discern the significance of the body of Christ.

I don't see how (in context) this command "to discern the Body" can possibly be understood as either 1) a failure to discern the location or mode of the flesh of Christ in the Sacrament, or 2) a failure to reflect adequately on His death during the meal. "Judging the body" is parallel to "judging ourselves" (1 Cor. 11:31). One fails to "judge the Body" when one "despises the Church of God" (1 Cor. 11:22). Paul's call to "discern the Body" is not a call to understand something about how the Lord's glorified flesh is somehow (if at all) connected to the elements of the Sacrament. Whenever the Sacrament is mentioned, it is mentioned as both body and blood. Verses 24–25 set out both elements. Then verse twenty-six says, "as often as you eat this bread and drink the cup." Verse twenty-seven says, "whoever eats the bread and drinks the cup of the Lord in an unworthy manner." Verse twenty-eight says, "he who eats and drinks, eats and drinks judgment." It is clear, then, that if Paul were referring to discerning something about the Sacrament, he would have written about "discerning the *body and blood* rightly." He didn't say this. He warns against not "discerning the Body" (1 Cor. 11:29). By referencing the "Body" only, he is signifying the body of Christ, that is, the Church.

Remember how Paul closes out the chapter with a summary exhortation: "So then, my brothers, when you come together to eat, wait for one another . . . . so that when you meet together it may not result in judgment" (1 Cor. 11:33–34). Paul does *not* summarize his warnings by reminding them to engage in rigorous, introspective self-examination before coming to the Table. He does *not* warn them against not participating in the Supper if they don't understand the correct interpretation of the "real presence" of the human body of Christ. Is it in heaven or in the bread and wine? He does *not* warn them about eating and drinking without having sufficient devotional preparation: "I see some of you looking around when you ought to have your eyes closed and head bowed in meditation on the death of Jesus." What he *does* tell them is to "wait for each other." Act like a community. Once again, this entire passage is about the manner in which the church at Corinth eats the Lord's Supper—they partake as a divided church. It is not about 1) children coming to the Table, 2) intellectually-challenged people coming to the Table, 3) people partaking who do not know the difference between the Reformed, Catholic, and Baptist theories of the presence of the humanity of Christ at (or in) the meal, or 4) people coming to the Table without adequately reflecting upon the death of Jesus. It is all about manifesting the unity of the Church at the Lord's family Table. We see this theme in one of the earliest post-apostolic Christian documents we have called the *Didache* or "The Teaching (*Didache*) of the Apostles,." What it says about the Lord's Supper is very brief, but the emphasis is on the oneness of the community. "On every Lord's Day—his special day—come together and break bread and give thanks, first confessing your sins that your sacrifice may be pure. Anyone at variance with his brother must not join in, until they be reconciled, lest your sacrifice be defiled" (*Didache*, 14).

Discerning the body is best understood, therefore, as a reference to discerning the Church as Christ's body and not as a reference to discerning any physical presence (or absence) of Christ's glorified human nature in the bread or wine. A man "proves himself" when he shows that he "discerns the body" rightly and accordingly participates in the sacramental meal in a manner worthy of the significance of the Lord's Supper. What Paul has said in 1 Corinthians 12:12 must be made manifest at the Lord's Table: "For as the body is one and has many members, but all the members of that one body, being many are one body, so also is Christ. For by one Spirit we were all baptized into one body." Paul's warning is not a threat that if you don't thoroughly dredge up and confess every little sin before or during the Communion service, you will be judged. This is not meant to lay a heavy dose of self-introspection on every believer. The question is something very objective and concrete: How do you treat others in the church? Have you proven yourself to be one who promotes the unity of the body of Christ? Do your words and behavior in relation to others in the body of Christ show that you are one who judges the importance of the oneness of the Body? Are you reconciled with your brothers and sisters in Christ when you come to the Table? If not, you will be judged (1 Cor. 11:29–32). Hadn't Jesus said the very same thing? Paul's warnings simply unpack the significance of Jesus' teaching for the Church and her new Sacrament:

> But I say to you that every one who is angry with his brother shall be liable to judgment; whoever insults his brother shall be liable to the council, and whoever says, 'You fool!' shall be liable to the hell of fire. So if you are offering your gift at the altar, and there remember that your brother has something against you, leave your gift there before the altar and go; first be reconciled to your brother, and then come and offer your gift. (Mt. 5:22–24)

Paul's admonition includes the whole Church. In principle it applies to children as well. They, too, as members of the holy community must learn to eat in a manner that is fitting. But the specific focus of Paul's exhortation in 1 Corinthians 11 is the adults, who should have known better. They were flagrantly disrupting the unity of the Church and profaning the Lord's Sacrament by their behavior. If they did not "prove themselves" through repentance and changed behavior, they were in danger of eating and drinking judgment on themselves for "profaning the body and blood of the Lord" (1 Cor. 11:27–28). Even Charles Hodge, the great Princeton theologian of the last century notes: "All that is necessary to observe is that the warning is directly against the careless and profane, and not against the timid and doubting."[2]

---

[2] Charles Hodge, *A Commentary on 1 Corinthians* (Edinburgh: Banner of Truth Trust, 1958 [1857]), 231.

But if children are not guilty of the kind of misconduct described by Paul, then it follows that Paul's warnings do not apply to them. Of course, young children are capable of disobedience and even some form of the sin Paul deals with in 1 Corinthians 11. If they are found to be willfully divisive and unmindful of the unity of the body of Christ, then they should be warned. Nevertheless, there is no reason to think that Paul intended to bar covenant children from the Table, unless they too were manifesting disrespect for the body of Christ. Glenn Davies comments are to the point: ". . . if Paul had intended to prohibit children from the Lord's table then it would have contradicted his inclusion of children in the Old Testament equivalent of communion with Christ [1 Cor. 10:1ff]. Yet God's judgment upon Israel's unfaithfulness was that the adults perished in the wilderness; all those twenty years and upward (except Joshua and Caleb) perished (Num. 14:29–30). The adults who murmured against the Lord never saw the Promised Land. If then, the children of the old covenant were able to eat the same spiritual food, and drink the same spiritual drink without condemnation, how much more can the children of the new covenant eat and drink the body and blood of their Lord without condemnation."[3] This is an important point. It was not the *immature* with whom the Lord was not pleased, but the *disobedient*. Yahweh's judgment came upon the disobedient adults, not the children.

Conclusion

Let me close by trying to bring all this to bear upon the paedocommunion question. Does this text give us any reason to forbid our youngest covenant children from eating at the Lord's Table? Are our baptized children members of the body of Christ, the Church? Why then are they cut off from Communion with Jesus? Are they holy? If so, why are the barred from Holy

---

[3] Glenn Davies, "The Lord's Supper for the Lord's Children," *The Reformed Theological Review* 50.1 (1991): 12–20.

Communion? Why do we eat as a *divided* body? In truth, we don't eat as one body at all; rather, some eat and others watch! The older, more knowledgeable "approved ones" eat and drink while the weaker, intellectually poorer members of the body fast.

Far from being a proof text against admitting young baptized children, this passage judges traditional Presbyterianism as a church for "not discerning the body." Why is it that when we come together as a church there are divisions among us? A great big ugly division is manifest at the Table between adults and children, members of the Church and halfway members of the Church. We are divided between those who are in the covenant (adults) and those who are halfway in the covenant (baptized little children). When the family of God gathers around the Table to eat dinner with the Lord, why are the youngest children excluded? Do they not belong to Him? Why must they be told and sometimes even forcibly hindered from eating and drinking with Jesus, the one with whom they are covenantally united? Are they in union with Christ (by Baptism) but not allowed communion with Him (at His Table)? Have they proven themselves to be schismatic or divisive? Do *they* fail to discern the unity of the body of Christ? If so, then by all means they should be excluded. If not, why are they denied access to the family Table? No, it is not the children who fail to discern the unity of the body of Christ. On the contrary, we, the adult leaders of the Church, are those who fail to judge the Body rightly. We traditional Presbyterians have for too long "despised the Church of God and humiliated those who have nothing" (1 Cor. 11:22).

The analogy with the family table is valid and powerful. All of my children have always eaten dinner with the family, even when they were one and two years old. They belong to my family. Therefore, I want them to eat and learn their place at the family table. Furthermore, they are all required to "prove themselves" before and at the family table. They are all required to "judge the body" of the family, so to speak. In other words, they are all required to respect the unity of the family. Even the babies and toddlers in the family learn this responsibility at the Table. So, for example, if any member of the family fails to discern the unity of the family and starts throwing food at a nearby sibling, then that member is disciplined. He or she will learn what it means to have the privilege of eating at the table. He must prove himself. He must "discern the body" before and at every meal. If he refuses, he may need to be disciplined.

Now, I have heard a Presbyterian minister say that he has "never encountered a three-year old who is able to examine himself." But I say that one-, two-, and three-year-olds evidence their ability to discern the importance of the family meal in countless Christian homes every night. We begin disciplining our children at very early ages because we believe that they are capable of self-examination, according to their age capacity. Because they are members of the family, they are graciously invited to the table to eat. In the context of this gracious setting, as they grow up, they gradually and with increasing maturity learn what it means to behave in accordance with the privilege of family table fellowship. They are able to "prove themselves." They begin to learn very early what the meaning and significance of the family meal is, and they learn how to behave in accordance with that significance. Surely, one can see the application to the Lord's Table.

Now, who really are those who are guilty of not "discerning the Lord's body"? Are they the little baptized children of the Church who have not yet attained intellectual maturity or are they those who bar such children from the Table? Who really is guilty of sinning against the "body of Christ"? Our covenant children? Or our theologians and pastors who deny them a place at their Lord's Table? Who really ought to be fenced from the Table? Christ's little ones or traditionalist Presbyterian theologians who continue to oppose the unity of the entire body of Christ, adults and children, around His Table? I am, of course, overstating the case somewhat. But not much. If while He was on earth Jesus was "indignant" with His disciples when they tried to hinder little covenant children from being brought to Him (Mk. 10:14), why should we think that His attitude has changed toward the little ones that are members of His Body today? If Paul's fundamental concern is the unity of the body of Christ around the Table, and if his admonition to "prove oneself" is directed at those who divide the Body at the Table, then, in my humble opinion, traditional Presbyterian theologians have some serious self-examination to perform before they come to the Lord's Table.[4]

---

[4] For more on the argument for restoring all covenant children to the communion table, see Tim Gallant, *Feed My Lambs: Why the Lord's Table Should be Restored to Covenant Children* (Grande Prairie: Pactum Reformanda Publishing, 2002); Peter J. Leithart, *Daddy, Why Was I Excommunicated?*, 2nd ed. (Niceville: Transfiguration Press, 1998); Christian L. Keidel, "Is the Lord's Supper for Children?" *Westminster Theological Journal* 37 (1975): 301–341; and Robert S. Rayburn, "Minority Report of the Ad-Interim Committee to Study the Question of Paedocommunion," in *PCA Digest: Position Papers 1973–1993*, ed. Paul R. Gilchrist (Atlanta: Presbyterian Church in America, 1993).

22
A Bibliographical Essay

Every book is a great action and every great action is a book!
—Martin Luther

I may as well begin this essay about books, with my deeply held conviction about how a ministerial student learns liturgical theology, indeed, how he learns any theology. What I have to say in this note pertains especially, but not only to students in training for the pastorate. In truth, it applies just as much to every Christian who aspires to "all the riches of the full assurance of understanding, to the knowledge of the mystery of God, both of the Father and of Christ" (Col. 2:2). I remember eating lunch one day years ago with a prominent Christian author. He had been thinking about how best to provide solid theological education for a few good Christian leaders. How could he get them to come on board with his specific theological agenda? He was anxious to change the world. He had come up with a new sure-fire method. His answer was to get as many Christians leaders as possible to agree to lock themselves away for a weeklong retreat. At this retreat they would spend every waking hour listening to lectures and reading solid books and articles on Reformed theology.

It would be one massive cram session. This would do it, he thought. Of course, this project lacked one important ingredient: *reality*. Reading books and listening to lectures is not the only, or even the most important way that men learn theology. Studying is crucial, to be sure; but it will not suffice, nor serve as a sufficient foundation.

Reading and Living in the Church

One of my mentors, James B. Jordan, once gave a series of lectures on how to read the Bible. One of the points he made in those lectures applies to all of our biblical and theological learning. He said that the proper way to learn the Bible was to read it, but especially to *hear* it read, preached, sung, and prayed in the heart of the kingdom, the Church. The Bible was written to be read aloud and heard in the local Christian congregation. We forget this. Most of the apostles' writings were written to pastors and elders to be read orally to the churches. There are a number of interesting ways to unpack the significance of this. But the one point that needs emphasis here, I believe, is that reading theology in the kingdom means reading it in the context of the liturgical worship of the Church. Hearing, reciting, praying, singing, speaking, receiving, tasting, seeing, and experiencing the Word within the liturgical life of the church will have a formative influence, not just the sermon, but the Divine Service as a whole. This, I have come to believe, is foundational for theological formation. Men must experience the liturgical consummation of theology. Theology is doxologically acquired and its primary function is doxological as well. Within the Divine Service theology is given, received, and offered in praise to God. Without this liturgical orientation theology becomes ideology and eventually heresy. And this begins with little "heresies" here and there, born of a man's reading and thinking outside of the context of the worshipping Church, whether it be alone in his study or in conspiracy with others in an academic context.

My recommendations to men who want to learn theology? Of course, books, books, and more books! But for every book, a dozen Sundays on your knees and at the Table. You see, along with the books there must be the formal, enthusiastic, participation in the life of a local church, particularly the self-abandonment of humble submission to the biblical order of God's service to His people in the weekly liturgy of worship. If the man is not in a church where the Lord draws His people to Himself through a participatory liturgy of confession, absolution, consecration, Communion (every week!), and benediction, then he will probably never come very near to my theological convictions. No liturgical worship, no working toward the consummation of his theological endeavor. No amount of reading can ever substitute for what is received from God and then offered back to Him in a biblical liturgical worship service. Period. Here I stand.

I am convinced that we have not even begun to think, in Reformed theological circles, about the massive influence of ritual(s) (especially those that we unthinkingly adopt in our typical evangelical worship services). We continue to do seminary without professors of Reformed Liturgy. This is amazing. It is ecclesiastical insanity. Our Reformed seminaries graduate men with little or no liturgical competence. We actively teach silly, sentimental pop worship, not realizing that one day we may, *because* of our pop worship (*lex orandi, lex credendi*), abandon the orthodox faith. My point here is that the weekly Lord's Day ritual has an enormous impact on the development of one's theological convictions. The student/pastor cannot hope to make any intellectual headway in this area by reading alone. He must faithfully and whole-heartedly hear, sing, pray, recite, and taste the Word of God in union with the body of Christ on the Lord's Day.

With that off my chest, the next question is: What about those books, books, and more books I mentioned above? What are some of the foundational books on worship that a ministerial student ought to read? Unfortunately, I cannot recommend only one or two books that will answer all of your questions. The study of liturgy and the history of liturgical forms ought to be the minister's life-long study. Moreover, the real issues in congregational worship cannot be answered by reference to a few proof texts in the Bible. I would encourage you to consider this subject very carefully before taking any public stands on controversial liturgical issues. Unfortunately, you almost surely will not receive the kind of education that you need in the history and theology of liturgy and worship in seminary. You will not even receive adequate instruction in traditional Reformed worship. Therefore, you must pursue these topics on your own. The study of what happens on the Lord's Day, when God's people are called into His presence, demands careful attention today on the part of young men in training for the pastorate. The wholesale rejection of the practice of common worship by post-modern Presbyterian evangelicals notwithstanding, changing the way one worships means changing one's confession of God. The *way* one worships one's god corresponds to *what* one thinks of that god (see chapters 6 and 7). You cannot separate form and content. This is foremost among the reasons why pastors ought to pay thoughtful attention to the form and order, as well as the content of their congregation's worship on the Lord's Day. Exactly what does our worship convey about the god/God we worship?

I have included all sorts of bibliographical references in the notes for the first two parts of this book, but here I want to provide a list of works every pastoral student and pastor ought to acquaint himself with, and even read at some point in preparation for and/or in the course of his ministry. I will not say a great deal about each of these books, but I can indicate very briefly what I have found useful in them. Some demand a careful reading, others can be skimmed, and still others ought to find a place on your shelf as trustworthy guides and reference works.

> A student who does not want his labor wasted must so read and reread some good writer that the author is changed, as it were, into his flesh and blood.

For a great variety of reading confuses and does not teach. It makes the student like a man who dwells everywhere and, therefore, nowhere in particular. Just as we do not daily enjoy the society of every one of our friends but only that of a chosen few, so it should also be in our studying.
—Martin Luther (Table Talk, No. 2894a, 1533)

The History and Development of Reformed Worship

For an insightful account of the development of Reformed worship, especially sixteenth century Reformed continental liturgy, see James Hastings Nichols, *Corporate Worship in the Reformed Tradition* (Philadelphia: Westminster Press, 1968). Nichols has also edited some works on the Mercersburg theology that examine how Philip Schaff and John Williamson Nevin attempted (not very successfully) to restore this older Reformed liturgical tradition in nineteenth century American Presbyterian and Reformed churches: James Hastings Nichols, *Romanticism in American Theology: Nevin and Schaff at Mercersburg* (Chicago: University of Chicago Press, 1961) and *The Mercersburg Theology* (New York: Oxford University Press, 1966). I lectured on the Mercersburg theology in 1993. The tapes may help you understand the significance of this movement ("The Mercersburg Movement" and "The Mercersburg Theology," are available from Biblical Horizons, P.O. Box 1096, Niceville, FL 32588, ph: 850–897–5299). The following works are also useful for understanding the theological commitments and liturgical revisions advanced by Nevin and Schaff: Jack Martin Maxwell, *Worship and Reformed Theology: the Liturgical Lessons of Mercersburg* (Pittsburg: The Pickwick Press, 1976); E. Brooks Holifield, "Mercersburg, Princeton, and the South: The Sacramental Controversy in the Nineteenth Century," *Journal of Presbyterian History* 54 (1976): 238–257; and B.A. Gerrish, "The Flesh of the Son of Man: John W. Nevin on the Church and Eucharist," chapter two in *Tradition and the Modern World: Reformed Theology in the Nineteenth Century* (Chicago: University of Chicago Press, 1978), 49–70.

The nineteenth-century Presbyterian theologian/pastor Charles W. Baird came back from his study in Europe having discovered the lost riches of the sixteenth-century Reformed worship and published a book called *Eutaxia* (renamed *Presbyterian Liturgies*, 1855) in which he sought to "remind" the Reformed churches of their true liturgical roots. The well-known professor of systematic theology at Princeton Seminary, Charles Hodge, also actively promoted this movement and gave Baird's book a very favorable review and commendation in old Princeton's theological journal (Charles Hodge, "Presbyterian Liturgies," *Biblical Repertory and Princeton Review* 28 [July 1855]: 445–467). Hodge even suggested that the Presbyterians produce an officially approved prayer book. Baird also compiled examples of Reformed liturgies: *The Presbyterian Liturgies: Historical Sketches* (Grand Rapids: Baker, 1957; previously published as an addendum to *Eutaxia* as *Chapter on Liturgies*, 1856). Similarly, Hughes Oliphant Old's doctoral dissertation seeks to uncover the post-apostolic, early Church foundation for the sixteenth-century Reformers' liturgical project: *The Patristic Roots of Reformed Worship* (Zurich: Theologischer Verlag, 1975). Books like these are in seminary and public libraries, but you may have to do a little searching.

While I'm on the topic of the early Reformers' liturgical reforms I should include: Carlos M. N. Eire, *War Against the Idols: The Reformation of Worship from Erasmus to Calvin* (Cambridge: Cambridge University Press, 1986); Hughes Oliphant Old, *The Shaping of the Reformed Baptismal Rite in the Sixteenth Century* (Grand Rapids: Eerdmans, 1992); Ronald S. Wallace, *Calvin's Doctrine of Word and Sacrament* (Edinburgh: Oliver and Boyd Ltd, 1953); William D. Maxwell, *The Litugical Portions of the Genevan Service Book* (Faith Press, 1965); William D. Maxwell, *John Knox's Genevan Service Book, 1556* (Edinburgh, 1931); the same author's *A History of Worship in the Church of Scotland* (London: Oxford University Press, 1955); James Hastings Nichols, "The Liturgical Tradition of the Reformed Churches," *Theology Today* 11 (1954): 210–224; and, finally, Bard Thompson, *Liturgies of the Western Church* (Philadelphia: Fortress, 1961). This last work by Thompson contains the liturgies of Luther, Calvin, Bucer, and Zwingli, among others. Frank C. Senn's article "The Reform of the Mass: Evangelical, but Still Catholic" in *The Catholicity of the Reformation*, ed. by Carl E. Braaten and Robert W. Jenson (Grand Rapids: Eerdmans, 1996),35–52, will provide the student with very useful summary descriptions of the various sixteenth-century attempts at liturgical reformation. I have purposefully left out references by Lutheran authors, which I have devoted a separate paragraph to below.

The Theology of Reformed Worship

By "Reformed" I mean not Lutheran and not Independent or "free" worship but those Reformation traditions that developed a form of worship in some way influenced by Calvin, including at least Swiss, French, Dutch, English, and Scottish liturgical traditions. For more general works on Reformed worship that seek to set forth some measure of systematic teaching on the subject, two slightly older systematic works on Reformed liturgy that deserve your careful attention: J.- J. von Allmen, *Worship: Its Theology and Practice* (New York: Oxford University Press, 1965) and Richard Paquier, *Dynamics of Worship: Foundations and Uses of Liturgy*, translated by Donald Macleod (Philadelphia: Fortress Press, 1967). Both the Swiss Reformed liturgist von Allmen and the French Reformed theologian Paquier tap into the older, "continental" Calvinistic tradition that takes seriously questions of ritual, dress, body posture, Sacraments, architecture, and the Church year—matters that are seldom addressed adequately in contemporary works on Reformed worship.

On this point do not fail to read Philip J. Lee, *Against the Protestant Gnostics* (Oxford: Oxford University Press, 1987). Michael Scott Horton addresses these types of issues as well in his new work, *A Better Way: Rediscovering the Drama of God-Centered Worship* (Grand Rapids: Baker Books, 2002). Donald Macleod, *Presbyterian*

Worship: Its Meaning and Method (Richmond: John Knox, 1965) remains an interesting attempt to articulate a doxological theology not only for the Sunday service but also for weddings, funerals, the Church year, and ecclesiastical architecture.

Robert G. Rayburn's *O Come Let Us Worship* (Grand Rapids: Baker, 1980) is still in print and useful, even if, as his son Robert S. Rayburn relates, he was urged by his publisher and others not to reveal the full extent of his convictions about the Church's need for liturgical reformation. If you can get your hands on the tapes or the transcribed manuscripts of *The Second Annual Conference on Worship*, February 23–25, 1996 (Nashville: Covenant Presbyterian Church, 1996), you should listen to/read Robert S. Rayburn's three excellent lectures: "Worship from the Whole Bible," "Worship and the Whole Man," and "Worship in the Early Church."

James B. Jordan's works are enormously significant. All of his essays, books, and lectures that touch on this topic are well worth owning. A complete catalog is available from Biblical Horizons, P.O. Box 1096, Niceville, FL 32588 or at the website (http://hornes.org/biblicalhorizons). Jordan also publishes newsletters that often deal with liturgical issues, especially *Biblical Horizons* and *Rite Reasons*. Four of Jordan's books may be singled out as helpful introductions to his work. First, in his *Theses on Worship: Notes Toward the Reformation of Worship* (Niceville: Transfiguration Press, 1994) Jordan outlines the basic argument for "covenant renewal worship." Jordan's *Liturgical Nestorianism* is a critical review of *Worship in the Presence of God* (mentioned above) in which he argues that an overly strict understanding of the "regulative principle of worship" is not only unbiblical and unworkable, but unfaithful to the practice of Reformed worship in history. Third, in *The Liturgy Trap: The Bible Versus Mere Tradition in Worship* he unmasks Roman Catholic and Eastern Orthodox worship as liturgical idolatry. Finally, there is his recent study on ritual and liturgy *From Bread to Wine: Toward a More Biblical Liturgical Theology*, Draft Edition 1.1 (Biblical Horizons, 2001).

Leading in Worship: A Sourcebook for Presbyterian Students and Ministers Drawing Upon the Biblical and Historic Forms of the Reformed Tradition, Terry L. Johnson, ed., (Oak Ridge: The Covenant Foundation, 1996) is a helpful source of prayers and liturgical examples. Terry is a PCA minister and the force behind the publication of the new *Trinity Psalter* (Pittsburgh: Crown & Covenant Publications, 1994). He has an excellent introduction to Psalm singing ("Why the Psalms") in that Psalter. His book *Leading Worship* contains a great deal of very practical source material for the Reformed pastor, including suggested orders of worship. Terry has also written a two-part series called "The Pastor's Public Ministry" in the *Westminster Theological Journal* 60 (Spring 1998): 131–52 and (Fall 1998): 297–325. One minor flaw in this journal article is Terry's attempt to order the elements of the worship service according to a "sensible, logical" way instead of allowing the order to arise out of the sacrificial, covenant renewal "logic" of Scripture. Whatever the shortcomings of Terry's approach, his "Gospel logic" produces what is, in effect, a covenant renewal worship service, probably because he has been guided by the biblical accounts of how God should be approached (i.e., Is. 6) as well as the traditional Christian order of liturgical worship. Apart from that caveat, his work is quite helpful.

On the other hand, *Worship in the Presence of God*, eds. Frank J. Smith and David C. Lachman (Greenville: Greenville Seminary Press, 1992) has some helpful chapters in it, but its usefulness is seriously impaired by an indefensibly narrow understanding of the "regulative principle of worship." The older symposium called *The Biblical Doctrine of Worship* (Reformed Presbyterian Church of North America, 1974) also defends the regulative principle in its stricter understanding (including exclusive Psalmody). The same kind of criticism might be made of D. G. Hart and John R. Muether, *With Reverence and Awe: Returning to the Basics of Reformed Worship* (Phillipsburg: Presbyterian and Reformed, 2002). There seems to be nothing at all wrong with traditional Reformed worship, according to the authors. No reforms are needed. Every-thing outside of the Reformed tradition is hopelessly muddled. The solution is to pound on the desk and yell "the regulative principle" at them all. Of course, that is something of an exaggeration. There are a few insightful criticisms of contemporary worship forms in the book. But the authors do not subject our tradition to a thorough biblical evaluation.

All of Hughes Oliphant Old's works are extremely useful, even if he falls short of arriving at an adequate defense of a biblical order of service: *Leading in Prayer: A Workbook for Worship* (Grand Rapids: Eerdmans, 1995*)*; and *Themes and Variations for a Christian Doxology* (Grand Rapids: Eerdmans, 1992); *Worship That is Reformed According to Scripture* (Atlanta: John Knox Press, 1984). Old's most recent works attempt a massive historical investigation into "an understanding of how preaching is worship, the service of God's glory": *The Reading and Preaching of the Scriptures in the Worship of the Christian Church*, vol. 1, *The Biblical Period* (Grand Rapids: Eerdmans, 1998) and vol. 2, *The Patristic Age* (1998).

Other interesting works include E. H. Van Olst, *The Bible and Liturgy* (Grand Rapids: Eerdmans, 1991); G. Vandooren, *The Beauty of Reformed Liturgy* (Winnipeg: Premier Publishing, 1980); and don't forget Peter Leithart's *The Kingdom and the Power* (Phillipsburg: Presbyterian and Reformed, 1993). Although not exactly a theology of worship, Leithart's *The Kingdom and the Power* does situate the Church's worship correctly at the center of human culture. Peter's book will give one the orientation necessary for understanding the centrality of Christian liturgy in the world. See also Leithart's "Against 'Christianity': For the Church" and "So-ciology of Infant Baptism," both of which are in *Biblical Horizons: Christendom Essays*, No. 100 (Dec. 1997): 29–50 and 86–106. I have already referred to his paradigm-shifting article "The Way Things Really Ought to Be: Eucharist, Eschatology, and Culture," *Westminster Theological Journal* 59 (1997): 159–76.

I have alluded to some of the older Presbyterian and Reformed liturgies that are available in a few of the edited collections already cited. In addition to these, a Reformed pastor ought to have the following Presbyterian and Episcopal service books in his library: *The Book of Common Worship* (Philadelphia: The Board of Christian Education of the Presbyterian Church in the United States of America, 1946); *Book of Common Worship* (Louisville: Westminster/John Knox Press, 1993), which was prepared for the Presbyterian Church (USA). I would also suggest both the older and the newest Episcopal Common Prayer books: *The First and Second Prayer Books of Edward VI*, 1549 & 1552 (London: J.M. Dent & Sons, 1968); The *Book of Common Prayer* (1928 Revision); and *The Book of Common Prayer* (1979 Revision). These works will serve you well in your selection of prayers, responses, and other liturgical elements for worship.

English Puritan, Scottish, and American Worship

An unhealthy mythology has developed concerning the "regulative principle of worship." Hagiographic accounts of the worship of the Puritans and Presbyterian Scots abound. The works I list here will help demythologize the history of Scottish and English Puritan worship. Hopefully, this will clear the way for a genuine appreciation of their contribution to our understanding of Christian worship as well as a serious attempt to overcome some of their characteristic errors. The basic textbook to own is Horton Davies, *Worship and Theology in England*. Originally published by Princeton University Press in five volumes, it has been reprinted in three books by Eerdmans. The first book covers the "Puritan" period (from Cranmer to Baxter and Fox, 1534–1690). If one wants to examine the English Puritans in particular, begin with the same author's *The Worship of the English Puritans* (Moran: Soli Deo Gloria 1997 [1948]). Davies shows how the Puritans did not always know or follow the older continental Reformed liturgical models. In reaction against their ecclesiastical enemies (the Catholics and

Episcopalians), the Puritans tended to adopt radical "separatist" positions (that ought not to bind us). I have alluded to their opposition to distinctive ministerial garb in my essay defending the ministerial robe.[1] From one who is very favorable to the Puritans, yet critical of their understanding of worship, see J. I. Packer's brief but trenchant ("The Puritan Approach to Worship, " in *A Quest for Godliness: The Puritan Vision of the Christian Life* [Wheaton: Crossway, 1990],245–257):

> The idea that direct biblical warrant, in the form of precept or precedent, is required to sanction every substantive item included in the public worship of God was in fact a Puritan innovation, which crystallized out in the course of the prolonged debates that followed the Elizabethan settlement. It is an idea distinct from the principle that tainted ceremonies, which hide the truth from worshipers and buttress superstitious error, should be dropped, as both dishonoring God and impeding edification. (247)

John Frame's *Worship in Spirit and Truth* (Phillipsburg: Presbyterian and Reformed, 1996) is helpful in so far as he provides a biblical critique of a strict use of the traditional regulative principle of worship. But Frame's analysis is seriously flawed, in my humble opinion, by faulty presuppositions and biases in favor of informality, spontaneity, and an unjustified preference for the New Testament (see Terry Johnson's brief but helpful critique in *Leading in Worship*,26–27 [note 26]).

Ralph J. Gore examines Puritan principles of worship in a more systematic way in his doctoral dissertation "The Pursuit of Plainness: Rethinking the Puritan Regulative Principle of Worship" (Ph.D. diss., Westminster Theological Seminary, 1988). It may be that Gore's argument against "the regulative principle" goes too far. The problem is not so much *that* the Bible regulates our worship, but exactly *how* it does so. I believe that the Bible as a whole (Old and New Testaments) does indeed provide us with regulative precepts, principles, and examples for corporate worship. Abandoning

---

[1] See chapter 19, "A Ministerial Robe and Collar."

a too-strictly construed Puritan principle of worship does not mean "anything goes." Gore's dissertation is available in *Covenantal Worship: Reconsidering the Puritan Regulative Principle* (Phillipsburg: Presbyterian and Reformed, 2003).

Peter J. Leithart examines how the Bible "regulates" our worship in two works: "Synagogue or Temple? Models for Christian Worship," *Westminster Theological Journal* 64 (2002), and *From Silence to Song: The Davidic Liturgical Revolution* (Moscow: Canon Press, 2003). Leithart critiques the common argument that the synagogue is the model for the church's worship in the New Covenant. The synagogue itself appears to have embodied the order and content of the sacrificial rituals. It is inaccurate to pit the synagogue against the temple to argue that liturgical worship is not true to the synagogue model. The situation in the Old Testament as well as the first century of the early Church is more complex than what is commonly taught.

I should note the very profitable study of American Puritan sacramental theology by E. Brooks Holifield, *The Covenant Sealed: The Development of Puritan Sacramental Theology in Old and New England, 1570–1720* (New Haven: Yale University Press, 1974). Reading Holifield one can get an idea of the degeneration of sacramental theology and worship during this time period.

It is always eye opening to examine the actual liturgical texts used in the past. This holds true especially for older Reformed worship. Nothing substitutes for the text itself. I've mentioned Baird's discovery of pre-Puritan liturgies already. One should also take some time to examine liturgical texts from the Scottish Reformation and Puritan period as well. A few books will help you get into these texts: Stephen A. Hurlbut, ed., *The Liturgy of the Church of Scotland Since the Reformation* (Washington, D.C.: St. Albans Press, 1950); William D. Maxwell, *John Knox's Genevan Service Book, 1556* (Edinburgh, 1931); John M. Barkley, *The Worship of the Reformed Church: An Exposition and Critical Analysis of the Eucharistic, Baptismal, and Confirmation Rites in the Scottish, English-Welsh, and Irish Liturgies* (London: Lutherworth Press, 1966). As for the history of worship in Scotland, see *Studies in the History of Worship in Scotland,* Duncan Forrester and Douglas Murray, eds,(Edinburgh: T&T Clark, 1984); William McMillan, *The Worship of the Scottish Reformed Church, 1550–1638* (London, 1931); and W. D. Maxwell, *A History of Worship in the Church of Scotland* (London: Oxford University Press, 1955). An examination of Knox's *Scots Confession* (1560) will show how much more "sacramental" the early sixteenth-century Reformed churches were than ours.

American Presbyterian worship owes much to the Puritan and Scottish traditions. There are not very many "histories" of American Presbyterian worship available. Apart from Julius Melton's *Presbyterian Worship in America: Changing Patterns Since 1787* (Richmond: John Knox Press, 1967) the student will have to search through other more general works on worship and American Presbyterian history for insight into the development of Reformed worship in this country. I have already referred to Mercersburg's attempt to restore an appreciation for pre-Puritan Reformed liturgies. (Melton provides a useful account of this and the reaction to it as well in chapters 4 and 5). The revivals had a substantial negative influence on worship practices in American Presbyterianism. A convincing argument has been made that the absence of a healthy liturgical life in the eighteenth-century Scottish Presbyterian church, particularly a participatory, sacramental worship service that engaged not only the minds but also the emotions and bodies of the congregation, was a major cause for the outbreaks of emotional fervor that swept through the infrequent "Communion seasons" in Scotland. Because American worship tended to be head-heavy, sermon-centered, and disembodied, the revivalists answered a genuine need when they offered Christian people an emotional, bodily outlet for their religious experience (see Leigh Eric Schmidt, *Holy Fairs, Scottish Communions and American Revivals in the Early Modern Period* [Princeton: Princeton University Press, 1989]).

Peter J. Leithart's "Revivalism and American Protestantism," in *The Reconstruction of the Church*, ed. James B. Jordan (Tyler: Geneva Ministries, 1985),46–84, analyzes the deleterious effects of the "revivals" on local American church life.

Although his work only deals incidentally with worship, Nathan O Hatch's *The Democratization of American Christianity* (New Haven: Yale University Press, 1989) is required reading for the pastor who would understand the "mind-set" of American evangelical Protestantism toward the role of worship, the ministry, and the Church. I do not hesitate to cite again E. Brooks Holifield's *The Covenant Sealed: The Development of Puritan Sacramental Theology in Old and New England, 1570–1720* (New Haven: Yale University Press, 1974). He argues that the Great Awakening stifled a sacramental renaissance within Reformed theology in the late seventeenth-century.

Light from the Lutherans

Do not neglect the Lutherans. Some of these works will be more helpful than the Reformed books I've already mentioned. This is because the Lutherans, unlike the Reformed, have maintained a tradition of Protestant liturgical scholarship and have sought to remain loyal to all that is beneficial in the catholic Christian liturgy. These first few books are indispensable and extremely useful. The first is Luther D. Reed, *The Lutheran Liturgy: A Study of the Common Liturgy of the Lutheran Church in America* (Philadelphia: Fortress Press, 1946). After a general introduction to Christian liturgy Reed provides a thorough commentary on the Lutheran liturgy of the *Service Book and Hymnal* (Minneapolis: Augsburg Publishing House, 1958). Even though others, especially the *Lutheran Book of Worship*, have replaced this extraordinary hymnal, it still holds its own as one of the most faithful and beautiful of all Protestant liturgies. Reed's commentary, although dated in places, has not been replaced by anything nearly so careful and comprehensive. Reed's more general work, *Worship: A Study of Corporate Devotion* (Philadelphia: Muhlenberg Press, 1959), is just as useful.

The Lutherans understand that only the priority of God's service to the congregation can deliver the congregation's service to God from Pelagianism. Their exposition of God's service to His people on the Lord's Day is exactly right, a healthy corrective to the lopsided misunderstanding of Christian liturgy as "the work of the people." This is why the Reformed pastoral student must study these Lutheran liturgical theologies carefully. In addition to Reed's theology of worship, one should also examine Peter Brunner, *Worship in the Name of Jesus* (St. Louis: Concordia Publishing House, 1968) and Vilmos Vajta, *Luther on Worship* (Philadelphia: Muhlenberg Press, 1958). Reed, Brunner, and Vajta will provide you with a rich theology of worship. I also recommend the collection of essays *Lutheran Worship: History and Practice*, ed. Fred L. Precht (St. Louis: Concordia Publishing House, 1993). The Eastertide 1993 edition of the Lutheran theological journal *Logia* is dedicated to "The Divine Service" and contains some thought-provoking essays, especially Norman Nagel, "Whose Liturgy Is It?" *Logia* 2/2 (April 1993): 4–8. Frank C. Senn's latest book *Christian Liturgy: Catholic and Evangelical* (Minneapolis: Fortress Press, 1997) takes one through the history of worship in some detail (over seven hundred pages) with a Lutheran slant. Philip H. Pfatteicher writes an excellent book on how the liturgy of the church serves to form Christian character: *The School of the Church: Worship and Christian Formation* (Valley Forge: Trinity Press International, 1995) and also a newer book called *Liturgical Spirituality* (Valley Forge: Trinity Press International, 1997).

You might wish to consult two judicious Lutheran critiques of the marketing-oriented worship of the contemporary "church growth" movement: Ernie V. Lassman, "The Church Growth Movement and Lutheran Worship," *Concordia Theological Quarterly* 62 (Jan. 1998): 39–67, and John T. Pless, "Six Theses on Liturgy and Evangelism," *Concordia Theological Quarterly* 52 (Jan. 1988). Of course, one should also read what Luther himself said about Christian worship and liturgy in volume fifty-three of the

American Edition of *Luther's Works,* ed. Ulrich S. Leupold, (St. Louis: Concordia Publishing House; Philadelphia: Fortress Press, 1965).

Every Reformed pastor ought to have at least four Lutheran service books in his library: *Service Book and Hymnal* (Minneapolis: Augsburg Publishing House and the Board of Publication for the Lutheran Church in America, 1958); *The Lutheran Hymnal* (St. Louis: Concordia Publishing, 1941); *Lutheran Book of Worship* (Minneapolis: Augsburg Publishing House and Board of Publication, Lutheran Church in America, 1978); and *Lutheran Worship* (St. Louis: Concordia Publishing and the Commission on Worship of the Lutheran Church Missouri Synod, 1982). The *Lutheran Book of Worship* (LBW) has an excellent commentary as well: Philip H. Pfatteicher, *Commentary on the Lutheran Book of Worship: Lutheran Liturgy in Its Ecumenical Context* (Minneapolis: Augsburg Fortress, 1990).

Liturgical Theology and General Studies on Worship

There is some disagreement among liturgical scholars about just what "liturgical theology" stands for. I use it here to refer to the discipline of studying the theological meaning of the Christian liturgy. Some, like David W. Fagerberg in *What is Liturgical Theology: A Study in Methodology* (Collegeville: The Liturgical Press, 1992), argue for limiting the phrase "liturgical theology" to the theology embodied in the liturgy itself as *performed* by the Church. Every Christian who participates in the liturgy participates in a deeply theological activity as he listens, speaks, prays, recites, etc. Here, however, I have in mind not that "first order" theological discourse of the content of worship itself, but the academic, scholarly theological explanation of the Christian liturgy. Here are some works that explain the art and practice of liturgical theology, seek to set out a theology of the liturgy, or seek to explain the theology behind Christian common worship. Most of these works are not by Reformed scholars. Since this is a theological discipline that

Reformed theologians have shamefully neglected, the student will have to learn from men with whom he will no doubt occasionally have substantial disagreements.

I consider the following four books indispensable: Louis Bouyer, *Liturgical Piety* (Notre Dame: University of Notre Dame Press, 1954); Aidan Kavanagh, *On Liturgical Theology* (New York: Pueblo Publishing, 1984); Geoffrey Wainwright's *Doxology: The Praise of God in Worship, Doctrine, and Life* (New York: Oxford University Press, 1980) is a marvelous book stuffed full of biblical, historical, and systematic theological insights (you may not read this straight through, but you must have it on your shelf for reference); and Alexander Schmemann, *Introduction to Liturgical Theology* (Crestwood: St. Vladimir's Seminary Press, 1986 [1966]). Although Eastern Orthodox, I have found Schmemann's work to be particularly stimulating. In addition to his *Introduction to Liturgical Theology*, his popularly written *For the Life of the World* (Crestwood: St. Vladimir's Seminary Press, 1973) is stuffed with astonishing biblical insights. Schmemann's other liturgical/theological works are also well worth pursuing, especially *The Eucharist* (Crestwood: St. Vladimir's Seminary Press, 1988), *Liturgy and Tradition: Theological Reflections of Alexander Schmemann* (Crestwood: St. Vladimir's Seminary Press, 1990), *Of Water and the Spirit: A Liturgical Study of Baptism* (Crestwood: St. Vladimir's Seminary Press, 1974), and *Liturgy and Life: Christian Development Through Liturgical Experience* (New York: Orthodox Church in America, 1983).

In a similar way, although Roman Catholic, I have also found the works of Louis Bouyer to be challenging and insightful. In addition to his *Liturgical Piety* mentioned above, take note of these influential works: his monumental study on the eucharistic prayer of thanksgiving before the Lord's Supper: *Eucharist: Theology and Spirituality of the Eucharistic Prayer*, trans. by Chalres Quinn (Notre Dame: University of Notre Dame Press, 1968); *Life and Liturgy* (London: Sheed and Ward, 1956); *The Word, Church, and*

Sacraments in Protestantism and Catholicism (New York: Desclee Company, 1961); and *The Spirit and Forms of Protestantism*, trans. by A.V. Littledale (Cleveland: Meridian Books, 1964). Gregory Dix's *The Shape of the Liturgy* (London: A&C Black, 1945), although out of date as far as the development of the study of liturgy goes, still retains its impressiveness as a comprehensive study of Christian liturgy.

One general reference work that everyone ought to have is *The Study of Liturgy*, eds, Cheslyn Jones, Geoffrey Wainwright, and Edward Yarnold (London: SPCK, 1992). This is a large book with essays on just about everything concerning the history and theology of the Christian liturgy.

You should probably have the following reference works in your personal library. You may not sit down and read through them page by page, but you will certainly profit from them as reference tools. First, there is the huge one-volume edition of *The Church At Prayer: An Introduction to the Liturgy*, ed. Aimé Georges Martimot (Collegeville: The Liturgical Press, 1992). This is written from a Roman Catholic viewpoint, but this 1300–page tome has articles on everything, absolutely everything. As for dictionaries, see *The New Westminster Dictionary of Liturgy and Worship*, J. G. Davies, ed., (Philadelphia: The Westminster Press, 1986); *The New Dictionary of Sacramental Worship*, Peter E. Fink, ed., (Collegeville: Liturgical Press, 1990); and Philip H. Pfatteicher, *A Dictionary of Liturgical Terms* (Philadelphia: Trinity Press International, 1991). This last paperback may be a good place to start if you have no other liturgical dictionaries.

There are a number of works on Christian worship that do not seem to fit very nicely into any of the other pigeonholes in this bibliographical essay. The works of Notre Dame's liturgical scholar James F. White are useful for gathering general information: *Introduction to Christian Worship* (Nashville: Abingdon Press, 1980); *Protestant Worship: Traditions in Transition* (Louisville: Westminster/ John Knox Press, 1989); and *Documents of Christian Worship:*

Descriptive and Interpretive Sources (Louisville: Westminster/ John Knox Press, 1992). The last book organizes various traditional sources under the headings of time, space, daily prayer, service of the Word, Sacraments, Baptism, Eucharist, and occasional services. The chapter "Space as Communication" shows how different liturgical functions (and conceptions) each produce a different kind of "space." White's *A Brief History of Christian Worship* (Nashville: Abingdon Press, 1993) is one of the most succinct histories of the liturgy available. Though sometimes his conclusions are dated, a concise, accurate history of the development of worship can still be found in the Scottish liturgist William D. Maxwell's *An Outline of Christian Worship: Its Developments and Forms* (New York: Oxford University Press, 1936). Gordon S. Wakefield's *An Outline of Christian Worship* (Edinburgh: T & T Clark, 1998) is a deliberate attempt to bring Maxwell's older work up to date.

D. A. Carson has edited two books on worship: *Worship: Adoration and Action* (Grand Rapids: Baker, 1993) and *Worship by the Book* (Grand Rapids: Zondervan, 2002). In the first book there are useful essays in Part II, "Reflections on Worship in the Heritage of the Magisterial Reformation" by Klaas Runia, Edmund Clowney, and others. The second book is a mixed bag. The essay by Mark Ashton on Cranmer deserves careful attention. The others are somewhat predictable.

Both of Marva J. Dawn's books on worship are worth consideration: *Reaching Out Without Dumbing Down: A Theology of Worship For the Turn-of-the-Century Culture* (Grand Rapids: Eerdmans, 1995) and the sequel *A Royal "Waste" of Time: The Splendor of Worshipping God and Being the Church for the World* (Grand Rapids: Eerdmans, 1999). She attempts to lasso in the seemingly invincible forces of "contemporary" worship in popular evangelicalism by calling the Church back to a more faithful form of distinctively Christian worship. Other authors before her have also sought to alert evangelicals to the danger of worship conformed to the spirit of the age. See Douglas D. Webster, *Selling Jesus: What's*

Wrong With Marketing the Church (Downers Grove: InterVarsity Press, 1992) and Philip D. Kenneson and James L. Street, *Selling Out the Church: The Dangers of Church Marketing* (Nashville: Abingdon Press, 1997).

Thomas Howard's books are a mixture of brilliant analysis, insightful theological passages, and specious Roman Catholic arguments. The latter should not keep the careful Reformed student from reading his works. His writing style is delightful and engaging. Howard's analysis of American "free style" worship is quite devastating. *Evangelical is not Enough* (Nashville: Thomas Nelson, 1984) is something of an autobiographical account of his discovery of the liturgical traditions of the Christian Church. Some chapters are priceless. Even in the midst of an erroneous argument for the veneration of Mary, a passage like that found on page 87, denouncing "parsimonious notions of God's glory," will likely stick with you for good. Howard's *Chance or Dance: A Critique of Modern Secularism* (Wheaton: Harold Shaw, 1969) is technically not about liturgy per se, but about the liturgical, dance-like nature of all of God's creation. It wonderfully trumps the reductionistic humdrum of our technologically fixated culture with the older typological world view of pre-modernism, where everything and everyone participates mysteriously in the orderly, beautiful dance of God's providential order.[2] Much of what Howard writes in this book will serve as presuppositional groundwork for our appreciation of the riches of traditional Christian worship. Like Howard, Robert E. Webber has also tried to capture some of the reasons for American evangelicals' interest in classical worship in his *Evangelicals on the Canterbury Trail: Why Evangelicals Are Attracted to the*

---

[2] I hope the reader will forgive me for adding a footnote to a bibliographical essay, but the mention of beauty reminds me that I have not said much about the aesthetics of liturgical worship. This issue demands its own separate treatment. Nevertheless, a few choice insights from the Orthodox liturgist Alexander Schmemann will help illumine the importance of beauty for "modern" man. "The liturgy is, before everything else, the joyous gathering of those who are to meet the risen Lord and to enter with him into the bridal chamber. And it is this joy of expectation and this expectation of joy that are expressed in singing and ritual, in vestments and censing, in that whole 'beauty' of the liturgy which has so often been denounced

Liturgical Church (Dallas: Word Books, 1985). Webber has also written some other books on worship, the most useful of which is probably *Worship: Old & New* (Grand Rapids: Zondervan, 1982), but the new revised version (1994) seems to go too far in embracing trendy American practices.

There are many more works that could be referenced in this category, but none are as significant as those that I have mentioned. The last one I will cite is William H. Willimon, *Worship as Pastoral Care* (Nashville: Abingdon Press, 1979). I do not always agree with Willimon's conclusions, but he poses all the right questions and sometimes surprises you with gutsy, profound answers.

Early Church, Roman Catholic, and Orthodox Works

You will have to sit at the feet of the Catholic and Orthodox Christian scholars to learn about early, post-apostolic worship. The benefits, however, are worth it. In the study of the history and theology of liturgy there is no room for denominational provincialism. When it comes to the church's liturgical heritage, especially the early Church tradition, it is as much ours as it is theirs. Nevertheless, their scholars have done the lion's share of work on the development of liturgy. There are certain well-respected, seminal studies that you should be familiar with. I have already referenced some of these men: Schmemann, Bouyer, Kavanagh, and others. Paul F. Bradshaw's *The Search for the Origins of Christian Worship: Sources and Methods for*

---

as unnecessary and even sinful. Unnecessary it is indeed, for we are beyond the categories of the 'necessary.' Beauty is never 'necessary,' 'functional,' or 'useful.' And when, expecting someone we love, we put a beautiful tablecloth on the table and decorate it with candles and flowers, we do all this not out of necessity, but out of love. And the church is love, expectation, and joy. It is heaven on earth, according to our Orthodox tradition; it is the joy of recovered childhood, that free, unconditioned and disinterested joy which alone is capable of transforming the world. In our adult, serious piety we ask for definitions and justifications, and they are rooted in fear—fear of corruption, deviation, 'pagan influences,' whatnot. But 'he that feareth is not made perfect in love' (1 Jn. 4:18). As long as Christians will love the Kingdom of God, and not only discuss it, they will 'represent' it and signify it, in art and beauty" (Alexander Schmemann, *For the Life of the World* [Scarsdale: St. Vladimir's Seminary Press, 1973], 29–30). Although I have lost the location, this next quotation also comes from one *the Study of Early Liturgy* (New York: Oxford University Press) would be necessary for no other reason than to give the student an appreciation for how complicated and difficult reconstructing the content and development of early Christian liturgies can be. Simple authoritative appeals to the "early Church" are extremely problematic.

The literature on the study of early Church worship can be overwhelming, so here I will suggest a few foundational works. If one desires to study this further, he can pursue the footnotes in these books. Here are some works that are well-respected that I have found most useful: Josef A. Jungmann, *The Early Liturgy to the Time of Gregory the Great*, trans. by Francis A. Brunner (Notre Dame: University of Notre Dame Press, 1959); Josef A. Jungman, *The Mass of the Roman Rite: Its Origin and Development*, 2 vols (Dublin, Ireland: Four Courts Press, 1951 [1949]); Oscar Cullman, *Early Christian Worship* (London: SCM Press, 1953); Thomas K. Carrol and Thomas Halton, *Liturgical Practices in the Fathers* (Wilmington: Michael Glazier, 1988); Jean Daniélou, *The Bible and the Liturgy* (Notre Dame: The University of Notre Dame Press, 1956); and Gregory Dix, *The Treatise on the Apostolic Tradition of St. Hippolytus of Rome* (London: SPCK, 1968 [1937]). Of course, some of the general liturgical histories previously cited in this essay may also contain useful information on worship in the early Church.

---

of Schmemann's works. "Evangelical and Modern Christianity are constantly referring to 'modern man' as the one to whom they are directing their 'ministries.' This 'modern man' is the one who uses electricity and computers, who has been shaped by the new technological society and the scientific worldview. He is the one who is stressed out, burned out, and has all these 'needs.' The modern man has come of age as a deadly serious adult, conscious of his suffering and alienation (or constantly being reminded of them), conscious of sex but not of love, of science but not of mystery, of the function of this or that but never of the beauty of this or that. . . . Based on this analysis, 'modern man' needs therapy, money, housing, a job, etc. No mention is ever made of beauty, poetry, art, singing. Damning omissions which condemn the modern technological and therapeutic world-view, for all its 'practicality,' as being a very truncated view of life indeed."

Medicine against the iconolatry virus can be found in James B. Jordan's succinct criticisms of the Eastern Orthodoxy and Roman Catholic violation of the second commandment. See James B. Jordan, *The Liturgy Trap: The Bible Versus Mere Tradition in Worship* (Niceville: Transfiguration Press, 1994) and especially his studies on the first and second commandments of the Decalogue: "The First Word," *Rite Reasons* 31–32 (February/April 1994), and the five in-depth essays on liturgical idolatry: "The Second Word I-V," *Rite Reasons* 33–36 (June-December 1994) and 57–59 (May-September 1998).

I would recommend reading a few respected works on Augustine for a taste of the context of worship and preaching in the late fourth and early fifth century. Above all, study carefully Peter Brown's awe-inspiring biography, *Augustine of Hippo* (Berkeley: University of California Press, 1967). Brown summarizes Augustine's liturgical program as "removing habits that give rise to false opinions" (p. 345). In addition to Brown, Ferdinand Van der Meer's *Augustine the Bishop* (London: Sheed and Ward, 1961) describes in some detail Augustine's practice of preaching and worship (Parts 2, 3, and 4).

Worship in the Old and New Testaments

Most of the exegetical and biblical theological work done on worship has been extremely disappointing. For example, David Peterson's *Engaging With God: A Biblical Theology of Worship* (Grand Rapids: Eerdmans, 1992) gets the whole purpose of sacrificial worship *exactly* wrong. We don't engage God, as Peterson thinks; rather, He engages us. The whole book is flawed because of this one-sided, Pelagian perspective. Then we have all those "biblical" works produced under the influence of critical historical scholarship, like Hans-Joachim Kraus, *Worship in Israel: A Cultic History of the Old Testament* (Richmond: John Knox Press, 1965) and Harold H. Rowley, *Worship in Ancient Israel: Its Forms and Meaning* (Philadelphia: Fortress Press, 1967). Most of these books are pretty worthless since they parcel out the Old Testament to various fictional authors imaginatively spun-out of the minds of English and German unbelieving scholars. They construct fictional developmental accounts of how the worship of Israel and the Church evolved and so get just about everything wrong. Rowley, for example, like all liberals, thinks that the ultimate meaning of the Old Testament sacrificial system has to do with encouraging ethical obedience. Roland de Vaux's *Ancient Israel*, vol. 2, *Religious Institutions* (New York: McGraw-Hill, 1965) is better, although still tinged by higher-critical presuppositions. He does, however, bring together a large amount of biblical detail and makes the details of Israel's ritual order accessible. Probably the best one-volume study on the sacrifices is J. H. Kurtz, *Sacrificial Worship in the Old Testament* (Grand Rapids: Baker Book House, 1980 [1863]). In addition, one should consult two good commentaries on Leviticus: Gordan J. Wenham, *The Book of Leviticus* (Grand Rapids: Eerdmans, 1979) and the Jewish commentator, Jacob Milgrom, *Leviticus 1–16*, vol. 3 of *The Anchor Bible* (New York: Doubleday, 1991).

James B. Jordan's books, essays, and lectures are indispensable for understanding the symbolism and ritual of the Old Testament. These are available from Biblical Horizons, P.O. Box 1096, Niceville, Florida 32588. See especially his *Through New Eyes: Developing a Biblical View of the World* (Brentwood: Wolgemuth & Hyatt, 1988) and "The Whole Burnt Sacrifice: Its Liturgy and Meaning," Biblical Horizons Occasional Paper No. 11 (Biblical Horizons, P.O. Box 1096, Niceville, FL 23588). Peter Leithart interacts with Milgrom's commentary in his 1993 lectures on Leviticus. I should stop here and highly recommend the lecture tapes from two conferences: "Worship & Sacrifice" (*Biblical Horizons Bible Conference*, August 17–21, 1992) and "Temple & Priesthood" (*Biblical Horizons Bible Conference*, July 12–16, 1993). For my money, these are indispensable for understanding the meaning of the sacrifices and rituals of the Old Testament.

I have a lecture in the 1993 conference called "Ritual and Redemptive History," where I puzzle over the disturbing, but pervasive practice among Reformed theologians, from the Reformation on, of disparaging Old Covenant sacrificial ritual by identifying it too closely with Roman Catholic errors. As noted earlier, this erroneous identification became more and more prominent in the seventeenth and eighteenth centuries. Even though it is not about worship per se, I highly recommend Henning Graf Reventlow's *The Authority of the Bible and the Rise of the Modern World* (Philadelphia: Fortress Press, 1985). Reventlow chronicles the rise of deism in England and Germany as the precursor to higher criticism. In the process of his research he shows how English Protestants, particularly the Puritans, displayed a deep-seated hostility to anything that smacked of material ceremony and ritual, and that they read the Old Testament with these colored lenses such that they tended to interpret Old Testament religion as a kind of Catholicism before Rome. Furthermore, this moralistic, anti-ceremonial bias fed right into (or possibly even "caused") the rising humanistic antipathy to revealed religion, particularly that of the Old Testament, leading to the rise of higher critical methodologies that deconstruct the first four-fifths of the Bible. At any rate, Reventlow's research on the anti-ritual "spiritualism" of the English post-Reformation theologians is extremely troubling. This work reveals something of the shortcomings of our own anti-liturgical, spiritualistic heritage.

I dealt with this briefly in Chapter sixteen on the "regulative principle of worship," but the works that deconstruct the Reformed polemics concerning the normative status of the synagogue are well worth a students careful study. See especially Peter J. Leithart, "Synagogue or Temple? Models for Christian Worship," *Westminster Theological Journal* (forthcoming), as well as his new book *From Silence to Song: The Davidic Liturgical Revolution* (Moscow: Canon Press, 2003). John W. Kleinig's *The Lord's Song: The Basis, Function and Significance of Choral Music in Chronicles* (JSOT Supplement #156; Sheffield: JSOT Press, 1993) and

Donald D. Binder, *Into the Temple Courts: The Place of the Synagogue in the Second Temple Period* (SBL Dissertation Series 169; Atlanta: Society of Biblical Literature, 1997) are both helpful in tracing the links between temple and synagogue in Old Testament worship.

As for studies in New Testament worship, the situation is not much better. Most scholars assume some sort of initial formless, "prophetic" kind of religion without ritual or ceremony. As if apostolic and post-apostolic worship was something like a contemporary charismatic service and only later, under the influence of alien Hellenistic presuppositions, did the Church adopt the forms and rituals of their culture. This is imaginative nonsense. It has no basis in fact. In fact, any attempt to determine what "New Testament" worship was like apart from a consideration of the Old Testament is doomed to failure. If we cannot get the Old Testament right, we will surely misunderstand the New. You will find a little help in the following works: C. E. B. Cranfield, "Divine and Human Action: The Biblical Concept of Worship," *Interpretation* 22 (1958): 387–98; Joacham Jeremias, *The Eucharistic Words of Jesus* (Philadelphia: Fortress Press, 1966); Charles Francis Digby Moule, *Worship in the New Testament* (Richmond: John Knox Press, 1961); Donald L. Williams, "The Israelite Cult and Christian Worship," in *The Use of the Old Testament in the New and Other Essays*, ed. James M. Efird (Durham: Duke University Press, 1972); and *The Making of Jewish and Christian Worship,* eds. Paul F. Bradshaw and Lawrence D. Hoffman (Notre Dame: University of Notre Dame Press, 1991).

Calvin and the Lord's Supper

John Calvin set us on the road to a healthy Eucharistic theology. Unfortunately, his theological grandchildren have not always appreciated Calvin's robust sacramental theology. In the mid-nineteenth century, for example, when John Williamson Nevin sought to reintroduce American Reformed theologians and pastors to Calvin's sacramental theology, a stormy controversy ensued. Nevin and his companion Philip Schaff even faced heresy charges in their denomination. They were accused, among other things, of harboring and promoting "Romanizing" tendencies (see James Hastings Nichols, *Romanticism in American Theology: Nevin and Schaff at Mercersburg* [Chicago: University of Chicago Press, 1966], 84ff; and E. Brooks Holifield, "Mercersburg, Princeton, and the South: The Sacramental Controversy in the Nineteenth Century," *Journal of Presbyterian History* 54 [1976]: 238–257).

When Nevin's book, *The Mystical Presence* (1846), was reviewed by Charles Hodge, the professor of theology at Princeton Seminary, he dismissed the results of Nevin's thorough historical scholarship by suggesting that what Nevin had uncovered was nothing but "an uncongenial foreign element" in Calvin's sacramental theology, probably derived from Calvin's overly familiar relations with the Lutherans. For more on this controversy consult the following works: John W. Nevin, *The Mystical Presence: A Vindication of the Reformed or Calvinistic Doctrine of the Holy Eucharist* (Philadelphia: J. B. Lippincott & Co., 1846); reprinted and supplemented in John W. Nevin, *The Mystical Presence and Other Writings on the Eucharist*, ed. Bard Thompson and George H. Bricker, vol. 4 of *Lancaster Series on Mercersburg Theology* (Philadelphia: United Church Press, 1966); Charles Hodge, "Doctrine of the Reformed Church on the Lord's Supper" [A Review of *The Mystical Presence: A Vindication of the Reformed or Calvinistic Doctrine of the Holy Eucharist*, by John W. Nevin] *Princeton Review* 20 (1848): 251–52; and especially B. A. Gerrish, "The Flesh of the Son of Man: John W. Nevin on the Church and Eucharist," chapter two in *Tradition and the Modern World: Reformed Theology in the Nineteenth Century* (Chicago: University of Chicago Press, 1978), 49–70. It is not difficult to demonstrate that Calvin looked up to and learned from Luther as the "pathfinder" of the Reformation.

For Calvin's evaluation of Luther see B. A. Gerrish, "John Calvin on Luther," in *Interpreters of Luther*, Jaroslav Pelikan, ed.

(Philadelphia, 1968), 67–96. Even during his debates with the arch- (or hyper-) Lutherans Westphal and Heshusius, Calvin was deeply concerned about Lutheran-Reformed relations; he argued that his treatises against "fanatics" like Westphal were not intended to be attacks on Lutherans as such (Wulfert de Greef, *The Writings of John Calvin: An Introductory Guide*, trans. Lyle D. Bierma [Grand Rapids: Baker Books, 1993], 190–193). Calvin was convinced that there was essential continuity between his theological program and that of Luther and Melanchthon. He believed this to be true, despite differences of emphasis, even in the area of sacramental theology.

After Calvin's death Reformed and Lutheran sacramental theologies begin to diverge. The reasons for this parting are complex and demand much more scholarly attention. For more on this see Jill Raitt, *The Colloquy of Montbeliard: Religion and Politics in the Sixteenth Century* (Oxford: Oxford University Press, 1993); her "Probably They are God's Children: Theodore Beza's Doctrine of Baptism," in *Humanism and Reform: The Church in Europe, England, and Scotland, 1400–1643,* ed. James Kirk (Oxford: Blackwell, 1991); Lewis W. Spitz and Wenzel Lohff, *Discord, Dialog, and Concord: Studies in the Lutheran Reformation's Formula of Concord* (Philadelphia: Fortress, 1977); and Mark D. Tranvik, "Jacob Andreae's Defense of the Lutheran Doctrine of Baptism at Montbeliard," *Lutheran Quarterly* 6 (1992): 425–437.

Calvin clearly held to an instrumental understanding of the efficacy of the Sacraments. Strictly speaking, the instrumental nature of the Sacraments was not the issue between Calvin and later Lutheran theologians like Westphal and Heshusius. In his *Secunda defensio* of 1556, Calvin explains his instrumental view of Baptism to Westphal: "But as Baptism is a solemn recognition by which God introduces his children into the possession of life, a true and effectual sealing of the promise, a pledge of sacred union with Christ, it is justly said to be the entrance and reception into the Church. And as the instruments of the Holy Spirit are not dead,

God truly performs and effects by Baptism what he figures" (Calvin, *Second Defense of the Faith Concerning the Sacraments in Answer to Joachim Westphal* [1556]; CO 9:41–120; cited in Willem Balke, *Calvin and the Anabaptists Radicals*, trans. by William Heynen [Grand Rapids: Wm. B. Eerdmans, 1981], 221.

But Calvin did debate sacramental instrumentality with other Reformed theologians, particularly those influenced by Zwingli. In the years leading up to the *Consensus Tigurinus* (1549), Calvin's debate with Bullinger was precisely over the instrumentality of the Sacraments. Bullinger, like his predecessor Zwingli, denied that God bound Himself to the Sacraments. The Sacraments did not confer grace; rather, they *pictured* and *testified* to God's grace. There is an analogy between God's work of grace and the Sacraments, Bullinger conceded, but certainly no necessary or *causal* connection. Like Zwingli, Bullinger insists that the "Spirit works on the soul directly, without crass intermediaries like implements or canals for grace . . . . He explicitly rejects the terminology of instrument [*instrumentum*] and implement [*organum*]" (Paul E Rorem, "The *Consensus Tigurinus* [1549]: Did Calvin Compromise?"in *Calvinus Sacrae Scripturae Professor*, Wilhelm H. Neuser, ed. [Grand Rapids: Wm. B. Eerdmans, 1994], 82–83). We can see how close Warfield is to Zwingli and Bullinger. Calvin set himself against this view. Calvin and Bullinger exchanged a massive amount of correspondence on this issue up until the *Consensus Tigurinus* or *Zurich Consensus* of 1549. Throughout this debate Calvin consistently and persistently argues for a strong doctrine of the Sacraments' instrumentality. Consider the following excerpts from Calvin's letters:

> There is union complementary with the thing figured, lest the sign be empty, because that which the Lord represents in a sign he effects at the same time [*simul efficit*], and executes [*impletque*] in us by the power of the Spirit. (Letter to Bullinger, 25 February 1547 [#880]; *CO* 12:482; cited in Rorem "The *Consensus*," 78. Rorem mistakenly cites the *CO* reference as *CO* 2. It is actually *CO* 12.)

> What indeed do we abrogate or take away from God when we teach that he acts through his instruments [*per sua instrumenta*], indeed he alone. (Letter to Bullinger, 25 February 1547 [#880]; *CO* 12:485)

> God works . . . through the Sacraments as instruments . . . . The Spirit is the author, the Sacrament is truly the instrument used. (*CO* 7:702)

We see, then, that Calvin insisted that a Sacrament ought to be called a means (*media*), an instrument (*instrumentum*), a vehicle (*vehiculum*), or an implement (*organum*), through which God's grace is conveyed. Bullinger, on the other hand, like Zwingli before him, refused to allow God to use material instruments. Warfield, therefore, carries on the Zwinglian/Bullingerian, not the Calvinian tradition.

I believe that there is a profound connection between the obvious embarrassment of later Reformed theologians with respect to Calvin's positive evaluation of Luther and his theology and their gradual abandonment of Calvin's hearty sacramental theology. B. A. Gerrish points out that even as early as Beza we discover something of an mild annoyance with Calvin's sacramentalism. As the editor of Calvin's correspondence, Beza "censored" certain portions of Calvin's correspondence that seemed to him to be evidence of too much compromise with Luther (*The Old Protestantism and the New: Essays on the Reformation Heritage* [Edinburgh: T. & T. Clark, 182],32, 285). In addition to this, under Beza's leadership Calvin's doctrine of predestination takes a more central, defining place within Reformed theology. This may have precluded later Reformed theology from fully utilizing Calvin's robust theology of sacramental instrumentality. A modified Zwinglian view, which is more compatible with a centralized doctrine of predestination, seems to make headway in the late sixteenth century.

This is a subject that demands more research. Did the heirs of Calvin move away from their master? Did they develop tendencies already present in Calvin? Did later Lutheran theologians remain true to Luther and Melanchthon? Did Melanchthon remain true to

Luther's theology of the Sacraments? It is worth noting that it was not until the Formula of Concord, when the Lutheran confession explicitly attacked Reformed theology, particularly Reformed baptismal theology, that Reformed theologians felt the need to "answer" any Lutheran confessional book or catechism. Before that, Reformed churches tended to accept the Augsburg Confession, including it within their collections of confessions and creeds (see Philip Schaff, ed., *The Creeds of Christendom*, vol. 3, *The Evangelical Creeds* [Harper and Row, 1931; reprint, Grand Rapids: Baker Books, 1990],354–355).

The ministerial student must fill out his sacramental theology with a careful investigation into these matters. I suggest that he start by digesting some of the works listed above (by Nevin, Schaff, Gerrish, Holifield, etc.) as well as the following essays and books: Peter Leithart, "The Way Things Really Ought to Be: Eucharist, Eschatology, and Culture," *Westminster Theological Journal* 59 (1997): 159–76; Ronald S. Wallace, *Calvin's Doctrine of Word and Sacrament* (Edinburgh: Oliver and Boyd Ltd, 1953); and, "Eating Gracefully: A Reformed Perspective on How to Be the Church," *Pro Ecclesia* 2 (1993): 21–36). For more on Calvin's instrumental theology of the Sacraments see my discussion in Jeffrey J. Meyers, "Baptism & Justification: Sacramental Instrumentality in John Calvin Compared With the Pre-Concord Lutheran Confessions and Catechisms" [Unpublished Seminar Paper, Concordia Theological Seminary, 1995]). The question of God's use of "instruments" or "means" has historically been connected with discussions on the Sacraments. The student who wants to investigate Calvin's instrumental theology of the Sacraments should read the articles by B.A. Gerrish on this topic in his three books: *Tradition and the Modern World: Reformed Theology in the Nineteenth Century* (Chicago: University of Chicago Press, 1978), esp. chapter two; *The Old Protestantism and the New: Essays on the Reformation Heritage* (Edinburgh: T. & T. Clark, 182), chapters 5–7; and *Grace and Gratitude: The Eucharistic Theology of John Calvin* (Minneapolis:

Fortress Press, 1993). Calvin's commitment to God's use of human and physical instruments can be clearly seen in his extended correspondence with Bullinger, in which he tries to convince Bullinger of this very truth (see Paul E. Rorem, "The *Consensus Tigurinus* (1549): Did Calvin Compromise?" in *Calvinus Sacrae Scripturae Professor,* Wilhelm H. Neuser, ed. (Grand Rapids: Wm. B. Eerdmans, 1994),72–90.

Music and Hymnody

There is too much self-serving fluff out there on "worship music." A few good books and articles will serve the pastoral student well in his resistance to powerful temptations to dumb down the Church's music and hymnody in favor of cultural relevance and so-called contemporary "intelligibility." Unfortunately, you can readily find any number of works that defend introducing the popular, mass-culture style of music in the Church. What I will reference here are works that question the wisdom of such a move. First, for an orientation to the problems and what's at stake, read James B. Jordan, "Church Music in Chaos," in *The Reconstruction of the Church* (Tyler: Geneva Ministries, 1985),241–265. Duck Schuler, Director of Music at Christ Church Moscow, Idaho (CRE) and Fellow of Music and College Choral Conductor at New Saint Andrews College, and former elder and choir director here at Providence, provides an Introduction to Musical Style and a compilation of Psalms, Hymns and Service Music in the *Cantus Christi* (Moscow: Canon Press 2002). Dr. Schuler may also be willing to share his Th.M. thesis outline: "In His Image: Music In Worship (1992). See also Dr. Schuler's critique of the *New Trinity Hymnal*: "A Review of the Trinity Hymnal, Parts I, II, & III," in *Rite Reasons: Studies in Worship* 16–18 (August-December 1991). In Part I one of his critique Duck provides a helpful biblical/theological orientation to Church music. Leonard Payton has a number of very helpful articles on Church music: "Reforming Worship Music," in *Modern Reformation* (March/April 1994): 20–31; "Music

Technology and Worldliness," *Reformation & Revival* 4 (Fall 1995): 105–115; "Is it a Prelude or a Quaalude?" *Modern Reformation* (Jan/Feb 1995): 10–16; and "The Pride of Simplicity," *Modern Reformation* (July/August 1995): 30–31. Payton also has a critical review of the *New Trinity Hymnal* (www.christpresbyterian.org/library/payton/). James B. Jordan discusses music in the Reformed Puritan heritage in "Puritanism and Music," *Journal of Christian Reconstruction* 6 (Winter 1979–80): 111–133.

If you want to discover how bad some of the Gospel hymns that we have inherited from the nineteenth century really are and why they are so theologically dangerous (and sometimes heretical) read both Sandra S. Sizer's *Gospel Hymns and Social Religion: The Rhetoric of Nineteenth-Century Revivalism* (Philadelphia: Temple University, 1978) and especially Ann Douglas's *The Feminization of American Culture* (New York: Knopf, 1977).

Eric Routley's works are always a stimulating corrective to the pop styles so prevalent in contemporary Christian music. Routley thinks about Church music and hymnody by taking the Reformation theological perspective seriously. Take for example the doctrine of total depravity. Music is an artistic, cultural work of man and as such music is not neutral. The idea that all music is God's music is not true. Music will inevitably reflect the perspective, motivation, goal, and commitments of the artist. That means music can go wrong. It can serve to embody idolatrous commitments or it can be just plain immature or ugly. The worldview and personality of those who compose music is always revealed to some degree in their music. Routley says, "The doctrine of 'total depravity,' greatly scorned and abused by some, is theological 'shorthand' for the truth that there is no activity of man which is exempt from this influence toward evil . . . . Now music . . . is an activity of mankind and therefore falls under the influence of sin . . . . Once touched by human hands it can go wrong" (Erik Routley, *The Church and Music: An Inquiry in the History, the Nature, and the Scope of Christian Judgment on Music* [London: Gerald Duckworth, 1967], 224, 225). Routley argues that sin introduces confusion and nonsense in the

musical realm. Sin is man's attempt to tamper with the divine order, which leads to humanly introduced confusion and nonsense in
the musical realm. Moreover, he argues from such passages as
Ephesians 4:14–15, James 1:4, and Hebrews 5:12–14 that maturity in music is the standard for the Church's hymnody: "We now
have some useful guides for judging church music . . . . We have the
principle that the Christian's goal must be maturity in Christ. Our
Lord could not have been clearer about His, and Paul found constantly (as apparently did other apostolic teachers) that to fallen
human nature the status of slave is attractive, while that of the son
is demanding. His father, we remember, did not permit the prodi-
gal son, despite his bad record, to take the job in the kitchen he asked
for. He had to wear the robe and the ring and like it . . . . We are
therefore on firm ground in saying that where church music inhibits
the growth of the Christian community to maturity it is to be cen-
sured" (*Church Music and The Christian Faith*, 20). Much of modern contemporary praise music falls under this ban. It inhibits the
mature growth of Christian communities. Routley has published
numerous works on Church music. The following are those that I
have found challenging: Eric Routley, *Church Music and the Christian Faith* (Carol Stream: Agape, 1978); *Christian Hymns Observed:
When in Our Music God is Glorified* (Princeton: Prestige Publications, 1982); and *Divine Formula* (Princeton: Prestige Publications,
1986).

A few more general books will provide you with arguments to
resist and flee the musical devil in our midst: Linda J. Clark,
Music in Churches: Nourishing Your Congregation's Musical Life (New
York: The Alban Institute, 1994); James Rawlings Sydnor, *Hymns
& Their Uses* (Carol Stream: Agape, 1982); and Calvin M.
Johansson, *Music & Ministry: A Biblical Counterpoint*, second edi-
tion (Peabody: Hendrickson, 1998). Finally, James L. Brauer has
an excellent article on how music works in the "seeker-sensitive,"
market-driven churches of modern American evangelicalism: "The
Role of Music in Seeker Services," *Concordia Theological Journal*
(Jan. 1998): 7–20.

Finis Coronat Opus

My hope and prayer as I conclude is that my explanation of the Lord's Service and these concluding essays may truly help you make progress in your understanding of the riches of Christian liturgical theology and practice. When I was young I did not understand Augustine's remarks in his *On Christian Instruction*. Now, I think I do. It really was *necessary* for me to write this book. If it serves you, then the end will have truly crowned the work.

Everything that is not exhausted by being given away is not yet owned as it ought to be, so long as we hold on to it and do not give it away. "For," Jesus has said, "He that has to him shall be given more." Therefore, he will give to those who already have; that is, he will increase and heap up what he has given, when they dispense with generosity what they have received. There were five loaves of bread and, on another occasion, seven loaves, before they were distributed to the hungry multitude. Afterwards, although the hunger of so many thousands was satisfied, they filled baskets and baskets. And so, just as that bread increased after it was broken, the Lord has now granted me the thoughts that are necessary for beginning this work, and they will be increased by His inspiration when I have begun to dispense them. As a result, I shall not only suffer no poverty of thought in this ministry of mine, but shall even exult in a remarkable abundance of ideas. (*De Doctrina Christiana,* 1.1)

† St. Augustine, *Christian Instruction,* trans. John J. Gavigan, The Fathers of the Church, vol. 2 (Washington D.C.: The Catholic University of America Press, 1947),26–28.

Scripture Index

Genesis

Exodus

Leviticus

Numbers

Deuteronomy

Titus

1   269
1:4   238

Hebrews

1:1   49
4:2   293
4:12   55, 67, 84, 195, 207, 364
4:14–16   211
4:15–16   211
5:12–14   431
6:4–6   226
6:20   59, 60
7:18   60
7:22   60
8:1–2   59
8:5   60, 132
8:6   35
8:6–13   60
8:10   35
9:1–10:4   60
9:3–4   82
9:4   35, 82
9:6   75
9:9   75, 364
9:9–10   57
9:14   60
9:15   55, 60
9:18   55
9:18–20   35
9:20   55
9:22   83
9:25   75
9:26   57
9:27   259
10:1   59
10:2   75
10:5   63

10:5–10   60
10:12   57
10:24   60
10:29   35
11:7   259
11:21   137
12:14   195, 363
12:22   132, 171
12:22–24   197
12:24   35, 55, 60
12:28   75
12:28–29   28
13   345
13:1–6   60
13:5   66
13:7   338
13:15   67, 239
13:15a   60
13:15b   60
13:16   28, 60, 66
13:17   338
13:18–21   345
13:20   55
13:22   345
13:22–24   345

James

1:4   431
2:10   201
4:4   208
4:8   208

1 Peter

1:7   370
1:11   259
2:5   59, 62, 66, 171, 206, 274, 311
2:9   206, 274
3:1–7   98, 272